"*Baptist Foundations* is a book whose time has come. In fact it has been needed for quite a while! Written by both scholars and practitioners, this book is biblical, theological, and practical. And, it is thorough. Do not be intimidated by its length. Read it at your leisure and be sure to consult it again and again when you have important ecclesiological questions. The odds are it has a helpful word."
Daniel L. Akin, president,
  Southeastern Baptist Theological Seminary

"When it comes to biblical ecclesiology, Mark Dever, Jonathan Leeman, and 9Marks offer this generation's gold standard. *Baptist Foundations* is perhaps the most biblically robust and historically informed book on church government on the market today. I would encourage everyone who serves or loves the local church to read this book and implement its message."
Jason K. Allen, president,
  Midwestern Baptist Theological Seminary and College

"When I teach students the doctrine of the church, and when I talk with pastors about the challenges that they face in their ministry, several issues always come to the forefront: how the leaders of the church—pastors, elders, deacons—and its members exercise authority in their respective spheres; the what/when/who/where/why/how of baptism and the Lord's Supper; and how to start or restore church discipline. The book you now have in your hands deals specifically with those issues! It is an accessible, easy-to-follow book that provides a solid foundation for Baptist pastors and laypeople who love the church of Jesus Christ."
Gregg R. Allison, professor of Christian Theology,
  The Southern Baptist Theological Seminary

"Mark Dever and Jonathan Leeman are to be commended and congratulated for putting together this extremely significant book, one that deserves a wide readership among Baptists and all interested in these vital matters of ecclesiology. The book as a whole makes a most significant contribution to the understanding of church polity and congregationalism, church membership, and church government, as well as the meaning of the ordinances and the nature of the church. The depth and serious reflection represented in the various chapters will pave the way for ongoing engagement, research, and conversation that will be immensely helpful for theologians, ministers, and church leaders, while strengthening churches across denominational lines. I am quite pleased to recommend this impressive and important volume."
David S. Dockery, president,
  Trinity International University

"Here is a superb collection of essays on Baptist congregationalism showing that 'church polity' is about more than organization, structure, and 'how to' matters of group dynamics. I commend this book to every Baptist pastor and church leader concerned with following Jesus Christ in a covenanted community of faithful disciples."
Timothy George, dean,
  Beeson Divinity School

"In *Baptist Foundations*, Mark Dever and Jonathan Leeman offer a treasure trove of wisdom and practical advice regarding a highly neglected subject: ecclesiology and church governance. Church leaders will find themselves returning to these essays repeatedly for guidance on topics such as elders, deacons, membership, baptism, and the Lord's Supper."

Thomas S. Kidd, professor of History,
   Baylor University

"The theological crises of our increasingly secular times are growing in both number and intensity. The collapse of cultural Christianity looms as one of the great events of our times. At the same time, we see a resurgent interest in the nature of the authentic church as displayed in Scripture, and this is exactly the right time for an urgent recovery of Baptist polity. To paraphrase Samuel Johnson, there is nothing like a theological emergency to clear the theological mind. This invaluable new work on Baptist polity is urgently needed, faithful in content, and comprehensive in scope. *Baptist Foundations* is the right book for the right time, written and edited by just the right team. I celebrate its arrival."

R. Albert Mohler Jr., president,
   The Southern Baptist Theological Seminary

"Historically informed, exegetically careful, and theologically substantial, *Baptist Foundations* tackles perennial issues in ecclesiology with verve and conviction. The church's nature, polity, ordinances, leadership, and attributes are ably treated and pastorally applied. Baptist pastors, ministry students, reflective church leaders, and professors will benefit from this significant volume."

Christopher W. Morgan, dean and professor of Theology,
   School of Christian Ministries, California Baptist University

"This edited volume by Mark Dever and Jonathan Leeman is much needed and fills a growing hole in the thinking and experience of present-day Baptists. This book will be valuable for every minister, and especially for seminarians, as they reflect upon and put into practice what it means to be a part of the church of the living Christ. Addressing issues of ordinances, organizational structures, and polity, the authors provide a powerful resource for those who want to live faithfully under the authority of the local church as the people of God."

Robert B. Sloan Jr., president,
   Houston Baptist University

Foreword by
James Leo Garrett Jr.

BAPTIST FOUNDATIONS

Church
Government
for an
Anti-Institutional
Age

B&H
ACADEMIC
NASHVILLE, TENNESSEE

EDITED BY MARK DEVER AND JONATHAN LEEMAN

Contents

Foreword vii
Editors and Contributors xiii
Preface. xv
      Mark Dever and Jonathan Leeman
Abbreviations xxiii
Introduction—Why Polity?. 1
      Jonathan Leeman

PART 1   CONGREGATIONALISM. 25

Chapter 1
Some Historical Roots of Congregationalism. 27
      Michael A. G. Haykin

Chapter 2
The Biblical and Theological Case for Congregationalism . 47
      Stephen J. Wellum and Kirk Wellum

PART 2   THE ORDINANCES. 79

Chapter 3
Five Preliminary Issues for Understanding the Ordinances 81
      Shawn D. Wright

Chapter 4
Baptism in the Bible. 91
      Thomas R. Schreiner

Chapter 5
Baptism in History, Theology, and the Church 107
      Shawn D. Wright

Chapter 6
The Lord's Supper in the Bible 131
      Thomas R. Schreiner

Chapter 7
The Lord's Supper in History, Theology, and the Church. .145
      Shawn D. Wright

PART 3   CHURCH MEMBERSHIP AND DISCIPLINE. . .165

Chapter 8
The Why and Who of Church Membership 167
      John Hammett

Chapter 9
The What and How of Church Membership. 181
      John Hammett

Chapter 10
The Why, How, and When of Church Discipline 199
      Thomas White

PART 4   ELDERS AND DEACONS 227

Chapter 11
Elders and Deacons in History 229
      Mark Dever

Chapter 12
The Scriptural Basis for Elders 243
      Benjamin L. Merkle

Chapter 13
The Biblical Qualifications for Elders 253
      Benjamin L. Merkle

Chapter 14
The Biblical Role of Elders. 271
      Benjamin L. Merkle

Chapter 15
Practical Issues in Elder Ministry. 291
      Andrew Davis

Chapter 16
The Office of Deacon 311
      Benjamin L. Merkle

Chapter 17
Practical Issues in Deacon Ministry 325
      Andrew Davis

PART 5   THE CHURCH AND CHURCHES 331

Chapter 18
A Congregational Approach to Unity, Holiness, and
Apostolicity: Faith and Order. 333
      Jonathan Leeman

Chapter 19
A Congregational Approach to Catholicity: Independence
and Interdependence 367
      Jonathan Leeman

Name Index. 381
Subject Index. 385
Scripture Index. 390

Foreword

The doctrine of the church, or ecclesiology, has always been a major concern for the people called Baptists. This statement is neither pure speculation nor pious denominational rhetoric. Rather it can be established by incontrovertible evidence.

First, Baptist confessions of faith have normally allotted considerable space to ecclesiology, as ten examples indicate: "A Declaration of Faith of English People remaining at Amsterdam in Holland" (1611), written by Thomas Helwys, consists of twenty-seven articles, thirteen of which pertain to the church.[1] "Propositions and Conclusions concerning True Christian Religion" (1612–14), written by John Smyth's party, contains 100 articles, of which nineteen are ecclesiological.[2] In the First London Confession of Particular Baptists (1644), fifteen of the fifty-three articles relate to the church.[3] "The Faith and Practice of Thirty Congregations" (1651), framed by General Baptists in the English Midlands, has seventy-five articles, and twenty-eight apply to the church.[4] In the Standard Confession of General Baptists (1660), nine of the twenty-five articles pertain to the church.[5] The Second London Confession of Particular Baptists (1677), a modification of the Westminster Confession (1646), contains thirty-two articles, some of which have lengthy subsections, and five are ecclesiological.[6] The New Hampshire Confession (1833), with two articles added in 1853, consists of eighteen articles, of which two relate to the church.[7] The 1925 Baptist Faith and Message (BF&M) of the Southern Baptist Convention (SBC) contains twenty-five articles, of which either three or six concern the church.[8] The 1963 BF&M of the

---

[1] William L. Lumpkin, *Baptist Confessions of Faith* (Philadelphia: Judson, 1959), 116–23.
[2] Ibid., 123–42.
[3] Ibid., 144–71.
[4] Ibid., 171–88.
[5] Ibid., 220–35.
[6] Ibid., 235–95.
[7] Ibid., 360–67.
[8] Ibid., 390–98.

SBC consists of seventeen articles, two of which have three subsections, and six are ecclesiological.[9] Finally, the SBC's 2000 BF&M has eighteen articles, of which one has three subsections and another has four, and six articles pertain to the church.[10]

Second, Baptists have repeatedly written and published treatises on ecclesiology. The following is a considerable, though not a complete, listing of these:

- Thomas Collier, *The Right Constitution and True Subjects of the Visible Church of Christ* (London, 1654)
- Benjamin Keach, *The Glory of a True Church and Its Discipline Display'd* (London, 1668)
- John Gill, *A Body of Practical Divinity*, books 2, 3 (London, 1770)
- William Bullein Johnson, *The Gospel Developed Through the Covenant and Order of the Churches of Jesus Christ* (Richmond: H. K. Ellyson, 1846)
- James Lawrence Reynolds, *Church Polity, or the Kingdom of Christ in Its Internal and External Development* (Richmond: Harrold and Murray, 1849)
- John Newton Brown, *The Baptist Church Manual* (Philadelphia: American Baptist Publication Society, 1853)
- Francis Wayland, *Notes on the Principles and Practices of Baptist Churches* (New York: Sheldon, Blakeman, & Co., 1857)
- John Leadley Dagg, *A Treatise on Church Order* (Charleston: Southern Baptist Publication Society, 1858)
- Edward Thurston Hiscox, *The Baptist Church Directory* (New York: Sheldon, 1860)
- James Madison Pendleton, *Church Manual: Designed for the Use of Baptist Churches* (Philadelphia: American Baptist Publication Society, 1867)
- William Williams, *Apostolic Church Polity* (Philadelphia: American Baptist Publication Society, 1874)
- Edwin Charles Dargan, *Ecclesiology: A Study of the Churches* (Louisville: Charles T. Dearing, 1897)
- Harvey Eugene Dana, *A Manual of Ecclesiology* (Kansas City, KS: Central Seminary, 1941)

---

[9] Lumpkin, *Baptist Confessions of Faith* (rev. ed.: Valley Forge, PA: Judson, 1969), 390–400.

[10] *Baptist Faith and Message of the Southern Baptist Convention, Adopted . . . June 14, 2000* (Nashville: LifeWay, 2000), 1–22. See also www.sbc.net/bfm2000.

- Norman Hill Maring and Winthrop Still Hudson, *A Baptist Manual of Polity and Practice* (Valley Forge, PA: Judson, 1963)
- Everett C. Goodwin, *The New Hiscox Guide for Baptist Churches* (Valley Forge, PA: Judson, 1995)
- Mark E. Dever, ed., *Polity: Biblical Arguments on How to Conduct Church Life* (Washington, DC: Center for Church Reform, 2001)
- John S. Hammett, *Biblical Foundations for Baptist Churches: A Contemporary Ecclesiology* (Grand Rapids: Kregel, 2005)
- Mark Dever, *The Church: The Gospel Made Visible* (Nashville: B&H, 2012)
- Gregg R. Allison, *Sojourners and Strangers: The Doctrine of the Church* (Wheaton: Crossway, 2012)

Third, although during the nineteenth century among Southern Baptists ecclesiology was not considered to be an integral part of systematic theology, the prevailing Baptist pattern has been to reckon ecclesiology as an essential component of systematic theology. John L. Dagg's *A Manual of Theology*[11] did not include any treatment of the church, but his ecclesiology was fully developed in a companion volume, *A Treatise on Church Order*.[12] James Petigru Boyce did not treat ecclesiology in his *Abstract of Systematic Theology*,[13] but his colleague E. C. Dargan subsequently produced a full-length textbook on ecclesiology.[14]

Fourth, most of the beliefs that have ever been claimed as Baptist distinctives are ecclesiological in nature; for example, regenerate church membership, believer's baptism by immersion, various forms of close or strict Communion, congregational polity and autonomy, religious liberty, separation of church and state, and so forth. Robert Stanton Norman's studies have made this clear.[15]

The twentieth century was not the finest epoch in Southern Baptist history with respect to ecclesiological practice. As urban churches increased in numbers of members, stress was placed on church efficiency. In the admission of members, there was less care and greater laxity, while corrective church discipline was abandoned and the use of

---

[11] (Charleston, SC: Southern Baptist Publication Society, 1857).

[12] (Charleston, SC: Southern Baptist Publication Society, 1858).

[13] 2 vols. (Louisville: C. T. Dearing, 1882); 1 vol. (Philadelphia: American Baptist Publication Society, 1887).

[14] *Ecclesiology: A Study of the Churches* (Louisville: C. T. Dearing, 1897). No attempt will be made to list the numerous Baptist systematic theologies that include ecclesiology.

[15] "A Critical Analysis of the Intentional Efforts of Baptists to Distinguish Themselves Theologically from Other Christian Denominations" (PhD diss., Southwestern Baptist Theological Seminary, 1997); *More than Just a Name: Preserving Our Baptist Identity* (Nashville: B&H, 2001).

church covenants became less frequent. Numerous members were inactive and/or nonresident, but their names were kept on church rolls. In larger urban churches, full-time ministers with specialized tasks assisted the pastors so that the "church staff" came to be. Certain other Baptist conventions and unions chose to identify with conciliar ecumenism and its goal of more visible transdenominational union, but the SBC declined to do so—eliciting the unfavorable epithet "problem child of American Protestantism"—and the conciliar movement faded in significance. Later in the century numerous megachurches developed, usually with multiple worship services and multiple sites and with the demise of congregational polity. In the final decades of the century, as Southern Baptists found more affinity with American evangelicals, they found that ecclesiology was a weakness, not a strength of evangelicals. Increasingly moral failure, both in the membership and in the leadership, became common in Southern Baptist churches, with church members having the same percentage of failures as nonmembers.

The call for the thoroughgoing renewal of the doctrine and practice of the church, especially as to membership and discipline, has never been made more aptly or clearly than by Al Jackson, the pastor for thirty-five years of Lakeview Baptist Church of Auburn, Alabama. He wrote, "A generation ago Southern Baptists . . . won the battle for the Bible. This generation faces a task even more daunting, to reclaim our heritage regarding regenerate church membership and the practice of church discipline."[16]

Mark Dever and Jonathan Leeman and their colleagues are to be commended for providing another carefully prepared volume that moves toward that goal. Aspects of their book will be widely accepted. The case for congregational autonomy will likely prove to be noncontroversial, whereas the democratic elements of congregationalism may be disputed. Some churches have surrendered congregational governance but are proudly independent. The restatements concerning baptism and the Lord's Supper will likely elicit wide concurrence, even though open membership has more advocates now than in the twentieth century, the *de facto* policy regarding open Communion is lacking in precise definition, and many may be slow to welcome a Calvinistic as well as a Zwinglian interpretation of the Supper. The call for interdependence as well as independence of congregations will likely get a good response,

[16] Endorsement for John S. Hammett and Benjamin L. Merkle, eds., *Those Who Must Give an Account: A Study of Church Membership and Church Discipline* (Nashville: B&H, 2012).

whereas the four classic marks of a true church may still sound strange to most Baptist ears.

The book's major challenge will likely be for the recovery of strict church membership and of both positive discipleship and corrective discipline with nineteenth-century Baptist life as a model. Here seminaries, universities, and LifeWay are limited in what they can do. The congregation is where the reform will be won or lost, and leadership is crucial.

The book's most controversial topic will be plural elder governance. Contributors reckon it as biblical and therefore proper, despite the long history of single elder (pastor)-deacons leadership in Baptist churches. But the twentieth-century advent of church staffs in larger urban churches testifies to the need for multiple leadership. Among contributors there are differences: deacons as assistants to elders versus deacons as servants of the congregation and absolute equality of elders versus a *de facto* (if not *de jure*) role particularity for a senior pastor or senior elder.

This book invites serious discussion and dialogue—biblical, theological, and practical—and indeed is worthy of such. May God use it to help many congregations discover what it truly means to be the church of Jesus Christ!

James Leo Garrett Jr.
May 2014

Editors and Contributors

Editors

MARK DEVER, senior pastor, Capitol Hill Baptist Church; president, 9Marks; occasional adjunct professor, The Southern Baptist Theological Seminary

JONATHAN LEEMAN, editorial director, 9Marks; occasional lecturer, Southeastern Baptist Theological Seminary; adjunct professor, The Southern Baptist Theological Seminary

Contributors

ANDREW DAVIS, senior pastor, First Baptist Church, Durham, North Carolina; visiting professor of historical theology, Southeastern Baptist Theological Seminary

JOHN HAMMETT, John L. Dagg Senior Professor of Systematic Theology and associate dean for theological studies, Southeastern Baptist Theological Seminary

MICHAEL A. G. HAYKIN, professor of Church History and Biblical Spirituality, The Southern Baptist Theological Seminary

BENJAMIN L. MERKLE, professor of New Testament and Greek, Southeastern Baptist Theological Seminary

THOMAS R. SCHREINER, James Buchanan Harrison Professor of New Testament Interpretation and professor of Biblical Theology and associate dean of the School of Theology, The Southern Baptist Theological Seminary

KIRK WELLUM, principal and professor of Theology, Toronto Baptist Seminary

STEPHEN J. WELLUM, professor of Christian Theology, The Southern Baptist Theological Seminary

THOMAS WHITE, president and professor of Theology, Cedarville University

SHAWN D. WRIGHT, associate professor of Church History, The Southern Baptist Theological Seminary

Preface

Mark Dever and Jonathan Leeman

This is an antipolity age, perhaps more than any other time in the history of the church. Mind you, human beings have not been fans of any authority but their own since the fall in Genesis 3. Nonetheless, a number of trends have conspired to make the latter half of the twentieth century and the early twenty-first century especially anti-institutional among otherwise well-meaning Christians.

- Since the dawn of the seventeenth-century Enlightenment, the Western mind has been trained to doubt all external authorities.
- Since the middle of the nineteenth century, scholars in theology departments of elite European universities have assumed that the churches of the New Testament were in a state of flux, their polities were inconsistent, and they offer no normative model for today. And when biblical norms vanish, pragmatism steps into the void.
- Church leaders in the twentieth century, therefore, found themselves enticed and eventually intoxicated by the methods of the booming American marketplace. Every few years a new church growth philosophy hit the bookshelves and conference circuit promising the latest and greatest way to grow a church in five easy steps.
- Beginning in the 1950s, the so-called neoevangelicals separated themselves from their separatist and fundamentalist parents by establishing their own seminaries, magazines, evangelism organizations, publishing houses, and other parachurch institutions.

Their hope was to fulfill the Great Commission in a more culturally engaged way while downplaying the things that divide us such
as church government and baptism. Evangelicals often favor mere
Christianity and mere ecclesiology. These work well for our para-
church-driven movement.

This list could go on, and we have not even mentioned the Internet,
social media, MP3 preachers, and their effect on the institutional structures of Christianity around the world.

Beginning in the 1950s, Robert Schuler, a church marketing master-
mind, began the trend of dropping grumpy old words like "Baptist" and
"Presbyterian" and "Methodist" from church signs and replacing them
with the gentler and family-friendly "Community" or "Valley Way."[1]
That trend has only accelerated in recent years as churches have taken
to giving themselves a mysterious and intelligently urban aura with
names like Perimeter and Karis. These days evangelicals do not identify
themselves so much by the old denominations, which divide over polity.
They define themselves by their "tribes." Tribes offer different lifestyle
choices. They are defined by the tone of their preachers, the style of their
music, the topics of frustration on their websites, and the general attire
at their conferences.

As such, to tell the members of the younger generation that they
should read their Bibles to figure out whether they are Baptist, Anglican,
or something else sounds both eccentric and futile. To say that they
might want to put one of those words back on their church sign sounds
positively archaic. Shall we ride in horse-drawn buggies as well?

The Gift of Authority

One thing that's missing from our antipolity age is any recognition of
God's gift of authority to his people and to creation. Church polity, most
fundamentally, is about exercising God's authority after him. The congregation is called to exercise one kind of authority, the elders or pastors
another kind. To celebrate the ordinances requires an exercise of authority, as does receiving and disciplining members. Those are the topics of
this book, and if people today are especially suspicious of authority, it's
no wonder this is an antipolity age. Polity is about authority.

---

[1] See John Hardin, "Retailing Religion: Business Promotionalism in American
Christian Churches in the Twentieth Century," PhD diss., University of Maryland at
College Park, 2011.

But what if there is a gift here, waiting to be unwrapped? What if God in fact means to create life in us through the authoritative structures of our churches?

I (Mark) remember once being chilled in a conversation with a lecturer at Cambridge University when the topic of authority arose. He was speaking in anger at length over a recent decision by the city council, which was fairly typical of this friend in matters of authority. So I asked him, "Do you think authority is bad?" Normally, an academic like him would respond to such an unnuanced question with a puzzled look, a condescending sniffle, and a heavily qualified, meandering answer. This time—shocking to me—he shot back just as directly, "Yes."

On the other hand, I (Jonathan) remember being chilled when Mark, my pastor, asked me to trust him in a church vote. I was an immature, perhaps a nominal, Christian at the time, and he had made a decision in the church to which I objected, so I planned on voting against him in an upcoming members' meeting. I was much like that academic friend of Mark's at Cambridge! Then in a Sunday afternoon informational meeting concerning that upcoming vote, he explained that, by being a member of the church, every one of us in that room had accepted him as our God-appointed pastor. He said that, as he prepared to give an account to God, he could not imagine taking a different course of action than the one he was recommending. And so calmly, meekly, he asked us to trust him in the course he was recommending. It was my rich young ruler moment. I didn't have a lot of money, but I, a lifelong nonconformist, had a high estimation of my ability to think and make decisions. And now here this guy was, in effect, asking me to follow Jesus by following him! What?! It was a crucial moment, as my universe of self-rule versus someone else's rule hung in the balance. (I did eventually vote with Mark, and how the Lord blessed me spiritually following that time.)

It is good and healthy for Christians to recognize the fallen nature of authority and its abuses in this world. Power apart from God's purposes is always demonic. In fact, abuses of authority lie about God as much as if not more than most sins because he is the one with all authority.

But to be suspicious toward all authority is both naïve and harmful to oneself and others. Really it reveals more about the skeptic than about the authority. It shows a cancerous degeneration in our capacity to operate as those made in God's image. To live as God meant us to live, we must trust him, and—to no small extent—trust those made in his image. Everyone in the Bible from Adam and Eve to the rogue rulers in the book of Revelation showed their evil fundamentally by denying God's authority and usurping it as their own.

Good authority authors life. It creates and empowers and uplifts. Yes, authority places boundaries on the road and writes rules for the game, but it does that so the game can be played and the destination reached.

Good authority is the coach who trains the runner to run faster, the teacher who teaches the student to build better. Again, authority authors life. Isn't this precisely what God did with his authority by creating the world? And isn't this what he meant for everyone created in his image to do by giving dominion to humanity? God's authority is nothing if not generous. And so should ours be.

King David, who had his share of experiences with both good and bad authority, offered these observations on the topic: "The one who rules the people with justice, who rules in the fear of God, is like the morning light when the sun rises on a cloudless morning, the glisten of rain on sprouting grass" (2 Sam 23:3–4 HCSB). One can picture the shafts of sunlight slanting downward from the sky, warming a green field, sparkling off the residue of the night's rain, and nourishing the grass, giving life and strength. Could that truly be what God means good authority to do?

It would seem that rejecting authority, as so many in our day do, is shortsighted and self-destructive. A world without authority is a world where desires have no restraints, cars have no controls, intersections have no traffic lights, games have no rules, lovers have no covenants, organizations have no purpose, homes have no parents, and people have no God. Such a world might last for a little while, but how quickly it would become pointless, then cruel, and finally tragic.

When we exercise proper and loving authority through the law, around the family table, in our jobs, on the baseball team, in our homes, and especially in the church, we help display God's image to the world. It speaks of his nature and character.

The difference between what people call "community" and what the Bible calls the "church" comes down to the question of authority. Jesus actually gave authority to the local assembly called a church (Matt 16:13–20; 18:15–20; Heb 13:7, 17; 1 Pet 5:1–5). This assembly is not only a fellowship but an accountability fellowship. It's not just a group of believers at the park; it preaches the gospel and possesses the keys of the kingdom for binding and loosing through the ordinances. It declares who does and does not belong to the kingdom. It exercises oversight. And exercising such affirmation and oversight *meaningfully* means gathering regularly and getting involved in one another's lives.

The Christian life will grow best, flower most beautifully, when nourished in the greenhouse of this accountability fellowship. That is why our Christianity should be congregationally shaped. Discipleship to Christ involves submitting ourselves to his Word and his people.

Heeding Scripture

So what exactly does the Bible say about polity?

I (Mark) remember using the word *polity* in an eighth-grade paper. My twenty-four-year-old English teacher circled it as an error. It was with juvenile glee that I took the dictionary to her, opened it, and read her something like "the organization created for managing affairs, especially public affairs; government." (Can you imagine how a kid like me fit in!) Polity, then, is management, organization, government, and structures of authority.

As Christians, we know we should strive to establish our lives on the teaching of Scripture. We must therefore ask, does Scripture deal clearly with questions about the polity, or organization, of the church? If so, what does it teach? Of course, we believe Scripture is sufficient for our preaching and discipling, for our spirituality and joy in following Christ, for family life and evangelism. But does Scripture intend to tell us how to organize our lives together as Christians in churches, or is polity a matter of biblical indifference, so that we are left to figure out our own best practices? "Does this work? What about that? Oops, just crushed a sheep. Anyone got a better idea?"

Indeed, precisely because this heavenly gift of authority can be used for such great good or such great abuse, God does speak to this topic. He has revealed in his Word everything we need to know in order to love and serve him, and this includes how we should organize our churches. For centuries, therefore, the confessions of Baptists, Congregationalists, Presbyterians, and many others have affirmed the sufficiency of Scripture for the corporate life of our churches. That does not mean different groups went to the Bible assuming their practices were correct and then sought to justify them biblically. Rather, it means generations and generations of Christians opened the Bible, read it carefully, and discovered that it addresses some basic aspects of structure and organization. Then they organized their churches accordingly. We should be slow to think we are wiser than so many of them.

The New Testament, in fact, is filled with references to polity. In its pages we find that churches held corporate meetings (Acts 20:7; Heb 10:25) and elections (Acts 1:23–26; 6:5–6). They had officers (Acts 20:17, 28; Phil 1:1), practiced discipline (1 Corinthians 5), collected money (Rom 15:26; 1 Cor 16:1–2), gave and received letters of commendation (Acts 18:27; 2 Cor 3:1), administered the ordinances (Acts 2:41; 1 Cor 11:23–26), baptized and received members (Matt 28:19; Acts 2:47), and more. Clearly God has given directions in his Word about many aspects of the church's corporate life and structure.

And it is wonderful that he does! Knowing that God's Word means to regulate our lives together, even in the organization of our churches, frees us from the tyranny of the latest fashion. Some pastors may feel that we *must* have youth groups and committees and that we *might* have sermons and membership. God's Word, though, realigns our thinking on the church. It lays out clear parameters for our instruction (though within those parameters there is flexibility). We learn that we *must* have preaching and membership and we *might* have choirs and committees.

Nineteenth-century Baptist pastor John L. Dagg (1794–1884) wrote:

> Church order and the ceremonials of religion, are less important than a new heart; and in the view of some, any laborious investigation of questions respecting them may appear to be needless and unprofitable. But we know, from the Holy Scriptures, that Christ gave commands on these subjects, and we cannot refuse to obey. Love prompts our obedience; and love prompts also the search which may be necessary to ascertain his will. Let us, therefore, prosecute the investigations which are before us, with a fervent prayer, that the Holy Spirit, who guides into all truth, may assist us to learn the will of him whom we supremely love and adore.[2]

Love prompts our obedience, and love prompts the search.

After all, right polity strengthens Christians and their ties to one another. Wrong polity weakens them and their ties.

Right polity properly situates a Christian under the rule of Christ during the time of his or her discipleship in this world. Wrong polity either wrongly imposes human rule where Christ does not mean for it to be, or it evacuates his rule from a certain area of the Christian's life where it should be.

---

[2] John L. Dagg, *Manual of Church Order* (Harrisonburg, VA: Gano Books, 1990; orig. pub. 1858), 12.

Right polity hems us in and keeps us from our excesses while also providing a platform for growth and ministry and freedom. Wrong polity erases the lines we should not cross while undermining those platforms that God intends for us to stand on and blocking the paths where we hope to walk.

Right polity protects the gospel from one generation to the next. It is the platinum prongs that hold the diamond of the gospel in place. Wrong polity loosens those prongs so that the diamond of the gospel eventually falls to the ground and gets lost. It leaves heresies and hypocrites unchecked. It lets hurting sheep wander off and fall into canyons.

Right polity protects the path of life. Wrong polity, over time, helps to lay the path for authoritarianism and moralism in one direction and nominalism, liberalism, and atheism in another.

Again, love prompts our obedience, and love prompts the search—love for God and love for our fellow Christians.

This Volume

It is not difficult to imagine a number of ways to order this volume and a rationale for each. But we have begun with congregationalism because we are convinced God gives final earthly authority to the church. Everything else, in a sense, falls under that, including the ordinances. The ordinances signify the existence of a congregation, and so these chapters come next. The ordinances mark off a church's boundaries in the waters of baptism then silently declare the congregation's source of life in the Lord's death at the Table. The ordinances, in other words, make the membership visible, and church discipline occurs through the ordinances. So the chapters on membership and discipline follow the ordinances. All this occurs under the oversight of the elders or pastors. They lead the congregation in their use of authority and in the ordinances, in membership, and in discipline. These chapters therefore come next. Finally, the book's posture turns from inward looking to outward looking. How does a local church view its relationship with other churches and Christians? Are they independent, interdependent, or both?

We intend this polity to be a distinctively Baptist volume, good for seminarians, church leaders, and interested members. Therefore we asked professors from three major Baptist seminaries to contribute a chapter or two (though Thomas White has since left Southwestern Baptist Theological Seminary and gone to lead Cedarville University, sadly ending our Southwestern representation). That said, the careful reader might find subtle disagreements between the authors rising up now and then, wholly (as we recall) at secondary levels of implication or application. There is broad agreement on all the basic planks, but the reader should not assume that every author agrees across the board with every other author. Indeed the editors don't. Yet, as we said, the level of agreement is fairly high indeed, both in terms of our polity and also in terms of our philosophies of ministry, such that the reader can receive this book as representing a single perspective or ministerial worldview.

In the final analysis God means to bless his people through the structures of a church. Dare we think he intended harm? Or that he was being foolish when he inspired certain forms of authority to be held by admittedly fallen human beings?

Frank Lloyd Wright was quite a controlling architect. He not only designed houses and rooms in houses; he designed furniture for those rooms and specified exactly where that furniture should be. But as residents moved into house after house, most of them found that Lloyd Wright's architecture was better than his furniture design.

The opposite will be true as we explore the house of God. The divine Architect has perfectly designed each room and perfectly placed each piece of furniture for the good of the inhabitants and the display of his own glorious character of holiness and love. Somehow the rudiments of polity in our local churches will, by God's transforming power, yield the new Jerusalem, the city descending from heaven in the Bible's final chapters.

Abbreviations

BDAG	W. Bauer, F. W. Danker, W. F. Arndt, and F. W. Gingrich. *Greek-English Lexicon of the New Testament and Other Early Christian Literature*. 3rd ed. Chicago: University of Chicago Press, 2000.
BSac	*Bibliotheca Sacra*
BNTC	Black's New Testament Commentaries
EDT	*Evangelical Dictionary of Theology*
JTS	Journal of Theological Studies
NICNT	New International Commentary on the New Testament
NIGTC	New International Greek Testament Commentary
Presb	Presbyterion
SecCent	Second Century
TDNT	*Theological Dictionary of the New Testament*
TNTC	Tyndale New Testament Commentaries
WBC	Word Biblical Commentary

Introduction—Why Polity?

Jonathan Leeman

The difference between a local church and a group of Christians is nothing more or less than church polity. To argue for polity is to argue for the existence of the local church. That is not to say that polity only references the local church—one must also account for the relationship between churches. But it is to say, no polity, no local church. It should hardly be surprising, therefore, that in an era in which we give little attention to polity, we also play fast and loose with the local church.

All organizations and social groups possess some type of polity, some governing structure that constitutes the group and organizes its members, even if that structure is fairly minimal.[1] To be "a people" or "a group" in any sense whatsoever, formal or informal—whether a nation-state, an advertising agency, a chess club, or the high school cool-kids' clique—means that some criteria exist for distinguishing members from nonmembers and that some rule structure guides behavior within the group. Indeed, these rules constitute a group as a group, even though "the rules may be so basic, so elemental, that members of the group may be unaware of them."[2]

---

[1] Nick Barber, *The Constitutional State*, in Oxford Constitutional Theory, ed. Martin Loughlin, John P. McCormick, and Neil Walker (Oxford, UK: Oxford University Press, 2010), 67.

[2] Ibid. The more formalized a group becomes, the more "aware" group members will be of the rules that constitute them as a group.

To put this another way: a "group" with no polity—no governing structure—is not in fact a group. Without criteria for membership, rules for governing behavior, a self-conscious sense of shared identity, a common purpose or guiding objective, there is no group. There is only a bunch of individuals. Social rules and social groups are inextricably connected: "Groups can only exist where they are constituted by social rules. But, conversely, social rules can only exist in the context of a social group, a group defined by—at minimum—their common acceptance of the rule, coupled with an awareness of their common acceptance."[3]

All this to say: every local church has some polity—some way to constitute itself, to maintain criteria for membership, and to make decisions—because its very existence depends in part upon that polity. Those who disavow the institutional church, or who profess disinterest in the topic of church polity altogether, are a bit like those who profess disinterest in God. It only means they prefer some other polity, or perhaps their own rule, rather than the one "on the books," as the deniers of God actually prefer some other god. Polity is inevitable. The only question is whether one's polity is coherent, orderly, and, most of all, biblical.

Traditionally, Christians have viewed church polity as addressing several areas of church life:

- A church's polity establishes who possesses authority over the processes of membership and discipline and what role baptism and the Lord's Supper play in signifying and constituting members as members and the church as a church.
- Polity creates leadership offices in the church, demarcates their responsibilities and jurisdictional boundaries, specifies who is eligible to serve in those offices, and stipulates the selection process.
- Polity dictates how significant decisions in the life of the church will be made.
- And polity delineates the nature of the relationship between a church and other churches or denominational structures, whether those ties are formal or informal, binding or nonbinding.

All these matters, typically, are laid out in what is variously referred to as a church constitution, book of church order, or book of discipline.

We will discover in this introduction that discipling other Christians and evangelizing non-Christians, too, are related to polity. Polity's significance, in other words, reaches beyond the few bureaucratic matters that

---

[3] Ibid., 69.

Christians force themselves to think about once a year in some church business meeting they attend out of a sense of duty. Rather it plays a crucial role in the Christian life. The present generation of Christians would do well to begin reconceiving their Christian discipleship in the institutional language of polity.

The purpose of this introduction, then, is not to argue for one form of polity over another but to provide an apologetic for the topic in general. It presents four reasons polity is important.

1. Polity Establishes the Local Church

Lest someone argue that local churches are not necessary, we should observe that Scripture treats them as normative: "tell the church"; "the report about them reached the ears of the church in Jerusalem"; "they . . . gathered the church together"; "he went up and greeted the church"; "greet also the church that meets in their home"; "to God's church at Corinth"; "when you come together as a church"; "to the churches of Galatia."[4]

Polity is what constitutes the local church as a local church. Put another way, polity provides the nexus between the universal church and the local church. The movement from the universal church to the local church is a movement *into* polity. To unite a group of previously unattached Christians or members of the universal church into a local church is to "polity-ize" them. It is to place individual Christian relationships inside of the binding identity and rule structure we call the local church. (One can almost picture a science-fiction movie where a ray gun called the Polity-izer fires upon a group of individual Christians and turns them into a church. A good movie for youth groups perhaps?)

The church on earth, we might therefore say, is constituted in two moments. First comes the invisible moment in which God creates a Christian, a member of the universal church, through the preaching of the gospel. The church is in this sense a creature of the word, as Protestants have long said.

Yet this is not the "only constitutive moment for ecclesiology."[5] The church at this first moment remains an abstract idea without a palpable

---

4 Matt 18:17; Acts 11:22; 14:27; 18:22; Rom 16:5; 1 Cor 1:2; 11:18; Gal 1:2. Unless otherwise indicated, all Scripture passages are taken from the HCSB.

5 John Webster, "The 'Self-Organizing' Power of the Gospel: Episcopacy and Community Formation," in *Community Formation: in the Early Church and in the Church Today*, ed. Richard N. Longenecker (Peabody, MA: Hendrickson, 2002), 183.

and public presence. It is not yet visible. For the church to be visible on earth, a mechanism is necessary for identifying both its individual members and its corporate embodiment, its gatherings. Were all the organized collectives we call local churches in the world to suddenly vanish, we who are saints would have no way of knowing who "we" were. The people of the old covenant had circumcision, Sabbath keeping, and eventually a land to identify them, to say nothing of their familial and ethnic ties. What do the people of the new covenant have? How do you exercise border patrol in a kingdom with no borders and no land?

In other words, the church's first constitutive moment is not enough. A group of Christians must still gather and constitute themselves (or be constituted) as a congregation and affirm one another as believers.

Which brings us to the second moment. "A church is born when gospel people form a gospel polity," observes Bobby Jamieson.[6] That is to say, a local church is created when a group of Christians gather together, someone explains the gospel, everyone agrees to it, and they mutually affirm one another's agreement through the ordinances. Different Protestant traditions disagree about whether elders or bishops are necessary for that formal affirmation, and they disagree about whatever else the ordinances may signify. But all agree that the ordinances publicly identify, recognize, or affirm the members of the universal church on earth. They effectually create something that didn't exist before—not salvation but a public and local reality. "The ordinances," says Jamieson, "make it possible to point to something and say 'church' rather than only pointing to many somethings and saying 'Christians.'"[7] Of course, they also make it possible to point to the many somethings and say "Christians." The ordinances, in other words, show us where a church is, and a church shows us who the Christians are.

The ordinances are the beginning of polity. To administer baptism or the Lord's Supper is to make an authoritative pronouncement: "Based on your confession of the gospel, you are with Christ." That pronouncement is the first act of governance in a church because it constitutes the church.[8]

---

[6] Bobby Jamieson, *Going Public: Why Baptism Is Required for Church Membership* (Nashville: B&H Academic, 2015).

[7] Ibid.

[8] We leave aside for now the question of whether elders or bishops must be involved in that constituting act (cf. Acts 14:23; Titus 1:5). Obviously, if one adheres to some concept of apostolic succession through the bishops or elders, a transmission of authority through ordination must precede any act of administering the ordinances and constituting a church.

In short, the church's palpable and public presence depends on its polity.[9] Polity grants believers a recognized status before one another and the nations. That means it is insufficient to say, "The local church is a people." It is also an organized collective, a people bound together by polity. In J. L. Dagg's parsing, "A church is an *organized* assembly."[10]

Some writers today argue that Christians don't need to join churches because they can find Spirit-filled fellowship through more casual and spontaneous associations. Sadly, many "Christians" today practice such church-less-ness, whether or not they have read these authors. All these individuals, however, are trading on the work of identification that local churches do, work that yields an identifiable body of people on earth known as "Christians." Economists might call them free riders—people who benefit from the goods of others without paying for that benefit.

The movement from universal church to local church, then, is the movement from faith to order (though noncongregationalists offer a slightly more complicated picture). The universal church is united in faith. The local church is united in faith and order.[11] Christ's kingly authority is regnant in the universal church, but it is given concrete expression in the local church. It is "put on" through the order or polity of a congregation, as the positional status of being righteous in Christ is "put on" existentially in individual acts of righteous-ness.[12] What's important to observe, though, is that faith and order "are not different entities—the latter, perhaps, clothing the former, but bearing no essential or intrinsic relation to it," as if a church may just as well put on one set of polity clothes as another.[13] Christ's authority is part and parcel of the gospel, which means church order is an outgrowth of Christian faith.

---

9 Membership is always the first and most basic matter of polity and governance because it is the members, bound together in a particular fashion and for a particular end, who constitute a polity. Every other matter of church polity—concerning offices, decision making, and a church's relationship to other churches—derives from this first matter. Cf. Michael Walzer, *Spheres of Justice: A Defense of Pluralism and Equality* (New York: Basic Books, 1983), 31. Speaking of political communities more broadly, Walzer writes, "The primary good that we distribute to one another is membership in some human community. And what we do with regard to membership structures all our other distributive choices: it determines with whom we make those choices, from whom we require obedience and collect taxes, to whom we allocate goods and services."

10 J. L. Dagg, *Manual of Church Order* (Harrisonburg, VA: Gano Books, 1990; orig. pub. 1858), 80, ital. orig.

11 See the extended discussion of this idea in this book, my chapter, "A Congregational Approach to Unity, Holiness, and Apostolicity."

12 See the extended discussion of this idea in Jonathan Leeman, *The Church and the Surprising Offense of God's Love: Re-introducing the Doctrines of Church Membership and Discipline* (Wheaton: Crossway, 2010), 200–16.

13 Webster, "'Self-Organizing' Power," in Longenecker, *Community Formation*, 183.

The gospel produces a certain social ordering among believers, a certain polity.[14]

Different traditions argue over what exactly that "social shape" is, but it's an argument worth having because there is a connection between faith and order.[15] So the Bible's explicit statements on polity must be treated as normative in and of themselves. Yet we should also expect those statements to make systematic sense in light of the gospel. We should expect our gospel and our polity to be logically consistent and mutually reinforcing. More specifically, church order should fit together with the promises of the new covenant, the work of the Spirit, the doctrines of sin and *sola fide*, the lordship of Christ, the priestly regency of believers, the already-not-yet realities of inaugurated eschatology, and more. These pieces of our systematic theology, properly related, will yield *this* polity rather *that* polity. Relating doctrines in order to formulate a polity is one task the authors of this volume seek to accomplish.

2. Polity Guards the Gospel What and Who

Three implications follow from polity's role in establishing the local church. And these provide the second, third, and fourth reasons polity is important. Second, polity is important because it guards the *what* and the *who* of the gospel—what the gospel message is and who the gospel believers are.

Contemporary Christians often ignore polity. We reason that the gospel alone is essential for salvation. But consider once again that movement from the universal to the local church, which I characterized as a movement *into* polity. That movement into polity separates the church from the world. It distinguishes the church's gospel message and gospel people from the world's false gospels and nongospel people. It addresses what I earlier called the problem of identification and accountability by identifying believers and their message. That is to say, church order formally recognizes and marks off the *what* and the *who* of the gospel and, in so doing, protects them.

Polity's gospel-recognizing and gospel-protecting work first shows up in Matthew 16:13–20, where Jesus essentially confronted the apostles

---

14 Webster writes, "Church order is the social shape of the converting power and activity of Christ, which is present as Spirit." Ibid., 183.

15 See David W. Hall, "The Pastoral and Theological Significance of Church Government," in *Paradigms in Polity: Classic Readings in Reformed and Presbyterian Church Government*, ed. David W. Hall and Joseph H. Hall (Grand Rapids: Eerdmans, 1994), 26–28.

with two questions: *What* is a right confession of who I am? And *who* of you knows it? He then affirmed both Peter and Peter's gospel words, saying they came from the Father in heaven. He promised to build his church on confessors confessing the same confession as Peter (the correct *who* and *what*). And finally he gave Peter and the apostles the keys of the kingdom for binding and loosing. With keys in hand, they could render this same formal affirmation on the *who* and *what* of the gospel.[16]

This authoritative pronouncement, which the apostolic church makes through baptism and the Lord's Supper, is the beginning of polity, as I said a moment ago. It separates, distinguishes, and identifies the church before the nations, thereby protecting and preserving the gospel *what* and *who* from one generation to the next: "Yes, that's the gospel; we'll baptize you" or "No, that's not the gospel; we won't baptize you."

Jesus, without a doubt, is deeply concerned about churches because his name is tied to these key-wielding assemblies: "I assure you: Whatever you bind on earth is already bound in heaven, and whatever you loose on earth is already loosed in heaven. . . . For where two or three are gathered together *in My name*, I am there among them" (Matt 18:18, 20, italics added). These gatherings and their members specially represent Christ and his glory before the nations, just like Israel specially represented Yahweh before the nations. Through the keys of binding and loosing, a church exercises its own border patrol and passport distribution among kingdom people who possess no land. A church guards his name, his message, and everyone united to his name. Membership in this community begins, after all, with "baptizing them *in the name* of the Father and of the Son and of the Holy Spirit" (Matt. 28:19, italics added; see also Acts 2:21, 38; 4:12; 5:41; 8:12; 10:48; etc.).

Paul, following the Lord's lead from Matthew 18:20, reminded the Corinthian church that they should exercise the keys through church discipline when the church is formally gathered in Christ's name: "When you are assembled *in the name* of our Lord Jesus and I am with you in spirit, and the power of our Lord Jesus is present, hand this man over to Satan" (1 Cor 5:4–5a ESV, italics added). Paul wanted them "to judge" (v. 12) a man wrongly identifying himself with Christ's name: "But now I am writing you not to associate with anyone who claims to be a believer who is sexually immoral or greedy, an idolater or verbally abusive, a drunkard or a swindler. Do not even eat with such a person" (v. 11).

---

16 For a fuller discussion of this text, again see my chapter "A Congregational Approach to Unity, Holiness, and Apostolicity"; for an even fuller treatment, see my *The Church and the Surprising Offense of God's Love*, 178–95, or *Political* (Downers Grove: IVP Academic, 2016), chap. 6.

The church's call to be separate for the sake of God's name has its background in the Old Testament. God specially identified himself with the Israelites, and they were to represent his name to the nations by being obedient, clean, pure, holy, and consecrated to him. When they defiled his name, he cast them out of the land. Yet even in exile, they profaned his name, so God promised a new covenant precisely for the sake of his name: "It is not for your sake that I will act, house of Israel, but for My holy name, which you profaned among the nations where you went" (Ezek 36:22). Paul, interestingly, looked back to the Old Testament purity laws and holiness requirements for temple worship and treated them as typological for the church. He reemployed this cultic language to argue that Christians should be a marked-off people:

> Do not be mismatched with unbelievers. For what partnership is there between righteousness and lawlessness? Or what fellowship does light have with darkness? What agreement does Christ have with Belial? Or what does a believer have in common with an unbeliever? And what agreement does God's sanctuary have with idols? For we are the sanctuary of the living God, as God said: "I will dwell among them and walk among them, and I will be their God, and they will be My people. Therefore, come out from among them and be separate, says the Lord; do not touch any unclean thing, and I will welcome you. I will be a Father to you, and you will be sons and daughters to Me, says the Lord Almighty." (2 Cor 6:14–18)

Because God is utterly concerned with his own name and reputation, Christ has authorized churches to wield the keys of the kingdom. He has deputized them to mark off the *what* and the *who* of the gospel through baptism and the Lord's Supper. Perhaps two illustrations will make this point concrete. Illustration 1: a Sunday school teacher begins teaching a false gospel—a false *what*—and refuses to be corrected. This heresy, if it spreads through the church, will undermine that church's gospel witness. Illustration 2: a young single man spends time in the home of an older church member who treats his wife and children abusively. The older man appears to be a false *who*. This hypocrisy, if never corrected, will undermine the church's gospel witness in the younger man's life. Quite possibly the younger man will conclude that gospel people are no different from nongospel people, so why bother with the gospel!? In both cases the church should employ the keys to correct the gospel error, first with verbal warnings and eventually, if necessary, with removal from membership and the Lord's Table.

Several lessons follow. First, polity protects churches from heretics and hypocrites, and so protects the gospel. By pounding the gavel and rendering a verdict on false gospel professions, the church clarifies its message.

Second, the *what* and the *who* of the gospel are the most significant matters of polity, even more than who the leaders are. The church *is* its gospel-believing members, and their everyday lives and words will impact the nations' opinion of Jesus more than bad headlines about fallen church leaders. Yes, my congregationalist convictions are seeping through here, but I believe any Protestant could affirm this with the right qualifications.

Third, a Christian never leaves the so-called institutional church behind, even when he scatters during the week, because the institutional church's affirmation of faith publicly unites the rest of his life (such as how he treats his wife and children, works at the office, interacts with neighbors, spends time on vacation) to the name of Jesus. Our membership in a church *makes our whole life speak about Jesus*. Members recognize one another as Christians because of the church's institutional work of baptism and the Lord's Supper. In short, we cannot so cleanly separate the "institutional church" and the "organic church."

That means, fourth, our Christian discipleship is shaped by church polity whether we intend it to be or not. We will further explore this fourth lesson in a moment.

Suppose, alternatively, that churches as the Bible describes them didn't exist and that gatherings of Christians were only that, casual groups of Christian individuals with no authority to bind or loose one another in the faith through baptism and the Lord's Supper. Instead, every Christian was left to self-identify. The state of Christianity in the world would be a mess, to say the least. Born-again Christians (or the universal church) could hypothetically exist, but they would have no good way of identifying one another or living out the corporate body life. One individual says that Jesus is God. Another individual says Jesus is the first of all God's creations. Both identify as Christians. And who would there be to say both aren't! Neither Christians nor non-Christians would have a good way of sorting out the false teachers from the true, or the false professors from the true. Does that spousal abuser, philanderer, or embezzler who names the name of Jesus in fact represent him? Who's to say he doesn't!? And which gatherings are the Christian ones? Is it the gatherings of Unitarians or Mormons or Americans? If they said they were Christians, who could say otherwise? In all this, Christianity would have an even larger public relations problem than it already has. There would be no way to "track" Christ's people, no way to reach out and put your arms around the phenomena of Christianity.

Again, how foolish are the contemporary voices who argue that the local church is unnecessary and that all Christians need is a little self-selected fellowship. How foolish, too, are the many so-called Christians who fail to submit themselves to a local church. Are they really so confident in their own faith and their own grasp of the gospel? Are they confident in every other so-called Christian's grasp of the gospel?

Paul assumed that the churches of Galatia should be able to discern the difference between a true and a false gospel. And he assumed that they had the authority, in one form or another, to insist that the true gospel be preached (Gal 1:6–9). Paul thought the Corinthian church should be able to recognize a life that was ethically out of step with the gospel, and he called them to protect the reputation of the gospel by removing an unrepentant sinner from membership (1 Corinthians 5). He was counting on these churches, in one way or another, to act authoritatively to protect the gospel and its witness in the lives of the saints. He was expecting them to employ their polity.

To be sure, some polities guard the *who* and the *what* of the gospel better than others, which is why debates over polity are important. Speaking from my own congregationalist and baptistic perspective for a moment, I believe regenerate church membership protects the gospel because it restricts membership in the church to believers, not believers and their children. Congregationalism protects the gospel, I believe, because it insists on equipping the saints for the work of the ministry, as I will argue in a moment. But the larger picture is that any polity is better than no polity because an irregular church is better than no church. A formally unattached group of Christians might gather occasionally and enjoy their shared participation in the gospel together. But let a year or two pass, let a controversy arise, let all the usual sins that occur between Christians occur in their fellowship, let the preachers come and go, let hypocrites and heretics enter their unorganized assembly, let one generation give way to the next, and see how firmly this group holds onto the gospel together. Would they even last a year? Would their members continue to stand firm in the gospel? A few of them perhaps.

Church polity, in short, protects the definition and articulation of the gospel. It guards the gospel message, like the prongs of a ring hold a jewel in place. And church polity protects the people of the gospel. It tells them when their lives contradict their professions, and it points them to the men who are exemplars of gospel living because they are "above reproach" (1 Tim 3:2). All this protects and strengthens the church's gospel witness in the neighborhood, the city, the nation.

3. Polity Gives Shape to Christian Discipleship

There is a third reason church polity is crucial: if polity constitutes the local church as the local church and if the New Testament teaches that believers should be united to churches, it would seem that church polity should shape the Christian's discipleship.

Christians are not accustomed to thinking this way, in part, because our discussions of church government often emphasize only one half of government's work, the work of constraining sin.[17] But church polity is about commissioning as much as constraining, authorizing as much as holding accountable, saying do as much as saying don't. God intended for both his old- and new-covenant people to be priests and kings—to represent his rule to the nations. The people of the new covenant, moreover, have been given an outpouring of his Spirit for these royal ends. Their whole lives are to be used for propagating his government and, therefore, fall within the rubric of church polity. We considered this idea above when we observed that our church membership makes our whole life speak about Jesus. The larger point is that joining a church means assuming an office. Elder and deacon aren't the only "offices." Membership is also an office, I will argue below. Polity, in other words, isn't only about who makes the decisions; it's about authorizing people to do the work of representing Jesus with their entire lives.

To contemporary ears, the claim that polity should shape Christian discipleship will sound strange. Too often, Christian discipleship is conceived in individualistic—by which I mean antiauthority—terms. Christians view their friends, pastors, and churches as aids to personal growth and discipleship, but there is a difference between pragmatic aids from which one picks and chooses and a structured accountability that binds and looses. That difference is nothing more or less than the local church. The church exists to place "fellowship" inside an authority structure.

Today's average evangelicals, however, often prefer their *koinonia* without *politeia*. I have argued elsewhere that we have been dramatically

---

17 Hall, "The Pastoral and Theological Significance of Church Government," in Hall and Hall, *Paradigms in Polity*, 13–17.

influenced by the broader cultural milieu that is deeply antagonistic to any authority outside the autonomous individual. Novel after novel and movie after movie rehash the same liberation narrative of the brave and heroic individual standing against oppressive governments or traditions. The consumer is accustomed to choosing from among thirty-one flavors. All truth claims have been debunked, and pragmatism rules the day.[18] Serious and nonserious Christians alike too often fail to place our discipleship in *submission* to the local church and its leaders. We might enjoy casual fellowship, but we don't deliberately build relationships for the purposes of discipling, equipping, transparency, and accountability. We don't invite instruction and discipline. We don't make ourselves known to the elders so that they can watch over us. We don't consult their wisdom when making major life decisions; indeed, the programmatic structures of too many churches work against such known-ness. We move to cities based on job or school opportunities without asking whether a healthy church exists. We purchase homes or rent apartments without considering their geographic proximity to a healthy church or concentrations of its members. We make budgetary decisions with little thought for generosity to church members in need or helping the church as a whole to make its budget. We don't inconvenience ourselves. We join churches lightly and exit them lightly—church hop—seldom stopping to weigh the consequences of our departure on others. Just take your purchase back to the checkout counter.

Contemporary spirituality focuses on individual expression and self-actualization. We read books and attend conferences that tell us to listen to God's voice. Pursue the plans he has for us. Discover our unique gifts. Journal our story. Practice God's presence in the quiet of conscience. Experience him. And take a step into the unknown for his sake. The question that drives us is not, What responsibilities and obligations do I have to the family of God? but, How can I be everything God intends for me to be?

Question 2 is a good one to ask. But the answer to question 2 depends, in good measure, on the answer to question 1. Our approach to spirituality tends to miss this, which leads to Christian lives that are often misshapen, misdirected, and unbiblical. Biblical discipleship requires laying down our lives for one another (see John 13:34–35). It requires us to relinquish the role of captain, or at least to steer our ships in formation with the armada.

Christian spirituality, sanctification, and discipleship should be both Word driven and church shaped. And a significant component of being

---

18 See *The Church and the Surprising Offense of God's Love*, chap. 1.

church shaped depends on polity. What then does it mean to say that polity should shape Christian discipleship?

The short answer is, it means the Christian life should be placed inside the accountability and authorizing structures of the local church both because Jesus commands it and because that's how both the individual and the body grow best. It means that, from the perspective of living out the Christian life, the words *Christian* and *church member* should be almost interchangeable. The individual Christian lives his or her life *in* and *through* the relationship structures that are the local church.

It's not enough to say that a Christian's discipleship must occur in the context of *relationships*. There are different kinds of relationships: husband-wife, employer-employee, governor-citizen, parent-child, friend-friend, and so forth. What makes these relationships different from one other is the combination of obligations and privileges that constitute and characterize each. A child's obligations and privileges with a parent, for instance, are distinct from an employee's with an employer. To say that Christian discipleship should be shaped by polity means (1) ascertaining exactly what privileges and responsibilities characterize the different kinds of relationships inside a local church (such as elder-member, member-member, deacon-elder, etc.) and then (2) submitting one's discipleship and growth to those relational structures.

So deep are the individualistic grooves in our cultural consciences, however, that we need to consider what it might mean to "think institutionally," as political scientist Hugh Heclo has put it.[19] Heclo says institutional thinking is *not* the modern impulse to critically challenge, question, unmask, expose, and demystify everything that is placed in front of us. It is not a hermeneutic of suspicion. Instead, says Heclo, institutional thinking involves three things: faithful reception, the recognition of value, and lengthened time horizons.

Faithfully Receiving Rather Than Continually Inventing

First, thinking in institutional terms involves a posture of faithful "receiving rather than inventing or creating." The individualist wants to think of everything for himself or herself: new discoveries, new stories, new doctrine, new expressions, new songs. The institutional thinker, however, recognizes that "what has been received from those who preceded carries

---

[19] Hugh Heclo, "Thinking Institutionally," in *The Oxford Handbook of Political Institutions*, ed R. A. W. Rhodes, Sarah A. Binder, and Bert A. Rockman (New York: Oxford University Press, 2006), 731–42. Heclo also has a 2011 Oxford University Press book titled *On Thinking Institutionally*.

authority." The past's institutions and traditions do not arrive in the present willy-nilly; their survival typically suggests some measure of wisdom and that they should be given a fair hearing, maybe even a *prima facie* judgment in their favor. A posture of faithful receiving does not mean no room exists for innovation or fresh thinking: "To be submissive to what has been received is a distinctly unfashionable idea, but it does not mean being servile." It simply means one should always seek to faithfully receive the wisdom of the past before venturing into new circumstances—where new questions and answers, of course, are inevitable.

What might "faithful receiving" look like in the Christian life? For starters, it might mean reading a book on church polity! More broadly, faithful receiving involves an acceptance of doctrinal orthodoxy, which is to say, an implicit acceptance of traditional doctrinal formulations, at least until new and better formulations can acquire a broad consensus. It might involve the use of old hymns, at least where they exist in one's cultural context. Christians from the past have much to teach us about understanding God and approaching him, and we don't want to squander their wisdom. Faithful receiving sees value in submitting one's Christian discipleship to older, more experienced Christians, as well as to the collective wisdom of the whole congregation. Faithful receiving involves putting oneself into relational situations where one might be contradicted or corrected, as uncomfortable as that can be. Faithful receiving places a premium on conversation and reasoning together. It involves asking questions and then listening intently to the answers. It precludes feeling entitled to our own way and being convinced of our own rightness. Faithful receiving means moving carefully and deliberately. It requires being quick to listen, slow to speak. It means being teachable and learning the art of leadership by being led, knowing that godly leadership, first and foremost, is submissive. Faithful receiving requires not demanding a higher office but recognizing that everything we receive is a gift. Faithful receiving entails submitting to the elders' decisions, even if one is an elder. It involves accepting limitations, boundaries, and lost votes.

Recognizing Theological and Moral Realities Beyond Personal Preference

Second, says Heclo, thinking institutionally involves recognizing the existence of certain values and moral realities that are larger than one's personal preferences. Institutions, which I define as rule structures that impact behavior and identity,[20] fix certain theological and moral valuations into place. They embed those valuations into expectations for behavior, requiring people to act not only out of convenience but obligation and responsibility. Institutional structures can represent the complacencies or the power mongering of past administrations, surely, but more often than not they serve to protect and promote something. This is true in everything from rules for aircraft safety to the norms and customs that constitute a particular vocation, such as lawyer, doctor, or teacher.

Consider, for instance, what it means to think as a "parent." To become a parent is to be placed inside of an identity and rule structure—an institution—that requires one to forfeit personal preference and value something larger. A baby crying at 2:00 a.m. is not just a physical imposition; it's a moral imposition. One can refuse it, as absentee fathers do, but the sense of moral responsibility pulls most people out of bed. To think as a "spouse," too, is to adopt an institutional identity that governs one's behavior based on a multitude of theological and moral valuations. When a society dismisses the significance of marriage or the family, what it's dismissing is a particular set of moral valuations that, theretofore, governed marriage and family.

How do these observations help us think about Christian discipleship through the lens of polity? Quite simply every area of polity listed as a bullet point at the beginning of this introduction represents a host of theological and moral valuations, and these valuations in turn impose various obligations and bestow various privileges on Christians:

Office of Church Member: Christianity is commonly characterized among evangelicals as a "personal relationship" with Jesus. This is a legitimate description, but what kind of relationship is it? There are many kinds of relationships, I observed above. Scripture gives this personal relationship with Jesus quite a bit of institutional specificity through the labels it gives Christ: Shepherd, firstborn, Messiah. One of Scripture's most prominent themes is Christ as the King of the kingdom. His kingship means that Christians relate to Jesus as citizens relate to a king (e.g., Eph 2:19; Phil 3:20). To become a Christian is to be given the institutional identity and office of kingdom *citizen*, a word that communicates the idea of being ruled while sharing in rule.[21] How then does someone publicly assume the office of *kingdom citizen* or *ruled ruler*

---

[20] See Elizabeth Sanders, "Historical Institutionalism," in Rhodes, Binder, and Rockman, *The Oxford Handbook of Political Institutions*, 38.

[21] Scripture sometimes uses the word *citizen* explicitly. More commonly the idea of being a ruled ruler is wrapped up in the theme of imaging God (e.g., Gen 1:28; Psalm 8; 1 Cor 15:49; 2 Cor 3:18; 2 Tim 2:12; Rev 5:10; 22:5).

between Christ's ascension and return? They become a church member. Through the ordinances of baptism and the Lord's Supper, the local church employs the keys of the kingdom to bind and loose on earth what's bound and loosed in heaven (see Matt 16:19; 18:17–18). The church affirms someone as belonging or not belonging to Christ's kingdom through membership.[22]

Church membership, then, is an office. It's the job of representing Jesus as one of his ruled rulers, as Jesus was a ruled ruler on behalf of the Father. Like all offices, its occupants possess a calling to the work and the mission of the organization. They have responsibilities and duties. Want to act like a Christian? Fulfill your church responsibilities. What are those responsibilities? Broadly, each church member is to be a Jesus representative. That's the membership office we enter upon baptism. We now wear his name and care about his name, and to that end we are called to do both the constraining and commissioning work of church government. This is why Jesus gives assemblies of two or three gathered in his name (churches) the keys of the kingdom (Matt 18:18–20). He intends for those two or three to guard and watch over his reputation by carefully attending to the *what* and *who* of the gospel. And he intends for them to represent his name through discipling and evangelism.

A church member's job, to put it another way, is to know the gospel, to only support teachers who teach the gospel, to live by the gospel in word and deed, to help other church members do the same, and to call non-Christian neighbors to the obedience of repentance and faith in Christ the Savior-King. We help other church members by knowing them, by involving ourselves in their lives, and by speaking "only what is good for building up someone in need, so that it gives grace to those who hear" (Eph 4:29). This is the picture of a body "building up itself in love by the proper working of each individual part" (Eph 4:16). Yes, Christians do this to some measure with Christian friends who belong to other churches, but we do so without the advantages of the formal accountability and discipline of the local church. Hopefully, those friends belong to churches of their own where their fellow members love them within the context of such formal accountability.

Offices of Leadership: In addition to the office of church member, Scripture establishes the offices of deacon and elder. Varying traditions treat these offices differently, and some even add a third office to the mix, but the offices always represent sets of theological and moral

---

[22] Jonathan Leeman, *Church Membership: How the World Knows Who Represents Jesus* (Wheaton: Crossway, 2012); *Political Church*, chap. 6.

valuations. Suppose we adopt the two offices advocated in this volume, whereby elders attend to the Word-intensive work of preaching, prayer, and oversight while deacons attend to the physical needs of the congregation. What theological and moral valuations are in play? We could name many: Word ministry is a priority and must never be hindered even by physical need; Christian growth is fueled by God speaking through godly teachers; oversight should belong to those who are formally recognized as proficient with the Word; the church should care for members in physical need; and so forth. Submitting to the leadership of elders and deacons involves internalizing these theological and moral valuations. The Christian "disciple" who decides not to polity-ize his or her discipleship by joining a church is effectively renouncing these theological and moral claims. He or she is effectively saying, for instance: "No, my Christianity does *not* require oversight by someone who has been formally recognized as being proficient in the Word. I am the best judge of my own life and Scriptural proficiency." Hopefully, the reader is by now acquiring some sense of how deeply arrogant anti-institutional, anti-polity thinking is.

Decision Making: Even the way church polity specifies a church's decision-making process assumes a set of theological and moral valuations that Christian disciples do well to internalize. Heclo's discussion of "rule-following" is worth quoting at length here:

> Because it is attentive to rule-following rather than personal strategies to achieve personal ends, thinking institutionally enhances predictability in conduct. Predictability in turn can enhance trust, which can enhance reciprocating loyalty, which can facilitate bargaining, compromise, and fiduciary relationships. Because institutional thinking goes beyond merely contingent, instrumental attachments, it takes daily life into something deeper than a passing parade of personal moods and feelings. In the end, the advantages of institutional thinking come down to what is distinctly human. The point is not that it is wrong to see institutions as cages of human oppression, but that this is a dangerously incomplete half-truth. Institutions can also be the instruments for human liberation and enriched, flourishing lives . . . . For example, without institutions upholding private property, even the most liberated individual will soon find his or her freedom an empty slogan. But it goes beyond that. By its nature, institutional thinking tends to cultivate belonging and common

life. It leads to collective action that not only controls but also expands and liberates individual action. Humans flourish as creatures of attachments, not unencumbered selves.[23]

To transpose this into the domain of church polity, we might say that submitting oneself to a book of church order or church constitution for the process of decision making, even if it recommends something as prosaic as Roberts Rules of Order, is a way of affirming the good of the church's corporate activity, the limits of any one individual, the necessity of the whole body, the value of trust and unity among the redeemed people of God, and more.

Other Churches: For a church to recognize any connection to other churches, whether formal or informal, is to acknowledge that the kingdom of God is bigger than one's own congregation. It is to acknowledge other believers with whom one can fellowship and cooperate for kingdom purposes. The precise nature of the connection to other churches, furthermore, speaks to a church's understanding of Christian unity, whether it depends on faith or upon faith and order.

Lengthening Our Time Horizons Beyond the Now

Third, Heclo argues that "institutional thinking values continuity and long-term over short-term calculations." Its time horizons stretch backward and forward, requiring us to acknowledge that much of what we have we have been given and we will give to others. We receive and we bequeath, which means we must always pay attention to questions of precedent. We live under the obligations of usufruct, says Heclo, the right to enjoy what belongs to another without destroying or wasting it. Institutional thinking places us inside a larger "us" that includes the living, the dead, and the unborn. It promotes solidarity.[24]

Again, it is not difficult to transpose Heclo's wisdom into the realm of discipleship and polity. Taking the long view attends to church history, as mentioned above, its orthodoxy and hymnody. It recognizes the continuity we share with those who came before us, and so it tries to learn from them. But taking the long view also means being careful about the precedents we set for those still to come. It may keep us from adopting seemingly "prudent" structures that work in our situation because a quick forward glance suggests they could easily mislead future generations. It

---

[23] Heclo, "Thinking Institutionally," in Rhodes, Binder, and Rockman, *The Oxford Handbook of Political Institutions*, 739–40.
[24] Ibid., 737.

nudges us back to the sufficiency of Scripture. It discourages us from designing flashy programs that produce quick decisions and reap nominal Christianity. It encourages us instead to work for a "long obedience in the same direction," as the phrase goes. Taking the long view should prompt us to rely on the ordinary means of grace and God's promise to work through his Word and Spirit, even if change comes slowly. In that sense the long view promotes patience and keeps us from manipulating people in an effort to accumulate results, statistics, and proof of conversions now.

A biblical concept that sums up Heclo's proposal for "institutional thinking" and these three postures—faithfully receiving, recognizing moral value, lengthening one's time horizons—is maturity. The screaming infant offers the paradigmatic picture of short-time horizons and a preoccupation with personal preferences.

Consider by way of contrast Paul's statement, "When I was a child, I spoke like a child, I thought like a child, I reasoned like a child. When I became a man, I put aside childish things" (1 Cor 13:11). Throughout the letter of 1 Corinthians, Paul addressed a church that had succumbed to factionalism and one-upsmanship. In chapters 12–14, where we find this verse, he reminded the church of each member's dependence on every other member (chap. 12) and of the premium they should place on practices that build up the body (chap. 14). That, apparently, is what it means to act like an adult and not a child. Childishness is individualistic. It is indifferent to the needs of the body and pursues its own desires. Maturity is body minded. It seeks to serve and recognizes its dependence on the whole.

The immature and individualistic mind-set, whether in its Christian or secular form, conceives of an ironically small universe. It makes *me* bigger and wiser than all those rules and structures and traditions and institutions that would bind me. I become the judge and lord of them all, which presumes that the boundaries of my mental universe encompass everything. My whole universe, then, becomes as big as . . . me—a small universe, indeed. But the moment I acknowledge that some rules and traditions or institutions are bigger than me, my universe has the potential to grow. To submit to the institution of marriage means caring not only for myself but for another. To submit to the institution of family means caring for children and parents. To submit to a church means caring for a whole group of believers to whom I'm joined not by blood but by freely elected covenant. Each of these institutional roles restricts activity in one direction but expands it in another. It's hardly surprising that an individualistic and antiauthority age is experiencing growing divorce rates and absentee parenting and church hopping.

When Christian discipleship confines itself inside the structures of church polity, it gains access to the platforms and tools that will expand, grow, and enlarge the soul. Polity hems in the soul in some ways, but it hems it in as a sculptor's chisel might or a gardener's shears. Its restrictions, over time, produce the body, the blossom. No, you may not be a member until you repent of your sin. No, you may not be an elder until you manage your household well. Yes, you must work toward a consensus. Yes, you must strive to persuade those who disagree. Here's what life inside the new humanity looks like. Now come!

Authority in a fallen world is often abused. But that does not change the inevitable-as-gravity fact that, according to Scripture, growth occurs through submission. Jesus even tells us that the basic shape of faith is submission (Matt 8:10). What is faith, after all, but believing and acting on the word of a higher authority? It's through the polity of a local church that Christians have the chance to exercise their faith muscles as they submit to one another (see Eph 5:21). The self-guided Christian life, on the other hand, has comparatively less opportunity to exercise and grow one's faith muscles because every spiritual step is taken on one's own terms. But the young couple who heeds the elder's instruction or the young woman who listens to the congregation's rebuke or the young man who rises to the older man's charge is learning to trust a voice other than his or her own, and that trust will yield a harvest of righteousness and peace (see Heb 12:11 NIV).

A polity-shaped approach to Christian discipleship, finally, is consistent with a Word-driven understanding of Christian growth.[25] Faith begins when we kneel before Jesus' claim to be Savior and Lord. It begins with our obedience to a word.[26] And it grows as we increasingly submit to everything he commands (Matt 28:20). Church polity and a polity-shaped understanding of Christian discipleship are nothing more or less than our obedience to a word—the Word of Christ in Scripture and then the delegated and authorized word of a church and its leaders.

---

[25] See Jonathan Leeman, *Reverberation: How God's Word Gives Light, Freedom, and Action to His People* (Chicago: Moody, 2011).

[26] See John 6:63; Rom 10:9–10; 2 Cor 4:6; Jas 1:18, 21; 1 Pet 1:23.

4. Polity Strengthens a Church's Witness

An irony of late-modern, liberal culture is that for all the emphasis on autonomy and tolerance, we place a high premium on ideological conformity, and we disdain anything reeking of sectarianism.[27] Evangelicals have their own version of this: impatience toward denominational or polity differences. That impatience might be the sincerely pious child of a desire for gospel outreach and unity, but Christians of the past didn't seem to worry that their convictions over polity would yield such trouble. Neither should we.

In fact, polity's work of establishing the local church actually propagates gospel work throughout the nations—the fourth reason polity is important. As stated several times now, institutions not only constrain; they commission. They provide platforms for activity or channels for growth. A church's polity should serve the church's mission, just like the governing structure of any organization should serve the end for which that organization exists, whether it is a computer manufacturer or a baseball team. Christians today sometimes disagree over how broadly or narrowly the church's mission should be defined, but virtually all would agree that its mission includes evangelism.

In every polity, baptizing people into the Christian church identifies them with Jesus' name and sets them apart for the work of representing Jesus through evangelism. The first biblical step of making an evangelist is baptism into church membership. It is like handing out a team jersey. People don't typically connect polity with evangelism, but the two are clearly connected. Institutional identification precedes and enables the work of evangelistic representation. The office of church member is an ambassadorial office.

In every polity, recognizing teachers of the Word leads to equipping of the saints for evangelism and witness more broadly. Pastors, elders, or bishops equip the saints for the work of ministry by teaching them (see Eph 4:11–16). Deacons, too, advance the church's evangelistic ministry by serving the needs of the saints and thus helping to build church unity. When the Hebrew- and Greek-speaking widows were threatened with

---

[27] On this point, see Colin E. Gunton, *The One, the Three, and the Many: God, Creation and the Culture of Modernity* (New York: Cambridge University Press, 1993), esp. 28–37. E.g., "The heart of the paradox of the modern condition is that a quest for the freedom of the many has eventuated in new forms of slavery to the one. . . . When God is no longer the one who holds things together, demons rush in to fill his place. An impersonal one replaces the despised one of traditional theism, and the slavery is greater than before" (34, 36).

disunity because of an inequitable distribution of food, deaconlike individuals worked to unite the church (see Acts 6:1–7).

In this final category of discussion, my own congregationalist perspective must again break the silence and speak. Congregationalism, when combined with the safety of regenerate church membership, best propagates a church's evangelistic work and witness.

What distinguishes congregationalism from any form of presbyterianism or episcopalianism, most fundamentally, is that it gives final authority to recognize the *who* and *what* of the gospel to the gathered church. It says the keys belong jointly to the whole congregation: "For where two or three are gathered" (Matt 18:20), and "When you are assembled in the name of the Lord Jesus . . . with the power of the Lord Jesus" (1 Cor 5:4). And this requires two things of every member. First, it requires every member to study the gospel and know it. That way they can discern any departures from it. Hence, Paul was "astonished" that the members of the Galatian churches had begun listening to another gospel (Gal 1:6–9 ESV). They should have known better! Second, it requires Christians both to understand the relationship between the gospel and obedience and to work to know their fellow members. That way they can exercise their shared authority over one another with integrity. Hence, Paul was grieved when the Corinthian members failed to root out a little bad yeast (1 Corinthians 5).

In other words, congregationalism, like no other form of church government, forces leaders to work hard at equipping the saints to do their jobs well. This is what builds a healthy church. One might liken a noncongregational church and a congregational church to two different exercise classes. In the noncongregational church, the instructor skips rope and lifts weights while the class sits on lawn chairs watching. In the congregational church, the instructor demonstrates the exercises and then walks around the room inspecting the rope jumping and weight lifting of the class members. Which of these two classes will be more equipped and stronger? Pushing the final locus of authority concerning the *who* and *what* of the gospel upward from the congregation, to the session, to the Presbytery, or to the bishop enervates the congregation and undermines their work of evangelism. It tempts the congregation to laziness and complacency because it effectively fires them from their jobs. Indeed, the higher the authority goes, the more we can expect complacency, nominalism, and eventually liberalism in the pews. Church history seems to testify to as much.

The new covenant removed the priest, the king, and any other tribal mediator from his position between God's people and God. There is now only one mediator, one priest, and one king, who is Christ. Through our union with Christ, all of God's people are made priests and kings. As such, "No longer will one teach his neighbor or his brother, saying, 'Know the LORD,' for they will all know Me, from the least to the greatest of them" (Jer 31:34). To put it another way, every member of the new covenant is made responsible for the *who* and the *what* of the gospel. But that responsibility cannot be properly exercised where there is no authority commensurate with the responsibility. Congregationalism, I propose, best fits the structures and promises of the new covenant. It best protects and propagates the evangelistic work of the church because it insists on equipping all the saints for the work of the church. It more decidedly and explicitly installs every Christian into office.

Conclusion

One newspaper opinion writer, reviewing Eric Liu's book *A Chinaman's Chance*, made this observation about America's public square, marketplace, and civic life: "American culture now has an excess of individualism, short-term thinking and prioritizing of rights over duties. [Liu] calls for 'a corrective dose' of Chinese values: mutual responsibility, long-term thinking, humility, moral character and contribution to society."[28] Anyone familiar with the individualistic and entitlement-driven nature of the American cultural landscape probably sympathizes with this author's interest in a corrective dose of these "Chinese" values. In the same way the purpose of this introduction—indeed, the purpose of this whole book—is to call for a corrective dose of polity thinking. Polity clearly will not provide evangelicals with everything we need for Christian discipleship and evangelistic witness, but it's a crucial piece.

Ultimately, God's goal in shaping Christian disciples and propagating their witness with the help of church polity is "that they might be for [God] a people, a name, a praise, and a glory" (Jer 13:11 ESV).

---

[28] Dana Milbank, "Battle Cry of the White Man," in the *Washington Post*, August 5, 2014. Accessed on August 22, 2014, http://www.washingtonpost.com/opinions/dana-milbank-battle-cry-of-the-white-man/2014/08/05/961858f4-1cd4-11e4-ab7b-696c295ddfd1_story.html.

PART 1

CONGREGATIONALISM

Michael A. G. Haykin
Kirk Wellum
Stephen J. Wellum

It is easy to caricature congregationalism and has been at least since the days of Theodore Bèza, as the first chapter below suggests. Of course, bad examples of congregational churches still abound that only aid the critics. In the past century many congregational churches seem to have learned more from democratic systems of government than from the Bible (not that congregationalism is the only form of church government that's open to abuse and distortion). They have treated their churches as some form of direct democracy, requiring the pastor to gain the whole church's approval on the most incidental expenses. Meanwhile, they treat their leaders with the suspicion given to politicians on Capitol Hill. A plurality of elders doesn't seem like such a good idea, then, because it's much easier to keep only one pastor in his place.

But it's not an unhealthy and distorted model of congregationalism we wish to defend. Instead, we defend the view that churches should be led and directed by biblically qualified elders, who in turn are accountable to the church as a whole. Ultimately, the congregation as a whole is accountable to the Word of Christ, ensuring that a faithful gospel ministry endures in that place. In short, organizational expression is given to the gospel reality that the church is a group of regenerate-but-not-yet-glorified Christians who are gathered together in the name of the Lord Jesus Christ.

In the chapters that follow, we will set the historical context and roots of congregationalism in Baptist life, spanning the years 1560–1720 and describing how congregationalism functioned and developed. Then we will turn to the biblical and theological case for congregationalism as the best form of church government for faithfully reflecting the nature of the church as the new covenant people of God. Throughout these chapters (and this book), the word *congregationalism* with a lowercased "c" refers to the doctrine, while the word with an uppercased "C" refers to a denomination.

CHAPTER 1

Some Historical Roots of Congregationalism

Michael A. G. Haykin

A comprehensive study of congregationalism, not simply as a denominational stream but as a conviction about church life that has been found in numerous Christian communities, would doubtless require a series of volumes. In what follows, I have taken my cue from Geoffrey F. Nuttall's brilliant study of congregationalism in the historical period between 1640 and 1660.[1] This present study, however, broadens the time frame to include congregationalist witness in the Reformation period as well as congregationalism among the most significant body of seventeenth- and eighteenth-century Baptists, the Particular Baptists. Essential to the Particular Baptist vision in these two centuries was a view of church government that they shared with their Congregationalist brethren, a view that they believed best reflected the scriptural teaching.

Jean Morély: An Early Proponent of Congregationalism

The massacre of St. Bartholomew's Day (August 24, 1572) and the weeks following, when thousands of French Protestants were slaughtered in cold blood, comprised a tragedy of immeasurable proportions. The slaughter decapitated the French Protestant community and

---

[1] *Visible Saints: The Congregational Way 1640–1660* (1957 ed.; repr. Weston Rhyn, Oswestry, Shropshire: Quinta Press, 2001).

radicalized those who survived. And in the long run it was detrimental to the well-being of the French nation.[2]

Among the victims in Paris were the chief supporters of Jean Morély (ca. 1524–ca.1594), one of the earliest known advocates of congregationalism, whose *Traicté de la discipline et police Chrestienne* (*A Treatise on Christian Discipline and Polity*) had created a firestorm of controversy within the French Reformed community since its publication at Lyons ten years earlier.[3] Morély was a member of the nobility. Some of his humanist education had been in Zurich, where he was probably converted between 1546 and 1548. After a brief stay at Wittenberg, where he studied under the German reformer Philipp Melanchthon (1497–1560), he completed his theological studies at Lausanne, where he became acquainted with Pierre Viret (1511–71), a close friend of John Calvin (1509–64). Between the early 1550s and 1561, Morély split his residence between Paris and Geneva, and in the latter city he completed his treatise on church government. He apparently showed it first to Calvin, but the French reformer was too involved in directing church planting and missions in France to read it.[4] Around 1561, Morély moved to Lyons, where Viret was pastoring. The latter gave Morély's manuscript a cursory read but did not study it closely enough to see any problems with its arguments. Morély thus went ahead in 1562 and had it printed in an elegant 350-page edition. He dedicated it to Viret[5] and presented it to the national assembly of the French Reformed Church, which was held in Orleans that year. The book was a bombshell.

Traicté de la discipline is divided into four books. In the first Morély argued for the necessity of church discipline.[6] He was concerned that the Reformed churches of his day had significantly inferior moral

---

[2] See Geoffrey Treasure, *The Huguenots* (New Haven, CT: Yale University Press, 2013), 167–75. Estimates of the slain vary from 5,000 to 30,000. We should probably think in terms of between 5,000 and 10,000.

[3] The best treatment of his life is Philippe Denis and Jean Rott, *Jean Morély (ca. 1524–1594) et l'utopie d'une démocratie dans l'église* (Geneva: Librairie Droz, 1993). See also Robert Kingdon, *Geneva and the Consolidation of the French Protestant Movement, 1564–1572* (Madison: University of Wisconsin Press, 1967), 43–137, and S. K. Barker, *Protestantism, Poetry and Protest: The Vernacular Writings of Antoine de Chandieu (c. 1534–1591)* (Farnham, Surrey/Burlington, VT: Ashgate Publishing, 2009), 195ff.

[4] On this mission, see Michael A. G. Haykin and C. Jeffrey Robinson Sr., *To the Ends of the Earth: Calvin's Missional Vision and Legacy* (Wheaton: Crossway, 2014), 65–70.

[5] *Traicté de la discipline et police Chrestienne* (Lyons, 1562), [i–vi]. Subsequent references to Morély's *Traicté de la discipline* will cite book and chapter where relevant and place the pagination in brackets.

[6] *Traicté de la discipline* 1 [1–72].

and lifestyle standards in comparison to the early church (*la primitive Église*).[7] But how was one to recover the moral ethos of the early church? Morély argued that churches needed to recover the type of governance that marked those halcyon days in the church's history, namely, "democratic government" (*gouvernement Democratique*), where authority is vested in the hands of the congregation. Unlike today, the term *democracy* and its cognates were freighted with deep-seated negative connotations in the sixteenth century. Centuries of political reflection about the ideal type of government in late Antiquity and the medieval era led to the consensus that a monarchical arrangement was best. As a result there was an instinctive rejection of any type of governance that gave the people a major role in decision making. Such governance was regarded as little better than anarchy, lacking both a permanent body of law and administrators for that legal framework.[8] Morély sought to circumvent this instinctive dislike by insisting that the church government he had in mind was not a true or "pure" democracy in the ancient sense because there was a body of law—to be found in the Scriptures—and a body of administration, namely, the pastors and elders of the local church.[9] He further defined the local church as that "union of truly blessed souls chosen in Jesus Christ from eternity for eternal life, who assemble for the preaching of the Word and the administration of the sacraments, who are a part and image of the universal church."[10]

Book 2 focused on the church's implementation of discipline as it related to excommunication and heresy. To whom has Christ given the authority to receive new members into the local church, or expel them if necessary? Morély is clear: such decisions are ultimately the responsibility of the local church. Pastors and elders must then execute decisions that come from the congregation.[11] On this point Pierre Viret took a similar stand to Morély, but during the controversy sparked by Morély's ideas, Viret kept his views to himself. To have done otherwise would have meant conflict with his closest friends, including Calvin in Geneva.[12] If the powers of reception and excommunication belong ultimately to the congregation, then it follows, as Morély argued in book 3,

---

[7] *Traicté de la discipline* 1.8 [30–33].

[8] Robert M. Kingdon, "Calvinism and Democracy: Some Political Implications of Debates on French Reformed Church Government, 1562–1572," *The American Historical Review* 69:2 (1964): 396.

[9] *Traicté de la discipline* 1.8 [32–33].

[10] *Traicté de la discipline* 1.12 [61–62], translation Michael A. G. Haykin.

[11] *Traicté de la discipline* 2.17 [166–69].

[12] Tadataka Maruyama, *The Ecclesiology of Theodore Beza, The Reform of the True Church* (Geneva: Librairie Droz, 1978), 97–98.

that the congregation also has the power to elect its own officers, pastors, elders, and deacons. And for scriptural proof Morély turned to the election of Matthias in Acts 1 and the election of Stephen in Acts 6.[13] The "voice of the church" elects its leaders.[14] The final book looks at a variety of ecclesiological issues: the role of ministerial meetings and synods,[15] how the church should take care of the poor,[16] the need for formal theological education,[17] and the importance of catechizing.[18]

Morély's book was printed in March 1562. A few weeks later, at the national synod of the French Reformed churches held in Orleans, it was condemned for its "wicked doctrine," doctrine that would subvert the Reformed cause in France if implemented.[19] Morély was asked to appear before the company of pastors in Geneva to give an account of his views. When he eventually did in July 1563, he offered to recant his views only if they were rejected publicly by the three recognized leaders of the French Reformation, namely, Calvin, Viret, and Guillaume Farel (1489–1565). Viret, as mentioned, sympathized with Morély, while Calvin refused to enter the discussion lest he undermine the synodal decision already made by the French elders at Orleans. The Genevan consistory, therefore, continued to press Morély to abandon his congregationalism. His response, Luther-like, was to refuse unless he was shown to be wrong by the Scriptures. In the face of such obstinacy, the consistory believed it had no choice but to condemn Morély as a schismatic and excommunicate him.[20]

Morély left Geneva for Paris, where he soon acquired an influential circle of friends, including Odet de Coligny (1517–71), the Protestant cardinal of Châtillon; Jeanne d'Albret (1528–72), the queen of Navarre; and the philosopher Pierre Ramus (1515–72). But his book was deemed serious enough that during the 1560s his main opponents proved to be Théodore de Bèza (1519–1605), Calvin's lieutenant and theological heir in Geneva, and Antoine de la Roche Chandieu (1534–91), leader of the Protestant cause in Paris, who wrote a harsh rejoinder to Morély, *La confirmation de la discipline ecclésiastique observée ès églises réformées du royaume de France* (*The Confirmation of the Church Discipline*

13 *Traicté de la discipline* 3.1 [174–76].
14 *Traicté de la discipline* 3.2 [186–87].
15 *Traicté de la discipline* 4.4–8 [280–305].
16 *Traicté de la discipline* 4.9–13 [305–22].
17 *Traicté de la discipline* 4.14–15, 17 [322–34, 337–39].
18 *Traicté de la discipline* 4.16 [334].
19 Robert M. Kingdon, *Geneva and the Consolidation of the French Protestant Movement 1564–1572* (Madison, WI: University of Wisconsin Press, 1967), 64.
20 Ibid.

Observed in the Reformed Churches of the Kingdom of France). The essence of Chandieu's argument was that excommunication and church discipline, the determination of orthodoxy, and the election and dismissal of church officers were entirely within the purview of the ministerial consistory, not that of the gathered community.[21] Bèza, on the other hand, undertook a letter-writing campaign to destroy Morély's support and reputation. In a lengthy letter to the Swiss German reformer Heinrich Bullinger (1504–75), for example, Bèza focused on Morély's use of the term *democracy*. Bèza accused Morély of calling the French Reformed churches an "oligarchy" or "tyranny" and told Bullinger that if Morély had his way, he would undermine these churches by means of a "most troublesome and most seditious democracy." Bullinger admitted he had actually never heard of Morély but concluded from what Bèza told him that he must be a dreadful Anabaptist![22] Morély's conduct in this early controversy over church government, in turn, was far from blameless. In a letter to a Reformed pastor in Orleans, he called Bèza "this new Antichrist."[23] Little wonder that when Bèza discovered this, he told Morély point-blank in a final letter to him: "It is you who have violated the virginity of the French churches."[24]

Although Morély did not perish with many of those who supported him in the St. Bartholomew's Day massacres, the debate between him and Chandieu and Bèza was over, and the latters' presbyterian position had won the day. After the horrific savagery of 1572, Morély fled to England, where he lived until his death around 1594. Further research is needed to see what influence Morély's ideas may have had on English Separatists in the 1580s. But whatever the outcome of such research, Morély still needs to be recognized as a key pioneer of the way of congregationalism.

The Congregationalist Legacy of the Separatists

The Reformation came to England during the reign of Henry VIII (r. 1509–47), although it was not until the reign of his son Edward VI (r. 1547–53) and his daughter Elizabeth I (r. 1559–1603) that it gained a firm foothold. Elizabeth's ascension to the throne affirmed that

---

21 *La confirmation de la discipline ecclésiastique observée en églises réformées de France* (Geneva, 1566), 149, 155, 205.

22 Kingdon, "Calvinism and Democracy," 398–99.

23 Treasure, *Huguenots*, 126.

24 Ibid., dated March 25, 1567.

England would firmly fall into the Protestant orbit. The question that arose, though, was to what extent the Elizabethan state church would be reformed. Elizabeth was content with a church that was "Calvinistic in theology, [but] Erastian in Church order and government [i.e., the state was ascendant over the church in these areas], and largely mediaeval in liturgy."[25] As a response to this "settledness" in the Church of England, the Puritan movement arose.

Initially Puritanism sought to thoroughly reform the Elizabethan church after the model of the churches in Protestant Switzerland, especially those in Geneva and Zurich. These continental churches were attempting to include in the church's worship only that which was explicitly commanded by Scripture. For instance, John Calvin declared that "nothing pleases God but what he himself has commanded us in his Word" concerning a church's worship.[26] As Douglas Kelly has noted, this concern with proper worship arose out of the fact that Puritanism was a revival movement. In his words:

> They [i.e., the Puritans] were so concerned with worship because they were so concerned with God. Puritanism budded during a revival movement, an outpouring of the Holy Spirit, which gave them an immediate sense of the nearness, the holiness, the beauty and the grace of the Triune God. . . . Everything less than God was secondary to knowing and serving Him aright. Worship was first; even the most legitimate concerns were second. If worship was of such supreme significance, what could matter more than to do it in a way that would please God?[27]

As the sixteenth century wore on, though, the goal of fully reforming the English state church seemed no closer. Consequently, in the latter part of that century, a number of Puritans concluded that the Church of England would never be fully reformed and decided to separate from the state church and organize their own congregations. These Puritans

---

[25] Robert C. Walton, *The Gathered Community* (London: The Carey Press, 1946), 59.

[26] T. H. L. Parker, trans., *Daniel I (Chapters 1–6)* Calvin's Old Testament Commentaries, vol. 20 (Grand Rapids: Eerdmans/Carlisle, Cumbria, UK: Paternoster Press, 1993), 130. Compare, though, the remarks of Douglas Kelly on Calvin's position: "The Puritan Regulative Principle and Contemporary Worship" in *The Westminster Confession into the 21st Century, Essays in Remembrance of the 350th Anniversary of the Westminster Assembly*, ed. J. Ligon Duncan III (Fearn, Tain, Ross-shire, Scotland, UK: Mentor, 2004), 71–72.

[27] Kelly, "Puritan Regulative Principle," in Duncan, *Westminster Confession into the 21st Century*, 73.

were known as Separatists, and they argued for what was essentially a congregationalist form of church government.

One of their earliest leaders was Robert Browne (c.1550–1633), who in a tract entitled *A Treatise of Reformation Without Tarrying for Anie* (1582), provided the "clarion-call" of the Separatist movement.[28] In this influential tract Browne set forth the views that became, over the course of the next century, common property of all the theological children of the English Separatists, including the Independents or Congregationalists and the Baptists. First of all, Browne conceded the right of civil authorities to rule and to govern. However, he drew a distinct line between their powers in society at large and their power with regard to local churches. As citizens of the state, the individual members of these churches were to be subject to civil authorities. However, he emphasized, these authorities had no right "to compel religion, to plant Churches by power, and to force a submission to ecclesiastical government by laws and penalties."[29]

Then Browne conceived of the local church as a "gathered" church, a company of Christians who had covenanted together to live under the rule of Christ, the risen Lord, who made his will known through his Word and Spirit. Finally, the pastors and elders of the church ultimately received their authority and office from God, but they were to be appointed to their office by "due consent and agreement of the church . . . according to the number of the most which agree."[30]

Although Browne later recanted these views under torture in England, he had started a movement that could not be held in check. Browne's mantle fell to three men in particular—John Greenwood (c. 1560–93), Henry Barrow (c. 1550–93), and John Penry (1559–93)[31]—all of whom were hanged in 1593 for what was regarded by the state as an act of civil disobedience, namely secession from the established church. When Penry was being examined by the state authorities, he was adamant that

---

28 B. R. White, *The English Separatist Tradition from the Marian Martyrs to the Pilgrim Fathers* (London: Oxford University Press, 1971), 42. On Browne, see White, *English Separatist Tradition*, 44–66, and Alan P. F. Sell, *Saints: Visible, Orderly and Catholic, The Congregational Idea of the Church* (Allison Park, PA: Pickwick Publications, 1986), 13–16.

29 White, *English Separatist Tradition*, 59.

30 Michael R. Watts, *The Dissenters: From the Reformation to the French Revolution* (Oxford: Clarendon Press, 1978), 30.

31 On Barrow and Greenwood, see Sell, *Saints*, 16–20. For a study of Penry, see Geoffrey Thomas, "John Penry and the Marprelate Controversy" in *The Trials of Puritanism, Papers Read at the 1993 Westminster Conference* (London: The Westminster Conference, 1993), 45–71.

a true church was "a company of those whom the Word calleth Saints, which do not only profess in word that they know God, but also are subject unto his Laws and Ordinance indeed." This was a veiled criticism of the idea of a parish church whose membership consisted of everyone who lived within the geographic boundaries of the parish.[32] One gets a sense of how committed these men were to their understanding of the Bible from words spoken by Penry shortly before his execution. He affirmed that "imprisonment, judgments, yea, death itself, are not meet weapons to convince men's consciences, grounded on the word of God."[33]

Before their deaths, the preaching and writings of these three men led a significant number in London to adopt Separatist principles. The English Baptist historian Barrie White has noted, "For many it was but a short step from impatient Puritanism within the established Church to convinced Separatism outside it."[34] To curb the growth of these Separatists, state and ecclesiastical authorities passed a law in April 1593 requiring everyone over the age of sixteen to attend their local parish church. Failure to do so for an entire month meant imprisonment. If a person still refused to conform three months following his or her release, the person was given a choice of exile or death. The Elizabethan church and state hoped to rid itself of the Separatist problem by sending the recalcitrant into exile.

Understandably, when faced with a choice of death or exile, most Separatists chose the latter and initially emigrated to Holland. From there a number of them sailed across the Atlantic in 1620 heading for Virginia. Blown off course, they landed after sixty-six days at sea at Plymouth in Cape Cod Bay. In 1691, Plymouth Plantation was absorbed into another Congregationalist colony, Massachusetts.

A Consistent Congregationalist, Oliver Cromwell

The first settlers of the Massachusetts Bay colony landed at Salem in 1628. Unlike the Separatists at Plymouth Plantation, though, these Puritans were congregationalists who had remained in the Church of England, seeking to reform her from within. During the 1630s, however, William Laud (1573–1645), the archbishop of Canterbury, used savage

---

[32] *The Examinations of Henry Barrow, John Greenwood, and John Penry, Before the High Commissioners and Lords of the Council* (London, 1635), 41.

[33] Watts, *Dissenters*, 39.

[34] White, *English Separatist Tradition*, 84.

measures to repress the Puritans, both presbyterians and congregationalists, in order to bring about religious uniformity within the state church.
Many of the Puritans thus quit England to find religious freedom in the
new world of New England. Twenty or so years later, the quintessential
Puritan Oliver Cromwell (1599–1658) recalled why they went and why
those who had stayed in England had taken up arms against their sovereign Charles I (1600–49) in the British Civil Wars (1642–51):

> Is not Liberty of Conscience in religion a fundamental? . . .
> Indeed, that hath been one of the vanities of our contests. Every
> sect saith, "Oh! Give me liberty." But give him it, and to his
> power he will not yield it to anybody else. Where is our ingenu-
> ity? Truly, that's a thing ought to be very reciprocal. The mag-
> istrate hath his supremacy, and he may settle religion according
> to his conscience. And I may say it to you, I can say it: All
> the money of this nation would not have tempted men to fight
> upon such an account as they have engaged, if they had not had
> hopes of liberty, better than they had from Episcopacy, or than
> would have been afforded them from a Scottish Presbytery, or
> an English either. . . .
> This I say is a fundamental. It ought to be so; it is for us, and
> the generations to come. And if there be an absoluteness in the
> imposer, without fitting allowances and exceptions from the
> rule, we shall have our people driven into wildernesses, as they
> were when those poor and afflicted people, that forsook their
> estates and inheritances here, where they lived plentifully and
> comfortably, for the enjoyment of their liberty, and were neces-
> sitated to go into a vast howling wilderness in New England,
> where they have for liberty sake stript themselves of all their
> comfort and the full enjoyment they had, embracing rather loss
> of friends and want, than to be so ensnared and in bondage.[35]

Such religious liberty, afforded under Cromwell's leadership, proved
fertile ground for the development of congregationalism. Cromwell had
made similar remarks about religious freedom at the outset of a military

[35] *Speech to Parliament* (September 12, 1654) in Thomas Carlyle, *Oliver Cromwell's
Letters and Speeches with Elucidations* (New York: Charles Scribner's Sons, 1897),
3:147–48. There are a multitude of biographies of Cromwell. See especially John
Buchan, *Oliver Cromwell* (London: Hodder and Stoughton, Ltd., 1934); Antonia Fraser,
Cromwell, Our Chief of Men (London: Weidenfeld and Nicolson, 1973); and recently,
Martyn Bennett, *Oliver Cromwell* (London/New York: Routledge, 2006).

campaign he had undertaken in Scotland in 1650–51. He was reluctant to enter into war against the presbyterian Scots because he shared the Reformed faith with them. Yet he utterly opposed how they exalted their distinctives and desired to coerce others into embracing them. Presbyterianism or any forms of church government, he told the Scots,

> are not by the Covenant to be imposed by force; yet we do and are ready to embrace so much as doth, or shall be made appear to us to be according to the Word of God. Are we to be dealt with as enemies, because we come not to your way? Is all religion wrapped up in that or any one form? Doth that name, or thing, give the difference between those that are the members of Christ and those that are not? We think not so. We say, faith working by love is the true character of a Christian; and, God is our witness, in whomsoever we see any thing of Christ to be, there we reckon our duty to love, waiting for a more plentiful effusion of the Spirit of God to make all those Christians, who, by the malice of the world, are diversified, and by their own carnal-mindedness, do diversify themselves by several names of reproach, to be of one heart and one mind, worshipping God with one consent.[36]

The Christian is called to love all in whom Christ dwells regardless of their denominational affiliation. After all, such denominational divisions, Cromwell felt, originate in worldliness and fleshly reasoning. Cromwell overlooked the fact that sometimes genuinely positive reasons exist for developing differing ecclesial bodies. For instance, godly congregations should leave a church connection that has abandoned the vital truths of the faith. But Cromwell was certainly correct to say that a significant amount of disagreement among genuine Christians is carnal narrow-mindedness. Waiting (and praying?) for an outpouring of the Spirit to unify God's people in love was thus an essential aspect of Cromwellian spirituality. Cromwell's final words were to pray for God to give his people "one heart and mutual love."[37]

Thus, it's no surprise that Cromwell, when appointed Lord Protector in 1653, sought to create a climate that made room for the differences

---

[36] *A Declaration of the Army of England upon Their March into Scotland, To All that Are Saints, and Partakers of the Faith of God's Elect, in Scotland* (July 19, 1650) in Wilbur Cortez Abbott with Catherine D. Crane, *The Writings and Speeches of Oliver Cromwell* (Cambridge: Harvard University Press, 1939), 2:285–86.

[37] Carlyle, *Oliver Cromwell's Letters and Speeches*, 4:204–5.

of conviction between professing Christians. Scholars differ over Cromwell's motives as well as the parameters of his policy of religious toleration.[38] There is, however, little gainsaying the fact that Cromwell had a burning desire for an atmosphere of religious toleration that precious few in his day were willing to sanction. Probably the most noteworthy statement by Cromwell in favor of such toleration is his 1652 remark that he "had rather that Mahumetanism [i.e., Mohammedanism] were permitted amongst us, than that one of God's children should be persecuted."[39] Cromwell believed that if Christians could not be immediately united, then liberty of conscience was an acceptable second best.[40] This statement also reveals, as Geoffrey F. Nuttall has noted, a sturdy faith in the might of the Holy Spirit to lead Christian men and women of differing views into unity.[41] Thus Cromwell could write to the governor of Edinburgh Castle, Walter Dundas, "Your pretended fear lest error should step in, is like the man that would keep all the wine out of the country lest men should be drunk. It will be found an unjust and unwise jealousy, to deny a man the liberty he hath by nature upon a supposition that he may abuse it."[42]

Oliver Cromwell never actually belonged to a specific congregation, but his religious convictions were definitely those of the Independents or Congregationalists. His one-time chaplain, John Owen (1616–83), expressed those convictions regarding religious liberty well when he wrote in the preface to *The Savoy Declaration*: "The Spirit of Christ

---

38 See, for instance, Robert S. Paul, *The Lord Protector: Religion and Politics in the Life of Oliver Cromwell* (Grand Rapids: Eerdmans, 1955), 324–33; H. F. Lovell Cocks, *The Religious Life of Oliver Cromwell* (London: Independent Press Ltd., 1960), 45–63; George A. Drake, "Oliver Cromwell and the Quest for Religious Toleration" in *The Impact of the Church upon Its Culture*, ed. Jerald C. Brauer (Chicago: University of Chicago Press, 1968), 267–91; Roger Howell Jr., "Cromwell and English Liberty" in *Freedom and the English Revolution, Essays in History and Literature*, eds. R. C. Richardson and G. M. Ridden (Manchester: Manchester University Press, 1986), 25–44; Blair Worden, "Toleration and the Cromwellian Protectorate" in *Persecution and Toleration*, ed. W. J. Sheils (Oxford: Basil Blackwell for the Ecclesiastical History Society, 1984), 199–233; J. C. Davis, "Cromwell's Religion" in *Oliver Cromwell and the English Revolution*, ed. John Morrill (London/New York: Longman, 1990), 191–99; and Michael A. G. Haykin, *"To Honour God": The Spirituality of Oliver Cromwell* (Dundas, ON: Joshua Press, 1999).

39 Cited Roger Williams, "To the Truly Christian Reader" in *The Fourth Paper, Presented by Maior Butler, To the Honourable Committee of Parliament, for the Propagating the Gospel of Christ Jesus* (London: Giles Calvert, 1652), ii.

40 Davis, "Cromwell's Religion," in Morrill, *Cromwell and the English Revolution*, 198–99.

41 *The Holy Spirit in Puritan Faith and Experience*, 2nd ed. (Oxford: Basil Blackwell, 1947), 127.

42 Carlyle, *Oliver Cromwell's Letters and Speeches*, 2:235; dated September 12, 1650.

is in himself too *free*, great and generous a Spirit, to suffer himself to be used by any human arm, to whip men into belief; he drives not, but *gently leads into all truth*, and *persuades* men to *dwell in the tents of like precious Faith*; which would lose of its preciousness and value, if that sparkle of freeness shone not in it."[43]

The Congregationalism of the Particular Baptists

Among those Christian communities that espoused a congregational polity during the era of Oliver Cromwell were the Particular or Calvinistic Baptists. By the mid-1640s there were at least seven Particular Baptist congregations, all of them coming out of a Puritan background and all of them located in the metropolis of London.[44] Among their key leaders in the early years of their existence were such men as John Spilsbury (1593–c. 1668), William Kiffin (1616–1701), and Samuel Richardson (fl. 1643–58). Because of their commitment to baptizing believers, many in London confused them with the Anabaptists of the previous century. In order to dispel this confusion, refute other charges that had been leveled against them, and demonstrate their fundamental solidarity with Calvinists throughout western Europe, these Particular Baptists issued the First London Confession of Faith in 1644.[45] As the exemplary historical research of Barrie R. White has shown, this confession gave these early Particular Baptists an extremely clear and self-conscious sense of who they were, what they were seeking to achieve, and how they differed from other Puritan bodies.[46] This First London Confession also

---

[43] "Preface" to *The Savoy Declaration* (1658), accessed January 7, 2014, http://www.creeds.net/congregational/savoy.

[44] For the full story of the emergence of the Calvinistic Baptists from the Puritan-Separatist matrix, see especially B. R. White, *The English Baptists of the Seventeenth Century*, rev. ed. (London: The Baptist Historical Society, 1996).

[45] For a readily accessible copy of this confession, see William L. Lumpkin, *Baptist Confessions of Faith*, rev. ed. (Valley Forge, PA: Judson Press, 1969), 153–71. The confession was issued as the Westminster Assembly was meeting and went through at least two printings in its first year of existence. It was then reissued in a slightly amended second edition on November 30, 1646 (four days after the Presbyterian Westminster Confession of Faith had been completed, though not yet published). Two further editions subsequently appeared in the early 1650s. See Murray Tolmie, *The Triumph of the Saints, The Separate Churches of London 1616–1649* (Cambridge: Cambridge University Press, 1977), 61–65; B. R. White, "The Origins and Convictions of the First Calvinistic Baptists," *Baptist History and Heritage*, 25:4 (1990), 45.

[46] See, in particular, the following publications by White: "The Organisation of the Particular Baptists, 1644–1660," *Journal of Ecclesiastical History* 17 (1966): 209–26; "The Doctrine of the Church in the Particular Baptist Confession of 1644," *The Journal of Theological Studies*, n.s., 19 (1968): 570–90; "Thomas Patient in Ireland," *Irish*

demonstrated for many that the Particular Baptists were not guilty of heterodoxy or fundamental error.

The local church, article 33 of the confession affirms, "is a company of visible Saints, called & separated from the world, by the word and the Spirit of God, to the visible profession of the faith of the Gospel, being baptized into that faith, and joyned to the Lord, and each other, by mutuall agreement."[47] In other words, the local church should consist only of those who have experienced conversion and who have borne visible witness to that experience by being baptized. As Benjamin Keach (1640–1704), a General Baptist who became the single most important theologian of the Particular Baptist movement at the end of the seventeenth century, put it: an essential part of a local church's "Beauty and Glory" is the fact that it is built with "all precious Stones, lively Stones; all regenerated Persons."[48] Especially noteworthy in the article from the First London Confession is the "mutualism" in the description of the church.[49] Believers are "joined to the Lord, and each other, by mutual agreement," says the confession. A church is envisaged as not simply a group of individuals who have put their faith in Christ. It is a community of belief—men and women who have owned Christ, been baptized as believers, and in so doing committed themselves to one another.[50]

This vision of the church clearly ran counter to a major aspect of the *mentalité* of seventeenth-century Anglicans, Presbyterians, and even the Congregationalists in New England, namely the idea of an ecclesio-political establishment, where religious uniformity was maintained by the arm of the state and infant baptism all but required for citizenship. Baptists were convinced that the church is ultimately a fellowship of those who have personally embraced the salvation freely offered in Christ, not an army of conscripted men and women who have no choice in the matter. Placing the phrase "being baptized into that faith" after the words "profession of the faith of the Gospel" in the above text underscores this conviction. Only those who have knowingly professed faith

---

Baptist Historical Society Journal 2 (1969–70), 36–48, especially 40–41; "Origins and Convictions of the First Calvinistic Baptists," 39–47; *English Baptists of the Seventeenth Century*, 59–94.

47 Lumpkin, *Baptist Confessions*, 165.

48 *The Glory of a True Church, and Its Discipline Display'd* (London, 1697), iii, 56.

49 For this term, see Charles E. Hambrick-Stowe, "'A Company of Professed Believers Ecclesiastically Confederate': the Message of the Cambridge Platform," accessed January 7, 2014, http://www.ucc.org/beliefs/theology/a-company-of-professed.html. This paper was given as part of a conference marking the 350th anniversary of the *Cambridge Platform* (1649).

50 Ibid.

should be baptized. Given the Cromwellian regime's understanding of religious liberty, it is not surprising that these Baptists flourished during the era when Cromwell ruled.

Articles 36 and 42–45 in this confession offer a classic description of congregational church government. On the basis of Matthew 18:17 and 1 Corinthians 5:4, the confession affirms that "Christ has . . . given power to his whole Church to receive in and cast out, by way of Excommunication, any member; and this power is given to every particular Congregation, and not one particular person, either member or Officer, but the whole."[51] The members of the local church acting together have the authority and power to receive new members into their midst as well as to excommunicate those who refuse to walk under Christ's lordship. Furthermore, "every Church has power given them from Christ, to choose to themselves meet persons into the office of Pastors, Teachers, Elders, Deacons."[52] It was also stressed that "none other have power to impose" leaders on the congregation from the outside. While later editions limited the names of the leaders of the congregation to "Elders" and "Deacons," there was no retreat from the fact that "the ministry was . . . firmly subordinated to the immediate authority of the covenanted community."[53] White has pointed out that these early Baptists maintained a jealous concern for congregational autonomy out of a deep desire to be free to obey Christ and not be bound by the dictates of men and human traditions.[54] Undergirding this was a profound concern for God's freedom to be Lord of his church. They regarded human religious traditions that were not sanctioned by God's Word as affronts to God's sovereign freedom and violations of his prerogatives.[55]

Balancing this strong affirmation of congregational autonomy, which could easily lead to isolationism, was article 47, which declared that "although the particular Congregations be distinct and several Bodies, every one a compact and knit City in itself; yet are they all to walk by one and the same Rule, and by all means convenient to have the counsel and help of one another in all needful affaires of the Church, as members of one body in the common faith under Christ their only head."[56] The

---

[51] First London Confession of Faith XLII (Lumpkin, *Baptist Confessions*, 168).

[52] First London Confession of Faith XXXVI (Lumpkin, *Baptist Confessions*, 166).

[53] White, "Doctrine of the Church," 581, and his "Origins and Convictions of the First Calvinistic Baptists," 46. On the fact that there should be only two church offices, those of elder and deacon, see the remarks of Keach, *Glory of a True Church*, 15–16.

[54] "Doctrine of the Church," 584.

[55] Philip E. Thompson, "People of the Free God: The Passion of the Seventeenth-Century Baptists," *American Baptist Quarterly* 15:3 (1991): 226–31.

[56] Lumpkin, *Baptist Confessions*, 168–69, modernized.

autonomy of each local congregation was recognized as a biblical given but so was the fact that each congregation ultimately belonged to only one body and each shared the same head, the Lord Christ. It was incumbent upon local congregations, therefore, to help one another.[57]

Baptists Covenanting Together— The Praxis of Congregationalism

An excellent window into early Baptist thinking about belonging to a Christian community can be found in their church covenants. These used to be common in Baptist churches but have fallen into disuse in recent days. But a good number of seventeenth- and eighteenth-century Baptist churches sought to promote and safeguard their experience as communities of Christian disciples by adopting written covenants.[58] Champlin Burrage, writing on this subject in 1904, suggested that the idea of a church covenanting together may well have originated among German Anabaptist communities in the 1520s.[59] Be this as it may, by the seventeenth century, written covenants were common to both Scottish Presbyterians—where they eventually took the form of a national covenant rather than ones agreed to by individual local congregations—and the Puritans who had separated from the Church of England, among whom were the Baptists.[60]

---

[57] The sort of help envisioned by the authors of this confession can be discerned in the proof texts that were placed alongside this article in both its 1644 and 1646 editions. The first edition cited, among others, 1 Cor 16:1, which refers to the collection of money that Paul gathered from congregations in Greece and Asia Minor for the poor in the church at Jerusalem, and Col 4:16, in which the church at Colossae is urged to share Paul's letter to them with the church at Laodicea and vice versa. In the 1646 edition, some proof texts were dropped and among those added were Acts 15:2–3, which deals with the Jerusalem Council, and 2 Cor 8:1, 4, which has to do with the collection of money for the church at Jerusalem. In other words the authors of this confession envisioned the churches helping one another in areas of financial need as well as giving advice with regard to doctrinal and ethical matters. Ultimately the churches were bound together by their determination to walk according to the "one and the same Rule," that is, the Scriptures. See further White, "Doctrine of the Church," 583–84.

[58] For the views of those Baptist leaders who felt that a church need not have a written covenant, see Champlin Burrage, *The Church Covenant Idea: Its Origin and Its Development* (Philadelphia: American Baptist Publication Society, 1904), 113–21, 124–25; Charles W. Deweese, *Baptist Church Covenants* (Nashville: Broadman Press, 1990), 26–27; Gwyn Davies, *Covenanting with God, The Story of Personal and Church Covenants and Their Lessons for Today* (Bryntirion, Bridgend, Mid Glamorgan: Evangelical Library of Wales, 1994), 51–52.

[59] *Church Covenant Idea*, 13–25. See also Deweese, *Baptist Church Covenants*, 20–21.

[60] Davies, *Covenanting with God*, 39; Deweese, *Baptist Church Covenants*, 22–23.

The heart and substance of these church covenants usually consisted of a series of carefully formulated commitments that were biblically based and that church members voluntarily made to God and to one another. Whereas confessions of faith are centered mainly on vital doctrinal issues, these covenants deal primarily with Christian conduct.[61] In the words of Charles Deweese, a Southern Baptist historian, they were designed to "deepen the quality of a church's fellowship, sharpen a church's awareness of vital moral and spiritual commitments, clarify biblical standards for Christian growth, and create and maintain a disciplined church membership."[62]

Church covenants greatly aided in the attempt to form Christian disciples. First of all, they served as filters by which a local church could determine to some degree who was or who was not a disciple of Christ.[63] The covenant was also a means of reclaiming recalcitrant members who had left the pathway of discipleship. It could be used to remind such individuals of what they had once promised to do and to observe.[64] Finally, covenants gave expression to a distinct view of the Christian life as one of a voluntary, wholehearted commitment to God and to his church. Christian discipleship begins with dedicating the entirety of one's being to God. And the best piece of evidence of this dedication is found in living wholeheartedly for him in the context of the local church.[65]

---

[61] Deweese, *Baptist Church Covenants*, viii–ix; David Fountain, "Can the Old Church Covenants Help Us Today?" *Sword & Trowel* (December 4, 1985), 8.

[62] Deweese, *Baptist Church Covenants*, x.

[63] Thus, William Carey (1761–1834), plagued by drunken deacons and bitter strife among a number of unruly members in his pastorate at Leicester, proceeded to recommend the dissolution of the church in September 1790. This was agreed to by a majority of the members. Then, with the support of this majority, the church was reconstituted on the basis of a covenant, so as "to bind them to a strict and faithful New Testament discipline, let it affect whom it might." The result, according to Carey's grandson, was that "they filled the fellowship with faithful love" and the "nettles gave place to the Spirit's flowers and fruits." See S. Pearce Carey, *William Carey* (London: Hodder and Stoughton, [1923]), 57–60.

[64] Davies, *Covenanting with God*, 52. In the concluding words of the church covenant drawn up by Benjamin Keach for his London congregation: "Can anything lay a greater obligation up the Conscience, than this Covenant, what then is the sin of such who violate it?" (cited Deweese, *Baptist Church Covenants*, 121). When Christmas Evans (1766–1838), who for more than forty years was the most celebrated Baptist preacher in Wales, arrived in the island of Anglesey, off the northern coast of Wales, he found the life of the Baptist churches there at quite a low ebb. His response was to hold a day of prayer so that the members of these churches might be brought to repentance and a recommitment to the promises they had made when they signed their church covenants. See Davies, *Covenanting with God*, 53.

[65] Fountain, "Church Covenants," 8–10.

While some of these church covenants were general, many of them were fairly detailed. A good example of the latter is that of the Baptist cause at Bourton-on-the-Water, Gloucestershire, dated January 30, 1720.[66] After the death of their pastor Joshua Head in 1719, who had served in this capacity for the previous nineteen years, the church was divided over the choice of a successor to Head. So deep was the division that the church actually dissolved for a brief period of time. In January 1720, though, a majority of the members formally recommitted themselves to one another as a body of believers and Christian disciples: "We ... freely & heartily give up our selves afresh," they declared, "to God the Father & his only Son our Lord and Lawgiver; & to one another according to his will." Documenting this act of recommitment was a covenant composed of thirteen articles.

Nearly a quarter of the articles commit members to preserving their unity in Christ, perhaps because of their recent experience of fractious disagreement over the choice of a new pastor. "We will, to the utmost of our power," they affirm in the first article, "walk together in one Body, & as near as may be with one mind, in all sweetness of Spirit, and saint-like love to each other, as highly becomes the disciples of Christ." Article 3 draws on the language of Ephesians 4:3, a classic text with regard to church unity, to make essentially the same point: "We will with all care, diligence, & conscience labour & study, to keep the unity of the Spirit in the bond of peace, both in the Church in general, & in particular between one another."

This concern for church unity, however, did not mean indiscriminately embracing all who affirmed that they were Christian disciples. Those who signed this covenant declared their readiness to "shun those that are seducers & false preachers of errors and heresies" (article 4). And in the second article the signators stated their determination to "jointly contend, & strive together for the Faith & purity of the Gospel," which they further defined as "the truths of Jesus Christ, & the order, ordinances, honour, liberty, & privileges of this his Church." The fifth and sixth articles asked them to promise to bear one another's burdens and weaknesses because doing this fulfilled "the end of our near relation." In other words, "being there" for one another was part of their *raison d'être* as a community of believers. Christian discipleship and the Christian pilgrimage cannot exist in isolation—they require community.

---

[66] For a copy of this covenant, see either "The Bourton Church-Covenant," *Transactions of the Congregational Historical Society* 1 (1901–4), 270–74, or Deweese, *Baptist Church Covenants*, 122–24. In the citations from it that follow, the spelling and capitalization have been modernized.

Article 7 addresses persecution:

> We will, as our God shall enable us, cleave fast to each other to
> the utmost of our power; & that if perilous times should come,
> & a time of persecution . . . we will not draw back from our
> holy profession, but will endeavour to strengthen one another's
> hands, & encourage one another to perseverance.

For any in the Bourton church who were roughly fifty years of age or
older, persecution for the faith was a vivid memory because, apart from
the brief period when England had been ruled by Cromwell in the 1650s,
genuine religious toleration had not existed until 1688. In fact, in 1714,
only six years before this covenant was drawn up, Anglican diehards had
unsuccessfully attempted to close down all of the academies and seminaries run by anyone outside of the Church of England.[67] This pledge
takes seriously that a Christian disciple's ultimate loyalty is to Christ.
He or she must be prepared to give up everything for his sake. But also
noteworthy is the communal context in which this test of discipleship is
placed. The persecution of a believer affects the entire community. And
as God gives them grace, these believers promise to stand alongside one
another in suffering for the gospel.

Then members vow to be circumspect in speaking about the church's
inner life to outsiders: "We do promise to keep the secrets of our Church
entire without divulging them to any that are not members of this particular Body, though they may be otherwise near & dear to us." The reason
given for this is drawn from the imagery of the Song of Solomon 4:12:
"For we believe the Church ought to be as a garden enclosed & a fountain sealed." This comparison of the local church to an enclosed garden
was commonplace in seventeenth- and eighteenth-century Baptist documents that talked about the nature of the church.

The next vow, article 9, is based on 2 Corinthians 6:14 (where Paul
urged Christians not to be "unequally yoked together with unbelievers,"
NKJV) and 1 Corinthians 7:39 (Paul's command to marry "only in the
Lord," NKJV). Members promise not to marry an unbeliever, for, they
state, "We believe it to be a sin to be unequally yoked, that it is contrary to the Rule of Christ, & the ready way to hinder our souls' peace,
growth, & eternal welfare." The tenth article pledges them to help one
another materially, while article 11 focuses on the spiritual help believers must give one another. The latter is designed especially to encourage

---

[67] For details, see Watts, *Dissenters*, 265–66.

a pastoral attitude on the part of the members toward one another. If they see a brother or sister harboring a sinful lifestyle, they promise "to remove it by using all possible means to bring the person to repentance & reformation of life." In article 12 the church members committed themselves to worshipping "on the Lord's days" and on other occasions the church deemed fit. The final commitment, article 13, entailed a promise to engage in private devotion, including prayer for one another, the growth of the church, and especially for their "ministers & the success of their ministry."

This covenant, like other Baptist church covenants of this era, gives expression to a distinct view of the Christian life: it is a voluntary, wholehearted commitment to God and to his church. Christian discipleship involves dedicating the entirety of one's being to God, the evidence for which is demonstrated in the context of the life of the local community of believers.[68]

Much more could be said about the historical development of congregationalism in this era. However, in contrast to other Reformed conceptions of the church, these early congregationalists viewed the church as a regenerate community, born of the Holy Spirit and united to Christ. Given this understanding of the church's nature, its government should follow. As a result, proponents of congregationalism contended that the church is comprised of all of God's people covenanting together and making decisions under the supreme authority of the head of the church, our Lord Jesus Christ, and under the leadership of Christ's appointed leaders within individual churches. Yet the entire congregation has a role to play in these decisions and in governing the affairs of the church because they are a regenerate people.

Historically this is how congregationalism developed. Yet ultimately Scripture should drive our view of church governance, as these early proponents of congregationalism made clear.

---

[68] Fountain, "Church Covenants," 8–10.

CHAPTER 2

The Biblical and Theological
Case for Congregationalism

Stephen J. Wellum and Kirk Wellum

Whether we want to admit it or not, churches are often influenced by the leadership and organizational models present in the surrounding culture. In our day these range from authoritarian structures to easy-come-easy-go arrangements. Sometimes churches deliberately move in the opposite direction of the culture in order to guard against cultural distortions of the biblical model. At other times they adopt the dominant cultural models in order to make church relevant to the people they want to reach with the gospel.

Neither of these moves, by themselves, is right. There is a time and a place to counterbalance the culture, and there are places we should contextualize to it. But the main goal must always be biblical faithfulness. As in all areas of the Christian life, faithfulness to the Bible in leadership and church structure is essential for the long-term health and usefulness of local congregations.

Thankfully, there has lately been an important recovery within evangelical Baptist circles of what early congregationalists gave their lives to defend, namely, the biblical model of a plurality of elders who govern the church along with deacons in a supporting role.[1] Although this basic

---

[1] See for example Mark Dever and Paul Alexander, *The Deliberate Church* (Wheaton: Crossway, 2005). This helpful book outlines the important features of the biblical model found in the New Testament. Also, see the fine discussion of this point in Gregg R.

47

model can be expressed in a number of ways, typically the pastor or pastors function as elders whose primary work is preaching and teaching, and they work alongside other elders to shepherd and direct the affairs of the church (see 1 Tim 5:17). Together these men are assisted by deacons who are responsible for organizing and implementing practical ministry objectives in the life of the congregation. And all of this occurs within the context of a congregation who possesses final authority.

This model is similar to but different from the sole pastor model of church government, in which the pastor alone is the elder and all the other leaders are known as deacons. This latter model can work well depending on the individuals involved, but it falls short of the New Testament's teaching of the plurality of elders taught in passages such as Act 14:23 and 20:17; 1 Timothy 4:14; Titus 1:5; James 5:14; and 1 Peter 5:5.[2]

It's also different from the authoritarian twist taken lately by a number of churches, where the elders take control and minimize, even exclude, the congregation's involvement. The ostensible goal of this authoritarian power shift is to tilt the balance of power toward the spiritually mature. It also allows for a more efficient and streamlined chain of command, and it seems to protect leaders from those who might oppose their teaching or policies.[3] But this model, too, is problematic.[4]

It is difficult to argue that the direct nature of this command structure is not more efficient, but we don't believe this model of leadership is biblical. It doesn't take into account the nature of the church as a new covenant community. And it doesn't provide adequate checks and balances against abuse of power by the small group of men to whom all authority is ceded. While these men may have the best of intentions, they are sinners who also need organizational structures that are compatible with the spiritual realities that exist at this time in redemptive history.

Allison, *Sojourners and Strangers: The Doctrine of the Church* (Wheaton: Crossway, 2012), 205–47.

[2] For a discussion and defense of elders and deacons, see part 4 in this volume.

[3] For example, see the provocative blog post by James MacDonald, "Congregational Government Is from Satan," accessed September 22, 2014, http://theelephantsdebt.files. wordpress.com/2012/06/congregational-government-is-from-satan.pdf.

[4] In today's discussion often a distinction is made between *elder led* within a congregational rule and *elder rule* without congregational involvement. This chapter defends the former, not the latter model, while numerous churches today adopt the latter. The leaders of these churches may be well intentioned, but this form of governance is highly problematic. In worst-case scenarios leaders treat questions as a sign of disloyalty. When healthy discussion is ended, churches will soon become highly dysfunctional.

The purpose of this chapter, then, is to argue in favor of a congregational form of church government. The congregationalism we defend is *not* what is sometimes caricatured as congregationalism. It's not some radical form of individualism in which everyone does what is right in his or her own eyes. It's not a "direct democracy" in which every decision concerning every issue must be put to a congregational vote, thus displacing any role for God-ordained leaders/elders.[5] Instead, we defend the view that, under the lordship of Christ and under the authority of divinely given elders who lead, the last and final court of appeal in matters related to the local church is the congregation itself.[6]

The key to understanding congregationalism, and the key contribution this chapter hopes to make, is to focus attention on the church's identity as God's new covenant people. The church belongs to a new time in redemptive history, and it is constituted as a regenerate and believing people. Here then is the key point: the redemptive developments of the new covenant necessitate a new leadership paradigm.

This new paradigm should simultaneously recognize that "all know God," as Jeremiah put it, without any specially called mediators; and it needs to leave a place for checks and balances, to borrow language again from the field of democratic theory. The new covenant era is an "already not yet" era. It's begun, but it's not yet been consummated. The church and its leaders might be constituted as a regenerate and believing people, but they are not perfected. A fully biblical model of church government, it turns out, reflects both of those realities.

The risen and ascended Christ is the ultimate Lord and head of the church. He saves his people and rules over them by his Word and his Spirit. He gives gifts to his church, including those who are called to teach, to provide oversight, and to serve. Yet he gives final earthly authority to his regenerate new covenant people for guarding the gospel.

In order to understand what Scripture teaches about church governance, it's important to first focus on what the church *is*. We therefore begin with five points of a basic New Testament ecclesiology on the

---

5 Often this is the caricature of congregationalism by those who reject it. For example see Robert L. Reymond, "The Presbytery-Led Church" in *Perspectives on Church Government: Five Views of Church Polity*, eds. Chad O. Brand and R. Stanton Norman (Nashville: B&H, 2004), 135–16, and James MacDonald, "Congregational Government Is from Satan" at http://theelephantsdebt.files.wordpress.com/2012/06/congregational-government-is-from-satan.pdf..

6 For helpful definitions and discussions of congregationalism, see Allison, *Sojourners and Strangers*, 277–95; Mark Dever, *The Church: The Gospel Made Visible* (Nashville: B&H, 2012), 47–61; and John S. Hammett, *Biblical Foundations for Baptist Churches: A Contemporary Ecclesiology* (Grand Rapids: Kregel, 2005), 135–215.

nature and identity of the church. Once that picture is in place, we can turn to five further points on how this best fits with congregational governance. Governance depends on nature.

What Is the Church? A Basic New Testament Ecclesiology

Not all Christians agree on the answer to the question, What *is* the church? In fact, most ecclesiastical divisions, including differences over church government, are directly tied to different conceptions of the nature of the church. To complicate things further, differences over the nature of the church are related to larger disagreements over entire biblical-theological systems such as dispensational and covenant theology and how those systems characterize the relationship between Israel and the church as well as the biblical covenants more broadly.[7] We don't need to discuss these differences at length, but it's important to realize that church government (and our defense of congregationalism) is *not* an isolated piece of ecclesiology but part of a larger discussion that wrestles with the continuity-discontinuity question regarding the biblical covenants.[8]

To summarize, the church is part of the one people of God and the one plan of redemption centered in Christ. However, the church must be viewed differently than Israel under the old covenant in at least two significant ways. First, the church is *new* in a redemptive-historical sense precisely because it is the community of the *new* covenant. With the coming of our Lord Jesus Christ—the last Adam and true Israel— all of the previous covenants reached their fulfillment, terminus, and *telos*. The salvation realities Jesus achieved and applies to his people are *not* exactly the same as those under the old covenant. The newness of the church, then, is rooted in Jesus the Messiah, who won our eternal redemption in his obedient life and atoning death, secured the new covenant promise and gift of the Spirit, and gave birth to a new community.

---

[7] For helpful summaries of the history and development of dispensational theology, see Craig A. Blaising and Darrell L. Bock, *Progressive Dispensationalism* (Wheaton: BridgePoint, 1993), and Craig A. Blaising and Darrell L. Bock, eds., *Dispensationalism, Israel and the Church: A Search for Definition* (Grand Rapids: Zondervan, 1992). For some introductory books on covenant theology, see Michael Horton, *God of Promise* (Grand Rapids: Baker, 2006); Peter Golding, *Covenant Theology: The Key of Theology in Reformed Thought and Tradition* (Ross-Shire: Mentor, 2004); and O. Palmer Robertson, *The Christ of the Covenants* (Grand Rapids: Baker, 1980).

[8] For a more in-depth treatment of these issues, see Peter J. Gentry and Stephen J. Wellum, *Kingdom Through Covenant: A Biblical-Theological Understanding of the Covenants* (Wheaton: Crossway, 2012).

Second, the New Testament church is new because, unlike old covenant Israel, it is formally comprised of a regenerate, believing people rather than a "mixed" group of believers and unbelievers. True members of the new covenant community are only those who have entered into union with Christ by repentance and faith. Churches, to the best of their ability, identify true members by their professions of faith and visible signs of conversion, and they excommunicate individuals who appear to be false professors. Furthermore, the covenant sign of the new covenant church, baptism, is applied to believers. Even though circumcision and baptism are both covenant signs, they do not signify the same realities due to their respective covenantal differences.

But let's unpack this understanding of the nature of the church with five statements, which will allow us then to turn and observe how what the church *is* best fits with congregationalism.[9]

1. The Church Belongs to the One People of God

It's important to establish from the outset that there is only *one* elect people of God throughout time. Some have disputed this point in the past, but today most don't. People in the Old Testament era, as in the New, were saved by grace through faith in the promises of God. The difference between the two eras is that now the promises of God are Christologically defined with greater clarity due to the unfolding nature of God's redemptive plan (see Gen 15:6; Rom 4:9–12; Gal 3:6–9; Heb 11:8–19). "Promise" has given way to "fulfillment," which means we cannot savingly know God apart from faith in Christ (John 5:23; Acts 4:12; see 1 John 2:23; 4:2–3).

Evidence of continuity between Old and New Testament saints (see Rom 1:1–2, 11; Phil 3:3, 7, 9) can be found in the language used to describe each. Descriptions of Israel as God's covenant people are applied to the church through its identification with Jesus the Messiah (e.g., Exod 19:6; Deut 32:15; 33:12; Isa 43:20–21; 44:2; Jer 31:31–34; Hos 1:6, 9–11; 2:1, 23; see Rom 9:24–26; Gal 3:26–29; Eph 2:12, 19; 3:4–6; 1 Thess 1:4; Heb 8:6–13; 1 Pet 2:9–10). For instance, the Old Testament sometimes uses the Hebrew word for "assembly" to characterize Israel, which translates as "church" (cf. *qāhāl* and *ekklēsia*; e.g., Deut 4:10; Josh 24:1, 25; Isa 2:2–4; Matt 16:18; 1 Cor 11:18; Heb

---

[9] These five statements are taken from, with some revision, Stephen J. Wellum, "Beyond Mere Ecclesiology: The Church as God's New Covenant Community," in *The Community of Jesus: A Theology of the Church*, ed. K. H. Easley and C. W. Morgan (Nashville: B&H Academic, 2013), with permission.

10:25).[10] And the New Testament describes the church, comprised of Jewish and Gentile believers, as the Israel of God (Gal 6:16).[11]

2. The Church as the New Covenant Community Really Is New[12]

However, all this does not mean Israel and the church are the same *kind* of communities. There are important differences, as attested by the Old Testament prophets as well as by the New Testament. The church is the people of the new covenant, and it really is new.

The new covenant is anticipated throughout the prophets, especially in the language of "everlasting covenant" and in the expectation of the coming new creation, Spirit, and saving rule of God among the nations. The new covenant is viewed in these texts as both national (Jer 31:36–40; 33:6–16; Ezek 36:24–38; 37:11–28) and international (Jer 33:9; Ezek 36:36; 37:28). Its scope is treated as universal, especially in Isaiah (42:6; 49:6; 55:3–5; 56:4–8; 66:18–24). And the Isaiah texts in particular project the ultimate fulfillment of the new covenant's divine promises onto an "ideal Israel"—a community tied to the Servant of the Lord located in a rejuvenated new creation (Isa 65:17; 66:22). This "ideal Israel" picks up God's promises to Abraham, and it's presented as the climactic fulfillment of the covenants God established with Adam, the patriarchs, the nation of Israel, and David's son (Isa 9:6–7; 11:1–10; Jer 23:5–6; 33:14–26; Ezek 34:23–24; 37:24–28). It's the fulfillment of all of God's promises.[13]

The most famous Old Testament "new covenant" text is probably Jeremiah 31:29–34. It signals a change in the *structure* and the *nature* of

---

[10] For a detailed development of this point, see G. K. Beale, *A New Testament Biblical Theology* (Grand Rapids: Baker, 2011), 651–749. Also see, Edmund P. Clowney, *The Church* (Downers Grove: IVP, 1995), 27–36.

[11] For a defense of this identification, see Beale, *A New Testament Biblical Theology*, 670–72, 719–24. Also see Andreas Köstenberger, "The Identity of the *Israel tou theou* (Israel of God) in Galatians 6:16," *Faith and Mission* 19:1 (2001): 3–24.

[12] The word "new" is taken from the important new covenant text, Jer 31:31–34. There is much debate over the meaning of the word (Hb., *hadas*; LXX, *kainos*) and hence the "newness" of the new covenant. Some argue that the word only means "renewed" (e.g., Lam 3:22–23), and others argue that it means "new" in a qualitatively different sense (Exod 1:8; Deut 32:17; 1 Sam 6:7; Eccl 1:10). Ultimately the "newness" of the new covenant must be contextually determined. On this debate see William J. Dumbrell, *Covenant and Creation: A Theology of the Old Testament Covenants* (Carlisle, Cumbria, UK: Paternoster, 1984), 175; Beale, *A New Testament Biblical Theology*, 727–49.

[13] For an in-depth defense of these points see, Gentry and Wellum, *Kingdom Through Covenant*.

God's people in moving from Israel to the new covenant people. Let us look at each of these changes in turn.

First, Jeremiah 31 anticipates a time when the *structure* of God's people will change, a change that eventually leads to the New Testament teaching on the priesthood of all believers. Under the old covenant, D. A. Carson has noted, God's people were organized through a tribal structure, whereby God related to them through specially called mediators.[14] The Old Testament does pay attention to individual believers, particularly through the remnant theme. But in general the people's knowledge of God and their relationship with him depended on specially endowed leaders. The entire nation benefited when these leaders did right, and they suffered when they did not. Thus, the Old Testament does not emphasize God's Spirit being poured out on every individual believer but distinctively on prophets, priests, kings, and other designated leaders, as when the Spirit comes upon Saul or David.

All this changes with the new covenant. Jeremiah anticipated a day when this tribal-representative structure will come to an end: "In those days, it will never again be said: The fathers have eaten sour grapes, and the children's teeth are set on edge. Rather, each will die for his own wrongdoing. Anyone who eats sour grapes—his own teeth will be set on edge" (Jer 31:29–30).[15] Carson observes:

> In short, Jeremiah understood that the new covenant would bring some dramatic changes. The tribal nature of the people of God would end, and the new covenant would bring with it a new emphasis on the distribution of the knowledge of God down to the level of each member of the covenant community. Knowledge of God would no longer be mediated through specially endowed leaders, for *all* of God's covenant people would know him, from the least to the greatest. Jeremiah is not concerned to say there would be no teachers under the new covenant, but to remove from leaders that distinctive mediatorial role that made the knowledge of God among the people at large a secondary knowledge, a mediated knowledge.[16]

---

[14] See D. A. Carson, *Showing the Spirit* (Grand Rapids: Baker, 1996), 150–58; cf. idem, "1–3 John," in *Commentary on the New Testament Use of the Old Testament*, eds. G. K. Beale and D. A. Carson (Grand Rapids: Baker, 2007), 1,065; Beale, *New Testament Biblical Theology*, 733–37, refers to it as "democratization."

[15] Unless otherwise stated, all quotations from Scripture are from the Holman Christian Standard Bible.

[16] Carson, *Showing the Spirit*, 152. From the context it is best to view the "knowledge" spoken of as a *salvific* knowledge so that *all* within the covenant community

The new covenant is a mediated covenant—it is mediated in and through Christ—but it's not mediated through specially endowed leaders. Every member of the covenant has direct, immediate access to God in Christ. And in contrast to the "mixed" nation of Israel, every covenant member knows the Lord. Verse 34 states, "No longer will one teach his neighbor or his brother, saying, 'Know the LORD,' for they will all know Me, from the least to the greatest of them."

Furthermore, it is no longer the case that God's Spirit merely empowers prophets, priests, kings, and other designated leaders for acts of service. Rather, the Spirit first empowered the Messiah (Isa 11:1–3; 49:1–2; 61:1ff) and then the Messiah's people (see Ezek 11:19–20; 36:25–27; Joel 2:28–32; cf. Num 11:27–29).[17] That is, he empowers and gifts every member for service. The distribution promises to be universal (Joel 2:28–32).

This universalization is precisely what occurs in the New Testament. John the Baptist announced this coming age (Matt 3:11), the cross work of Christ procured and secured it (John 7:39; 16:7; Acts 2:33), and then Pentecost inaugurated it with the giving of the Spirit (Acts 2). The Spirit gives life to the New Testament saints, equips them to be priests with the knowledge of God, and empowers them with gifts for ministry and mediating the knowledge of God to the unbelieving nations (1 Cor 12:4–7; 1 Pet 2:9). The role Israel was supposed to play is now fulfilled in us, the church, by the Spirit.[18] Everyone within the new covenant community is given the Spirit as the seal, down payment, and guarantee of their promised inheritance (Eph 1:13–14). To be a member of the new covenant community, the church, is to be united to Christ and to have the Spirit. In fact, *not* to have the Spirit is *not* to have Christ or to be his people (Rom 8:9).

This is not to say that there were no believers prior to Pentecost, or that the Spirit was not active. The lives of people like Abraham, Moses, Joshua, Hannah, Ruth, David, and others attest otherwise. Yet what is unique about the day of Pentecost in Acts 2 was the extent to which the Spirit was given, the fact that he was given to people permanently, and the fact that the entire community received the promised Holy Spirit, fulfilling the words of both the prophet Joel and Jesus (Joel 2:28–32; Acts 1:4–5; cf. John 7:37–39). Pentecost also fulfilled what Moses

---

savingly know God. See Dumbrell, *Covenant and Creation*, 177–78; Paul R. House, *Old Testament Theology* (Downers Grove: IVP, 1998), 317–21.

[17] On this point see Max Turner, "Holy Spirit," in *New Dictionary of Biblical Theology*, eds. T. D. Alexander et al. (Downers Grove: IVP, 2000), 551–58; David F. Wells, *God the Evangelist* (Grand Rapids: Eerdmans, 1987), 1–4; Anthony A. Hoekema, *The Bible and the Future* (Grand Rapids: Eerdmans, 1994), 55–67.

[18] See Thomas R. Schreiner, *Romans*, Baker Exegetical Commentary on the New Testament (Grand Rapids: Baker, 1998), 395–468.

longed for many centuries before: "I wish that all the LORD's people were prophets and that the LORD would put his Spirit on them!" (Num. 11:29 NIV). On that occasion the Lord had taken the Spirit that was on Moses and distributed it among the seventy elders of Israel. But what Israel ultimately needed was not more leaders or even more Spirit-endued leaders. The nation needed to know the Lord and be filled with the Spirit. Then, at Pentecost, Moses' hopes were realized. The Spirit was abundantly poured out on *all* members of the covenant community. Wouldn't this seem to suggest the need for a new leadership paradigm?

Second, Jeremiah 31 anticipates a change in the *nature* of the covenant people: they are regenerate. The entire community will know the Lord directly because God will write his law on every member's heart (which is another way of saying that all are "circumcised in heart" or regenerate [see Deut 10:16; 30:6; Jer 4:4; 9:25]), and he will forgive their sin (vv. 33–34).

Under the old covenant there was a distinction between the physical seed and the spiritual seed of Abraham (see Rom 9:6). Both of these "seeds" received the covenant sign of circumcision, and both were viewed as full covenant members in the national sense. But only the spiritual seed—the remnant—truly believed in a salvific sense. What's more, "for every David there were a dozen Ahabs; for every Josiah a legion of Manassehs," James White has observed. He elaborates: "Unfaithfulness, the flaunting of God's law, the rejection of the role of truly being God's people, the rejection of His knowledge, and the experience of His wrath, were the *normative* experiences seen in the Old Covenant."[19] This does not mean no Old Testament saint knew God or God did not regenerate or forgive any Israelite of sin. There was a forgiven remnant.[20] Yet Israel, again, was a "mixed" group by nature.

What was true only for Israel's remnant (elect) would now be true of the entire covenant community and in greater ways. To be united to

---

[19] James R. White, "The Newness of the New Covenant, Part 2," *Reformed Baptist Theological Review* 2:1 (2005): 88.

[20] Under the old covenant the nation's remnant (elect) would have been regenerate and forgiven—typologically through the sacrificial system and by faith in the covenant promises of God. However, they only had access to God through the priesthood and tabernacle/temple structures; it was not immediate as it is now in Christ. Plus, the entire community was not regenerate, as every member of the new covenant is. And even the elect did not experience the full new covenant realities of the Spirit's work as the New Testament saints do, especially in regard to the indwelling of the Spirit. (On this point see, James M. Hamilton Jr. *God's Indwelling Presence: The Holy Spirit in the Old and New Testaments* [Nashville: B&H, 2006].) They were declared just before God (see Gen 15:6) but only as they believed God's promises and looked forward to God's provision of a greater sacrifice to come (see Rom 3:21–26; Heb 9–10).

the new covenant community is to be forgiven and to be regenerated, promises fulfilled in Christ and his people (Matt 26:17–30 par.; Acts 2; Hebrews 8–10). The church, therefore, should be viewed as *new*, constituted as a believing, regenerate people, not a "mixed" community.[21]

3. The Church as the New Covenant Community Is God's Eschatological Assembly

The newness of this new covenant community is reinforced by the New Testament's description of the church as an eschatological and gathered community (hence, *ekklēsia*).[22] It identifies the church with the dawning of the kingdom and the "age to come." It's an already-not-yet reality: it has already arrived in Christ, and it will be consummated in his return. Its identity does not depend on "this present age," which is passing away, but upon the "age to come," which has now arrived in the saving reign (kingdom) of Christ.[23] Those who place their faith in Christ are now citizens of the new, heavenly Jerusalem and have already begun to gather there.

This is the point of Hebrews 12:18–29. In contrast with the Israelites who gathered at Mount Sinai under the old covenant (vv. 18–21), new covenant believers have already gathered to meet God at the "heavenly" Jerusalem (vv. 22–24). This heavenly Jerusalem is still future but in a profound sense is already here.[24] As the church,[25] we are already begin-

---

21 See House, *Old Testament Theology*, 317–21, who rightly observes that Jeremiah 31 provides a profound shift in the definition of the elect. In Israel one can think of the nation as consisting of believing and unbelieving persons, a situation that creates the notion of a remnant. However, in the new covenant, the idea of the remnant or the elect within the community is not what Jeremiah anticipates. Also see White, "The Newness of the New Covenant: Part 2," 88, who makes this same point.

22 See D. A. Carson, "Evangelicals, Ecumenism, and the Church," in *Evangelical Affirmations*, eds. Kenneth S. Kantzer and Carl F. H. Henry (Grand Rapids: Zondervan, 1990), 363–67, as well as the helpful discussion in P. T. O'Brien, "Church," in *Dictionary of Paul and His Letters*, eds. Gerald F. Hawthorne et al. (Downers Grove: IVP, 1993), 123–31; and Clowney, *The Church*, 27–33.

23 For a thorough discussion of inaugurated eschatology and its application to the church, see Schreiner, *New Testament Theology* (Grand Rapids: Baker, 2008), 41–116, 675–754.

24 "You have already come" (*proselēluthate*) is in the perfect tense, which stresses the point that believers have come to their final destination even now starting with conversion. In other words, we *already* participate in new covenant realities as the gathered people of God, even though we await the consummation of those realities. On this point see P. T. O'Brien, *The Letter to the Hebrews*, Pillar New Testament Commentary (Grand Rapids: Eerdmans, 2010), 482–85.

25 In the NT, *ekklēsia* is used in the plural and singular. Both usages can be used for specifying local assemblies, as in "the church in Corinth" or "the churches of Galatia." But the singular usage can also be used in reference to our participation in the heavenly eschatological church, i.e., the *heavenly* Zion or the *new* Jerusalem, that which is

ning to enjoy, by faith, the privileges of that city. We await the consummation of the ages in Christ's return (see Heb 13:14), but we already experience the realities of the end.

How do we enjoy that heavenly city now? We enjoy it by faith. To speak of coming to the heavenly Jerusalem and participating in its realities is to speak about belonging to the new covenant and the new creation. It's to speak of already having been raised and seated with Christ in the heavenly realms (see Eph 2:5–6; Col 2:12–13; 3:3). And it's difficult to imagine someone doing all this who is not regenerate and believing. Salvation transfers us from being "in Adam" to being covenantally "in Christ" with all the benefits of that union.[26] And in the Bible new covenant people receive the benefits of Christ's work in one way: through individual repentance toward God and faith in Christ. Nowhere does the New Testament envision someone who is a member of the new covenant and "in Christ" who is not regenerate, effectually called by the Father, born of the Spirit, justified, holy, and awaiting glorification.

Where do we enjoy that heavenly city now? We enjoy it in the local church, which brings us to the relationship between the local church and the eschatological, heavenly gathering. D. A. Carson starts with what that relationship is not:

> [E]ach local church is not seen primarily as one member parallel to a lot of other member churches, together constituting one body, one church; nor is each local church seen as the body of Christ parallel to other earthly churches that are also the body of Christ—as if Christ had many bodies.[27]

Then he explains how we should view the relationship:

> [E]ach church is the full manifestation in space and time of the one, true, heavenly, eschatological, new covenant church. Local churches should see themselves as outcroppings of heaven, analogies of "the Jerusalem that is above," indeed colonies of

identified with the "age to come" and which is now here. In this latter sense the language of *heavenly* or *new* Jerusalem is not a spatial image but an eschatological one, identifying the people of God with the eschatological realities that Jesus has won for us in his finished work. See, O'Brien, "Church," in Hawthorne et al., *Dictionary of Paul and His Letters*, 123–31.

[26] On the reality of union with Christ and all that it entails, see Sinclair Ferguson, *Holy Spirit* (Downers Grove: IVP, 1996), 93–138; Wayne Grudem, *Systematic Theology* (Grand Rapids: Zondervan, 1994), 840–50.

[27] Carson, "Evangelicals, Ecumenism, and the Church," in Kantzer and Henry, *Evangelical Affirmations*, 366.

the new Jerusalem, providing on earth a corporate and visible expression of "the glorious freedom of the children of God."[28]

The gathered and believing local church, in other words, is where we go to see a "manifestation of the one true, heavenly, eschatological, new covenant church" now.

And if local churches are the manifestation of this new covenant people, how can we say they are, *by design*, a mixed people, like Israel of old?

Carson has noticed one more implication that would follow if this biblical and theological understanding of the church were right: "The ancient contrast between the church visible and the church invisible, a contrast that has nurtured not a little ecclesiology, is either fundamentally mistaken, or at best of marginal importance."[29] To understand Carson's remark, one must realize that the invisible/visible distinction is often used in conjunction with an unmixed/mixed distinction, as if to say the invisible and universal church is pure, while the visible and local church is designed to be mixed, like ancient Israel. Now, it is no doubt true that not everyone who professes faith in Christ is regenerate, and some people who are admitted into church membership later show themselves not to be Christians: "If they had belonged to us, they would have remained with us. However, they went out so that it might be made clear that none of them belongs to us" (1 John 2:19). The New Testament knows of false professions and spurious conversions. In fact, that's why Paul exhorted, "Examine yourselves to see whether you are in the faith" (2 Cor 13:5 NIV; see also 2 Pet 1:10). Still the New Testament views the church on earth as a *heavenly* (tied to the "age to come" and the new creation) and *spiritual* (born of and empowered by the Spirit) community. It is "the outcropping of the heavenly assembly gathered in the Jerusalem that is above."[30] Scripture simply does not treat it as a mixed community of believers and unbelievers like ancient Israel. It is constituted as a regenerate people who profess to have crossed from death to life, to have been united to Christ, to be participants in the new creation and the new covenant age.

---

[28] Ibid. Also see O'Brien, "Church," in Hawthorne et al., *Dictionary of Paul and His Letters*, 123–31.

[29] Carson, "Evangelicals, Ecumenism, and the Church," in Kantzer and Henry, *Evangelical Affirmations*, 367.

[30] Ibid., 371.

4. The Church as the New Covenant Community Is God's New Temple

It is difficult to overestimate the importance of the theme of tabernacle and temple in Scripture.[31] This theme, too, reinforces the newness of the new covenant people.

At the heart of the covenant relationship is the triune God dwelling with his special people. In the Old Testament the tabernacle/temple was the means by which this holy God dwelt among his covenantal but sinful people without destroying them. It was where he offered a place for them to atone for their sin through the mediation of the priesthood and the sacrificial system. And this unique covenantal presence by an omnipresent God distinguished Israel from all the other nations (see Exod 33:15–16).[32] The nation assembled annually in Jerusalem to attend the place where God dwelt (Pss 42:2; 63:2; 65:1–2).

When the nation went into exile and the temple was destroyed, it was as if the entire covenant had come to an end. But the prophets reminded the people that God's presence was not limited to a place; the temple/tabernacle itself was only a type and pattern of something greater (see Exod 25:40; cf. Ezek 11:22–23; Heb 8:3–5).

The New Testament then presents Jesus Christ as the one who fulfills all of the hopes and expectations of the prophets in at least two important ways.[33] First, he is the fulfillment and replacement of the temple (John 1:14–18; 2:19–22).[34] He is the dwelling of God with us (Matt 1:23; John 1:14). He brought the purpose and function of the earthly temple to its end through his life, death, and resurrection (Matt 27:51; Heb 9:1–10:18).

Second, he is the temple builder and Lord of the house who now builds a people for himself from every nation, tribe, and tongue (Matt 16:18; Eph 2:11–22; Heb 3:1–6; cf. Rev 5:9–10). The church becomes God's house/temple by being transferred from one covenant head to another—from Adam to Christ. By the agency of the Spirit who regenerates and indwells, we have become God's *new* temple both individually

---

[31] For a development of the temple theme in Scripture, see G. K. Beale, *The Temple and the Church's Mission: A Biblical Theology of the Dwelling Place of God*, New Studies in Biblical Theology (Downers Grove: IVP, 2004); R. J. McKelvey, "Temple" in Alexander et al., *New Dictionary of Biblical Theology*, 806–11.

[32] On this point see Clowney, *Church*, 32–33.

[33] For a development of these points, see the excellent article by Edmund Clowney, "The Final Temple," *Westminster Theological Journal* 35 (1972–73): 156–89.

[34] See Paul M. Hoskins, *Jesus as the Fulfillment of the Temple in the Gospel of John* (Eugene, OR: Wipf & Stock, 2007).

as Christians and corporately as Christ's church (1 Cor 3:16–17; 6:19; 2 Cor 6:16; Eph 2:21; Heb 3:6; 1 Pet 2:5).

One cannot stress enough how incredible this truth is, and it once again points to the newness of the new covenant people. First, nowhere in the Old Testament are the people of Israel described as the temple of God in which God's Spirit dwells. The temple was a building. People traveled there. Now the temple is identified with a specific person (Jesus Christ) and, by virtue of union with him, a people (the church).[35] In Christ the church is God's temple people, who now have direct access to the Father through Christ by the Spirit (Eph 2:18; Heb 4:14–16; 10:19–22).

Second, the church must be a regenerate, believing people and not a "mixed" body. It only makes sense to call a *people*, as opposed to a *building*, the temple of God in whom the Spirit dwells if, in fact, they have been brought from death to life by the calling of the Father, the new birth of the Spirit, and union with Christ by faith—a union that is permanent and secure (see Rom 8:28–39; Eph 1:3–14). The New Testament knows nothing of unbelievers who are described in this way. True, some profess faith and don't persevere, but in so doing they demonstrate that they never truly belonged to the church (1 John 2:19; cf. Col 1:21–23; Heb 3:6, 14).

5. The Church as the New Covenant Community Is God's New Humanity

Finally, the New Testament presents the church as God's "new man" or new humanity. This description is especially clear in Ephesians 2:11–22,[36] and it nicely sums up the previous four points, capturing elements of both *continuity* and *discontinuity* between the church and Israel.

---

[35] The description of the church as God's new temple because of our union with Christ and our indwelling by the Spirit is close to another New Testament description of the church as "the body of Christ." Biblically and theologically it is best to understand the body imagery in covenantal terms: Christ is our representative head, and we are his body, i.e., his covenantal people. Headship has more to do with representation, primacy, and authority than merely that Christ is the top member of the body. This is clear from the fact that when Paul, for example, speaks of the members of the body he includes ear, eye, and nose—technically all parts of the head (1 Cor 12:16–21). This is also borne out in the fact that Paul thinks of the church as a body in terms of one whole man in Christ, not merely in terms of one part of the body in relation to other parts.

[36] For helpful exegetical treatments of this important ecclesiological text, see P. T. O'Brien, *The Letter to the Ephesians*, Pillar New Testament Commentary (Grand Rapids: Eerdmans, 1999), 182–221; John R. W. Stott, *The Message of Ephesians*, Bible Speaks Today (Downers Grove: IVP, 1986), 89–112.

The element of continuity is found in the fact that, while the Gentile Christians were once excluded from "the citizenship of Israel" and "foreigners to the covenants of the promise," they have now been "brought near" (vv. 12–13). They have come alongside believing Jews as "fellow citizens with the saints, and members of God's household, built on the foundation of the apostles and prophets, with Christ Jesus Himself as the cornerstone" (vv. 19–20). A note of newness resounds through all of this, of course, but it's built upon the old.

The element of discontinuity is in the newness. Jew and Gentile together are God's "one new man" and are being built as a new temple "for God's dwelling in the Spirit" (vv. 15, 22). The new community is not simply an extension of Israel. It is not an amalgam of the best elements of Israel and the Gentiles. It is a new humanity and part of the dawning new creation, a third entity that is neither Jewish nor Gentile but Christian (see Paul's self-understanding as a Christian in 1 Cor 9:19–23). It transcends the two old entities, even though unbelieving Israel and disobedient Gentiles continue to exist. That means the church is not simply a replacement for Israel, or a "renewed" instantiation of it, or merely one phase in God's redemptive plan to be interrupted in the future when God returns to his previous plan for Israel. God's old plans always anticipated the creation of this new humanity. Christ fulfilled the old covenant and identified the new humanity with himself by inaugurating a new and better covenant.

God's new humanity, once again, really is new. This is attested throughout the New Testament. For instance, Matthew's first major block of Jesus' teaching describes the radical transformation expected of those who belong to the new covenant. They are poor in spirit, mourn over sin, are meek in character, hunger and thirst for righteousness, are merciful and pure in heart and peacemakers, and are persecuted for their faith (5:3–12). Hence, they are the "salt of the earth" and the "light of the world" (5:13–16). Indeed, they are not like the Israelites of old who did not produce fruit in keeping with repentance and would therefore be cast out (e.g., 3:7–10; 8:11–12).

John's Gospel teaches the same, as when Jesus told Nicodemus that he must be born again of water and of the Spirit if he hoped to enter the kingdom of God—things which apparently he should have known from the Hebrew Scriptures (John 3:1–15; cf. Ezek 36:25–27). Entrance into the kingdom would not be gained on the basis of national identity or physical parentage. It is entered individually as one experiences the life-changing power of God for those who believe (3:16–21).

This new humanity, furthermore, is characterized by new kinds of relationships, which inevitably require a new kind of governance. God is their Father, such that congregations are composed of sons and daughters of God in the full salvific sense. Jesus is their brother, such that congregations are composed of men and women who are being conformed into his moral image and likeness. And the congregation as a whole is likened to a body on which there are different parts. Each part has its own function, each part is necessary, and all the parts must work together for the overall health and efficiency of the body (cf. Eph 1:22–23; 4:11–16; 1 Cor 12:1–31). Leaders must lead, but God has built interdependence into church relationships such that the leadership must operate in conjunction with the church as a whole. Damage comes when leaders forge ahead on their own without considering the health of the group as a whole.

The basic thesis of these chapters, we should recall, is that this new, born-again humanity necessitates a new leadership paradigm. And as we will see, congregationalism is most consistent with the fact that we have this new matrix of relationships.

But at the center of all this is Jesus Christ. One cannot understand the *identity* and *nature* of the church or its newness apart from Jesus Christ. The progression across redemptive history from type to antitype and through the covenant heads Adam, Noah, Abraham, Moses-Israel, and David culminated in Jesus' person and work and the new age that he inaugurated. He is the head of a new covenant, the people of which become the "one *new* man." Through its union with him, the new covenant church is a new assembly and new temple who are born, empowered, and indwelt by the Spirit. The church is not a mixed entity but a regenerate, believing community precisely because all whom Christ calls come (John 10:27). And all who come he keeps (v. 28). Those who are not his sheep don't hear and don't come (v. 26).

From What the Church Is to Congregationalism

These five points provide a basic New Testament ecclesiology. They are incredible truths, reminding us who we are, but they also provide the theological underpinning for congregationalism. Congregationalism presents a picture of each local church governing its own affairs, under the lordship of Christ, and living out what it means to be the full manifestation of the one, true, heavenly, eschatological church.

Why then does this description of the church's identity and nature best fit with congregationalism in contrast to other forms of church government? We can answer this question in five more points. None of these points are new and have been developed at greater length elsewhere.[37] However, it's important to see how they are organically related to the nature of the church.

1. Christ Is the Only Head and Mediator of the New Covenant Church

He bought the church with his blood (Eph 5:25–27). He builds it (Matt 16:18). He is its foundation, its cornerstone, and the chief Shepherd over those who lead it (1 Cor 3:11; Eph 2:20; 1 Pet 5:4). As the church's only mediator and Lord, Christ's direct headship precludes "any human mediators between God and his redeemed people," Gregg Allison rightly notes. "The church functions directly under the mediatorial lordship of Jesus Christ."[38] This is not the case with other hierarchical forms of church government that insert other human mediators, as in Roman Catholic theology. In the new covenant there is a direct relationship between Christ and his people so that the *entire* congregation has immediate access to God. God's grace and presence are not mediated through various leaders to the people. The latter may be true of the old covenant, but it is not true of new covenant realities.

Even the apostles, who were arguably the most authoritative human voices in the early church, did not function in the church as the mediators of the old covenant did, and the apostles' authority was not without limit. As D. A. Carson rightly observes, "A Peter could prove inconsistent in practice (Gal. 2:11–14), and a Paul could be mistaken in judgment (Acts 15:37–40; cf. 2 Tim. 4:11). The objective truth of the gospel, Paul insists, enjoys an antecedent authority; if even an apostle tampers with that, he is to be reckoned anathema (Gal. 1:8–9)."[39] No doubt, the apostles served as Christ's chosen instruments to interpret the Old Testament, to write the New Testament, and to pass on the gospel that had been given. Yet their authority rested not in themselves but in the triune God who acted in and through them to give an authoritative text to govern the

---

[37] For the most recent defenses, see Allison, *Sojourners and Strangers*, 205–317; Dever, *The Church*, 47–61; and Hammett, *Biblical Foundations for Baptist Churches*, 135–215.

[38] Allison, *Sojourners and Strangers*, 281.

[39] D. A. Carson, "Church, Authority in," in *Evangelical Dictionary of Theology*, ed. Walter A. Elwell (Grand Rapids: Baker, 1984), 228.

life of the church (see 2 Tim 3:16–17). In no way did they function as mediators or dispensers of grace.

In the new covenant Christ directly governs his church. The *entire* people of God are under his direct sovereign rule and authority, including various leaders in the church, whether apostles, elders, or deacons. Only Christ's authority is absolute, and any transgressing of his authority by a church leader requires God's people to obey Christ alone and not men (Acts 5:29).

2. Each Local Church Must Govern Its Own Affairs

That means no outside ecclesiastical authority possesses jurisdiction over the local church. Why? For the simple reason that every local church is God's new *ekklēsia*. Each one is the full manifestation in space and time of the one, true, heavenly, eschatological, new covenant church. Or, as John Hammett nicely states, "Each local congregation is fully *ekklēsia* in itself."[40] And the fact that each congregation manifests the one heavenly and eschatological church, fully *ekklēsia* in itself, explains a number of things in the New Testament:

(1) It explains why there is no evidence in the New Testament that the local church is ruled by a larger organization called "the church." The Bible knows nothing, says James White, of a "God-established hierarchical structure above the local church."[41] Instead, the New Testament views each local church as having been given sufficient gifts in its people and leadership to govern its own affairs.

(2) It explains why Christ's New Testament church comes to expression in visible local assemblies where fellow believers covenant together, affirm those leaders who rightly preach the gospel (see Gal 1:6–9), practice the ordinances (Acts 2:42; 1 Cor 11:26), exercise discipline (Matt 18:15–20; 1 Cor 5:1–12), and in all these ways govern their own affairs.

(3) It explains why most of the New Testament letters (except Philemon and the Pastorals) were written to local churches and not merely to church officers or some larger ecclesiastical

---

[40] Hammett, *Biblical Foundations for Baptist Churches*, 30.

[41] James R. White, "The Plural-Elder-Led Church: Sufficient as Established—the Plurality of Elders as Christ's Ordained Means of Church Governance," in Brand and Norman, *Perspectives on Church Government*, 260. Cf. Allison, *Sojourners and Strangers*, 277.

body.[42] Church leaders surely possess unique responsibility in a congregation. Still, the letters were written to instruct the entire congregation of their responsibilities to govern themselves, to protect themselves against false teachers, and to watch over people's lives.

(4) It explains why Paul in Galatians expected this young church to sit in judgment of angelic and apostolic authority *if* they should preach something other than what they have heard (Gal 1:8). As Mark Dever notes, "[Paul] doesn't write merely to the pastors, to the presbytery, to the bishop or the conference, to the convention, or to the seminary. He writes to the Christians who compose the churches, and he makes it quite clear that not only are they competent to sit in judgment on what claims to be the gospel, but that they *must*!"[43]

The same conclusion may be drawn from Revelation 2 and 3. Jesus addressed independent churches and not just their leaders or outside church hierarchies. Allison has noticed that Christ addressed each of these churches individually and treated them as independent, that is, self-governing and responsible for their own affairs. Allison writes:

> In his letters to the seven churches (Revelation 2-3), Jesus Christ addressed each one as an individual entity. When he rebuked the church, the reprimand was directed at the church for trouble that it had brought upon itself. . . . In turn, when the Lord corrected a church, his expectation was that the church itself would repent (2:5, 16, 22; 3:3, 19) and set straight its own matters. . . . No call for help from any other church was needed to rectify the sinful situation and bring about restoration. The churches had gotten themselves into trouble, and they were expected to depart from their former trouble and embrace the right path. There is no indication of any necessary assistance from the outside in terms of other churches or structures; each church had resources of its own for making the change.[44]

---

[42] White, "The Plural-Elder-Led Church," in Brand and Norman, *Perspectives on Church Government*, 262, makes this same point when he writes, "The apostolic epistles exhort the churches as churches and not in the context of any overarching ecclesiastical body."

[43] Mark Dever, *A Display of God's Glory: Basics of Church Structure—Deacons, Elders, Congregationalism, and Membership*, 2nd ed. (Washington, DC: 9Marks Ministries, 2001), 35.

[44] Allison, *Sojourners and Strangers*, 280.

3. The Final Court of Appeal Is the Congregation

Biblically and theologically this follows from what the church *is* as God's new covenant community. We observed that this community is different from old-covenant Israel in both *structure* and *nature*. And both of these changes provide the theological rationale and grounding for congregationalism.

Think first of the *structural* changes of the new covenant: all of God's people are empowered and gifted by the Spirit; all have access to God; all know God; and all are priests. As such the entire congregation should be involved in the governance of the church. That does not negate the importance of divinely ordained and gifted leadership offices in the church. But it is to say that these leaders do not function in an old covenant sense, namely, as distinctive mediators between God and the people, or even as authoritative rulers over God's people without involvement from the people. Rather they function as fellow believers, gifted by God for a specific task to lead the people of God but in concert with the entire Spirit-born-and-gifted congregation. Both elders and congregation are accountable to the lordship of Christ, but the congregation remains the final earthly court of appeal. To give this authority to only the elders undermines what the church *is* as God's new covenant people. It returns the church to old covenant categories where various leaders acted for and on behalf of the people.

We also observed that the *nature* of the new-covenant community is different from that of the old. It is a regenerate, believing community. Now some writers take hold of the already-not-yet explanation of redemptive history and wrongly apply it to the new covenant. They say the church is here now only in an inaugurated form, such that it's presently a "mixed" community such as Israel but will someday be a regenerate community.[45] But this explanation mistakes *width* for *length*. No doubt every member of the new covenant awaits the full *length* of his or her redemption—everything in the "not yet." But the beginning of that redemption is still community-*wide*. The community that is "already" here is constituted as a believing, justified people, born of the Spirit and united to Christ, our covenant head. With Christ's coming, the new covenant community is now here; the Spirit has been poured out on the entire community, everyone knows God, and all have been justified by God

---

[45] See Richard L. Pratt Jr., "Infant Baptism in the New Covenant," in *The Case for Covenantal Infant Baptism*, ed. Gregg Strawbridge (Phillipsburg, NJ: P&R, 2003), who makes this argument. For detailed and helpful critique of Pratt, see White, "The Newness of the New Covenant: Part 2," 97–103.

(Acts 2; Rom 8:1; Eph 2:18; Heb 10:19–25). What does all this have to do with the church's governance? God's purpose for his regenerate people is to restore them to what he intended for humanity in the first place, namely, to act as his image bearers who exercise dominion over this world for the sake of his glory. All humanity was originally called to "govern," but now the task falls to members of the new covenant. In other words it involves the entire community, not just a few within the community. Everyone is involved in this image-bearing work of ruling, judging, and putting all things under our feet as we live under the lordship of Christ, the pioneer, champion, and trailblazer of our salvation (see Heb 2:5–18).

The whole community's work of governance explains why the entire congregation sits in judgment and exercises authority over false teachers (2 Cor 10–13; 2 John), even apostolic preachers (Gal 1:8), as well as over people's lives (Matt 18:15–20; 1 Cor 5:1–13; 2 Cor 2:5–11).

Consider for instance the fact that the whole local church is involved in matters of church discipline. Before Jesus ascended and poured out the Spirit, he spoke about the church's having authority to bind and loose. Initially this authority was given to Peter and by extension to the other apostles as men (see Matt 16:19). But later, when speaking about dealing with sin in the assembly, Jesus laid out a disciplinary pattern that initially starts small but then grows to involve more people if the situation cannot be resolved in a satisfactory manner. As a last resort the matter must be brought before the whole church, and their judgment is considered final. Church discipline is carried out by the entire church— under the authority of its leaders, to be sure, but not apart from the congregation either (Matt 18:18–20).

First Corinthians 5:1–13 then provides a practical example in the early church of how the entire church was called to be involved in discipline. It begins with Paul's rebuking the whole church for not doing anything about a situation that was wrong even by pagan standards. Then he told them what they must do to remedy the situation. They are to assemble as a group in the name of the Lord and hand the perpetrator over to Satan for the destruction of the flesh in the hope that his spirit will be saved on the Day of the Lord. He was unrepentant, and so he needed to be removed from membership. Membership, again, is for believers. The church is not to be mixed.

It's worth recalling once again that the New Testament writers were writing to whole churches. Writers like Paul believed every member in Corinth and elsewhere had a stake in the church and needed to participate in the overall affairs of the church. There is no *us* versus *them* mentality between leaders and members, nor are the church leaders told to read the letters behind closed doors and only tell the congregation what they think they need to know. For instance, when one stops to consider the nature of all the difficulties being experienced by the congregation in Corinth (division, sexual sin, lawsuits, questions about Christian freedom, arguments over the spiritual gifts, etc.), it really is remarkable that at no point in the letter did Paul stop and address the leaders separately. Rather, the truth of the gospel and its application is for all of God's people, and everyone needs to be involved. Some might possibly object that this makes godly leadership unnecessary, but, in fact, the opposite is true. Leaders must read and digest the contents of the letters and then work hard to make sure everyone understands what is being said and what is required in terms of compliance.

If the whole church should be involved in disciplinary action of the kind described in 1 Corinthians 5, it's no surprise that Paul was horrified when recounting in chapter 6 that the Corinthian church had been seeking the help of non-Christians to settle their own disputes. This is not what a people called to the image-bearing work of ruling, judging, and putting all things under Christ's feet should have to do. They shouldn't have to turn to rebels to resolve their disputes. Paul expected the Corinthians to act *now* according to what the church *is now* in Christ, which he made abundantly clear by a series of pointed questions:

> Don't you know that the saints will judge the world? And if the world is judged by you, are you unworthy to judge the smallest cases? Don't you know that we will judge angels—not to mention ordinary matters? So if you have cases pertaining to this life, do you select those who have no standing in the church to judge? I say this to your shame! (1 Cor 6:2–5a)

If one day they would judge the world, surely the congregation should be able to resolve smaller disputes now. Inside this community, the job of adjudicating these disputes begins today—for everyone. Again Paul's horror only makes sense if he assumed the entire church should be involved in these kinds of decisions, consistent with the nature of new covenant salvation. Each member, given who they are in Christ, has a role to play, which means the entire church is ultimately responsible as the final court of appeal for her own affairs under the lordship of Christ.

Later in 2 Corinthians 7:10–13, Paul praised the church for carrying out his instructions and for their godly repentance and zeal in dealing with the sin in their midst. He spoke of the encouragement he and others experienced because of the promptness and thoroughness of their actions.

Sadly, it is no doubt the case that churches do not always act like regenerate, new covenant communities, which is evident even on the pages of the New Testament. Congregations and their leaders fail to be diligent in preaching the gospel clearly, receiving members, and practicing church discipline in order to preserve the purity of the church as a regenerate body. They fail to help their members know what it means to be in Christ and to have received the new birth of the Spirit. When these failures occur, our churches end up receiving and keeping unregenerate members, which leads the church away from what it should be. And under such circumstances, it's no wonder congregationalism is rejected. Yet Hammett rightly observes, "The problem is not with *congregationalism* as a system of church government, but with particular *congregations* no longer composed exclusively of regenerate members. Congregational church government demands regenerate church membership."[46]

---

[46] Hammett, *Biblical Foundations for Baptist Churches*, 102. In this regard, recently, James MacDonald, pastor of Harvest Bible Fellowship, wrote a couple of provocative blog posts rejecting congregationalism. See his "Congregational Government Is from Satan" accessed September 22, 2014, http://theelephantsdebt.files.wordpress .com/2012/06/congregational-government-is-from-satan.pdf and "Responding to Satanic Attacks on My Post About Satanic Congregationalism," accessed September 22, 2014, http://www.igniteus.net/archives/818. MacDonald is tired of "carnal members" who "spew their venom" and destroy the work of Christ in the church. He views congregationalism as elevating the "fleshly and worldly," and in place of it, he argues for an elder *rule without* congregational involvement. In fact, tongue-in-cheek he observes that the only place where a pure congregational vote took place was in Numbers 14 (Israel against Caleb and Joshua) and Luke 23 (the people wanting Barabbas instead of Jesus), both occasions where unruly, unregenerate people stood against God's rule and caused havoc. He exhorts the church not to go in this "congregational" direction. However, at least two serious problems exist with MacDonald's assessment. First, even though he is not clear on this point, he acts *as if* the church is comprised of a "mixed" community, like Israel of old. No doubt the church does not always act as it ought, but to view the church as constituted by "carnal" and unregenerate people is simply to misunderstand the nature of the church. Second, even though he rightly acknowledges the important role of elders, he elevates them almost to an old-covenant status where they function as if they have the Spirit and the people do not, or it is through them that God works out his will for the church. But once again this is a failure to understand the structural changes that are crucial for understanding the New Testament church and its nature. A far better assessment of the limits of congregationalism, without an accompanying rejection of its God-given role, is Jonathan Leeman, "Congregationalism Is Used by Satan . . . like He Uses Everything Else" at http://www.9marks.org/blog/congregationalism-used-satanlike-he-uses-everything-else.

4. Elder Authority Depends on Pastoral Persuasion

The New Testament identifies three church offices: apostle, elder, and deacon. The office of apostle no longer exists in the church because the men specifically chosen by Jesus to serve in this capacity have died and are no longer with us. And the office of deacon, like the office of elder, will be discussed at length in a later chapter of this book. But a brief word here about an elder's authority in the church seems appropriate. An elder's authority is tied to the Word of God, and it depends on his work of persuading according to the Word.

The New Testament teaches that a plurality of elders should be in the church, as we have already seen. Also biblically mandated are the qualifications for elders. Men who are mature in the faith and who can conduct themselves in an exemplary fashion among God's people should hold the office of elder. This is borne out, for example, in the list of qualifications of church leaders (1 Tim 3:1–7; Titus 1:5–9). Carson has observed that "almost every entry is mandated elsewhere of *all* believers."[47] What is distinctive about the elder is that he must be "able to teach" and not a recent convert, but the whole congregation is expected to work at the other qualifications. In other words, the elders are not a special class within the congregation but men who "must excel in the graces and deportment expected of all believers," says Carson. After all, "he who would lead the church must himself be a good reflection of it, not a mere professional."[48]

It is best to understand the terms *elder*, *overseer*, and *pastor* to refer to the same office, though each term bears its own nuance.[49] But all three speak of experience, supervision, and nurturing care. Again, they're to be pictures of mature godliness, gentle oversight, and wise care befitting people who love the "chief Shepherd" and will follow him wherever he leads (cf. 1 Pet 5:4 and John 10:26).

There is a sense in which elders can make commands. But since they do not have the power of excommunication at their exclusive disposal, they cannot enforce their commands without the congregation's assent.

---

[47] Carson, "Church, Authority in," in Elwell, *Evangelical Dictionary of Theology*, 229.
[48] Ibid.
[49] In the New Testament the terms elder (*presbyteros*), pastor (*poimen*), and overseer or bishop (*episkopos*) probably all refer to the same office. Elders and pastors are linked in that they have teaching and shepherding responsibilities (see Eph 4:11 and 1 Tim 3:2; cf. Acts 20:28; 1 Pet 5:2–4). Paul uses the words *elder* and *overseer* interchangeably (see Acts 20:17, 28; Phil. 1:1; 1 Tim 3:1–2; 5:17; Titus 1:5–7; cf. Acts 14:23). The term *elder* speaks of maturity, *pastor* of nurture and care, and *overseer* of direction and guidance.

This protects them from abusing their authority because they are forced instead to rely on *persuading* church members according to the Word.

The authority of persuasion is consistent with the regenerate nature of the new covenant community; and along these lines the manner in which apostolic writers like Paul, Peter, and John addressed the church is instructive for elders. Sometimes the apostles spoke to the church as a father would speak to his children. They were affectionate, tender, and patient.[50] Other times they spoke as brothers to other brothers and sisters.[51] Although the apostles were to lead and shepherd the people of God, they were never arrogant in the letters, and they did not bully and push their own selfish agendas. They did not treat the church as if it was full of unregenerate people who must be controlled else they would get out of line and cause difficulty. Rather they appealed to them as those who belong to the same spiritual family and are destined to share in the salvation of God forever. A classic example is Paul's way of confronting Philemon: "Although I have great boldness in Christ to command you to do what is right, I appeal to you, instead, on the basis of love" (Phlm 8–9). Paul as an apostle could have commanded; instead he appealed on the basis of love. How instructive is this for elders, who don't have the ability to command in the same way Paul did!

The authority of an elder depends in large part on his faithfulness to God's Word both in doctrine and in life. Paul therefore instructed Timothy to set an example for the believers in speech, in conduct, in love, in faith, and in purity. Timothy was to be diligent in these matters and give himself wholly to them so that everyone may see his progress (1 Tim 4:11–16). Paul was instructing Timothy to lead in a way that wins the approbation of the whole congregation. He was to lead by example, and his leadership was to inspire others to follow in his footsteps.

In this regard it should be noted that the ethical exhortations found in the New Testament letters are also consistent with the regenerate nature of the new covenant community in that there is a notable absence of law-based exhortation.[52] Typically Christian believers are exhorted to be all they are in Christ Jesus (Rom 13:14). They are reminded of their union with Christ in his death, burial, and resurrection (Rom 6:1–4). They are told of the price that has been paid for their salvation (1 Cor

---

[50] See 1 Cor 4:15; Phil 2:22; 1 Thess 2:6–8; Phlm 10; 1 Pet 5:14; 1 John 5:21.

[51] See Rom 12:1; 15:14–16; 1 Cor 1:10; 15:58; 2 Cor 13:11; Gal 6:18; 2 Pet 1:10; 1 John 5:19.

[52] Eph. 6:1–3; cf. Exodus 20 where obedience to parents is enjoined because the command to honor father and mother is the first commandment with a promise that children will live long on the earth.

6:20; 1 Pet 1:18) and of the fact that God is committed to their complete renovation (Phil 1:6). They are told of their position in Christ, who is seated in heaven at the right hand of God, and encouraged to set their minds on things above and not on the things of this earth (Col 3:1–4). They are reminded of the contrast between what they were before they became Christians and what they are now that they have come to Christ (Eph 4:20–24). What is true for the congregation is true for church leaders as well. There is no special status or set of rules for the one group as opposed to the other. All are to love the Lord and serve him with all of their hearts. They are to work together to help one another be all that God wants them to be. There is no sign of any form of elitism in the church (1 Cor 3:1–23).[53]

5. Church Authority Divides Between Three Spheres: Christ's, the Congregation's, and the Elders'

The nature of elder authority in the context of congregationalism brings us to a fifth point, which gets at the balance between elder and congregational authority and how they are meant to work in concert. This last point also sums up the previous four. In short, church authority divides between three different "spheres of authority" that need to be carefully kept and balanced:[54] the ultimate authority of Christ, the final earthly rule of the congregation, and the everyday leadership of the elders or pastors.

As we have already argued, the church may be regenerate and every member empowered and gifted by the Spirit, but that does not negate the importance of divinely ordained and gifted leadership offices, specifically those of elder and deacon. We have sought to make clear that these church leaders do not function as leaders did under the old covenant, namely, as distinctive mediators between God and the people or as authoritative rulers over God's people without any involvement from the people. As such, there should not be a divide between clergy and congregation so that the Scriptures only come to the people through the mediation of "experts." In the new community all of the members have

---

[53] See Schreiner, *New Testament Theology*, 146. Schreiner writes, "The Corinthians do not belong to Paul, Apollos, or Cephas, for they are God's cultivated field and God's architectural masterpiece (1 Cor. 3:9). Boasting in human ministers is shallow and superficial, for the Corinthians have something infinitely better than weak human beings. Because they belong to Christ, they belong to God, and once someone belongs to God, then everything belongs to the believer—whether death or life."

[54] For the use of this expression, see Carson, "Church, Authority in," in Elwell, *Evangelical Dictionary of Theology*, 230; Allison, *Sojourners and Strangers*, 284.

the Spirit. There is no longer a *qualitative* difference between leaders and people. The entire new covenant community knows the Lord in a personal way. Right after observing that some will leave the church because they are not "of us," John observes, "But you have an anointing from the Holy One, and all of you have knowledge" (1 John 2:20). All are anointed. All have knowledge. Church leaders function then as fellow believers, gifted by God for a specific task in leading the people of God but in concert with the entire Spirit-born-and-gifted congregation. The realities of the new covenant era mean that God's people should be encouraged to read and study the Scriptures for themselves. Gifted preachers and teachers help them do this. The nature of the new covenant people of God requires that both leaders and people work together in the church and in this way express what we are in Christ, which is precisely what congregationalism affirms.

Turning to the story of the early church, particularly in the book of Acts, this is exactly what we find: leaders and members working and deciding matters of consequence together. In Acts 6:1–6 the twelve apostles were overburdened by the work of caring for the daily distribution of food to widows. They proposed that the congregation select seven men known to be full of the Spirit and wisdom so that the apostles could concentrate on prayer and the ministry of the Word. This proposal pleased *the whole group*, and *they chose* seven men and presented them to the apostles, who prayed and laid their hands on them. The whole congregation acted together with the apostles. How much more, then, with nonapostolic elders?

In Acts 13:1–3 God is directly involved in the selection of Paul and Barnabas from among a group of five prophets and teachers at Antioch for a special work of evangelism and church planting. Still the whole church at Antioch responded to the call of God on Paul and Barnabas's lives by fasting, praying, and placing their hands on them, and sending them off. Again, everyone in this new covenant community was *ruling* together.

In Acts 15:1–35, a council is called in Jerusalem to adjudicate a theological disagreement that had arisen regarding the relationship between circumcision and salvation. Involved in the process, again, are not only apostles such as Paul, apostolic representatives like Barnabas, and the elders, but other church members as well. To begin with, it appears the whole congregation at Antioch sent both Paul and Barnabas to Jerusalem to get answers and then received them upon their return (15:2, 20–31). When the delegation arrived in Jerusalem, they were welcomed by "the church and the apostles and elders" in that order (15:4 NIV). The apostles took the lead in the discussions that ensued while "the whole assembly became silent as they listened" (15:12 NIV), unlike most presbytery and elder meetings today, which are held behind closed doors. As important as this council was, it was not closed to nonapostles and nonelders. James offers a final pronouncement. The apostles and elders come to one accord (vv. 23, 25). But then "the apostles and elders, with the whole church" determine how to reply to Antioch (15:22 NIV). All told, this passage gives us a wonderful example of church leaders and people working together in the cause of the gospel. There was no secrecy or closed-door discussions. The church members were not treated as second-class citizens who were unable to enter into the debate even though it involved critical theological issues that lay at the heart of the Christian faith. And the final ruling clearly had the support of the whole church.

In Acts 17:10–12, Paul encountered a group of Jews in Berea who were described as more noble in character than those he had previously encountered in Thessalonica because, when they listened to the apostle, they heard him with great joy and then examined the Scriptures every day to see if what he said was true. Their examination and questions did not irk Paul, even though he was an apostle. Rather, he welcomed their scrutiny, and as a result of his careful teaching and their diligent inquiries, many people in that city believed in Jesus (v. 12). Here Paul embodied what it means not to lord his authority over the people of God.

Similarly, in Acts 18:24–26, we find the eloquent Apollos being instructed by Priscilla and Aquila in their home after they heard him speak and realized his understanding of the gospel was deficient. Apollos was not offended by their instruction; rather he was helped and made more useful by this remarkable married couple. It's a powerful example of a Spirit-filled preacher who is helped by other Spirit-filled members of the congregation.

Similarly, when we come to the pastoral letters of 1 and 2 Timothy and Titus, we find that although Paul was writing to Timothy and Titus, he had a message for the whole church. He told Timothy he was writing so he would know how people ought to conduct themselves in God's household (1 Tim 3:14–15). Also, assessing the fitness of office bearers could not be Timothy's or Titus's task alone but something that must be done in conjunction with the rest of the church (see 1 Tim 3:1–13; Titus 1:5–9). For example, elders must be above reproach within the church and have a good reputation with those outside the church; they must manage their families well and see that their children obey them, and do so in a way that is worthy of full respect. Determining the suitability of elders based on these qualifications will require the assessment of members. Paul also said that deacons "must first be tested; and then if there is nothing against them, let them serve as deacons" (1 Tim 3:10 NIV). As with assessing elders, such testing requires input from the congregation, not merely the leadership team.

Previously we noted that most New Testament letters were written to churches as a whole and not merely to church leaders. Many of them end with words of greeting and thanks that give us insight into the contributions and involvement of many in the congregation.[55] For example, at the end of Paul's letter to the Romans, both men and women are mentioned, those who opened their homes and provided the church with a place to meet, those who worked hard, those who were imprisoned alongside Paul, and those who became Christians before Paul did.

There is also much warmth, sharing, and mutuality that, while not erasing the need for biblically qualified leaders, is consistent with the rich descriptions of the new covenant community we find in the New Testament. The church is described as people who are chosen by God in Christ before the foundation of the earth (Eph 1:3–4), joined by faith to Jesus Christ (Eph 1:5–7), and filled with the Holy Spirit (Eph 1:13–14). They hear and obey the Good Shepherd's voice and follow him wherever he leads (John 10:26–27). They are the body of Christ (Eph 1:22–23), and to them he has given gifts and responsibilities (1 Cor 12:7–31). They are the bride of Christ whom he is cleansing and purifying from remaining sin (Eph 5:25–27, 32). They are temples of the living God in which he dwells by his Spirit (1 Cor 6:19–20). They are coworkers in God's service, God's field, and God's building (1 Cor 3:9). As Peter so eloquently puts it, "You are a chosen people, a royal priesthood, a holy nation, God's special possession, that you may declare the praises of him who called you out of darkness into his wonderful light. Once you were not a people, but now you are the people of God; once they had not received mercy, but now you have received mercy" (1 Pet 2:9–10 NIV).

In other words, the nature of this people requires a leadership structure that is compatible with who they are and where they are in redemptive history. While they are not perfectly holy yet, perfection is their destiny, and the practice of rule begins now. While they will always need human leaders in this life, their only King and Master is Jesus. He alone deserves their full allegiance. They are new creations in Christ Jesus

---

55 See Rom 16:1–16, 21–24; 1 Cor 16:19–20; 2 Cor 13:12–13; Phil 4:21–22; Col 4:7–18; 2 Tim 4:19–21; Heb 13:24; 1 Pet 5:12–14; 2 John 13; 3 John 14.

(2 Cor 5:17), they possess the Spirit of Christ (Rom 8:9), their sins have been forgiven, and they know the Lord (Heb 8:7–12; cf. Jer. 31:31–34). Spiritual gifts and abilities will vary—and not all are called to serve in positions of leadership—but all have a vital role to play in the church when it comes to taking the gospel into the world.

The elder's call to teach should not surprise us, nor should we think it conflicts with the congregation's final authority. It makes sense of the body imagery of the local church (see 1 Cor 12–14). Christ is the head of the church, but the church is comprised of many body parts (members). All members have an important place and role in the life of the church. All are gifted by the Spirit to carry out their God-ordained role but not in the same way, and ultimately all are part of the governing of the church, which is evidenced by the entire congregation's role in choosing leaders, guarding the gospel, carrying out church discipline, and so on.

In all this what we see are "spheres of authority" that are given in order for the church to function as the church. First and foremost is the authority of the Lord Jesus Christ who is the head of the church. All authority is his, and any authority we have is a derived and given authority from him. Second, there is the authority is given to the congregation as a whole, consistent with what the church is. Third, a divinely ordained authority is given to gifted leaders who are called to lead the church. What is crucial is not to pit these authorities against one another, particularly the last two. Both of them are ordained by the Lord of the church to function together, and what he brings together we should not rend asunder.

Final earthly authority goes to the church in a number of matters of judgment: church discipline, which ranges all the way from private admonition to excommunication (1 Cor 5:5; Gal 6:1; cf. Matt 16:19; 18:18); internal disputes (1 Cor 6:4); the selection of deacons and elders (Acts 6:3–6; 15:22; 1 Cor 16:3); the collection and distribution of monies for relief of the poor (1 Cor 16:1–4; 2 Cor 8–9); the administration of the Lord's Supper (1 Cor 11:20–26); setting apart and sending out specific people for certain responsibilities (Acts 11:19–24; 13:1–3; 14:24–28); the right preaching of the gospel (Gal 1:7–8; 2 Tim 4:3); and so on. But Christ also has ordained specific leaders to lead the church in concert with the congregation (e.g., Acts 14:23; 20:28; 1 Tim 5:17; Titus 1:7; Heb 13:7, 17; 1 Pet 5:2–3). Put together, then, the New Testament presents a picture of congregational *rule* that is elder *led*. The elders lead and guide the church to fulfill and carry out its responsibilities as the church.

Unfortunately, what often occurs in discussions of church government is that one side of the biblical evidence is elevated over against other biblical evidence. Either the rule of the congregation is elevated at the expense of the leadership, or the authority of the leadership is elevated without acknowledging the final authority of the congregation. Such reductionism must be rejected. We must do justice to all the biblical data, which better fits with a congregational-rule and elder-led structure.[56] Furthermore, if the church is functioning as it ought, a healthy balance will exist between the leaders and the congregation. Both will recognize their rightful place. The congregation will recognize the authority and gifts of the leaders, and on matters that are important and clear, the elders and the congregation will normally agree. On matters that are less clear, the congregation should trust their leaders as their leaders follow Christ and submit themselves to God's Word. But the elders should covet the prayers and seek out the wisdom of God's people as they, too, are new covenant members, born of the Spirit, united to Christ, and growing in grace.

Congregationalism: Concluding Reflections

The church is a Spirit-filled and Spirit-led body, and it requires leaders who are the same. Because there is no qualitatively spiritual difference between the leaders and the congregation, ecclesiological structures need to facilitate interaction between these two groups. Leaders are necessary because the church is still growing in conformity to Christ and there are many threats to that growth. However, leaders are also growing in their commitment to Christ, and therefore both groups need to balance one another as they share in governing the life of the church. Churches filled with unregenerate church members are a terrible problem, but so are churches whose offices and pulpits are filled with unregenerate church leaders.

Congregationalism locates authority in the church as a whole as it follows the directives of its Lord in the Scriptures. Elders and deacons provide leadership and guidance in the church's work. Where the church and its leaders are at odds with each other, one or both are wrong, and they need to go back to the Scriptures and sort out their differences. Although congregationalism may not be as efficient as other organizational models, we believe it is compatible with the nature of the

---

[56] For a nice description of this, see Dever, *The Church*, 59–61.

new-covenant people of God and all that is revealed about them and their leaders in Scripture. The church has been described as a "colony of heaven,"[57] and as such it should reflect the beauty of a people who are being transformed into the image of our Lord with ever-increasing glory (2 Cor 3:18). When all the biblical data regarding the church as the new-covenant people of God are collated and synthesized, the result should be a way of doing things that is "fitting and orderly" (1 Cor 14:40 NIV), which a healthy practice of congregationalism should yield.

Christians disagree on church governance, to be sure, and this has tempted some to relegate the topic to the category of indifference. But we must fight to bring every thought captive to Christ and his Word, including how we organize ourselves as the people of God. Even though most of these differences among us are not gospel differences, it is still imperative for us to make sure our ecclesiology conforms to Scripture and what the church *is* as God's new covenant people. Not only does God insist that we do, which is reason enough; doing so is for our good. The church will not fully live up to everything our glorious God intends for it to be in the *now* of redemptive history unless we organize ourselves in congregational terms. May our gracious triune covenant Lord enable us to do so, ultimately for his glory and also for the good of the church.

---

[57] Clowney, *The Church*, 72.

PART 2

THE ORDINANCES

Thomas R. Schreiner
Shawn D. Wright

Discussions about the ordinances of baptism and the Lord's Supper often fall into one of two opposite errors. On the one hand the ordinances can be emphasized too much. They become the *raison d'être* of Christianity and the means by which one has a relationship with Jesus. What becomes central in the life of the church is whether one was baptized and receives Communion. On the other hand the ordinances can be emphasized too little and treated as almost unnecessary additions for the vital Christian life. Other things—often good things like preaching or evangelism—receive all the attention.

But we need to avoid both errors—sacramentarianism and a barebones utilitarianism, respectively. A correct understanding of the ordinances must begin with a correct understanding of the work and person of Christ, which is right where part 2 begins with a discussion of five preliminary issues. The subsequent chapters will then work through the historical, biblical, and theological dimensions of baptism and the Lord's Supper, respectively.

CHAPTER 3

Five Preliminary Issues for Understanding the Ordinances

Shawn D. Wright

A biblical understanding and practice of the ordinances requires us to orient our thinking around five preliminary issues: Jesus' centrality in the church, the gospel, biblical interpretation of the ordinances, the role of church history, and the distinction between ordinances and sacraments.

The Centrality of Jesus Christ in the Church

The gospel, of course, is central. The gospel is the "good news" of God's act of rescuing sinners through the blood of his Son, Jesus. Apart from the gospel there would be no Christians.

But the gospel is never experienced in isolation; it is lived out in the community of the local church. God saves sinners and transports them into the kingdom of his beloved Son. This brings them into communion not only with Jesus but also with one another. And Jesus is the focal point of the church. We will avoid many errors in our thinking and practice by following this simple rule: nothing or no one else in the church should take the limelight away from Jesus. In its past (looking back to the cross), its present (experiencing Jesus' presence by his Spirit), and its future (anticipating being with the Lord forever), the church is focused on Jesus. Jesus is the Lord of his church.

But what is the church of Jesus Christ? That building down on Fourth and Main Street? Everyone in communion with the Bishop of Rome, Christ's vicar on earth? Wherever two or three brothers or sisters in Christ get together for encouragement and accountability? A couple of Baptist confessional statements on the nature of the church illustrate how Baptists have answered this question. The Second London Baptist Confession (1689) reads:

> The catholic or universal church is invisible in respect of the internal work of the Spirit and truth of grace. It consists of the whole number of the elect who have been, who are being, or who yet shall be gathered into one under Christ who is the church's head. The church is the wife, the body, the fullness of Christ, who "fills all in all."
>
> All persons throughout the world who profess to believe the gospel and to render gospel obedience unto God by Christ are, and may be called, visible saints, provided that they do not render void their profession of belief by holding fundamental errors or by living unholy lives; and of such persons all local churches should be composed.
>
> The Lord Jesus Christ is the head of the church. By the appointment of the Father, all authority requisite for the calling, establishment, ordering and governing of the church is supremely and sovereignly invested in Him.[1]

Similarly, the *Abstract of Principles* of The Southern Baptist Theological Seminary (1858) says this about the church:

> The Lord Jesus is the Head of the Church, which is composed of all his true disciples, and in Him is invested supremely all power for its government. According to his commandment, Christians are to associate themselves into particular societies or churches; and to each of these churches he hath given needful authority for administering that order, discipline and worship which he hath appointed.[2]

---

[1] Second London Baptist Confession 26.1–2, 4, http://www.founders.org/library/bcf/bcf-26.html.

[2] *Abstract of Principles* 14, http://www.founders.org/abstract.html.

From these historic Baptist descriptions of the church, we can draw out three essential characteristics of the church relevant to a discussion of the ordinances.

First, the church belongs to Christ. He is the head of the church, and the church is his body (Eph 1:22; 5:23; Col 1:18). Among other things this means that Christ is the final authority in his church. Not only has he saved it; he reigns over it as Lord. He has the right to regulate all the church does, including what it does when it gathers and how it practices baptism and the Lord's Supper. The body must follow its head. More specifically, as the inaugurator and mediator of the new covenant, Christ stipulates the covenantal conditions the church must follow, including the initiatory covenantal sign of baptism and the ongoing covenantal sign of Communion.[3]

Second, the church is composed of regenerated believers in the Lord Jesus Christ. Not everyone who claims to be a Christian truly is one, and false professors must sometimes be excluded from a church (see Matt 7:21–23; 18:15–20; 1 John 2:19). But only those who submit to Christ their Head and live under the reign of Christ their Mediator should be permitted to be members of the church and partake of the church's ordinances.

Third, the church is already risen with Christ but has not yet been fully raised to be with him.[4] In other words, the church experiences an already-not-yet reality. Members have been completely forgiven, are completely accepted by Holy God because of Christ's perfect atonement, and have fellowship with God through the present work of the Comforter. These are tremendous present blessings, but they are not yet experienced in their fullness. Sin, Satan, the attacks of the world—all these plague the church's joy and fellowship with the Lord. This already-not-yet nature of the church has several implications as we consider the ordinances. Christ reigns over their use as covenantal Lord, and believers have fellowship with Christ when they participate. Yet the ordinances do not grant believers access to Christ in his fullness. They are proleptic, pointing expectantly to something still to come. They point backward to the cross and resurrection and forward to the wonderful day when the bride

---

[3] See Stephen J. Wellum, "Beyond Mere Ecclesiology: The Church as God's New Covenant Community," in *The Community of Jesus: A Theology of the Church*, eds. Kendell H. Easley and Christopher W. Morgan (Nashville: B&H Academic, 2013), 183–212.

[4] On the already-not-yet paradigm, see George Eldon Ladd, *The Presence of the Future: The Eschatology of Biblical Realism*, rev. ed. (Grand Rapids: Eerdmans, 1974), and Thomas R. Schreiner, *New Testament Theology: Magnifying God in Christ* (Grand Rapids: Baker, 2008), 41–116.

of Christ has perfect, never-ending, and never-diminishing fellowship
with the bridegroom in heaven.

The Gospel

We have already begun talking about the gospel, of course, but a few
more points need to be made here.[5] One danger of placing too much
emphasis on the ordinances is treating baptism and Communion as what
saves people. This is wrong. Only trusting in Jesus' saving work on their
behalf will save. There are two implications of the gospel for the ordinances of the church.

First, the church makes the gospel visible, in part through the ordinances. Paul said baptism displays the death and resurrection of our Lord
(Romans 6). And Paul told us that partaking of the bread and wine in the
Supper proclaims Jesus' death until he comes again (1 Cor 11:23–26; cf.
Matt 26:26–29). The gospel is all about Christ's death for sinners, and
the ordinances visibly show unbelievers this gospel. The church—the
community of the ordinances—is therefore the gospel made visible.

Second, the gospel must set the paradigm for all discussions about
the ordinances. Problems arise when we speak about the power of the
ordinances apart from the gospel, as if they had some intrinsic ability
to effect good. The gospel bounds our thinking about the ordinances.
Christians are saved and nourished by the gospel; baptism and the Lord's
Supper testify to this. In other words the ordinances must be subservient
to the gospel. They portray the gospel, magnifying it and highlighting its
importance. The gospel is a higher priority than the ordinances because
it defines them and limits who may participate in them.

Hermeneutics and the Ordinances

Given the significance of the ordinances in the life of the church, and
also in debates that have occurred throughout the history of the church,
it may be surprising that there is little material in the New Testament on
either baptism or the Lord's Supper. The next chapters will cover this
material, but what about the dearth?[6]

---

[5] See Greg Gilbert, *What Is the Gospel?* (Wheaton: Crossway, 2010).

[6] Mark Dever helpfully outlines a Baptist view of the sufficiency of Scripture to
teach us about the church and its ordinances in *The Church: The Gospel Made Visible*
(Nashville: B&H Academic, 2012), xiii–xxix. This has been the historic position of
Baptists when it comes to their ecclesiology. For example, J. L. Reynolds states, "As the

First, we do not need a full-blown systematic theological presentation of a truth in the Bible to maintain a key biblical tenet. Scripture nowhere asserts that God is "one in essence or substance and three eternal, co-equal Persons." But this doctrine is supported by plenty of biblical material. In a similar way the ordinances are related to the gospel, and the gospel is the central message of the Bible, which means we have much material to inform our understanding of the ordinances.

Second, the Bible gives us all the information we need about the ordinances, particularly in relation to the gospel, which must be our guiding hermeneutical principal. Biblical practices will be those that highlight the supreme person and work of our Savior and call us to trust in him. In other words we must not interpret passages about the ordinances apart from what we know about Christ's atonement, justification by faith alone, conversion, and so forth.

Third, the fact that the Bible does not specify all we wish it did about the ordinances should lead us to exercise wisdom and charity with others regarding baptism and the Lord's Supper. Also, we should not bind men's consciences beyond what the Bible requires. Churches need to maintain everything the Bible teaches and to require their members to adhere to this teaching. Beyond that, we need to thoughtfully attempt to apply gospel principles and contextualize them in our particular local churches.

The Role of Church History in the Ordinances

As we seek to exercise wisdom in those areas where the Bible is not clear, and as we seek to understand the Bible rightly, how much should we look back to church history for help? This is a pertinent question because ecclesiastical tradition is a major component of much discussion about the ordinances.

On the one hand, knowing the history of the church's doctrine is helpful. We are instructed as we observe brothers and sisters from ages past attempting to understand and apply God's Word. History teaches

---

kingdom of Christ is a subject of pure revelation, it may justly be expected that every thing pertaining to its nature, and to the external organizations by which its principles are to be diffused among men, will be found in the inspired volume, in which that revelation is deposited. . . . The Scriptures are a sufficient rule of faith and practice. The principles of ecclesiastical polity are prescribed in them with all necessary comprehensiveness and clearness" (J. L. Reynolds, *Church Polity, or The Kingdom of Christ, in Its Internal and External Developments* [1849]; rpt. in *Polity: Biblical Arguments on How to Conduct Church Life*, ed. Mark Dever [Washington, DC: 9Marks, 2001], 305).

us humility. Others may have understood the Word of God better, and been more consistent in applying it, than we have. History is extremely valuable.

On the other hand, history is not authoritative, and we should not overvalue it. Even churches in the New Testament abandoned the truth. Instead of following the apostolic teaching and practice, they invented new understandings and new practices. It should in no way surprise us, then, that vast segments of the church have erred over time. And the New Testament promises that this will continue.

How, then, do we understand the historical relationship of Baptists to the rest of the church? Here are a few brief assertions, which, for the sake of time, we will not defend. The New Testament church was baptistic, holding to regenerate church membership and to the baptism of believers only. It also taught that the covenant meal of Communion was instituted to remember the death of Christ and to lead the church to renew their hope in the gospel.

In the centuries that followed, the church quickly erred in a number of significant ways—ecclesiologically, sacramentally, and doctrinally—concerning the gospel. As it moved toward a sacramentarian understanding of baptism, the church abandoned the emphasis on a regenerate church membership. Instead of being a marker that one had been saved, baptism became viewed as saving.

By the year 500, the church had begun to regularly baptize infants. Even earlier than that, the church's understanding of the Lord's Supper had become clouded in mysticism. Over the course of the centuries following Augustine (d. 430), the church lost her way on the doctrine of salvation, introducing both a semi-Pelagian understanding of salvation and the penitential system, which was how one could be sure he would go to heaven. Notable parties in the Middle Ages like the Waldensians, John Wycliffe, and Jan Hus called for reform for some of these abuses. But it wasn't until the Reformation of the sixteenth century that the gospel of justification by faith alone was clearly and consistently recovered.[7]

Church order, though, was not recovered. The Anabaptists of the sixteenth century were more biblical concerning the ordinances than the magisterial Reformers, but their understanding of the gospel and its implications for Christian living were still suspect. The English Puritans helpfully moved beyond the continental Reformed tradition with their dual emphasis on the necessity of being born again and on a covenanted

[7] See Marvin Anderson, *The Battle for the Gospel: The Bible and the Reformation, 1444–1589* (Grand Rapids: Baker, 1978).

community within the church. Baptists then flowed out of the English Puritan movement, arriving on the scene in the mid-seventeenth century. The Baptists adhered to the biblical gospel and tried to live that gospel out in a community of covenanted church members. As one older writer put it, Baptists are the "thorough Reformers" of the Reformation era.[8]

This means we are not Landmarkists. Landmarkism is a Baptist view arising in the nineteenth century, often identified with "the trail of blood," which argues for a direct historical connection from the ministry of John the Baptist, Jesus, and the apostles up to the present. According to Landmarkists, the gospel was preached, people believed and were baptized by immersion, churches were formed, and biblical ministers were rightly ordained—all through the history of the church. From the time of Constantine, such true churches were the persecuted minority (hence, the trail of blood), but they have always existed.[9] Although Landmarkism offers an interesting historical narrative, this narrative is simply not historical. There just were not many, if any, baptistic churches between the early centuries after the apostles and the period of the Protestant Reformation.[10] Baptists had a new, real genesis in the seventeenth century.

In saying this, we are not denying the Lord's promise that "the gates of Hades shall not prevail against" the church (Matt 16:18 NKJV). We do deny that the Lord meant there would be a continuous succession of biblical churches from his earthly ministry until his victorious return in judgment. The fact that there are now biblical churches that adhere to the faith once for all delivered to the saints (Jude 3) fulfills Jesus' words to Peter. Jesus is building his church now, for which we are humbly grateful.

Further, we are not declaring that everyone who lived between the first centuries and the seventeenth century is spending eternity in hell. We trust that God saved many over those centuries who understood that they were sinners and that Jesus was their only hope of salvation but

---

8 John Quincy Adams, *Baptists, The Only Thorough Religious Reformers* (1876; rpt., Rochester, NY: Backus, 1980).

9 See *The Trail of Blood: Following the Christians Down Through the Centuries*, or *The History of Baptist Churches from the Time of Christ, Their Founder, to the Present Day* (1931; rpt., Lexington, KY: Ashland Avenue Baptist Church, 1981); James A. Patterson, *James Robinson Graves: Staking the Boundaries of Baptist Identity* (Nashville: B&H Academic, 2012).

10 James Edward McGoldrick, *Baptist Successionism: A Crucial Question in Baptist History* (Lanham, MD, and London: American Theological Library Association and Scarecrow Press, 2000); John Thornbury, *The Doctrine of the Church: A Baptist View* (Pasadena, TX: Pilgrim, 1990).

who did not have a perfect understanding of the Scriptures (as we don't). Our concern here is with the biblical nature of the corporate church.

Ordinances or Sacraments?

Christians tend to call baptism and the Lord's Supper either "sacraments" or "ordinances." We think *ordinance* is the better term, even though *sacrament* has a long history in the church. *Sacramentum* is a Latin word, which one dictionary of Latin terms defines as "a holy rite that is both a sign and a means of grace" and "the visible Word of God, distinct but not separate from the audible Word or Holy Scripture." Sacraments must have three characteristics: "(1) they must be commanded by God (*a Deo mandata*), (2) they must have visible or sensible elements prescribed by God, and (3) they must apply and seal by grace the promise of the gospel."[11] In the history of the church, the so-called sacraments came to predominate over the gospel, which gives us some reluctance about the term. Also, the language of "signing and sealing" is ambiguous and needs to be defined carefully, or else the terms can lead to misunderstanding. For these reasons we believe *ordinances* is the better term.[12]

The term *ordinances* refers to the fact that Christ has "ordained" these rites as a means of visibly portraying the gospel. Of course Jesus commanded many things, but only baptism and the Lord's Supper display the gospel in such clear pictorial fashion. They are unique in this and thus are the only two ordinances we should practice in our churches.[13]

---

[11] Richard A. Muller, *Dictionary of Latin and Greek Theological Terms: Drawn Principally from Protestant Scholastic Theology* (Grand Rapids: Baker, 1985), 267–68. See Robert L. Reymond, *A New Systematic Theology of the Christian Faith* (Nashville: Thomas Nelson, 1998), 917–23; John S. Hammett, *Biblical Foundations for Baptist Churches: A Contemporary Ecclesiology* (Grand Rapids: Kregel, 2005); Gregg R. Allison, *Sojourners and Strangers: The Doctrine of the Church* (Wheaton: Crossway, 2012), 323.

[12] See Shawn D. Wright, "Baptism and the Logic of Reformed Paedobaptists," in *Believer's Baptism: Sign of the New Covenant in Christ*, ed. T. R. Schreiner and S. D. Wright (Nashville: B&H Academic, 2006), 208–13; Shawn D. Wright, "The Reformed View of the Lord's Supper," in *The Lord's Supper: Remembering and Proclaiming Christ Until He Comes*, ed. T. R. Schreiner and M. R. Crawford (Nashville: B&H Academic, 2010), 256–61.

[13] Some "footwashing Baptists" over the years have considered footwashing to be a third ordinance based on Jesus' example in John 13. They have always been a minority for good reason. Jesus does not say washing feet is a portrayal of the gospel, nor does he tell his disciples to wash feet until he returns. See J. L. Dagg, *Manual of Church Order* (1858; repr., Harrisonburg, VA: Gano, 1990), 226–31.

Only the church has the authority to practice the ordinances, but the ordinances do not exist by the authority of the church. They exist because Christ commanded the church to practice them. Jesus commanded baptism (Matt 28:18–20); his apostles prescribed it (Rom 6:3–4; Col 2:11–12); and the early church practiced it (Acts 2:41; 18:8; 20:7, 11). Jesus also commanded the Lord's Supper (1 Cor 11:23), as did the apostles (1 Cor 11:17–34). And it was the practice of the early church (Acts 2:42). The church, to be Christ's church, must practice the ordinances in the way Christ commanded. In both baptism and Communion the gospel becomes visible (e.g., Acts 2:41; 8:21; 18:8; Rom 6:3–7; 1 Cor 11:17–34; Col 2:11–12).

CHAPTER 4

Baptism in the Bible

Thomas R. Schreiner

T he meaning of baptism in the Scriptures has been debated for
centuries. A fresh survey of the Scriptures should prove helpful
because we construct our theology of baptism from these foundational
documents.

We first encounter baptism with John the Baptist. Surprisingly Jesus
himself asked to be baptized by John. Still, John recognized that his
baptism was inferior to the baptism Jesus would bring. The Gospels do
not, rightly interpreted, support infant baptism. Baptism, as the Great
Commission text indicates, is for those who have chosen to follow Jesus
Christ as Lord. In Acts baptism follows immediately upon conversion
and faith, being integrally related to the other elements of salvation. Acts
also uses the language of being baptized in Jesus' name, but we should
not view this as contradicting the trinitarian formula of Matthew 28:19.
This verse shouldn't be interpreted as if it became the formula that was
invariably and always used when baptisms were performed in the early
church.

The Epistles, like Acts, focus on baptism as an initiation rite. Those
who are baptized have died to sin, are clothed with Christ, and are
cleansed from their sin. Such remarkable statements indicate that the
Epistles offer no basis for infant baptism because these realities are true
only of believers.

Baptism in the Gospels

John's Baptism and Jesus' Baptism

Baptism appears on the scene with the person of John the Baptist.[1] The name attached to John ("the Baptist") indicates the centrality of baptism in his ministry. Scholars have debated whether John's baptism was patterned after proselyte baptism. We lack enough information to give a definite answer because we cannot determine from the sources whether proselyte baptism preceded or followed John's baptismal practice.[2] Some scholars have detected parallels between John's baptism and the washings described in the Dead Sea Scrolls, but the parallel fails because the washings at Qumran were repeated while John's baptism took place only once.

In the Gospels John functions as an Elijah-like figure (Matt 11:12–14; 17:10–13; Mark 1:6; Luke 1:17) who prepares Israel for the coming day of the Lord and for the new exodus prophesied in Isaiah (Isa 40:3–5; Mal 3:1; Mark 1:2–4). Isaiah, after all, had emphasized that Israel would only return from exile when their sins were forgiven (Isa 43:25; 44:22; 59:2, 12), and such forgiveness would be accomplished by the Suffering Servant of the Lord (Isa 52:13–53:12). John's ministry in the wilderness signified that Israel was in spiritual exile even though they lived in the land of promise (Mark 1:3). John baptized in the Jordan River to symbolize that Israel, so to speak, had to cross the Jordan again to experience the saving promises of the Lord (Mark 1:5). John's baptism was tied to Israel's need to have their sins forgiven (Mark 1:4–5).

The immersion of those baptized probably symbolized the cleansing and removal of their sins because the new exodus (the redemption of Israel) belonged only to those who were purged of their sins.[3] At the same time John was keenly conscious of the inadequacy of his baptism (Mark 1:7–8). He realized the kingdom would not be inaugurated under his ministry. Israel needed something more effective than immersion in water. They needed to be baptized with the Holy Spirit, which is the gift

---

[1] For an in-depth examination of the Baptist's ministry, see Robert L. Webb, *John the Baptizer and Prophet*, Journal for the Study of the New Testament: Supplement Series 62 (Sheffield: Sheffield Academic Press, 1991).

[2] See Scot McKnight, *A Light Among the Gentiles: Jewish Missionary Activity in the Second Temple Period* (Minneapolis: Fortress, 1991), 82–85.

[3] Baptism was by immersion during the New Testament era. See Robert H. Stein, "Baptism in Luke–Acts," in *Believer's Baptism: Sign of the New Covenant in Christ*, ed. T. R. Schreiner and S. D. Wright (Nashville: B&H Academic, 2006), 58–61; Andreas J. Köstenberger, "Baptism in the Gospels," in Schreiner and Wright, *Believer's Baptism*, 18, n21.

of the new creation (Isa 32:15; 44:3). And only Jesus of Nazareth could carry out such a mission.

Jesus' baptism by John is recorded in the Synoptic Gospels (Matt 3:13–17; Mark 1:9–11; Luke 3:21–22). Matthew tells us that John objected to Jesus' baptism, realizing that the roles should be reversed (Matt 3:13–14). Jesus, however, told him it was necessary "to fulfill all righteousness" (v. 15).[4] What does this mean? The most important clue comes from verse 17, where Jesus is identified as the Servant of the Lord in whom the Lord delights (Isa 42:1). Jesus is God's "beloved Son" (Matt 3:17), i.e., he is the true Israel who always obeyed the Lord. Jesus was not baptized so that his own sins would be cleansed. He was baptized by John to prefigure and anticipate his death as the Servant of the Lord by which he would atone for the sins of his people and inaugurate the new creation.

The Great Commission

In the famous Great Commission text, Jesus commands his followers to "make disciples of all nations" (Matt 28:19), and baptism is one of the means by which this command is carried out: "baptizing them in the name of the Father and of the Son and of the Holy Spirit" (Matt 28:19). The trinitarian character of baptism is striking. We also see that baptism is fundamental to discipleship. It is the initiation rite for entrance into the people of God, signifying that one has become a member of the new community and that one now belongs to the triune God.[5] It follows that the covenant sign should not be given to infants because it is limited to those who follow Jesus in faith and discipleship.

Children and Infants

Those who support infant baptism point to Jesus' welcoming of children. Jesus said one must be converted and humble like children to enter the kingdom (Matt 18:3–4). Children must be allowed to come to Jesus, "for to such belongs the kingdom of heaven" (Matt 19:14 ESV; cf. Mark 10:13–15; cf. Matt 18:5). Even more remarkably, Luke in the parallel text uses the term "infants" (*brephē*) (Luke 18:15).

Still the texts cited do not support infant baptism. First, they don't even mention baptism, and so baptism must be read into the text. Second,

---

4 Unless otherwise indicated, all Scripture passages are taken from the HCSB.

5 Baptizing infants, then, contradicts fundamentally what it means to be a disciple. For an exposition of this point, see Köstenberger, "Baptism in the Gospels," in Schreiner and Wright, *Believer's Baptism*, 24–26.

Jesus does not actually say children per se *are* in the kingdom. He says the kingdom belongs to those who are *like* children, that is, to those who are humble and warmly receive Jesus. The kingdom belongs to those who realize they depend on God for life. It does not teach that infants are in the kingdom without welcoming it and believing it for themselves.[6]

Baptism in Acts

Baptism is a regular feature in the narrative of Acts. Three themes surface regarding baptism. First, baptism as an initiation rite occurs immediately after belief. Second, baptism is integrally related to other aspects of conversion. Third, baptism does not follow the trinitarian formula of Matthew 28:19 but is invariably in Jesus' name. I will examine each of these themes and then briefly consider the significance of household baptisms in Acts.

The Immediacy of Baptism

We begin by noting how baptism occurs immediately after conversion. On the day of Pentecost, Peter called upon his hearers to be baptized for the forgiveness of sins (Acts 2:38); and the 3,000 who repented and received Peter's message were baptized immediately (Acts 2:41), signifying they were members of the people of God. In the same way the Samaritans believed the gospel proclaimed by Philip and were baptized (Acts 8:12–13, 16). The immediacy of baptism is also evident in the story of the Ethiopian eunuch (Acts 8:36, 38). He believed, was baptized, and then went on his way. It might be tempting to draw out a lesson from the fact that an individual apart from a church performed the baptism hereby, but the situation of the Ethiopian eunuch was unique and hardly normative. He lived in a country in which there were no churches! What we do see, however, is that baptism took place immediately after conversion.

When Paul believed, he was baptized (apparently three days after his conversion; Acts 9:18; cf. 9:9). When Cornelius and his friends believed, Peter, though astounded that the Spirit was given to Gentiles, instructed them to be baptized (Acts 10:47–48). Lydia, too, was baptized after she believed (Acts 16:15). The conversion of the Philippian jailer is interesting in this regard because he and his household believed in the middle of

---

6 Cf. here D. A. Carson, "Matthew," *Expositor's Bible Commentary*, ed. F. E. Gaebelein (Grand Rapids: Zondervan, 1984), 8:420.

the night, and yet he was baptized right then and there (Acts 16:30–33). The household of Crispus and many other Corinthians were also baptized when they believed (Acts 18:8). The case of the Ephesian Twelve is fascinating because they had received John's baptism but apparently not the Holy Spirit (Acts 19:1–7). Paul proclaimed the good news about Jesus to them and then baptized them in Jesus' name.

To sum up, every case is the same in Acts. Baptism invariably follows immediately upon conversion and belief in Jesus Christ. Baptism clearly signifies that one has been converted. Those who are baptized are new persons. They belong now to Jesus Christ and are members of the people of God.

Baptism and Conversion

The second theme is closely related to the first: baptism is integrally related to conversion and salvation.[7] The Philippian jailer believed to "be saved" (Acts 16:31), and salvation was ratified by baptism (Acts 16:33). We read in Acts 2:38 that baptism is required "for the forgiveness of . . . sins." There is no grammatical basis for the idea that the word "for" (*eis*) should be translated "because."[8] Luke is not teaching here baptismal regeneration or sacramental theology. Yet baptism is integrally tied to forgiveness, to the cleansing that comes when one is converted, to the acceptance of the word of the gospel (Acts 2:41; cf. Acts 10:43). Acts 22:16 says that sins are washed away in baptism. This should not be interpreted mechanically, as if immersion itself cleanses a person from sin. The water of baptism signifies the washing away of sins, the cleansing of the human being (Titus 3:4–5).

Baptism is also inextricably intertwined with belief. In fact, it always occurs *after* one believes, supporting the notion that baptism is only for believers. The Samaritans and Lydia were baptized after they believed (Acts 8:12–13; 16:15). Similarly baptism is given to the Philippian jailer and his household because they believed (Acts 16:31–34). Crispus and the Corinthians were baptized upon belief (Acts 18:8). Belief and repentance are two sides of the same coin in Acts, summarizing the appropriate human response to the gospel (Acts 2:38; 3:19; 5:31; 8:22; 11:18; 17:30; 20:21; 26:20). Calling on Jesus' name for salvation also demonstrates that one has believed because calling implies faith in the one who is petitioned for help (Acts 22:16; Rom 10:13–14).

---

[7] For an outstanding essay that unpacks this theme, see Stein, "Baptism in Luke–Acts," in Schreiner and Wright, *Believer's Baptism*, 34–58.

[8] Cf. here ibid., 49.

Baptism is also closely associated with receiving the Holy Spirit. Those who repent and are baptized receive the Holy Spirit (Acts 2:38). Space is lacking here to investigate what was going on in Samaria because it is highly unusual that the Samaritans believed and were baptized without receiving the Spirit (Acts 8:12–17). The situation here is unique and unrepeatable, but whatever one makes of the text, it is evident that baptism is associated with receiving the Spirit.[9] When Peter explained the good news about Jesus Christ to Cornelius and his friends, the Holy Spirit came upon them, and they received him (Acts 10:44–45, 47; 11:15). The connection between the Holy Spirit and baptism is clear: Peter concludes that Cornelius and his cohorts should be baptized since the Spirit was poured out on them. We also see a correlation between baptism in water and baptism in the Spirit in the same account (Acts 11:16). The two can be distinguished, but they were also inseparable realities in the early church. It was inconceivable that anyone would receive the Spirit and refuse water baptism. The account of the Ephesian Twelve also links baptism and the reception of the Holy Spirit (Acts 19:1–7). The Holy Spirit came upon those who believed, and they were baptized in water.

It is not our purpose here to work out an *ordo salutis* in Acts. The point is that baptism, forgiveness of sins, being saved, repentance, belief, and receiving the Holy Spirit are closely associated in Acts, and all occur at conversion. Because Cornelius and his friends received the Spirit before they were baptized, it is clear that baptism is not necessary for conversion. Cornelius and his friends were certainly Christians before they were baptized because the Holy Spirit's indwelling indicates that one is a believer (Acts 15:7–11; cf. Gal 3:1–5; Rom 8:9). Still, baptism is treated as a boundary marker by which one is transferred from Satan's realm to God's kingdom. In the New Testament period it was inconceivable that anyone would become a believer without being baptized. No one had a notion of baptismal regeneration, but baptism was integral to

---

[9] The reason the Samaritans didn't receive the Spirit immediately was to prevent a schism between Jerusalem and Samaria. Historically, Jews and Samaritans were separated from each other. The Samaritans even built their own temple on Mount Gerizim, but John Hyrcanus burned it down. It is instructive that the Spirit was not granted to the Samaritans through Philip's ministry, even though the Samaritans believed. We have no other instance where people believed and didn't receive the Spirit. It is also important to note that the Philip in view here is the Philip from Acts 6:5, and he was not one of the apostles, for the apostles stayed in Jerusalem (Acts 8:1). The Spirit was given to the Samaritans through the apostolic ministry of Peter and John. As a result, it was clear to the Samaritans that a rival church must not be established in Samaria. The authority for the church was apostolic, and the Spirit was given only through an apostolic ministry.

the process of becoming a Christian. Because all Christians got baptized right after conversion, there was no controversy over whether baptism was required for salvation.

Baptism in Jesus' Name

Third, the name in which believers were baptized stands out in Acts. The trinitarian formula of Matthew 28:19 is completely absent. Instead, believers were baptized "in the name of Jesus Christ" (Acts 2:38; 10:48) and "in the name of the Lord Jesus" (Acts 8:16; 19:5). We must beware of making too much of the difference here. On the one hand it certainly doesn't mean Luke denied the Trinity because there is ample evidence that he shared the same trinitarian conception found elsewhere in the New Testament (e.g., Matt 3:16–17; 28:19; 2 Cor 13:14). It may instead suggest that baptismal practice was not standardized at an early period. Such flexibility indicates that one could read Matthew 28:19 too mechanically. In any case, Luke emphasizes the fundamental role of Jesus in baptism, underscoring the centrality of Jesus in conversion. He is the only name through which salvation comes (Acts 4:12).

The Household Baptisms

Finally, we see several times in Acts that entire households were baptized (Acts 11:14; 16:15, 31, 34; 18:8). I don't think there are any clues from the Lydia passage that help us adjudicate the issue. It is common to argue that these texts support the baptism of infants because on three occasions the text says the entire household was baptized, and certainly the household included infants. This textual argument for the paedobaptist position doesn't stand alone, of course. It's tied to the covenantal view of baptism and the alleged connection to circumcision. Yet the purpose here is to assess whether household baptisms point to the baptism of infants. If we examine the text carefully, the answer is no. In the case of Cornelius, the household that is saved (Acts 11:14) is limited to those who repented (Acts 11:18), heard the word (Acts 10:44), received the Spirit (Acts 10:44–47; 11:15–17), and spoke in tongues (Acts 10:46).[10]

Nor does the baptism of the Philippian jailer's household in Acts 16:31–34 support infant baptism.[11] Verse 31 restricts salvation to those who believe. Should someone argue that the jailer's belief was sufficient to save his entire household, they would have no textual basis to limit

---

[10] Stein, "Baptism in Luke–Acts," 62.
[11] Ibid., 63.

that salvation to infants. On such a reading, the jailer's faith would save his *entire* household, and personal faith would not be required for inclusion in the church. Yet such a notion is foreign to Acts and the remainder of the New Testament. One person cannot be saved based on another person's faith. It appears instead that both the jailer and his whole household believed in God. Verse 34 offers an important piece of evidence that is often missed for interpreting this passage. It says the entire household "rejoiced." Such rejoicing is only possible for those who understood the significance and meaning of what had just happened, which would not include infants. The smiles of an infant without comprehension hardly fit with what Luke says here! Both belief and joy emanated from those who understood the message of the gospel and responded to it rightly.

The interpretation proposed for the Philippian jailer fits with the household of Crispus: "Crispus, the ruler of the synagogue, believed in the Lord, together with his entire household. And many of the Corinthians hearing Paul believed and were baptized" (Acts 18:8 ESV). Luke emphasizes that everyone in the household believed and does not limit belief to Crispus. The last part of the verse underscores the connection between faith and baptism, showing that baptism followed belief. When the evidence is investigated and assessed carefully, there is no warrant for the notion that household baptisms included infants.

Baptism in the Epistles

Baptism isn't mentioned often in the Epistles, but they clearly assume that every believer was baptized. An unbaptized Christian was an anomaly, and there is no evidence that believers rejected baptism.

The meaning of baptism of the dead in 1 Corinthians 15:29 continues to be debated, but it is certain that the early Christians thought baptism was important if they practiced baptism for the dead. No doctrine should be erected upon a verse that is unclear, especially since Paul's purpose here was not to discuss baptism but to defend the credibility of the resurrection.[12] Perhaps the Corinthians engaged in the practice because some of their beloved had died suddenly after coming to faith and were unable to be baptized.

---

[12] For various interpretations, see Rudolf Schnackenburg, *Baptism in the Thought of St. Paul: A Study in Pauline Theology*, trans. G. R. Beasley-Murray (Oxford: Blackwell, 1964), 95–102; Anthony C. Thiselton, *The First Epistle to the Corinthians*, New International Greek Testament Commentary (Grand Rapids: Eerdmans, 2000), 1240–49.

Union with Christ

What we see in the Epistles, just as we saw in Acts and the Gospels, is that baptism is tied closely to new life and union with Christ. As such it marks out those who belong to the church of Jesus Christ. Three passages in particular are worth exploring.

1. Romans 6:2–5

In this passage Paul tells his readers that they had "died to sin" and then reminds them of their baptisms, which symbolized their union with Jesus in his death and resurrection. Being plunged underneath the water symbolizes dying with Christ, and emerging from the water signifies rising with Christ. Paul argues, therefore, that the dominion, the tyranny, and rule of sin have been broken in those who are baptized. It is difficult to see how this can apply to infants because the power of sin has not been defeated in their lives. It seems clear that Paul limits what he says here to believers, to those who have experienced new life in Jesus Christ.

Is Paul teaching baptismal regeneration here? To many Baptists it sounds strange to say we died to sin in baptism. But he's not teaching baptismal regeneration. Unlike our own day, virtually all Christians were baptized shortly after their conversion.[13] Hence, another way of saying someone was a Christian was to say he or she had been baptized. In other words Paul could refer to one's baptism as shorthand for their conversion. Because unbaptized Christians didn't exist for all practical purposes, one could define what a Christian was by baptism.[14] This is not to deny, of course, that some who were baptized later fell away, revealing that they weren't truly saved.

Another passage offers a clue that baptism doesn't save. In 1 Corinthians 1:17, Paul announces that he didn't come to baptize but to proclaim the gospel. Apparently, the Corinthians were assigning

---

[13] See Schnackenburg, *Baptism in the Thought of St. Paul*, 125; G. R. Beasley-Murray, *Baptism in the New Testament* (Grand Rapids: Eerdmans, 1962), 298; Anthony R. Cross, "'One Baptism' (Ephesians 4:5): A Challenge to the Church," in *Baptism, the New Testament and the Church*, ed. S. E. Porter and A. R. Cross, Journal for the Study of the New Testament: Supplement Series 171 (Sheffield: Sheffield Academic Press, 1999), 192.

[14] See the important study by Robert H. Stein, "Baptism and Becoming a Christian in the New Testament," *Southern Baptist Journal of Theology* 2 (1998): 6–17. For the same point, see Anthony R. Cross, "Spirit- and Water-Baptism in 1 Corinthians 12.13," in *Dimensions of Baptism: Biblical and Theological Studies*, ed. S. E. Porter and A. R. Cross, Journal for the Study of the New Testament: Supplement Series 234 (London: Sheffield Academic Press, 2002), 120–48.

significance to whether Paul or Apollos or perhaps even Peter baptized them (1 Cor 1:13–16). Such an idea was repugnant to Paul. Baptism is in Christ's name, not the name of a mere human being! The one who actually performs the baptism is utterly insignificant. But what this passage also shows us is that baptism must be interpreted in light of the gospel. The gospel isn't interpreted in light of baptism. Hence, we must reject any understanding of baptism that contradicts the free grace of the gospel (such as baptismal regeneration or sacramental theology) because it does not accord with the gospel of Christ.[15]

2. Colossians 2:12

Like Romans 6, Colossians 2:12 teaches that baptism unites us to Christ in his death and resurrection: "Having been buried with him in baptism, in which you were also raised with him through faith in the powerful working of God, who raised him from the dead" (ESV). Those who are converted and transferred into God's kingdom have conquered death through union with Christ. They were buried with Christ in baptism and raised to new life at his resurrection (cf. Col 2:13). The new life, however, does not come *ex opere operato*. Paul says this life is ours only "through faith in the working of God" (Col 2:12). Again the evidence rebuts infant baptism since new life in Christ is only granted to those who believe. The objective work of God is never separated from the subjective appropriation of his work. Paul doesn't conceive of baptism having an effect apart from faith.

Paedobaptists, however, point to Colossians 2:11: "In him also you were circumcised with a circumcision made without hands, by putting off the body of the flesh, by the circumcision of Christ" (ESV). The parallel between circumcision and baptism (see v. 12 above), they claim, supports paedobaptism. Just as infants were circumcised in infancy under the old covenant, so too in the new covenant infants should receive the covenant sign of baptism. The argument is complex and will be examined in more depth in the theological section below, but a few things can be said here.[16]

First, finding a parallel here fails at an exegetical level. Paul does not draw a connection between baptism and physical circumcision. The link

---

[15] Obviously, I would need to introduce a number of other theological arguments to defend what is being stated here.

[16] For further argumentation, see J. P. T. Hunt, "Colossians 2:11-12: The Circumcision/Baptism Analogy, and Infant Baptism," *Tyndale Bulletin* 41 (1990): 227–44.

is between baptism and spiritual circumcision.[17] Physical circumcision was administered on the eighth day in Israel (Lev 12:3) and made one a member of the covenant people. But if the Old Testament is clear on anything, it's that those who are physically circumcised are not necessarily spiritually circumcised. Indeed, what Israel needed (Deut 10:16) and lacked (Jer 4:4) was a circumcised heart. Hence, the nation looked forward to the day when the Lord would circumcise their hearts in the new covenant (Deut 30:6; Jer 31:31–34). The significance of the Old Testament witness should be evident. Baptism finds its parallel with spiritual circumcision, which occurred when a person was regenerated. Regeneration did not take place when Israelites were physically circumcised. In fact, this was the problem with Israel. Although they were physically circumcised, they were not all spiritually circumcised.

Second, the so-called parallel between baptism and circumcision fails to observe the difference between the covenants. The old covenant was theocratic in nature so that Israel was both a political entity and a spiritual entity. Entrance into the covenant community was marked by circumcision, but those who were physically circumcised were not necessarily spiritually transformed. In the new covenant all know the Lord (Jer 31:31–34; cf. Heb 10:15–18). The new covenant is not theocratic but spiritual in the sense that all are indwelt by the Spirit and keep God's commands (Ezek 36:25–27). The proposed connection between baptism and circumcision is unconvincing.

3. Galatians 3:27

Finally, Galatians 3:27 teaches union with Christ: "For as many of you as were baptized into Christ have put on Christ" (ESV). What it means to be a Christian is to be clothed with Christ, and all those who are immersed into Christ via baptism belong to him. We see again that Paul simply assumes that all those baptized are converted.[18] Baptismal regeneration and sacramentalism are ruled out by Galatians 3:26, which emphasizes that we are God's sons "through faith." Those who are baptized are those who have believed, and they are thereby incorporated into Christ.[19]

---

[17] D. F. Wright, "Children, Covenant and the Church," *Themelios 29* (2004): 29.

[18] This is not to deny that some who were baptized later fell away, showing that they were not truly converted. It was not Paul's purpose to address this matter in Gal 3:27.

[19] For the importance of faith, see Beasley-Murray, *Baptism in the New Testament*, 156, 304; Schnackenburg, *Baptism in the Thought of St. Paul*, 116, 122–27.

Regeneration and Salvation

The parallel between baptism and spiritual circumcision mentioned by Colossians 2 brings us to the connection between baptism and regeneration. We see this even more clearly in Titus 3:5: "He saved us—not by works of righteousness that we had done, but according to His mercy, through the washing of regeneration and renewal by the Holy Spirit." Some scholars question whether washing refers to baptism, but such doubts aren't convincing. Because baptism was the universal experience of all believers, a reference to washing that hearkens back to the inception of the Christian life naturally brings to mind water baptism.[20] Salvation comes "through" the washing that occurs in baptism, and the term "washing" signifies the cleansing of sin that believers receive when they are saved. Here in Titus 3, washing is associated with regeneration and renewal. The nouns "regeneration" (*palingenesia*) and "renewal" (*anakainōsis*) both modify "washing," and these two nouns are synonyms. The physical washing that took place in baptism represents the new life granted at conversion. Paul emphasizes that such regeneration and renewal are supernatural. They come from the Holy Spirit.[21]

One of the most striking statements on baptism is found in 1 Peter 3:21:[22] "Baptism . . . now saves you, not as a removal of dirt from the body but as an appeal to God for a good conscience, through the resurrection of Jesus Christ" (ESV). Often this statement shocks readers because it sounds like a blatant statement of baptismal regeneration. If we recall, however, how virtually everyone was baptized in the early church, then the statement is not so astonishing. "Baptism," as we have seen in other texts, is tied to salvation. Finally, the verse itself does not teach that baptism mechanically saves someone. The mere removal of dirt from the body, which takes place in washing, doesn't rescue anyone from God's wrath. Baptism does not work magically or sacramentally. It is only effective when accompanied by an "appeal to God for a good conscience." The one receiving baptism calls out to God for the cleansing of his or her conscience, for the forgiveness of sins. Now it is possible that the word translated "appeal" (*eperōtēma*) by the ESV should be

---

[20] See here Stein, "Baptism in Luke–Acts," in Schreiner and Wright, *Believer's Baptism*, 46, n25.

[21] See here Schnackenburg, *Baptism in the Thought of St. Paul*, 10; Lars Hartman, *'Into the Name of the Lord Jesus': Baptism in the Early Church*, Studies in the New Testament and Its World (Edinburgh: T&T Clark, 1997), 113.

[22] It used to be common to see 1 Peter as a baptismal treatise, but such a view is not predominant today. See Thomas R. Schreiner, *1, 2 Peter, Jude*, New American Commentary (Nashville: B&H Academic, 2003), 42–43.

rendered "pledge" (HCSB).[23] If such is the case, the one who is baptized promises to live in a way that accords with his new status as a believer. In either case the subjective decision of the believer is included. As is the case throughout the New Testament, the subjective and objective belong together. Baptism without faith does not save. Baptism does not save in and of itself. Christ's death brings us to God (1 Pet 3:18); and hence salvation finds its roots in the death and resurrection of Jesus, and baptism testifies to that saving work.

Cleansing

Baptism witnesses to the washing or cleansing from sin that believers receive through Jesus Christ. "But you were washed, you were sanctified, you were justified in the name of the Lord Jesus Christ and by the Spirit of our God" (1 Cor 6:11). In this verse Paul reflects on the saving work of God—baptism, sanctification,[24] and justification—and the inception of the Christian life. At salvation believers are washed and cleansed from sin; they are placed into the realm of the holy; and they are declared right before God. All three metaphors highlight the truth that believers are forgiven of their sins and have a new relation to God. Baptism, in particular, reminds Christians that their sins have been washed away.

The picture of washing appears again in Ephesians 5:25–26: "Christ loved the church and gave Himself for her to make her holy, cleansing her with the washing of water by the word." Some have seen a reference to a bridal bath rather than baptism, finding an echo of Ezekiel 16:8–14.[25] There may be an allusion to this practice since the context of Ephesians 5 is marriage. Nevertheless, we should not opt for an either-or here because it is a common feature in the New Testament to denote baptism by washing.[26] And just as we saw in 1 Corinthians 6:11, holiness and washing are joined together. By virtue of Christ's work, believers are holy before God and cleansed of their sins. Baptism testifies to that saving work. The "word" in 5:26 most likely refers to the word of the

---

[23] For the latter view, see Paul J. Achtemeier, *First Peter*, Hermeneia (Minneapolis: Fortress, 1996), 270–72; John H. Elliott, *1 Peter*, Anchor Bible (New York: Doubleday, 2000), 679–80.

[24] When Paul says, "You were sanctified," he is referring to the definitive and positional sanctification that belongs to believers in Jesus Christ, not progressive sanctification.

[25] E.g., Harold H. Hoehner, *Ephesians: An Exegetical Commentary* (Grand Rapids: Eerdmans, 2002), 753–54.

[26] Rightly, Hartman, *Baptism in the Early Church*, 106; Beasley-Murray, *Baptism in the New Testament*, 201.

gospel. The cleansing occurs in accord with the word of the gospel, the good news of Christ crucified and risen.

Perhaps there is also an allusion to baptism in Hebrews 10:22: "Let us draw near with a true heart in full assurance of faith, our hearts sprinkled clean from an evil conscience and our bodies washed in pure water."[27] The body being "washed" refers to the whole person being washed and cleansed, which, as Hebrews 7:1–10:18 emphasizes, is accomplished through the death of Jesus Christ, who is the final and effective sacrifice for sins. Believers can look back to their baptism and be reminded that their sins were forgiven at the cross. Hence they can enter God's presence with assurance and confidence, knowing they are loved by God and that their sins do not separate them from him.

Baptism and Unity

Ephesians 4:5 says there is "one baptism." All believers enter the people of God the same way—through baptism. They are united together as sinners who have been washed and cleansed of their sin. Baptism, which is intimately tied to the forgiveness of sins and the work of Jesus Christ as the risen and crucified one, summons us to the truth that the church is a community of sinners who have been forgiven. They are united to one another as members of the church of Jesus Christ, and baptism is the initiation rite into the community. Baptism, then, is not just a vertical reality but also has a horizontal dimension. It signifies the unity believers share with one another through Jesus Christ.

The unity of believers is also taught in 1 Corinthians 12:13: "For in one Spirit we were all baptized into one body—Jews or Greeks, slaves or free—and all were made to drink of one Spirit" (ESV).[28] Baptism indicates that believers are members of the body of Christ, that they are members together in the church. Paul particularly emphasizes here the universality of such an experience. All believers without distinction and without exception are members of Christ's body. But doesn't Paul describe Spirit baptism here instead of water baptism? Driving a disjunction between these two is not Paul's intention because baptism in

---

[27] Some scholars see a reference to baptism in Heb 6:2, which refers to washings (*baptismōn*).

[28] For the interpretation proposed here, see Gordon D. Fee, *The First Epistle to the Corinthians*, New International Commentary on the New Testament (Grand Rapids: Eerdmans, 1987), 605–6. For another reading, see M. B. O'Donnell, "Two Opposing Views on Baptism with/by the Holy Spirit and of 1 Corinthians 12:13. Can Grammatical Investigation Bring Clarity?" in Porter and Cross, *Baptism, the New Testament and the Church*, 311–36.

the Spirit is coincident with water baptism.[29] Paul is not reflecting here on a precise *ordo salutis* but thinks of the events that occur at the inception of the Christian life in a general way. We see in Acts 10:44–48 that Spirit and water baptism are inevitably associated so that those who have experienced the former are candidates for the latter (cf. Acts 11:16). All those who have received the Spirit are members of the people of God. In fact, baptism is the *sine qua non* of membership in God's people (Acts 15:7–11; Rom 8:9; Gal 3:1–5).

1 Corinthians 7:14

Paedobaptists often appeal to 1 Corinthians 7. The paragraph in question is about the marriage of a believer to an unbeliever, and Paul exhorts the Corinthians not to initiate divorce, though divorce is permissible if the unbeliever forsakes the relationship. Apparently some of the Corinthians worried that sexual relations with an unbelieving spouse would defile them. How could they enjoy sexual union with someone who hated God? Some of the Corinthians likely reasoned that divorce would be preferable. Paul disagrees with them: "For the unbelieving husband is made holy because of his wife, and the unbelieving wife is made holy because of her husband. Otherwise your children would be unclean, but as it is, they are holy" (1 Cor 7:14 ESV). Paul assures them that marriage to an unbeliever is pleasing to God, for the unbelieving spouse is in the realm of the holy because they are married to a believer. Now this doesn't mean the unbelieving spouse is saved. Paul makes clear in verse 16 that there is no assurance that the unbelieving spouse will be saved. There is the hope of salvation, however, because they are in the realm of the holy.

From what has been said, it should be clear that the baptism of infants does not accord with this text. Paul does say they are "holy," but they are "holy" in the same way an unbelieving spouse is in the realm of the holy.[30] They enjoy the possibility of salvation because one of their parents is a believer. But there is certainly no grounds here for infant baptism. If the child is to be baptized for being holy, then the unbelieving

---

[29] Rightly Beasley-Murray, *Baptism in the New Testament*, 168–69. Against James D. G. Dunn, *Baptism in the Holy Spirit: A Re-examination of the New Testament Teaching on the Gift of the Spirit in Relation to Pentecostalism Today* (Philadelphia: Westminster, 1970), 129–31.

[30] Surprisingly, Wilson fails to see that the two terms are in the same semantic domain in his defense of infant baptism from this text. See Douglas Wilson, *To a Thousand Generations—Infant Baptism: Covenant Mercy for the People of God* (Moscow, ID: Canon Press, 1996), 50–51.

spouse should be baptized as well. But no one argues from this text that unbelieving spouses should be baptized. To justify baptism from this text introduces a foreign element to it, one that is determined by an a priori theology that doesn't accord with the purpose of the verse.

Conclusion

We see clearly in the Gospels, Acts, and the Epistles that baptism is by immersion and should be applied to believers. The baptism of believers fits with the nature of the new covenant and the character of the church as a community of believers. Baptism testifies to the new life enjoyed by believers. Those who are baptized are disciples of Jesus Christ. They have confessed him as Lord and Savior and have repented of their sins and put their faith in Jesus Christ. Those who are baptized have been clothed with Christ and have died to sin and have risen to new life in Christ. They have been regenerated and forgiven of their sins. Baptism symbolizes the cleansing of sin that takes place upon conversion. Those who are baptized have received the Holy Spirit and enjoy new life. Baptism belongs to the great complex of events that initiate one into the people of God, testifying to the great salvation believers enjoy through Jesus Christ as the crucified and risen Lord.

CHAPTER 5

Baptism in History, Theology, and the Church

Shawn D. Wright

The last chapter examined the New Testament's teaching on baptism, which prepared the way for this chapter. Here I will begin by noting two issues of a historical nature that inform our theological formulation, which in turn will help us define baptism theologically and make ecclesiological applications.

The Development of Infant Baptism

To begin it is worth looking at the rise of infant baptism and the baptismal theologies of Lutheranism and Reformed covenantal theology.

The Early Church

It is fair to say that, at best, great fluidity was in the church's baptismal theology from about AD 100 to 500. Various church leaders propounded different views, often leading to sharp geographical differences of opinion.[1] Rather than trace the flow of thought across the Patristic era, we

---

[1] This is the opinion of two paedobaptist historians who conclude that infant baptism was not the practice of the early church. See H. F. Stander and J. P. Louw, *Baptism in the Early Church*, rev. ed. (1994; rpt., Leeds, England: Reformation Today, 2004). The most comprehensive study of this subject, also concluding that paedobaptism was a later

shall merely note several instances that demonstrate the practice of the early church was to baptize converts to the faith. Along the way reasons for the growth of the novel practice of infant baptism will be suggested.

A document from the second century known as the *Didache* detailed the church's baptismal practice. It describes immersion as the preferred method of baptism and says the one being baptized should prepare himself before receiving baptism: "Before the baptism let the one baptizing and the one who is to be baptized fast, as well as any others who are able. Also, you must instruct the one who is to be baptized to fast for one or two days beforehand."[2] This would not, of course, apply to infants who would not be able to fast.[3]

In the middle of the second century, Justin Martyr echoed the idea that baptism was reserved for those who had made a commitment to follow Christ: "As many as are persuaded and believe that what we teach and say is true, and undertake to be able to live accordingly, are instructed to pray and to entreat God with fasting, for the remission of their sins that are past, we are praying and fasting with them. Then they are brought by us where there is water and are regenerated [i.e., baptized]."[4] Clearly, again, baptism was for those who had consciously committed themselves to follow Christ.

The third-century treatise by Tertullian, *On Baptism*, is the oldest extant work devoted to the ordinance of baptism. Tertullian wrote this treatise in opposition to a new practice showing up in some segments of the church: infant baptism. This new practice was fraught with difficulties: infants had no sin that needed to be cleansed; infants were unable to commit themselves to live a Christian life, which baptism called them to do; and their sponsors could not be held liable for the infants' potential future lack of pursuit of Christ.[5] Later in the same century, Cyprian

---

development, is Everett Ferguson, *Baptism in the Early Church: History, Theology, and Liturgy in the First Five Centuries* (Grand Rapids: Eerdmans, 2009). Some paedobaptists believe the historical evidence suggests an earlier date for the genesis of infant baptism. See, e.g., Sinclair B. Ferguson, "Infant Baptism View," in *Baptism: Three Views*, ed. David F. Wright (Downers Grove: IVP, 2009), 79–84.

[2] *Didache* 7.4 in *The Apostolic Fathers: Greek Texts and English Translations*, 3rd ed., ed. and trans. Michael W. Holmes (Grand Rapids: Baker, 2007), 355.

[3] Steven A. McKinion, "Baptism in the Patristic Writings," in *Believer's Baptism: Sign of the New Covenant in Christ*, ed. T. R. Schreiner and S. D. Wright (Nashville: B&H Academic, 2006), 169–70.

[4] Justin Martyr, *First Apology 61 in The Ante-Nicene Fathers*, vol. 1, ed. Arthur Cleveland Coxe (Peabody, MA: Hendrickson, 1994).

[5] McKinion, "Baptism in the Patristic Writings," in Schreiner and Wright, *Believer's Baptism*, 174. "Tertullian's primary concern was that infant baptism negated the church's practice, already seen clearly in the documents from the second century, of a time of

of Carthage penned his *Epistle 58* "to announce the decision of an African synod in AD 253 to require the baptism of infants."[6] Moving in a decidedly sacramental direction, Cyprian averred that "no one should be hindered from baptism and from the grace of God," suggesting that grace was given to infants at their baptisms.[7] Still, the fact that a regional synod was called to discuss infant baptism suggests that the practice was not universal, even in the mid-third century.[8]

Two later Christians' works will end our discussion of the patristic era. Gregory of Nazianzus (d. 389/390), one of the three "Cappadocian Fathers" and a central theologian in the East, is pertinent because of his *Oration* 40, which addressed baptism. In essence Gregory taught that the church should delay baptism until somewhere around the child's third year, so that the child could understand something of what was happening to him and of the commitment he was making. Infant baptism should only be performed if there was a high likelihood that the infant would die. As Steven McKinion notes, it is likely that Gregory was allowing for infant baptism as a pastoral compromise to aid families grieving the loss of a child.[9] This seems likely, especially given the fact that Gregory

---

preparation for baptism which included repentance from sin, fasting, and prayer. None of these necessary precursors to baptism was possible for infants. Each was possible, however, for young children and those who were older" (ibid., 176–77). Tertullian responded to one of the texts paedobaptists continue to use as support for their position: "The Lord does indeed say, 'Do not forbid them to come to me.' Let them come while they are growing up. Let them come while they are learning where they are coming. Let them become Christians when they have become able to know Christ" (*On Baptism*, 18).

6 McKinion, "Baptism in the Patristic Writings," in Schreiner and Wright, *Believer's Baptism*, 178.

7 Ibid., 179.

8 Ibid.

9 Ibid., 183. "Due to the dual pressures of infant mortality and evolving views of the sinfulness of even newborn infants, the novel practice of baptizing infants became widespread by the third century. This practice was not accepted as universal even by the fourth century, as infants' need for forgiveness continued to be questioned" (ibid., 188). Stander and Louw conclude their study in this way: "In the first four centuries of Christianity, the literature on baptism clearly shows how, in the majority of instances, it was persons of responsible age (generally adults and grown children) who were recipients of baptism. Emergency baptism and the eventual linking of baptism to circumcision, as well as the fact that baptism was believed to remove sin, occasioned the extension of baptism to small children and finally to infants. Though some authors (Tertullian and Gregory of Nazianzus) opposed this development, others (Cyprian) strongly advocated this trend, contending that no one is to be deprived of salvation and all the gifts of God's grace. Within this theological framework, baptism became . . . the most exclusive donator of Christian blessings. The symbol became the actual means. The rite of baptism itself, rather than Christ, became the guarantee of eternal salvation. . . . While the third century voiced objections against what appears to have been a growth in the number of infants being baptized, the fourth century seems to have accepted these baptisms along

himself was not baptized until he was thirty, even though his father was a bishop of the church.[10]

In the West, Augustine (d. 430) takes pride of place as the most important thinker from the early church. Although he had not been baptized as an infant, Augustine argued for paedobaptism. Against the Donatists he urged the parallel of infant baptism with circumcision. Against the Pelagians he averred that only infant baptism could cleanse the child of original sin and implant the life of Christ in him.[11] Even though Augustine argued forcefully for the historicity of paedobaptism, and even though his doctrinal exposition helped support the practice throughout the medieval period,[12] infant baptism was not the universal practice of the church during Augustine's life. However, the North African bishop's authority and ability to sway his readers seem to have helped move the broader church toward adopting paedobaptism in the years that followed.[13] In the Western church out of which Protestantism sprang, Augustine's teaching that original sin made infants liable to future punishment and concern about high infant mortality rates appear to have been the theological and pastoral impetuses, respectively, behind the universal adoption of infant baptism.

Martin Luther

Martin Luther (d. 1546) moved the church in new directions regarding the nature of authority (Scripture) and the means of salvation (faith,

with adult baptism which was still performed on a regular scale. It may, however, be said that since the fourth century infant baptism began to develop into a generally accepted custom" (Stander and Louw, *Baptism in the Early Church*, 183–84).

[10] McKinion, "Baptism in the Patristic Writings," in Schreiner and Wright, *Believer's Baptism*, 182.

[11] Ibid., 184–85. "The church was rescued from Baptist theology and practice by Augustine of Hippo" (Peter J. Leithart, "Infant Baptism in History: An Unfinished Tragicomedy," in *The Case for Covenantal Infant Baptism*, ed. Gregg Strawbridge [Phillipsburg, NJ: P&R, 2003], 258).

[12] See Jonathan H. Rainbow, "'Confessor Baptism': The Baptismal Doctrine of the Early Anabaptists," in Schreiner and Wright, *Believer's Baptism*, 190–91.

[13] "Before Augustine of Hippo, baptismal practice and theology assumed the active participation of converts; baptism of infants and children took place, but far from routinely and perhaps primarily in cases of illness. Augustine's early writings show that he, like other Christians of his time, had done little theological thinking about infant baptism. On baptism they are neither passionate nor profound. A new clarity came to his treatment of baptism after c.410 in his anti-Pelagian writings. Theologically he came to believe that infant baptism was the sole cure for the guilt of original sin; practically he came to advocate the universal baptism of infants soon after their birth. The result was a devaluation of baptism in the West which did much to determine the contours of Christendom" (David F. Wright, "Augustine and Transformation of Baptism," in *The Origins of Christendom in the West*, ed. Alan Kreider [Edinburgh: T&T Clark, 2001, 287]).

not works). Luther believed that faith and the power of the Word of God were both essential in baptism.[14] Faith was central to Luther, not an "alien faith" like the Catholics had taught but real, genuine faith: "Unless faith is present, or comes to life in baptism, the ceremony is of no avail. . . . Who should receive baptism? The one who believes is the person to whom the blessed, divine water is to be imparted." Rather than moving away from paedobaptism though, Luther taught that infants should be baptized because they really do believe: "In baptism the infants themselves believe and have their own faith." Apparently not seeing the illogic of his reason, he asserted:

> When the baptizer asks whether the infant believes, and it is answered "Yes" for him, and whether he wants to be baptized, and it is answered "Yes" for him . . . therefore it must also be he himself who believes, or else those who answer must be lying when they say "I believe" for him.[15]

Infants can only exercise faith because the word has created it within them. For Luther faith and the Word of God always work in tandem. As the word of the gospel was spoken in the baptismal ceremony, it penetrated the infant's heart and created faith. Infants are baptized because they really believe.

At least one early group of Protestants began to question Luther's baptismal practice. The Anabaptists believed the Protestant doctrine of justification by faith alone should result in the practice of baptizing only those who had exercised faith. They believed the New Testament everywhere supported their "confessor baptism" view. In opposition to these Anabaptists, a new paedobaptist argument was offered by Ulrich Zwingli, pastor of the Reformed church in Zurich.[16] Zwingli's thought

---

14 In the discussion of Luther and Zwingli's interaction with the Anabaptists, I am following the contours of Rainbow, "Confessor Baptism" in Schreiner and Wright, *Believer's Baptism*, 189–206. For a contemporary defense of Lutheran baptism, see Robert Kolb, "Lutheran View: God's Baptismal Act as Regenerative," in *Understanding Four Views on Baptism*, ed. John H. Armstrong (Grand Rapids: Zondervan, 2007), 91–109.

15 K. Brinkel, *Die Lehre Luthers von der fides infantium bei der Kindertaufe* (Berlin: Evangelische Verlagsanstalt, 1958), 44; quoted in Rainbow, "Confessor Baptism," in Schreiner and Wright, *Believer's Baptism*, 192.

16 Zwingli was the first person in the history of the church to sever faith from baptism. Prior to his teaching, people were baptized either because they exercised faith or because it was thought that faith was granted them at baptism. Zwingli, though, said faith was irrelevant in baptism. He was aware of the novelty of his position, as he pointed out in his 1525 treatise, *On Baptism*: "In this matter of baptism—if I may be pardoned for saying it—I can only conclude that all the doctors have been in error from the time of the

was later developed and elaborated by John Calvin. This Calvinistic argument is the most common evangelical defense of paedobaptism in our day.

Covenantal Paedobaptism

The Calvinistic paedobaptist doctrine is too vast to engage comprehensively here.[17] We will, rather, look at several key features that unite adherents of this perspective, offering correctives to the salient points of the position. Four of their major arguments will require our attention.

1. Denying Their Own Definition of Baptism

In the first place, covenantal paedobaptists must deny their own definitions of what baptism is. Calvin provided an illuminating example, beginning with a succinct definition: baptism is "the sign of initiation by which we are received into the society of the church, in order that, engrafted in Christ, we may be reckoned among God's children."[18] Baptism marks one as being united with Christ. It does so because baptism both demonstrates faith and confirms that one has exercised faith: "Baptism serves as our confession before men. Indeed, it is the mark by which we publicly profess that we wish to be reckoned God's people; by which we testify that we agree in worshiping the same God, in one religion with all Christians; by which finally we openly affirm our faith."[19] Faith is central: "From this sacrament, as from all others, we obtain only as much as we receive in faith. If we lack faith, this will be evidence of our ungratefulness,

apostles. This is a serious and weighty assertion, and I make it with such reluctance that had I not been compelled to do so by contentious spirits, I would have preferred to keep silence. . . . At many points we shall have to tread a different path from that taken either by ancient or more modern writers or by our own contemporaries." Baptists would do well to remind our paedobaptist friends that we are not the ones who've created a new theology of baptism. We're doing what Christians have done for centuries: baptizing because we think faith is present. They have created a new doctrine of baptism.

[17] Contemporary defenses of this position include Gregg Strawbridge, ed., *The Case for Covenantal Infant Baptism* (Phillipsburg, NJ: P&R, 2003); Richard L. Pratt Jr., "Reformed View: Baptism as a Sacrament of the Covenant," in Armstrong, *Understanding Four Views of Baptism*, 59–72; Ferguson, "Infant Baptism View," in Wright, *Baptism: Three Views*, 77–111. Reformed covenantalists are not monolithic. Meredith Kline's biblical-theological "oath sign" view is treated in Duane A. Garrett, "Meredith Kline on Suzerainty, Circumcision, and Baptism," in Schreiner and Wright, *Believer's Baptism*, 257–84.

[18] John Calvin, *Institutes of the Christian Religion*, ed. John T. McNeill, trans. Ford Lewis Battles (Philadelphia: Westminster, 1960), 4.15.1.

[19] Calvin, *Institutes* 4.15.13. Later Calvin notes that baptism "is given for the arousing, nourishing, and confirming of our faith" (*Institutes* 4.15.14).

which renders us chargeable before God, because we have not believed the promise given there."[20] Although faith can be a subjective act, three objective components to baptism are: baptism symbolizes and proves that a Christian has been cleansed of his sin;[21] it symbolizes that a believer has died to sin and been renewed in Christ;[22] and it demonstrates a disciple's union with Christ. Stressing the manner in which baptism symbolizes a Christian's union with Christ, Calvin averred that

> our faith receives from baptism the advantage of its sure testimony to us that we are not only engrafted into the death and life of Christ, but so united to Christ himself that we become sharers in all his blessings. For he dedicated and sanctified baptism in his own body in order that he might have it in common with us as the firmest bond of the union and fellowship which he has deigned to form with us.[23]

We think Calvin was correct in his exposition of the meaning of baptism. He reflected the New Testament's teaching well. How he could go on in the next chapter of *The Institutes* to advocate infant baptism is a mystery that baffles us and has stymied others too.[24] Calvin overturned his definition of baptism by advocating infant baptism.[25]

2. Reading Children into the Text

The second foundation of covenantal paedobaptists is not difficult to understand. They display a consistent penchant for reading children

---

[20] Calvin, *Institutes* 4.15.15.

[21] Calvin, *Institutes* 4.15.1–4.

[22] Calvin, *Institutes* 4.15.5.

[23] Calvin, *Institutes* 4.15.6. For a critique of Calvin's inconsistencies on the doctrine of baptism, see Shawn D. Wright, "Baptism and the Logic of Reformed Paedobaptists," in Schreiner and Wright, *Believer's Baptism*, 207–55.

[24] Karl Barth noted: "According to Calvin's own and in itself excellent baptismal teaching, baptism consists not only in our receiving the symbol of grace, but it is at the same time, in our *consentire cum omnibus christianis*, in our public *affirmare* of our faith, in our *iurare* in God's name, also the expression of a human *velle*. This without doubt it must be, in virtue of the cognitive character of the sacramental power. But then, in that case, baptism can be no kind of infant-baptism. How strange that Calvin seems to have forgotten this in his next chapter where he sets out his defense of infant-baptism, there commending a baptism which is without decision and confession" (*The Teaching of the Church Regarding Baptism*, trans. Ernest A. Payne [London: SCM Press, 1948], 48).

[25] See Wright, "Baptism and the Logic of Reformed Paedobaptists," in Schreiner and Wright, *Believer's Baptism*, 213–18, for similar critiques of other paedobaptist thinkers.

into baptismal passages and for reading baptism into passages that have nothing to do with this rite. Whether it is Jesus' welcoming of the little children, the promise of the coming of the Holy Spirit (Acts 2:39), the household baptisms in Acts, or Paul's words in 1 Corinthians 7:14, our paedobaptist friends seem to assume that wherever a child is mentioned baptism must be in view.

But of course that cannot be the case. Jesus compared the faith he desired to the faith of children, but he did not say anything about baptism.[26] The Spirit was dispersed on all sorts of people in Acts 2 in fulfillment of the new covenant promises of Ezekiel, Jeremiah, and Joel. A consistent paedobaptist analysis of Acts 2:39, as well as of 1 Corinthians 7:14, would lead to baptizing unbelieving spouses and "all who are far off."[27] Lastly, the households in Acts need not have contained infants, and indeed the members of the households believed before they were baptized.

We are left agreeing with Baptist theologian Roger Nicole's quip: "There are three types of passages in the NT: those which speak of infants, those which speak of baptism, and those which speak of neither."[28]

3. The Church's Mixed Character

In the third place, Reformed paedobaptists assume the church is of a mixed character—that it is composed both of believers and unbelievers. The argument here depends on a great measure of covenantal continuity across the canon: just as the people of God in ancient Israel were composed of both believers and unbelievers, so the people of God in the New Testament church are likewise made up of both wheat and tares. Membership in the covenant community, then, does not mean a person is saved. It means access to certain privileges, such as hearing the Word of the Lord, being around those who will pray for you, having good role models, and so forth. Membership is not an indication of whether or not one is bound for heaven.

This is a foundational argument for paedobaptists because abundant proof is in the Old Testament that this was indeed the situation for Israelites. Circumcision was a physical marker bringing one into a

---

[26] Timothy George rightly notes, "Jesus took a special interest in children, received them into his arms, and blessed them. He did not baptize them" ("The Reformed Doctrine of Believers' Baptism," *Interpretation* 47 [1993]: 252).

[27] Unless otherwise indicated, all Scripture passages are taken from the ESV.

[28] Nicole said this in lectures and conversations at Gordon-Conwell Theological Seminary, but I have not seen it in print.

national community. It did not indicate that someone was saved. God separately called the people to salvation by commanding them to circumcise their hearts. Time and again we read in the Old Testament about members of the covenant community (priests, kings, etc.) who were definitely not spiritually renewed. The "mixed" character of national Israel (with its entrance marker of circumcision), so the argument goes, is the paradigm for the church (with its entrance marker of infant baptism). This character of the church is essential to the paedobaptist argument. B. B. Warfield, for example, announced, "According as is our doctrine of the Church, so will be our doctrine of the Subjects of Baptism."[29] Pierre Marcel makes this point explicitly:

> Since the covenant is the same in both Old and New Testaments, and the sacraments have the same fundamental significance, another conclusion urges itself upon us where the objective elements of the covenant are concerned, namely, that through the course of history *the Church has been and remains one: the nation of Israel was the Church; the Christian Church, since it also comes under the covenant of grace, is the same Church.*[30]

The people of God, as well as the significance of the entrance marker into this covenant community, are one across redemptive history. Because of the reality of covenantal continuity, there is one people of God. This becomes a foundational argument for paedobaptism.[31]

We agree with Warfield that one's definition of the church will, in essence, determine one's doctrine of baptism. However, we also think our paedobaptist brethren are reading too much Old Testament background into the pages of the New Testament, especially the Epistles. The New Testament Epistles everywhere assume that those who are in the church are true believers. The Epistles address church members as "saints" or holy ones, and they point to clear objective realities that God has accomplished among them. In Ephesians, for example, they have

---

[29] Benjamin Breckinridge Warfield, "The Polemics of Infant Baptism," in *Studies in Theology* (1932; rpt, Grand Rapids: Baker, 2000), 389. Another paedobaptist theologian similarly notes that "the ongoing debate [between paedo- and credobaptists] is not about nurture but about God's way of defining the church" (J. I. Packer, *Concise Theology: A Guide to Historic Christian Beliefs* [Wheaton: Tyndale, 1993], 216).

[30] Pierre Marcel, *The Biblical Doctrine of Infant Baptism: Sacrament of the Covenant of Grace*, trans. Philip Edgcumbe Hughes (Cambridge: James Clarke & Co., 1953), 95 (emphasis his).

[31] See Wright, "Baptism and the Logic of Reformed Paedobaptists," in Schreiner and Wright, *Believer's Baptism*, 218–24.

been elected by the Father, redeemed by the Son, and sealed by the Spirit (Eph 1:3–14). Even in 1 Corinthians, surely written to one of the most dysfunctional churches of the apostolic era, Paul speaks of the church in objective categories that can only be applied to true believers. Nothing is hypothetical or potential in Paul's thinking. He addressed the letter to saints who are called by God and sanctified by Christ (1 Cor 1:2). He thanked God for the work he has already done in the people's lives (1:4). He implored them to live set-apart, holy lives because of the work God has done for them in Christ (1:10). And he directed them to excommunicate from the church a person who refuses to repent of known, flagrant sin (5:5). The New Testament speaks of the church as a redeemed community, set apart by God's sovereign will, to be his own peculiar people. They are not a mixed community.

4. The Covenant of Grace

The covenant argument serves as the primary foundation and warrant for infant baptism, specifically the argument that the "covenant of grace" ties all of Scripture together and thus justifies paedobaptism in the church.[32] This is the fourth and the major tenet of covenantal infant baptism. Stephen Wellum summarizes the covenant of grace well. It is, first of all, to be seen in contrast to the "covenant of works" made with Adam. As representative of the entire race, Adam sinned, plunging all his posterity into sin, death, and condemnation. Yet God is gracious, and he made a second covenant with the elect, the covenant of grace

---

[32] See Robert L. Reymond, *A New Systematic Theology of the Christian Faith* (Nashville: Thomas Nelson, 1998), 503–44. Covenantal paedobaptist Randy Booth summarizes the covenantal argument for infant baptism in the following five steps:

1. *Covenant Theology.* Throughout the Bible, God relates to his people by way of a covenant of grace. Covenant theology provides the basic framework for rightly interpreting Scripture.
2. *Continuity of the Covenant of Grace.* The Bible teaches one and the same way of salvation in both the Old and the New Testaments, despite some different outward requirements.
3. *Continuity of the People of God.* Since there is one covenant of grace between God and man, there is one continuous people of God (the church) in the Old and New Testaments.
4. *Continuity of the Covenant Signs.* Baptism is the sign of the covenant in the New Testament, just as circumcision was the sign of the covenant in the Old Testament.
5. *Continuity of Households.* Whole households are included in God's redemptive covenant (R. R. Booth, *Children of the Promise: The Biblical Case for Infant Baptism* [Phillipsburg: P&R, 1995], 8, cited by Wellum, "Baptism and the Relationship Between the Covenants," *Believer's Baptism: Sign of the New Covenant in Christ,* ed. T. R. Schreiner and S. D. Wright [Nashville: B&H Academic, 2006], 99).

"wherein the God of grace freely offered to sinners life and salvation through the last Adam, the covenantal head of his people, the Lord Jesus Christ."[33] This covenant of grace, which began immediately after the fall into sin, is the central covenant of God in Scripture. The nature of God's promise in the covenant of grace was revealed progressively in the covenants with Noah, Abraham, Israel, and David, and it was brought to fulfillment in the new covenant. Wellum summarizes covenantal thought this way:

> It is important to stress that even though there are different covenants described in Scripture, there is, in reality, only *one* overarching covenant of grace. That is why one must view the relationships between the covenants in terms of an overall continuity. Booth underscores this point in his comments on the "newness" of the covenant inaugurated by our Lord. He states, "the new covenant is but a new—though more glorious—administration of the same covenant of grace." Thus, under the old covenant administration of the covenant of grace, it was administered through various promises, prophecies, sacrifices, rites and ordinances (e.g., circumcision) that ultimately typified and foreshadowed the coming of Christ. Now in light of his coming, the covenant of grace is administered through the preaching of the word and the administration of the sacraments. But in God's plan there are not two covenants of grace, one in the Old Testament and the other in the NT, but one covenant differing in substance but essentially the same across the ages.[34]

The doctrine of the covenant of grace has several deficiencies that we will note briefly, ending with the most serious critique, which undercuts the doctrine of Reformed paedobaptists.[35] In the first place, the phrase "covenant of grace" is never used in the Bible, although the Scripture speaks much of covenants and of grace. To use this rubric as the final proof for infant baptism without seeking to prove its existence from the pages of the Bible is to force a theological category on the redemptive-historical flow of Scripture that does not allow the Bible to speak on its own terms. Wellum comments:

---

[33] Wellum, "Baptism and the Relationship Between the Covenants," 102.

[34] Ibid., 103, citing Booth, *Children of Promise*, 9.

[35] In addition to Wellum's cogent critiques, see Paul K. Jewett, *Infant Baptism and the Covenant of Grace* (Grand Rapids: Eerdmans, 1978); Gregg R. Allison, *Sojourners and Strangers: The Doctrine of the Church* (Wheaton: Crossway, 2012), 346–50.

When it comes to thinking of the "covenant," let us speak in the plural and then unpack the relationships between the biblical *covenants* vis-à-vis the overall eternal plan of God centered in Jesus Christ. We may then think through more accurately how the one plan of God, tied to the promises of God first given in Gen 3:15, is progressively revealed in history *through* the biblical covenants. For, in the end, to continue to speak of the "covenant of grace" too often only leads to a flattening of Scripture; indeed it results in a reductionism which has the tendency of fitting Scripture into our theological system rather than the other way around.[36]

We must read the Bible on its own terms. In addition, the doctrine of the covenant of grace fails to see the importance of the Abrahamic covenant in the development of biblical revelation, specifically the manner in which it points forward to the new covenant inaugurated by Jesus. Both the Mosaic and the Davidic covenants are "built on the backbone of the Abrahamic covenant," showing that the Abrahamic covenant was paradigmatic and the latter two focused the promises of the former one, first in the people of Israel and then in her king.[37] Movement from promise to fulfillment is seen in the various covenant administrations; covenant theology fails to see this.[38]

Most significantly, the doctrine of the covenant of grace fails to take account of the newness of the new covenant. Those who hold to the covenant of grace, according to Wellum, believe the new covenant is "new" because

> it expands the previous era, broadens its extent, yields greater blessings, but the basic continuity is still in place, particularly in regard to the nature of the covenant community. Additionally, this is why paedobaptists argue that the new covenant, like the old, is a *breakable* covenant which includes within it "covenant-keepers and covenant-breakers."[39]

This may fit well with a covenant of grace rubric that sees continuity in the makeup of covenant communities across both testaments. But Wellum's evaluation is pertinent:

---

36 Wellum, "Baptism and the Relationship Between the Covenants," 127.
37 Ibid., 130–31.
38 On this point, see the insightful critique of Wellum in ibid., 127–37.
39 Ibid., 138.

In the Old Testament promise of the new covenant (Jer 31:29–34) and its fulfillment in Christ (see Luke 22:20; Heb 8, 10), the nature of the covenant communities are not the same, which entails a difference in the meaning and application of the covenant sign. Specifically, the change is found in the shift from a *mixed* community to that of a *regenerate* community with the crucial implication that under the new covenant, the covenant sign must only be applied to those who are in that covenant, namely, believers. The covenant sign of circumcision did not require faith for all those who received it, for a variety of reasons, even though it marked a person as a full covenant member. However, the same cannot be said of baptism. Because the church, by its very nature, is a regenerate community, the covenant sign of baptism must only be applied to those who have come to faith in Christ. It is at this point that we see the crucial discontinuity between the old and new covenant communities, a point the paedobaptist fails to grasp.[40]

Fundamentally, Reformed paedobaptists fail to see that the nature of the covenant community has changed with the inauguration of the new covenant by our Lord Christ. The nature of the covenant community was mixed in the old covenant, as we have seen. However, the prophets looked forward to a day in which the Lord would pour out his Spirit in a new way to make the people of the community know him (Jer 31:31–34; Ezek 11:19–20; 36:25–27; Joel 2:28–32). This new covenant community, in which all the members know the Lord, is what Jesus inaugurated. Only those who know the Lord should receive the initiation sign of the covenant, baptism.[41] At the end of the day, then, our view of the makeup of the covenant community will determine who receives the ordinance of baptism. The New Testament's teaching on regenerate

---

[40] Ibid.

[41] See Wellum, "Baptism and the Relationship Between the Covenants," 137–53; Ware, "Believers' Baptism View," in Wright, *Baptism: Three Views*, 41–47; Wellum, "Beyond Mere Ecclesiology," in *The Community of Jesus*, ed. Kendall H. Easley and Christopher W. Morgan (Nashville: B&H, 2013), 195–202. Wellum notes: "The church is God's new covenant community; it is *new*, yet not ontologically so, given its relation to Israel of old. However, in contrast to covenant theology, one must say that the church is a regenerate, believing community now. It is not enough to say that the church, as God's new covenant community, is here now but only in an inaugurated form, so that presently it is a 'mixed' community, like Israel, but in the future it will be a *regenerate* community. Of course, we still await the not-yet aspects of our redemption, but the community is already constituted as a believing, justified people, born of the Spirit and united to Christ, our covenant head" ("Beyond Mere Ecclesiology," 201).

church membership is the most central reason we should only baptize those who profess faith in Christ.

A Definition of Baptism

We come then to a definition of baptism and a discussion of how this ordinance should be applied in the life of local churches. Anglican theologian J. I. Packer succinctly captures the essence of baptism in these words:

> Christian baptism . . . is a sign from God that signifies inward cleansing and remission of sins (Acts 22:16; 1 Cor 6:11; Eph 5:25–27), Spirit-wrought regeneration and new life (Titus 3:5), and the abiding presence of the Holy Spirit as God's seal testifying and guaranteeing that one will be kept safe in Christ forever (1 Cor 12:13; Eph 1:13–14). Baptism carries these meanings because first and fundamentally it signifies union with Christ in his death, burial, and resurrection (Rom 6:3–7; Col 2:11–12); and this union with Christ is the source of every element in our salvation (1 John 5:11–12). Receiving the sign in faith assures the persons baptized that God's gift of new life in Christ is freely given to them.[42]

Packer's definition is insightful, but he misses the ecclesiastical focus of the commitment the one baptized is making to follow Christ in the fellowship of the church. Two Baptist confessions fill that lacuna:

> Baptism is an ordinance of the New Testament instituted by Jesus Christ. It is intended to be, to the person baptized, a sign of his fellowship with Christ in His death and resurrection, and of his being engrafted into Christ, and of the remission of sins. It also indicates that the baptized person has given himself up to God, through Jesus Christ, so that he may live and conduct himself "in newness of life".[43]
>
> Baptism is an ordinance of the Lord Jesus, obligatory upon every believer, wherein he is immersed in water in the name of the Father, and of the Son, and of the Holy Spirit, as a sign of his fellowship with the death and resurrection of Christ, of remis-

---

[42] Packer, *Concise Theology*, 212–13.
[43] Second London Confession 29.1.

sion of sins, and of his giving himself up to God, to live and walk in newness of life. It is prerequisite to church fellowship, and to participation in the Lord's Supper.[44]

Baptists have rightly emphasized both God's sovereign work displayed in baptism and the personal commitments being made by the person baptized.

From the biblical, historical, and theological discussion above, we may summarize the New Testament's teaching about the meaning of baptism to include the following elements. In the first place, baptism symbolically associates the one baptized with the completed work of Christ in dying for sinners and rising for their justification.[45] Two further meanings flow from this symbolic union. Baptism symbolizes that a person has been cleansed from sin, that sins are forgiven and the person has been raised to new life in Christ. In addition to that, baptism entails the individual's pledge to faithfully follow after Christ in the new life. Finally, baptism signifies that Jesus has inaugurated his kingdom in this world; the new covenant has dawned. For this reason, baptism has a corporate, churchly component. Those baptized are to be members of the body of Christ expressed in local churches.[46]

Baptism in the Church

How then do we apply this understanding of baptism to the life of local churches?

I will answer that by noting four important aspects of baptism: its close relationship to the gospel, the subject of baptism, baptism's mode, and the relationship of baptism to church membership. These four matters, in turn, will help us to answer three significant questions: When

---

[44] *Abstract of Principles* 15. Nettles offers a concise definition: "Baptism is the immersion in water of a believer in Jesus Christ performed once as the initiation of such a believer into a community of believers, the church" (Thomas J. Nettles, "Baptist View: Baptism as a Symbol of Christ's Saving Work," in Armstrong, *Understanding Four Views on Baptism*, 25).

[45] E.g., Allison, *Sojourners and Strangers*, 354; although Allison also highlights the importance of the baptized person's identification with the triune God based on the trinitarian name into which one is baptized in Matt 28:19 (ibid., 353–54), we also note that in Acts often baptism was done in the name of the Son only (Acts 2:38; 8:16; 10:48; 29:5).

[46] See further John S. Hammett, *Biblical Foundations for Baptist Churches: A Contemporary Ecclesiology* (Grand Rapids: Kregel, 2005), 263–67; Allison, *Sojourners and Strangers*, 353–57; Mark Dever, *The Church: The Gospel Made Visible* (Nashville: B&H Academic, 2012), 30–36.

should a church baptize someone? Should children professing faith in Christ be baptized? And who should perform baptisms?

1. Baptism's Relationship to the Gospel

Baptism is significant for the life of the church and the individual Christian because it is a picture of the gospel. In baptism we are reminded once again of Christ's death for sinners. More than that, even, we are assured of Christ's forgiveness. This is Paul's logic in Romans 6:3–4.[47]

At the point of conversion, the Christian does not only receive what Christ has done for him; he is commanded to commit himself to living under the lordship of Jesus. Now that Christ has saved him, he is to live in obedience to him.[48] Baptism reminds the believer that he is no longer who he used to be, and so he should now live for Christ (Rom 6:1–4). He is a new creation, one who has been raised to "walk in newness of life."

In fact, baptism is so clearly tied with the death of Christ and the necessity of personal faith in him that sometimes the apostles could use shockingly strong language about it. For instance, Paul spoke of the symbol (baptism) as if it were the reality (forgiveness) itself. He declared, "And now why do you wait? Rise and be baptized and wash away your sins, calling on his name" (Acts 22:16). Of course, in Paul's mind baptism does not literally wash one's sins away like water washes away dirt. Rather, Christians' sins are forgiven because of Christ's death, the benefits of which they receive by personal faith alone (e.g., Rom 3:21–26; 5:1). But baptism is a clear picture of the fact that "if anyone is in Christ, he is a new creation" (2 Cor 5:17). The one baptized is saved by calling on the name of Christ, and baptism symbolizes that the one baptized has been reborn as a new creature in Christ. The old man was buried. The new man is risen with Christ.

For reasons such as these, we are compelled by the New Testament to stress the significance of baptism. Out of faithfulness to our Lord and his apostles, we must stress what they stressed. In its essence, then, baptism is a sign that the person baptized has died to sin and has been raised to new life in Christ. Moreover, the baptismal candidate pledges to walk in faithfulness to Christ from that time forward. Therefore, Paul said in very short fashion, "For as many of you as were baptized into Christ have put on Christ" (Gal 3:27).

---

[47] I have previously noted Col 2:11–12 and 1 Pet 3:21 in this regard.
[48] For example, Rom 12:1ff.; Eph 4:1ff; Col 3:1ff.

2. The Subject of Baptism

Who should be baptized? In the New Testament baptism is only contemplated for believers, as we have said throughout these chapters. Only those who have trusted in Jesus Christ for salvation should be baptized.[49] This is evident with Jesus' commission to his disciples in Matthew 28, the expansion of the early church in Acts, and the teaching of the Epistles. The New Testament lucidly requires that believers alone be baptized.

3. The Mode of Baptism

Baptism should be done by immersing the baptized person in water because the Greek word *baptizo* means "to dip," "to immerse," or "to plunge."[50] The New Testament authors could have used other words if they wanted to convey the meaning of "sprinkling" (Heb 9:13). Immersion in water was the practice of the New Testament (e.g., Matt 3:16; Mark 1:5; John 3:23; Acts 8:36–38).

We have already seen that baptism alone does not save anyone. No aspect of baptism—immersion or anything else—is intrinsically salvific. Nonetheless, immersion in water is significant because of the symbolic truth taught by putting a person under water and then bringing him up again. Three of the texts previously mentioned display the logic of immersion (Rom 6:3–4; Col 2:11–12; 1 Pet 3:21). Each of these passages draws our attention first of all to Jesus Christ and his completed work on behalf of believers. Jesus died, was buried, and was raised to life on the third day. This is the gospel we proclaim (see 1 Cor 15:1–4). Each component of it is essential to our salvation. Jesus died, bearing the wrath of God we deserved against our sin. His sacrifice was acceptable to God, so Jesus was raised to new life, just as he had promised before he died. Because he was raised, we know that those who put their faith in him will be justified (Rom 4:25).

They will be saved because they are united with Christ. Union with Christ is one of the keys to understanding the biblical doctrines of salvation and baptism. Union with Christ pervades the apostle's thought in Ephesians 1 and 2. Believers were chosen by God "in Christ" (1:3); they have redemption and an inheritance "in him" (1:7, 11); they have been sealed by the Holy Spirit "in him" (1:13). Paul said the foundation of this union is Christ's work for believers. As unbelievers, all persons

---

[49] Hammett, *Biblical Foundations*, 267–71; Ware, "Believers' Baptism View," 23–40.

[50] See Hammett, *Biblical Foundations*, 274–75; Nettles, "Baptist View," in Armstrong, *Understanding Four Views on Baptism*, 26–27; Ware, "Believers' Baptism View," 21–23; Allison, *Sojourners and Strangers*, 354.

are dead in sin and unable to save themselves (2:1–3). But because of God's great love for his people and his mighty power on their behalf, God raises them to new life in a parallel fashion to the way he raised Jesus to life on the third day (2:4–6). Thus God "made us alive together with Christ" (2:5) and "raised us up with him and seated us with him in the heavenly places in Christ Jesus" (2:6).

Believers have been united with Christ in his death and resurrection. As he died, so we were dead. And as he was raised to life, we have been raised to life in him. This is what being immersed in water portrays to us. We have died to our old self and have been raised to walk in new life following Christ our Lord. Immersion is important for what it shows us of this pattern of burial and resurrection. It portrays the gospel and reminds us of our union with our Savior.

4. Baptism and Church Membership

Baptism is closely tied to church membership. It is to be performed under the authority of a local fellowship, and it should be required of all those who seek membership in the church because of its connections to the gospel.

Baptism is essential because, according to Scripture, we publicly profess faith and commit to following after Jesus by being baptized. If a Christian has not been baptized following his conversion to Christ, he is not being obedient. The Lord summons his followers to be baptized, and so it's one component of observing everything he commanded (see Matt 28:18–20).

What is the relationship, then, between baptism and church membership? To answer this question, we need to recognize in the first place that the New Testament never contemplates any persons as members of the church except those who are regenerate, that is, who have been "born again." As I have argued previously, in the apostles' minds there is no such thing as a member of a local fellowship who is not a believer in Jesus Christ. Church members are those who have been born again, who are "children of light, children of the day" (1 Thess 5:5).[51]

In the second place, baptism is the entrance marker of a converted person into the membership and accountability of a local church.[52] A con-

---

[51] On the necessity of church membership, see Benjamin L. Merkle, "The Biblical Basis for Church Membership," in *Those Who Must Give an Account: A Study of Church Membership and Church Discipline*, ed. John S. Hammett and Benjamin L. Merkle (Nashville: B&H Academic, 2012), 31–52.

[52] "In summary, baptism is best understood as the rite of commitment. It is the ordained occasion when one confesses that she or he has made a faith commitment to

vert to Jesus should be baptized out of obedience to the New Testament. The New Testament never alludes to an instance of a person being a church member without having been baptized (e.g., Acts 2:41; 16:15, 31–33; 18:8; 19:5; Gal 3:27).

Biblical religion is a corporate affair, and baptism is a key marker of a new believer's entrance into the life of the church. It is his profession of faith in Jesus, publicly stating that he has committed himself to Christ and Christ's concerns, including Christ's church. This is a central part of walking in newness of life. Baptism also visibly portrays the church's commitment to the well-being and care of the newly baptized person as it receives him into membership.[53]

When Should a Church Baptize Someone into Membership?

The New Testament pattern is that baptism follows closely on the heels of a "credible profession of faith," as the accounts in Acts referred to above make clear. How closely? Although the New Testament does not give didactic material to help us answer this question, we can nonetheless draw out several principles.

First, the person who is baptized needs to understand the gospel. He does not need to be a theologian or even literate. But he must understand the gospel (including his sin, the necessity of Christ's death for him, that salvation is through faith in Christ alone, Christ's resurrection, and that he must repent of his sin and strive to follow Jesus). This means that we need to be careful not to rush baptism until we judge that the person has comprehended salvation well enough to understand and appreciate the symbolism of baptism. This does not mean that only adults can be baptized, for even young children can comprehend these things. But it does place a premium on our teaching persons so that they understand the gospel before their baptism.[54]

Additionally, those who are to be baptized should be presented to the fellowship for its approval before their baptism. One of the

---

[53] See Hammett, *Biblical Foundations*, 275–77. For this reason I oppose "open membership," in which a Baptist church allows a nonbaptized person (i.e., one not baptized after confessing faith in Christ) to join the church if he is not convinced that believer's baptism is required. Like many other aspects of church life (e.g., church government and whether women can serve as elders), baptism is a matter of corporate concern. The church should be able to decide its doctrine of baptism and require those who want to join its membership to submit to it in this matter.

[54] Ibid., 271–74.

responsibilities of a fellowship is to receive members. Because one who is baptized out of obedience to Christ should also join a local church out of obedience to Christ, we need to keep these two practices tied closely together. It is therefore the congregation's responsibility to hear the testimony of the one to be baptized so that they might then receive him into their membership in a meaningful way. When a church receives a person as a member, they are saying, "As far as we can tell, you are one of us. You have been born again. You are a pilgrim along with us on our way to heaven." Church members need to be satisfied that these things are true before they vote on receiving someone as a member.

We also need to be aware that, from the perspective of the New Testament, people may make false professions of faith in Jesus. God is the ultimate judge of a person's heart; we are not. Our responsibility as members of a fellowship is to be satisfied that a person is a Christian before voting to receive him into the church. But that person may deceive us; he may even deceive himself. For example, in the parable of the soils, our Lord spoke of those who "endure for a while; then, when tribulation or persecution arises on account of the word, immediately they fall away." He also mentioned others "who hear the word, but the cares of the world and the deceitfulness of riches and the desires for other things enter in and choke the word" (Mark 4:17–19). If it becomes clear to the church that someone they baptized made a false profession of faith (even though it may have been credible at the time), they must lovingly discipline the false professor and no longer regard him as a member of the church out of genuine love for that person and out of concern for the church's holiness.

When Should a Child Professing Faith in Christ Be Baptized?

It may be more difficult to discern if a child's faith is genuine than it is in the case of adults. Usually they have not developed overt sinful habits, which they forsake to follow Christ; so it is harder to tell by a changed life if they are truly converted than it is with adults. They usually are not as intellectually developed as adults, which makes their understanding of the gospel correspondingly basic. Additionally, there is the real concern that children may merely be mimicking their parents' ideas, or (rightly) trying to please their parents by saying the things they know their parents desperately want them to say. One might also ask if children can fulfill all the obligations of membership mentioned earlier in this chapter and in the chapter on congregationalism.

For these reasons and more, some Baptist churches advocate a policy of encouraging children who profess faith in Christ to wait to be baptized until they are recognized as independent adults. When the child is his own person, making life decisions for himself and experiencing independence from his parents' authority and protection, then he is ready to pursue baptism. Then the church can be more certain that his desire to pursue baptism and church membership is genuine and not the result of outside influence.[55]

One of the arguments used by those advocating this position is historical. In years past Baptists waited significantly longer to baptize than churches tend to today. Not only are we deviating from our heritage, but the decreasing age of baptisms in Baptist churches has been accompanied by other unhelpful practices.[56] Dever exposes the pastoral and ecclesiological issue at stake:

> Whatever the reason for the change in practice, Christians today should be careful about participating in a well-intended but ill-fated baptism that seems to have tragically resulted in the confirmation of millions of people in conversions that have evidently proved to be false. So-called Christians are deceived, churches are diminished in their power, and the witness of the gospel is confused and weakened.[57]

This may be one of the most difficult issues—emotionally and pastorally—for churches to face. Local churches need to exercise biblical wisdom as they seek to arrive at policies regarding the age at which they will baptize children professing faith. A few considerations, however, have led us to adopt a position slightly modified from the one noted above.

History has some weight in this matter. Dever is certainly correct to note the drastic shift in the average age of baptismal candidates in our churches, leading some to lament that Southern Baptists are almost becoming paedobaptists. The last thing we want to do is encourage laxity

---

[55] For example, see the policy of Capitol Hill Baptist Church in Washington, DC, "The Baptism of Children" (http://www.capitolhillbaptist.org/we-equip/children/baptism-of-children). See also, Mark Dever, "Baptism in the Context of the Local Church," in *Believer's Baptism*. For an opposite perspective, see Ted Christman, *Forbid Them Not: Rethinking the Baptism and Church Membership of Children and Young People*. Available online: http://www.hbcowensboro.org/mediafiles/uploaded/f/0e1609819_forbid-them-not-pdf.pdf.

[56] Dever, "Baptism in the Context of the Local Church," 346–47.

[57] Ibid., 347.

in the church concerning the baptisms of children. Yet we also think we should consider statements our Baptist forebears made suggesting that children professing faith should be baptized. For example, it is true that Charles Spurgeon was not baptized until he was fifteen years old and did not baptize his twin sons until they were eighteen.[58] Spurgeon's sermons lead us to the conclusion, though, that he did not think this was the model for all baptisms. In fact, he called on young children to trust in Jesus and be baptized. Apparently, he baptized a child as young as nine years old.[59]

This historical consideration is not as significant as the pastoral one. Everyone agrees the children can be saved by hearing the Word, repenting of their sin, and trusting in Christ. No disagreement exists there. The difference falls out over whether a church *is capable of discerning whether a profession is credible.* My own view is that a church is able to affirm a credible profession of faith. Furthermore, delaying a credible profession of faith can unduly harm the child. A child is saved by faith in Jesus, not by baptism, and so his or her salvation is secure even without baptism. But telling a child who wants to obey the Lord in baptism to wait risks communicating that salvation is not by faith alone but by faith and holiness and obeying one's parents. Because we do not want to

---

[58] Ibid., 346n24.

[59] "There may be some little children here—indeed, I am glad to see boys and girls mingling with the congregation. Listen to me, my children! I am always glad to see you and we preachers make a great mistake if we do not preach to you. Oh, dear John and Jane, Mary and Thomas—I wish you would come to Christ while you are yet young—and put your trust in Him and become young Christians. There is no reason why you should not! You are old enough to die; and you are old enough to sin; and you are old enough to believe in the Lord Jesus Christ! Why should you not do so at once?

"When I was just about 15 years of age I was helped by God's Spirit to cast myself upon Christ. And have I ever regretted that I came to Jesus so soon? No! I wish that I could have come 15 years before and that I had known Christ as soon as I learned to know my mother! Some of you have heard about Jesus from your infancy. His name was part of the music with which your mother sang you to sleep. Oh, that you may know Jesus by faith as well as by hearing! Do not think that you have to wait till you are grown up before you may come to Jesus. We have baptized quite a number of boys and girls of 10, 11 and 12. I spoke the other day with a little boy nine years of age and I tell you that he knew more about Christ than many gray-headed men do—and he loved Jesus most heartily!

"As the sweet child talked to me about what Christ had done for him, he brought tears into my eyes, to see how happily and brightly he could speak of what he had felt in his own soul, of the Savior's power to bless. You young children are like rosebuds and you know everybody likes a rosebud better than a full-blown rose. My Lord Jesus will gladly receive you as rosebuds! Offer yourselves to Him, for He will not cast you away! I am sure He never will" (Charles Spurgeon, "High Doctrine and Broad Doctrine" [sermon #1762], 5–6; http://www.spurgeongems.org/vols28-30/chs1762.pdf).

mislead children about the nature of salvation, we believe it is better—circumspectly, slowly, and with many different eyes on the child—to handle professions of faith on a case-by-case basis. There certainly are risks, but the bigger risk lies with both keeping the child from obedience and confusing him or her about the nature of salvation.

Based on these convictions, I recommend that the church handle each situation individually. My church adds one key step to the membership process when it comes to children. We have them go through a six-week study on the gospel with a teacher at our church, during which time they are exposed to the gospel and the teacher is given the opportunity to observe how they interact with the truths there: do they love Jesus or merely enjoy thinking about him? As long as the church is willing to exercise church discipline in the case of unrepented-of sin (which it must be willing to do both with children and adults!), even in the case of a teenager, for example, we see no problem and several advantages in handling each case separately and rejoicing in the Lord's work of regenerating children.

How Quickly Should Someone Be Baptized?

What I have said about children and baptism raises the question of how quickly to baptize someone after their profession of faith in Christ. In fact, the question is usually asked in a more pointed fashion: Because the New Testament pattern is profession of faith followed quickly by baptism, what right do we have to add a new step—prebaptism or church-membership classes, meeting with the pastor, and so on—to the process? Aren't we actually teaching new Christians to disobey Jesus' clear command if we delay baptism?[60]

There are several things to say in response to this question. On the one hand, we want to keep a person's initial faith and his baptism joined together as closely as possible. On the other hand, we should delay long enough that we're able to examine the person being baptized—to hear their profession of faith and to have some sense of their repentance. It is important to ensure that a person is not living in unrepentant sin. Suppose an unmarried man who is living with a woman asks to be baptized. He needs to move out before baptism can occur.

---

[60] For example, Saucy comments, "It is significant that every baptism in Acts took place almost immediately following the confession of faith" (Robert Saucy, *The Church in God's Program* [Chicago: Moody, 1972], 195, cited in Hammett, *Biblical Foundations*, 273.

Baptism not only symbolizes an individual's commitment to Christ. It indicates a person's commitment to live in communion with the local church and the church's commitment to receive the person into its membership. In other words, baptism has both individual and corporate aspects. At times the corporate orientation of baptism may need to slow down the individual's ability to demonstrate faith through baptism. We acknowledge that this may not be everyone's preferred course of action, but we believe it's sometimes pastorally wise.[61]

Furthermore, matters today are a bit more complicated than they were during New Testament times. Many years have passed since the days of the apostles, and we now have different conceptions of baptism circulating. Those who grow up in a culture with significant Christian influence may easily misunderstand baptism, thinking it as natural, say, as being an American. Hence, more instruction is needed.

---

[61] Hammett helpfully notes: "The baptisms in Acts, as far as we know, were of adults, and so there was not the need we have today to delay baptism of children. . . . The biblical evidence for immediate baptism is not particularly strong. There is nothing resembling a command to baptize immediately, and while there are instances of immediate baptism, there are other instances where the time factor is not clear (Acts 18:7–8) and where conversions are reported without any mention of an immediate baptism (4:4; 13:48); in fact, conversions are spoken of as a daily occurrence, but not baptisms (2:47; 16:5). There is some deliberate openness as to the timing of baptism. The case for believer's baptism is much stronger than that for immediate baptism, and if the purpose for delay is to ascertain as much as possible that those to be baptized are believers, the delay seems commendable, rather than questionable" (*Biblical Foundations*, 273).

CHAPTER 6

The Lord's Supper in the Bible

Thomas R. Schreiner

If baptism serves as the entrance marker into the Christian church, the Lord's Supper serves as the regular sign of the gospel. As with baptism the gospel is the primary rubric through which we should interpret the meaning of the Supper. In the history of the church, wrong ideas about the meaning of Communion flourished whenever the rite was divorced from the efficacy of Christ's death for sinners on the cross. But when we view the Supper through the lens of the gospel, as a means both for remembering Christ's sacrifice and for reminding one another of its sufficiency, we find the correct orientation toward Communion. Also as with baptism, we see that Christ is determinative for our theology and practice of the Supper. The Supper is the Lord's. He must determine what we think and experience in it. As the head of the new covenant community, Christ has the authority to regulate the meal to be practiced in the church until his return.

The Lord's Supper is different from baptism in this important dimension: it looks not only to the past (reminding us of our Lord's death for us) and the present (as we remember that he is ever ready to forgive us); it also has a future orientation. In the Eucharist we experience a meal with Jesus that looks forward to the wedding banquet the church will share with him in heaven. This past-present-future orientation of the Supper is important.[1] Christians constantly need the comfort and hope

---

1 "The renewal called for by the Lord's Supper thus looks back to the past in remembrance, looks around in the present to the fellowship we experience with Christ and the body of believers, and looks ahead to the consummation, when Christ returns" (John

that Jesus is still for us and will be for us forever. The Supper is hope inducing and comfort producing. This meal is communal. It is a family feast, not to be taken in isolation but in community. And in this communal meal we bolster one another's faith by looking together to Jesus in the present, based on his completed work for us in the past, knowing that he will take us to be with him in the future.

Once again, this discussion will begin where all doctrine and practice should start: the Bible. The next chapters will then ask some historical and theological questions Christians have wrestled with over the centuries.

A Word on Terminology

Baptism surfaces in many texts in the New Testament, but references to the Lord's Supper are relatively infrequent. We have the three parallel texts in the Synoptic Gospels where Jesus instituted Communion at his last Passover meal with his disciples. Scholars dispute whether breaking of bread in Luke–Acts refers to the Eucharist and whether the bread of life discourse in John 6 refers to the Lord's Supper. Finally, Paul referred to Communion in two texts (1 Cor 10:16–17, 21; 11:17–34). The aim here is not to provide a full exegesis of any of these texts but to highlight central themes that relate to the Eucharist.

A word about terminology might be helpful. Paul used the phrase "Lord's Supper" (*kyriakon deipnon*, 1 Cor 11:20). Historically, the word *Eucharist* has also been used to describe the Supper. Meaning "thanksgiving," this term is also fitting because Jesus gave thanks when he instituted the Supper (*eucharistēsas*, Matt 26:27; Mark 14:23; Luke 22:19; 1 Cor 11:24). Another term often used is *Communion*, stemming from another term Paul used (*koinōnia*, 1 Cor 10:16). Hence, all three terms that are common parlance today are found in the Scriptures and will be used in the discussion below.

The Lord's Supper in the Synoptics

Three parallel texts describe the institution of the Eucharist in the Synoptics (Matt 26:26–29; Mark 14:22–25; Luke 22:14–20). The Matthean and Markan accounts are similar, while Luke has some unique elements. Interestingly, Luke's version is similar to Paul's rendition in

S. Hammett, *Biblical Foundations for Baptist Churches: A Contemporary Ecclesiology* [Grand Rapids: Kregel Academic & Professional, 2005], 283).

1 Corinthians 11:23–26. It is not our purpose here to investigate the similarities and differences but to highlight the central themes regarding the Lord's Supper.[2] In the Synoptics six themes will be noted: (1) the connection of the Lord's Supper with Passover, (2) the figural character of the meal, (3) the covenantal dimensions of the Eucharist, (4) the emphasis upon atonement, (5) the eschatological slant in the accounts, and (6) the communal nature of the meal. These six themes are not discrete entities. They overlap, but these motifs are important enough to comment on each one individually.

First, most scholars agree that the Lord's Supper is a Passover meal.[3] In fact, the connection is explicit. Jesus said, "I have fervently desired to eat this Passover with you before I suffer"[4] (Luke 22:15; cf. Matt 26:17–19; Mark 14:12–16; Luke 22:13). What is particularly significant is the theological connection between the Passover and the Eucharist. The Passover recalled the great saving event for Israel as a nation from bondage to Egypt (cf. Exodus 12–14). To escape the scourge of the destroying angel, every Israelite had to apply the blood of a lamb to their house. However, the Passover pointed to a greater deliverance—to the great redemption and new exodus that would take place through the death of Jesus Christ (cf. Isa 11:11–15; 40:3–11; 42:16; 43:2, 5–7, 16–19; 48:20–21; 49:6–11; 51:10). Through Jesus' blood his people are saved from destruction just as Israel was saved from the destroying angel. Though it is not in the context of Communion, Paul picked up the same notion, saying, "For Christ our Passover has been sacrificed" (1 Cor 5:7).

One of the central themes of Passover was remembrance. It was part of the formalized ritual because children asked their parents in succeeding generations about the meaning of the Passover (Exod 12:26–27; cf. also Exod 10:2; 13:3, 8, 14–15; Deut 7:18–19; Ps 78:3–4). Remembering assured Israel that God was for them, granting them strength to trust him in the present and in the future. Evoking Passover traditions, so, too, Jesus calls upon his followers to remember his death (Luke 22:19; cf. 1 Cor 11:24–25). The goal of remembering is not merely to recall a past event with fondness but to recall how Jesus rescues his people from the slavery of sin so that they in turn are liberated to love and obey him.

---

[2] I am indebted in this section to Pennington, though there are some differences as well. See Jonathan T. Pennington, "The Lord's Last Supper in the Fourfold Witness of the Gospels," in *The Lord's Supper: Remembering and Proclaiming Christ until He Comes*, ed. T. R. Schreiner and M. R. Crawford (Nashville: B&H Academic, 2010), 43–58.

[3] See Andreas J. Köstenberger, "Was the Last Supper a Passover Meal?" in Schreiner and Crawford, *The Lord's Supper*, 6–30.

[4] Unless otherwise indicated, all Scripture passages are taken from the HCSB.

Second, the Eucharistic meal is figural and symbolic.[5] "Jesus took bread, blessed it and broke it, gave it to the disciples, and said, 'Take and eat it; this is My body'" (Matt 26:26; cf. Mark 14:22; Luke 22:19). The bread used in the Eucharist represents Jesus' body. Historically, the meaning of these words has been the subject of intense debate. Roman Catholics have interpreted them to support a doctrine of transubstantiation, which says that the elements actually become the body and blood of the Lord. Luther, too, argued in his debate with Zwingli that "is" should be translated literally and not symbolically, even though he did not endorse transubstantiation. The Lutheran position developed into what is called consubstantiation, meaning that Christ's presence is "with, in, and under" the substance of the bread and wine, as later Lutheran theologians put it. Both interpretations fail to see the figural character of what Jesus did here. He argued symbolically, indicating that the bread represents his body, which would be given over in death. Jesus "broke" the bread (Matt 26:26; Mark 14:22; Luke 22:19; 1 Cor 11:24), signifying that his body would be broken in death. He was surrendering his life for their sake and for their salvation. In other words, his body would be their "food" that would sustain them in life. They must "eat" the bread to live, finding their life in his death by believing in what he would do on their behalf. If they did not participate in his death by eating (i.e., believing), they would not benefit from what he would do for them.

The figural and symbolic character of Jesus' actions is confirmed with the cup. Jesus took the cup and invited his disciples to drink from it (Matt 26:27), explaining that the wine "is my blood of the covenant" (Matt 26:28 ESV; cf. Mark 14:23–24). The wine symbolizes the blood of Jesus that was shed to establish his covenant with those who belong to him. Luke's account confirms a figural reading, since Jesus said, "This cup is the new covenant in my blood" (Luke 22:20 NIV 2011; cf. 1 Cor 11:25). Certainly, Jesus did not mean that the cup itself *is* the new covenant. His point was that the cup *represents* the new covenant. We should apply the same rule when Jesus said that the bread *is* his body. The wine in the cup represents the blood of Jesus, the blood that inaugurates the new covenant.

Third, the Eucharist is covenantal in character. Jesus said, "For this is my blood of the covenant, which is poured out for many for the forgiveness of sins" (Matt 26:28 ESV; cf. Mark 14:24; Luke 22:20). The Sinai covenant was established with sacrifices and the sprinkling of blood on

---

5 Pennington calls it "an enacted parable of Jesus' impending sacrificial death" ("The Lord's Last Supper," in Schreiner and Crawford, *The Lord's Supper*, 44–47).

the altar and the people (Exod 24:5–8). So, too, Jesus inaugurated the new covenant with the shedding of his blood. Luke actually uses the term "new covenant" (cf. 1 Cor 11:25). The Supper evokes the new covenant promise of Jeremiah 31:31–34 where Yahweh promised to establish a new covenant with his people and write his law on their hearts and minds. He also promised a definitive and final forgiveness of sins. The sacrifices of the Sinai covenant clearly could not provide final and full forgiveness, and a superior sacrifice was needed (Heb 7:1–10:18). Christ came to give this new covenant.

Fourth, the Lord's Supper highlights the forgiveness of sins and the atoning work of Jesus on the cross. The focus on the atonement is present in the other themes we have investigated. The great deliverance at Passover pointed forward to Jesus' Passover sacrifice. But how did Jesus rescue his people? He did not rid Palestine of the Romans like Yahweh rescued Israel from the Egyptians. He did not cleanse Palestine of their enemies. He freed Israel by dying for his people. How does this free anyone? Just as the blood of the Passover spared Israel from the destroying angel, so Jesus' blood spares those who trust in him from the punishment God will inflict on the ungodly. In this sense Jesus' death is atoning because he accomplished forgiveness for his people and rescued them from judgment.

We also saw that the new covenant is tied to the forgiveness of sins. Yahweh said in the great new covenant promise of Jeremiah 31:34, "For I will forgive their wrongdoing and never again remember their sin." Such final forgiveness is realized in the death of Jesus. Jesus declared at the Last Supper, "For this is My blood that establishes the covenant; it is shed for many for the forgiveness of sins" (Matt 26:28; see also Mark 14:24; Luke 22:20). The Eucharist is a feast of thanksgiving because it recalls and rejoices in a once-for-all cleansing of sin. Believers remember that they cannot rescue themselves, and that Jesus gave his life so that their sins will be forgotten forever. Jesus experienced the penalty that sinners deserve to suffer.

Fifth, the Eucharist is eschatological. It points to the future consummation of the kingdom, to the realization of the kingdom in all its fullness, to a day when there will be no more sorrow or sighing. Jesus declared, "But I tell you, from this moment I will not drink of this fruit of the vine until that day when I drink it in a new way in My Father's kingdom with you" (Matt 26:29). Mark and Luke's versions are similar (Mark 14:25; Luke 22:18). The Lord's Supper not only looks back on what Jesus did in shedding his blood for his people. It also looks forward to the joy believers will experience in the kingdom of God. It is retrospective and prospective. Communion anticipates the day when joy will be complete, when believers will enjoy the Messianic banquet (Isa 25:6–8). And the point is that Jesus' new covenant and Passover sacrifice is the means by which this great promise for the future is secured. Jesus' past sacrifice procures forgiveness of sins and future joy, and therefore believers are strengthened in the present to live their lives for the sake of the kingdom. The future consists of endless happy tomorrows.

Sixth, Communion is communal. Disciples eat the bread together in community (Matt 26:26; Mark 14:22; Luke 22:19). They don't eat it alone in their houses, nor do they eat it only with family members. They eat of it in the assembly. Jesus said about the cup, "Drink from it, all of you" (Matt 26:27), and Mark tells us that "they all drank from it" (Mark 14:23; cf. Luke 22:17). The Lord's Supper is not merely a meal where I celebrate what Jesus did for me. It is a communal meal where the people of God, the church of Jesus Christ, give thanks for what Jesus did for us. A new family has been forged through the sweat and blood of the Savior.

All the themes touched on here could be explored in further detail, but the heart of what was accomplished was the forgiveness of sins. Jesus delivered his people as at Passover through his blood. The cup symbolizes his sacrifice for his people. The new covenant is realized through his blood, and future eschatological glory comes to pass because of the forgiveness of sins. And there is no community apart from forgiveness, for the church of Christ consists of forgiven sinners.

John 6 and the Lord's Supper

John 6 begins with the feeding of the 5,000, followed by Jesus identifying himself as the bread of life, declaring, "I am the bread of life" (John 6:35, 48). The vivid language about eating and drinking convinces some that John refers directly to the Eucharist. Jesus said that one must eat his flesh and drink his blood to have eternal life (John 6:53–56), claiming that "the bread that I will give for the life of the world is My flesh" (John 6:51). The Jews were scandalized at the thought of eating Jesus' flesh (John 6:52), but Jesus didn't modify his statements but spoke even more radically when he said that one must eat his flesh and drink his blood to have life.

One can see why transubstantiation is read out of the text. It is unlikely, however, that Communion is directly in view for at least three reasons.

First, if the Eucharist were described, the text would teach that partaking of Communion is necessary for eternal life, which is a thought found nowhere else in the New Testament. Further, baptism, not the Eucharist, is the initiation rite linked to conversion. And baptism is not necessary for eternal life.

Second, there is a recurrent motif in John of Jesus making a radical statement and his hearers misunderstanding him and taking him literally.[6] For example, Jesus' opponents believed he referred to destroying the temple, though the referent was actually his own body (John 2:19–22). Even the disciples failed to understand what Jesus meant until after the resurrection. Nicodemus thought Jesus was literally saying one must be born again (John 3:3–6) when he spoke of the necessity of new life spiritually. The Samaritan woman believed Jesus had in mind literal water when he said he had living water to give her (John 4:14–15). It is unlikely, given this pattern, that a literal eating and drinking are intended. Eating Jesus' flesh and drinking his blood call attention to the cross. His torn flesh and shed blood are the only pathway to life. A crucified Messiah is the scandal.

Third, John 6:35 fits with the interpretation offered here. "'I am the bread of life,' Jesus told them. 'No one who comes to Me will ever be hungry, and no one who believes in Me will ever be thirsty again.'" Eating Jesus' flesh and drinking his blood means that one trusts in him for salvation. It creates a vivid picture of dependence on Christ for life, showing us we are not saved by our self-sufficiency. And this trust is in Jesus as the crucified Lord, the One who returned to God via the cross.

John 6, then, is not directly about Communion, but in a derivative sense it relates to Communion because it's about the cross and Jesus giving his flesh and spilling his blood so believers might have life. During the Eucharist believers reflect on and give thanks for this great atoning work, and the narrative of John 6 reverberates with these Eucharistic themes.

Breaking of Bread in Luke–Acts

Quite often in Luke–Acts we find the expression "breaking bread" (cf. Luke 22:19; 24:30, 35; Acts 2:42, 46; 20:7, 11; 27:35).[7] Scholars have questioned whether the phrase refers to the Eucharist because it is clear in Acts 27:35 that it refers to eating an ordinary meal. Hence, the other

---

6 See here the important article by D. A. Carson, "Understanding Misunderstandings in the Fourth Gospel," *Tyndale Bulletin* 33 (1982): 59–91.

7 It occurs in both verbal and nominal phrases.

occurrences of the phrase in Luke–Acts (apart from Luke 22:19) *could* be interpreted similarly. It seems more likely, however, that they either refer or allude to the Eucharist. It should also be noted that a Eucharistic celebration does not preclude the eating of an ordinary meal as well because in the early church the Lord's Supper was celebrated in conjunction with a meal.[8]

The breaking of the bread at the Last Supper clearly symbolizes Jesus' death, where the broken bread symbolizes the breaking of his body for the salvation and forgiveness of his people (Luke 22:19). The next text where we find the breaking of bread is Jesus' meal with Cleopas and his companion after their walk to Emmaus (Luke 24:30, 35). They didn't recognize Jesus as they walked and talked, being prevented from identifying him. They were gloomy and discouraged because they were convinced that Jesus' death indicated that he wasn't the Messiah (Luke 24:17–24). Jesus unpacked for them Old Testament prophecy, explaining that a suffering Messiah accorded with what the Old Testament taught (Luke 24:25–27). It is highly significant in the narrative, then, that Jesus is disclosed to them "in the breaking of the bread." The language evokes Jesus' Last Supper with his disciples (Luke 24:35; cf. 24:30). Cleopas and his friend had rejected a suffering Messiah, but now they recognized Jesus in the breaking of the bread, and realized that Jesus had to suffer per the Old Testament so that Israel would be forgiven of their sins. To object that Cleopas and his friend were not at the Last Supper misses the point, for Luke makes a literary point here and is not concerned to explain to the readers how Cleopas and his friend grasped the matter.

We also find the breaking of bread in Acts 2:42 and 2:46. Apparently, it was the standard practice of Christians to break bread together as they met "from house to house" (Acts 2:46). The reference to houses does not preclude a reference to the Lord's Supper since the church met in houses, and thus the house meals point to a worship context. The meals, then, were something more than a potluck. In fact, the context of Acts 2:42 suggests that Communion is in view. Believers "devoted themselves to the apostles' teaching, to the fellowship, to the breaking of bread, and to the prayers." The other elements mentioned here—the teaching of the apostles, prayers, fellowship—describe the life of the church gathered together. It seems probable, then, that the breaking of bread isn't restricted to eating meals together. Given the antecedents in

---

[8] See B. B. Blue, "Love Feast," *Dictionary of Paul and His Letters*, ed. Gerald Hawthorne, Ralph Martin, and Daniel Reid (Downers Grove: IVP Academic, 1993), 579.

Luke (22:19; 24:30, 35), it seems that Luke has in mind the celebration of Eucharist.

Another instance where we find the breaking of bread is Paul's visit to Troas in Acts 20:6–11. Two references to breaking bread are found in this text (Acts 20:7, 11). Again, it is possible that Luke is talking about believers eating together without any reference to the Eucharist, particularly in Acts 20:11. But in verse 7 it seems probable that Communion is in mind, which suggests that the same is true in verse 11. Luke informs us that "on the first day of the week, [they] assembled to break bread." The first day of the week was the day of Jesus' resurrection (Matt 28:1; Mark 16:2; Luke 24:1; John 20:1, 19). There are hints, including Acts 20:7, that the first day very early became the day on which Christians met together in celebration of Jesus' resurrection (1 Cor 16:2; Rev 1:10). When we add to this the use of the word "gathered" in Acts 20:7, it seems that a formal occasion is contemplated, one in which the Lord's Supper was celebrated at the end of the meal.

If we summarize the use of breaking of bread in Luke–Acts, we find two of the themes that we found in the Last Supper texts. First, the Supper is where Jesus is recognized as the crucified Messiah who gave his life for the forgiveness of sins, as Cleopas and his friend discovered. Second, the Lord's Supper centers on the community life of disciples and their shared life together as Christians, as suggested in Acts 2:42, 46 and Acts 20:7, 11. A new community is formed and established on the basis of Jesus' death.

Communion and Paul

Outside of the Gospels and Acts, Paul was the only writer who mentioned the Lord's Supper, and he mentioned it in two texts in 1 Corinthians.[9]

1 Corinthians 10:16–17

The first text is located in a context where Paul was admonishing the Corinthians not to eat food sacrificed to idols in an idol's temple (1 Cor 10:16–17; cf. vv. 14–22). To do so constituted idolatry. Eating the food of the idol meant that one "benefits" from the idol, and behind the idols stood demons; and one could not share the table of demons and the table

---

[9] For a helpful and insightful exposition, see James M. Hamilton Jr., "The Lord's Supper in Paul: An Identity-Forming Proclamation of the Gospel," in Schreiner and Crawford, *The Lord's Supper*, 68–102.

of the Lord (1 Cor 10:21). The reference to the Lord's table brings up the subject of Communion. Paul drew an analogy between eating at the table of demons and partaking of Communion at the Lord's Table. Two truths about the Eucharist stand out here.

First, when believers drink of the cup, "is it not a sharing in the blood of Christ?" (v. 16). And when they break the bread, "is it not a sharing in the body of Christ?" (v. 16). The word translated *sharing* here is the term that is often translated as "Communion" (*koinōnia*). It is instructive as well that Paul used the phrase "breaking bread," suggesting that the phrase was common parlance for speaking of Communion. In any case, Paul's main point here was that believers share in the benefits of what Christ has done for them by drinking the cup and eating the bread. He was not thinking they share in the benefits sacramentally because in the context he criticized the idea that baptism and the Lord's Supper protect one magically from punishment (1 Cor 10:1–12). Rather, when believers eat and drink, they recall what the Lord has done for them and are spiritually strengthened and encouraged by the forgiveness they have obtained through the body and blood of the Lord.

Second, the Lord's Supper is communal, signifying the unity of the church. "Because there is one bread, we who are many are one body, for all of us share that one bread" (1 Cor 10:17). All believers derive their life from the Christ himself, and hence they are one body. The text gives us another piece of evidence that celebrating Communion occurs when the church gathers together. It is by definition a communal and not an individual matter, and hence it is to be shared when believers are assembled together. Believers testify together that their life depends on Jesus Christ.

1 Corinthians 11:17–34

The most extensive discussion of the Lord's Supper in the Epistles and actually in the entire New Testament is 1 Corinthians 11:17–34. The tradition Paul relayed here about the Supper is close to the Lukan tradition and most likely derives from it (cf. 1 Cor 11:23–26; Luke 22:14–20). The comments on this shared tradition will be brief because they were discussed in the synoptic section above. The purpose here is not to offer a full exegesis but to comment on five major themes in the text.

First, the Lord's Supper was celebrated when the church was gathered together. The verb "come together" (*synerchomai*) is used four times in this text (1 Cor 11:17, 18, 20, 33). It is evident that the church celebrated the Lord's Supper when they assembled. We see again that the celebration is communal and not individualistic. The church finds its common bond and identity in the work of Jesus Christ on its behalf.

Second, the communal nature of the church must be reflected in its life together, including its celebration of the Eucharist. What frustrated Paul was the social stratification that occurred between the rich and poor at the Supper (1 Cor 11:19). The rich were gorging themselves at the Supper and perhaps even getting drunk, while the poor were not finding enough to eat. And Paul was thoroughly embarrassed (1 Cor 11:21–22).[10] The Corinthians called it "the Lord's Supper," but it was certainly not the *Lord's* Supper because it became the platform for selfishness and blatant disregard of poorer members of the community (1 Cor 11:20). Communion is a place where members welcome and receive one another (1 Cor 11:33), not a place where distinctions are drawn. The behavior of the Corinthians contradicted one of the fundamental purposes of the Eucharist—to testify to the unity of the church of Jesus Christ and his self-giving love on the cross.

Third, the Supper is a remembrance of Jesus' death.[11] Twice Paul noted that in the celebration, the death of Jesus is remembered (1 Cor 11:24, 25). We are scarcely remembering the death of Jesus if we do not care for one another.[12] Remembering Jesus' death is not merely a "religious" event apart from everyday life; it manifests itself in how members of the church care for one another. Jesus' death testifies to his love for others. His body was broken for the salvation of those who believe in him (1 Cor 11:24). The word *blood* indicates that his death was sacrificial (1 Cor 11:25), with the result that the new covenant was inaugurated by his atoning sacrifice. Clearly, Paul taught that Jesus' death, which is remembered in the Supper, secured forgiveness of sins. The Lord's Supper recalls the atonement accomplished at Calvary. Hence, Paul could describe the Supper as a proclamation of Jesus' death (1 Cor 11:26). The broken bread and the wine symbolize the body and blood of Jesus given for the sake of his people.

---

[10] For this reading of what was taking place at the Supper, see Otfried Hofius, "The Lord's Supper and the Lord's Supper Tradition: Reflections on 1 Corinthians 11:23b–25," in *One Loaf, One Cup: Ecumenical Studies of 1 Cor. 11 and Other Eucharistic Texts*, ed. B. F. Meyer (Macon, GA: Mercer University Press, 1993), 90–92; David E. Garland, *1 Corinthians*, Baker Exegetical Commentary on the New Testament (Grand Rapids: Baker, 2003), 540–41; Hamilton, "The Lord's Supper in Paul," in Schreiner and Crawford, *The Lord's Supper*, 77–84.

[11] On the significance of remembering, see Garland, *1 Corinthians*, 547–48; Anthony C. Thiselton, *The First Epistle to the Corinthians*, New International Greek Testament Commentary (Grand Rapids: Eerdmans, 2000), 878–82.

[12] Rightly Hofius, "The Lord's Supper," in Meyer, *One Loaf, One Cup*, 109.

Fourth, the Supper is eschatological. As Paul said, "You proclaim the Lord's death until he comes" (1 Cor 11:26). When believers meet together, they don't only look back at what Jesus accomplished; they also look forward to what he secured. His death has a promissory element, so that it functions as the guarantee of a coming new creation. He is not only the crucified One but also the triumphant One. Death did not conquer him, but he conquered death.

Fifth, judgment will be meted out to those who eat unworthily. Those who eat in an unworthy way are "guilty of sin against the body and blood of the Lord" (1 Cor 11:27). They eat and drink "judgment" on themselves if they don't discern the body (1 Cor 11:29). Some scholars think discerning the body refers to discerning the church, but Paul probably referred to the physical body of Christ in light of verses 24 and 27. Discerning the body probably means the believers at Corinth did not realize in their everyday life the significance of Jesus' death symbolized in the Lord's Supper. In other words, partaking of the Lord's Supper is not simply a matter of trusting in and resting upon Christ during the ceremony. If one mistreats fellow Christians, then one does not perceive the significance of what Jesus has accomplished in giving his life for us. The two themes are closely connected in any case, for believers eat in an unworthy manner when they mistreat other believers.

Theologically, eating unworthily refers to any blatant sin that remains unconfessed. This should not be confused with perfection. All believers fall short in myriad ways (Jas 3:2), but if they are repentant, they are free to come to the table. Paul did not call for morbid introspection here. His point was that those who are living in blatant sin are partaking in an unworthy manner. Self-examination before the Lord will prevent believers from eating in a way that displeases him (1 Cor 11:28). The judgment threatened can be interpreted in two ways (1 Cor 11:29–32). It could refer to damnation, as if someone's act of eating unworthily demonstrated that the person was never a believer and did not belong to those who were "approved" or truly saved (*dokimoi*, 1 Cor 11:19).[13] Conversely, it could refer to a discipline that falls short of final judgment, and which spares believers from final condemnation. In any case, the consequences of eating unworthily and failing to examine oneself are significant. God will not tolerate treating holy things as common.

---

[13] So Hamilton, "The Lord's Supper in Paul," in Schreiner and Crawford, *The Lord's Supper*, 92–97. Given the use of *dokimoi*, Paul certainly referred to those who are true instead of false believers in 1 Cor 11:19. The question is whether the same applies to 1 Cor 11:29–32.

Conclusion

The Lord's Supper is a time of great joy and celebration, as believers remember and rejoice in the atoning sacrifice of Jesus offered on their behalf. The great deliverance at the Passover pointed to and anticipated the redemption accomplished in Jesus Christ. By his sacrifice Jesus inaugurated the new covenant and secured final and full forgiveness of sins. Those who share in the bread and wine are a new community in Christ. They are brothers and sisters and are to reflect this unity by the way they live together in the church of Jesus Christ. They reveal that they are "remembering" Jesus' death by their love for one another. The Eucharist is not limited to the past because the salvation gained by Jesus' death points to the final Messianic banquet and the day when Jesus comes and the kingdom is present in its fullness.

CHAPTER 7

The Lord's Supper in History, Theology, and the Church

Shawn D. Wright

E xactly what takes place in the Supper has been a subject of discussion and debate in the church for centuries. Lacking earlier definitions, the meaning of the Eucharist excited intense debates in the Middle Ages, leading to the Roman Catholic Church's doctrine of transubstantiation. The Protestant revolt against many Catholic errors at the time of the Reformation led to a variety of Eucharistic views among Protestants that continue to define the landscape to this day.

Views in the Early Church and the Middle Ages

The early church did not define the meaning of the Supper but seemed to agree generally about its significance: Christ was present in the Eucharist. According to Jaroslav Pelikan, Christians in the early centuries of the church believed in "the doctrine of the real presence of the body and blood of Christ in the Eucharist, which did not become the subject of controversy until the ninth century."[1] Although the church did

---

[1] Jaroslav Pelikan, *The Christian Tradition: A History of the Development of Doctrine: Vol. 1, The Emergence of the Catholic Tradition (100–600)* (Chicago and London: University of Chicago Press, 1971), 166. A helpful survey of patristic Eucharistic thought and practice is found in Michael A. G. Haykin, "'A Glorious Inebriation': Eucharistic Thought and Piety in the Patristic Era," in *The Lord's Supper: Remembering and*

not speak of Jesus' body and blood as more than symbols, "in the act of remembrance the worshiping congregation believed Christ himself to be present among them." The people's adoring of Christ in the elements "seems to have presupposed that this was a special presence, neither distinct from nor merely illustrative of his presence in the church."[2] The "real presence" of Christ was not defined in the first centuries, but it was closely tied to the notion that the Supper was a sacrifice of Christ that "would prepare the communicant for immortality."[3]

The debates in the medieval Roman Catholic Church tried to untie the knot of whether Christ was present spiritually or bodily in the elements of the Supper. For example, Ratramnus argued in the ninth century for the spiritual presence of Christ, while Radbertus opposed him by arguing that Jesus was in the elements bodily.[4] The outcome of these debates moved the church toward its definition of transubstantiation, which was formally affirmed at the Fourth Lateran Council in 1215. The Roman Catholic Church still maintains this.[5] Jesus Christ's "body and blood are truly contained in the sacrament of the altar under the forms of bread and wine. The bread is transubstantiated into the body and the wine into the blood by the power of God, so we may receive from him what he has received from us."[6]

Reformation Views

Undergirded by the cry of *sola Scriptura*, Protestants reacted to the dearth of scriptural warrant for transubstantiation. Three main positions

Proclaiming Christ Until He Comes, ed. T. R. Schreiner and M. R. Crawford (Nashville: B&H Academic, 2010), 103–26.

[2] Pelikan, *The Christian Tradition*, 1:167–68.

[3] Ibid., 168–69.

[4] See David S. Hogg, "Carolingian Conflict: Two Monks on the Mass," in Schreiner and Crawford, *The Lord's Supper*, 127–50. For an additional debate, see John D. Hannah, *Our Legacy: The History of Christian Doctrine* (Colorado Springs: NavPress, 2001), 279–80.

[5] Not only was transubstantiation affirmed in opposition to Protestants at the Council of Trent, but it was also restated in the aftermath of the Second Vatican Council. See Gregg R. Allison, "The Theology of the Eucharist according to the Catholic Church," in Schreiner and Crawford, *The Lord's Supper*, 152–64, 175–76.

[6] Ibid., 169. Thomas Aquinas especially explained the manner in which the mystery of transubstantiation occurred, having recourse to Aristotelian thought regarding the distinction between "substance" and "accidents": "He explained how conversion of one substance into another—something that is naturally impossible—can take place by divine power with the Eucharist. Though the substance changes, the accidents of the bread and wine remain. By joining Aristotelian philosophy with the church's theology of the Lord's Supper, Aquinas set forth the definitive Catholic view of the presence of Christ during the celebration of the Eucharist" (ibid., 169–70).

were offered instead.[7] Lutheran "consubstantiation" located the body of Jesus "in, with, and under" the elements without claiming that the elements' substance had been mysteriously changed into Jesus' body. Lutherans insisted that Jesus' words "this *is* my body" and "this *is* my blood" required a literal fulfillment. Both Zwinglians and Calvinists rapidly challenged this.[8]

Ulrich Zwingli's famous dissent culminated in the fateful Marburg Colloquy of 1529.[9] Reacting to what he felt were Luther's extrabiblical excesses, Zwingli taught that the Supper was best viewed as a memorial to the death of Christ. He argued "that Christ, having sacrificed himself once, is to eternity a certain and valid sacrifice for the sins of all faithful, wherefrom it follows that the mass is not a sacrifice, but is a remembrance of the sacrifice and assurance of salvation which Christ has given us."[10] Bruce Ware summarizes Zwingli's thought in this way:

> That Christ provided a fully sufficient atoning sacrifice in His death on the cross, and that we proclaim the Lord's coming in our eating of the Lord's Supper until the day of His return, join together, then, to bear witness that no further work need be done. Christ's atoning work is complete. The purpose of the Lord's Supper, then, must be seen most fundamentally in its commemorative function, of remembering just what has already happened in fullness, the reality of which is attested to further by Christ's future coming in glory. As Jesus said, when you take

---

7 Allison helpfully delineates five principle positions: "Catholic transubstantiation," "Lutheran consubstantiation," Zwinglian memorialism, Calvinist "spiritual presence," and Anabaptist and Baptist views (Gregg R. Allison, *Sojourners and Strangers: The Doctrine of the Church* [Wheaton: Crossway, 2012], 372–86). We think there is overlap in the memorialistic and Baptist views, as we will argue below. Letham organizes the views into four different schemes: "physical presence: transubstantiation," "physical presence: consubstantiation," "real absence: memorialism," and "real spiritual presence: communion." See Robert Letham, *The Lord's Supper: Eternal Word in Broken Bread* (Phillipsburg, NJ: P&R, 2001), 19–29.

8 On Luther's view, see Matthew R. Crawford, "On Faith, Signs, and Fruits: Martin Luther's Theology of the Lord's Supper," in Schreiner and Crawford, *The Lord's Supper*, 193–228. For background to the debate between Luther and Zwingli, see Heiko A. Oberman, ed., *Forerunners of the Reformation: The Shape of Late Medieval Thought Illustrated by Key Documents* (New York: Holt, Rinehart, and Winston, 1966), 243–78.

9 The background to the debate, as well as its best reconstruction, is found in Hermann Sasse, *This Is My Body: Luther's Contention for the Real Presence in the Sacrament of the Altar* (Minneapolis: Augsburg, 1959).

10 Zwingli, *Selected Works*, 112, quoted in W. P. Stephens, *Zwingli: An Introduction to His Thought* (Oxford: Clarendon, 1992), 95.

the bread, and drink the cup—recall, both elements stress this point—we must partake of these "in remembrance" of Him.[11]

As Ware and others have pointed out, though, the memorial element in Zwingli's thought is not "bare memorialism," as if all we are doing is intellectually recounting something we know occurred centuries ago. It is also a joyful celebration, only to be received in faith.[12]

The Reformed, or Calvinistic, view of the Supper is often labeled the "spiritual presence" position. In reality, though, there are varieties of opinion within Reformed churches about what exactly it means that Jesus is present in the Supper.[13] We can summarize the main trajectories of the Reformed position under four headings.[14] In the first place, Calvinists stress that the Supper is an objective means of displaying God's gracious character to his people. Just as the gospel is objectively true and its work is done extrinsic to us, so also the Supper objectively portrays the gospel to us, apart from what our subjective feelings about it might be. It sends "us to the cross of Christ" as we in "living experience" grasp the power of his death on our behalf.[15] In the second place, believers possess a true union with Christ when they receive the elements. Calvin stressed this point, saying things like this: "The signs are bread and wine, which represent for us the invisible food that we receive from the flesh and blood of Christ," and "salvation for us rests on faith in his death and resurrection, but also . . . by true partaking of him, his life passes into us and is made ours—just as bread when taken as food imparts vigor to the body."[16] Third, believers can have union with Christ

[11] Bruce Ware, "The Meaning of the Lord's Supper in the Theology of Ulrich Zwingli," in Schreiner and Crawford, *The Lord's Supper*, 231.

[12] Ibid., 231, 235–37. What's more, in the last years of his life, Zwingli went beyond his earlier memorialistic emphasis and stressed that Christ was spiritually present in the Supper. Believers thus have real communion with Jesus, who is present in the elements (Ware, 240–44).

[13] See Wright, "The Reformed View of the Lord's Supper," in Schreiner and Crawford, *The Lord's Supper*, 248–84, and the sources cited there. Robert L. Reymond, for example, critiques Calvin's view, especially his use of John 6 (*New Systematic Theology of the Christian Faith*, [Nashville: Thomas Nelson, 1998], 962–64). For fine expositions of Calvin's position, see W. Robert Godfrey, "Calvin, Worship, and the Sacraments (4.13–19)," in *A Theological Guide to Calvin's Institutes: Essays and Analysis*, ed. David W. Hall and Peter A. Lillback (Phillipsburg, NJ: P&R, 2008), 368–89; Timothy George, *Theology of the Reformers* (Nashville: Broadman, 1988), 238–39; François Wendel, *Calvin: Origins and Development of His Religious Thought*, trans. Philip Mairet (New York: Harper & Row, 1963), 329–55. Letham offers a fine introduction to the Reformed doctrine and practice of the Supper in Letham, *The Lord's Supper*.

[14] We are summarizing Wright, "The Reformed View of the Lord's Supper," 261–71.

[15] Calvin, *Institutes* 4.17.4.

[16] Ibid., 4.17.1, 5.

in Communion because in it they mysteriously eat Christ's body and drink his blood. Thomas Davis summarizes what this meant for Calvin:

> To speak of eating the body of Christ meant for Calvin that the Christian is nourished by and gains union with a real human body. There is, literally, a fleshly body involved in the Christian's spirit feeding on Christ (though the body is literal, the feeding itself, however, must be understood spiritually in the sense of nourishment rather than manducation [chewing]). That is why Calvin insisted on substantial partaking of the body of Christ in the Eucharist, for it is the human body of Christ that is the accommodated instrument of God's salvation. It is the thing by which righteousness comes to believers.[17]

The mysterious nature of the third point leads to Calvin's fourth emphasis, which is perhaps the most characteristic aspect of this view—Christ is present in the Supper for believers. He avers, "I freely accept whatever can be made to express the true and substantial partaking of the body and blood of the Lord, which is shown to believers under the sacred symbols of the Supper—and so to express it that they may be understood not to receive it solely by imagination or understanding of mind, but to enjoy the thing itself as nourishment of eternal life."[18] How this occurs is a mystery, but the Holy Spirit is the agent of the union of Christ with his people. Christ's flesh is in heaven, but at the Table believers have communion with Christ because the Spirit unites them: "Christ feeds his people with his own body, the communion of which he bestows upon them by the power of his Spirit," and we must "believe that it is through [the Spirit's] incomprehensible power that we come to partake of Christ's flesh and blood."[19] Because of the stress Calvin places on the role of the Spirit as well as the importance of the body of Christ, his view is often called the "spiritual presence" position.[20]

---

[17] Thomas J. Davis, *This Is My Body: The Presence of Christ in Reformation Thought* (Grand Rapids: Baker, 2008), 87.

[18] Calvin, *Institutes* 4.17.19.

[19] Ibid., 4.17.18, 33.

[20] For other treatments of Calvin's position, see Michael Horton, "Union and Communion: Calvin's Theology of Word and Sacrament," *International Journal of Systematic Theology* 11.4 (2009): 398–414; Michael Horton, *The Christian Faith: A Systematic Theology for Pilgrims on the Way* (Grand Rapids: Zondervan, 2011), 807–23; Allison, *Sojourners and Strangers*, 381–83.

Historic Baptist Views

Baptists are often labeled "Zwinglian" or "memorialist" when it comes to the Eucharist.[21] This may be the majority Baptist position of our day, but historically this has not been so. Certainly many Baptists have stressed the centrality of remembering Christ's sacrifice in the Supper. Others, though, have held that Jesus is uniquely spiritually present in the Supper.[22] In fact, the Second London Confession of Faith (1689) teaches both approaches. The first paragraph on the Lord's Supper highlights both the remembering ("perpetual remembrance") and the spiritual ("spiritual nourishment") aspects of Communion:

> The Lord's supper was instituted by the Lord on the same night in which He was betrayed. It is to be observed in His churches to the world's end, for a perpetual remembrance of Him and to show forth the sacrifice of Himself in His death. It was instituted also to confirm saints in the belief that all the benefits stemming from Christ's sacrifice belong to them. Furthermore, it is meant to promote their spiritual nourishment and growth in Christ, and to strengthen the ties that bind them to all the duties they owe to Him. The Lord's supper is also a bond and pledge of the fellowship which believers have with Christ and with one another.[23]

The spiritual aspect of the Supper is stressed again later:

> Those who, as worthy participants, outwardly eat and drink the visible bread and wine in this ordinance, at the same time receive and feed upon Christ crucified, and receive all the benefits accruing from His death. This they do really and indeed, not as if feeding upon the actual flesh and blood of a person's body, but inwardly and by faith. In the supper the body and blood of Christ are present to the faith of believers, not in any actual physical way, but in a way of spiritual apprehension, just as the

---

[21] See Allison, *Sojourners and Strangers*, 383–86.

[22] "Baptists have historically used language so rich about Christ's presence in the Lord's Supper for those who come by faith that little difference is perceptible between their position and the Reformed idea of Christ's spiritual presence" (Mark E. Dever, "The Church," in *A Theology for the Church*, ed. Daniel L. Akin [Nashville: B&H, 2007], 828).

[23] Second London Confession 30:1.

bread and wine themselves are present to their outward physical senses.[24]

By faith believers spiritually "receive and feed" on Christ who is "spiritually present to the faith of believers."

Although the "spiritual presence" view is not usually viewed as being Baptistic, it actually has a long Baptist pedigree. In England, especially, this was the majority view well into the nineteenth century, only being supplanted by memorialism later.[25] We see the presence view on the eve of the twentieth century in the thought and practice of the prominent English Baptist pastor C. H. Spurgeon. Peter Morden has argued that, for Spurgeon,

> the supper was far more than a "memorial." He certainly believed it *was* a memorial, and could talk in these terms. But he strongly resisted the drift towards what Timothy George describes as "eucharistic minimalism." This trend towards viewing the supper as primarily a "memorial to an absent savior" had actually begun in the last quarter of the eighteenth century, even amongst Calvinistic Baptists. But it was something Spurgeon resisted.[26]

Spurgeon had a rich theology of the presence of Christ in the Supper, eschewing both Catholic transubstantiationism and low-church memorialism, neither of which, he felt, expressed the true communion that believers had with Christ at the Table. In the Supper, as James Gordon notes, Spurgeon stressed "the present reality of the indwelling Christ and all the potential for a communion of love which his real presence conveyed."[27] Spurgeon explained what he meant by Christ's real, spiritual presence:

---

24 Second London Confession 30:7.

25 See Michael J. Walker, *Baptists at the Table: The Theology of the Lord's Supper Amongst English Baptists in the Nineteenth Century* (Didcot, UK: Baptist Historical Society, 1992); Michael A. G. Haykin, "'His Soul-Refreshing Presence': The Lord's Supper in Calvinistic Thought and Experience in the 'Long' Eighteenth Century," in *Baptist Sacramentalism*, ed. Anthony R. Cross and Philip E. Thompson (Carlisle, Cumbria, UK: Paternoster, 2002), 177–93.

26 Peter J. Morden, "The Lord's Supper and the Spirituality of C. H. Spurgeon," in *Baptist Sacramentalism 2*, ed. Anthony R. Cross and Philip E. Thompson (Milton Keynes, UK: Paternoster, 2008), 188, citing Timothy George, "Controversy and Communion: The Limits of Baptist Fellowship from Bunyan to Spurgeon," in *The Gospel in the World: International Baptist Studies* (Carlisle, Cumbria, UK: Paternoster, 2002), 56 (italics his).

27 J. M. Gordon, *Evangelical Spirituality: From the Wesleys to John Stott* (London: SPCK, 1991), 164.

> By spiritual we do not mean unreal. . . . I believe in the true and
> real presence of Jesus with His people: such presence has been
> real to my spirit. Lord Jesus, thou Thyself has visited me. As
> surely as the Lord Jesus came really as to His flesh in Bethlehem
> and Calvary, so surely does He come really by His Spirit to His
> people in the hours of their communion with Him. We are as
> conscious of that presence as of our own existence.[28]

This was clearly no mere memorialism.[29] In nineteenth-century America,
as well, whatever "memorialism" Baptists held regarding the Supper
was anything but "mere." Rather, they echoed the Second London
Confession in seeing the Supper as having both a "memorial" and a
spiritual nourishment function. Christians truly fed on Christ by faith at
Communion.[30]

Not only have Baptists historically struggled to answer the question, "How is Jesus present in the Supper?"; they have also vigorously
debated who the proper recipients of the elements should be. Were the
only proper recipients people who had been baptized by immersion
upon their profession of faith (so called "strict," "restricted," or "close"
Communion), or could anyone who demonstrated a living, vibrant
faith in Jesus receive the Supper ("open" Communion)?[31] Over three
centuries the debate raged. Close communionists included such lumi-
naries as Henry Danvers, William Kiffin, Abraham Booth, and Joseph
Klinghorn. John Bunyan, John Collent Ryland, Robert Hall Jr., and
C. H. Spurgeon were prominent open communionists.[32] Peter Naylor

[28] C. H. Spurgeon, "Mysterious Visits," in *Till He Come* (n.p.: n.d.), 17, cited in
Morden, "The Lord's Supper and the Spirituality of C. H. Spurgeon," in Cross and
Thompson, *Baptist Sacramentalism*, 189–90.

[29] For more on Spurgeon's theology of the Supper, see Walker, *Baptists at the Table*,
164–81.

[30] E.g., J. L. Dagg notes the design of the Supper in this way: "The Lord's Supper was
designed to be a memorial of Christ, a representation that the communicant receives
spiritual nourishment from him, and a token of fellowship among the communicants"
(*Manual of Church Order* [1858; rpt. Harrisonburg, VA: Gano, 1990], 209).

[31] A further degree of "close" communion is the "closed" position, which limits participation to members in good standing of the church in which the Supper is being practiced. It is usually associated with Landmarkism.

[32] The history of the debates between the two groups is helpfully laid out in Peter
Naylor, *Calvinism, Communion and the Baptists: A Study of English Calvinistic Baptists
from the Late 1600s to the Early 1800s* (Carlisle, Cumbria, UK: Paternoster, 2003),
94–163. Also see Walker, *Baptists at the Table*, 32–83; Robert W. Oliver, *History of the
English Calvinistic Baptists 1771–1892: From John Gill to C. H. Spurgeon* (Edinburgh
and Carlisle, PA: Banner of Truth, 2006), 58–88, 231–59, 357–59. In the latter nineteenth century, C. H. Spurgeon practiced open Communion. See Morden, "The Lord's
Supper and the Spirituality of C. H. Spurgeon," in Cross and Thompson, *Baptist*

helpfully summarizes the similarities and differences between the two positions in this way:

> The advocates of restricted communion agreed with their opponents in holding that baptism is not essential to salvation. . . . Further, all were quick to point out that they baptized solely upon a profession of faith, the discipline showing their disapproval of infant baptism. Nevertheless, the restricted communionists averred that the teaching of Christ and the unvarying practice of his apostles demand that only baptized believers be admitted to the Lord's Table. When challenged about their approach, all they could do, and felt that they needed to do, was to cite the precepts and practices of the New Testament. Their logic was simultaneously deductive and inductive.
>
> Open communionists usually claimed that the New Testament never demands as a term of admission to the Lord's Table anything that is confessedly not a condition of salvation. They contended that for this reason Scripture does not present immersion as a term of communion, and that they had been unable to discover a book, chapter and verse that clearly teach or imply the restriction. When challenged, all they felt that they needed to do was to turn back to what they believed to be the teaching, both explicit and implicit, of the New Testament.[33]

Throughout Christian history the church has restricted Communion to those who have been baptized. Baptists who insist on close Communion are following this principle. In addition, all evangelicals limit participation—or should!—to those who won't take the elements unworthily. Unless one opens the Table to everyone present, one is

Sacramentalism, 177, n15. Spurgeon's church had Communion every Sunday morning. "This was open to every Christian. Spurgeon said, 'Every man who became a member of a recognised Church of Christ had a perfect right to Christian ordinances, he had a right to baptism and the Lord's Supper, and the fact of a man's being unbaptised, was no reason why he should not have extended to him the fullest Christian fellowship.' Yet membership of the Tabernacle was restricted to those who had been baptised on profession of faith. Spurgeon again said that he 'would rather give up his pastorate than admit any man to the church who was not obedient to his Lord's command'" (Geoff Thomas, "The Preacher's Progress," in Tim Curnow, Erroll Hulse, David Kingdon, and Geoff Thomas, *A Marvelous Ministry: How the All-Round Ministry of Charles Haddon Spurgeon Speaks to Us Today* [Ligonier, PA: Soli Deo Gloria, 1993], 42–43, quoting C. H. Spurgeon, *Metropolitan Tabernacle Pulpit*, 1861, 260).

33 Naylor, *Calvinism, Communion and the Baptists*, 94. Dagg helpfully lists the main arguments for each position, arguing for close Communion. See Dagg, *Manual of Church Order*, 214–25.

limiting participation in some way. The debate between close and open Communion continues to rage in our day.[34]

The Meaning of the Lord's Supper

Some of the richness of the Supper is indicated by the fact that the New Testament refers to it by several different names. It is called the "breaking of bread" (e.g., Acts 2:42; 20:7; 1 Cor 10:16), the "eucharist" (Matt 26:27; Mark 14:23; Luke 22:17, 19; 1 Cor 11:24), "communion" (1 Cor 10:16), the "Lord's Supper" (1 Cor 11:20), and the "Lord's table" (1 Cor 10:21). Based on these passages, we can summarize the purpose of the Lord's Supper under several headings.[35]

First, the Lord's Supper visibly reminds us of Christ's death for us. As we've seen, ordinances function as visible reminders of the gospel. In the case of the Supper, the broken bread and the cup remind us that on the cross the body of Jesus was broken and his blood was shed for the remission of our sins. The Lord's Supper doesn't take our sins away, but it vividly reminds us that Christ did. This is why Paul said, "For as often as you eat this bread and drink the cup, you proclaim the Lord's death until he comes" (1 Cor 11:26).[36] So the Supper gives us assurance of our salvation. It reminds believers that Christ loves us individually. Just as we individually eat the meal, remembering Christ's death for us, we are each reminded that "I have been crucified with Christ. It is no longer I who live, but Christ who lives in me. And the life I now live in the flesh I live by faith in the Son of God, who loved me and gave himself for me" (Gal 2:20). Just as Jesus called us individually to himself in the gospel, so now he calls us individually to the Table, and there he reminds us of his love for each of us individually.

[34] John S. Hammett nicely points out the arguments on both sides of the debate, noting the strong appeal of the open Communion position, while finally concluding that the strict position is most biblically consistent. See Hammett, *Biblical Foundations for Baptist Churches: A Contemporary Ecclesiology* (Grand Rapids: Kregel, 2005), 283–88. Also arguing for a close position is Gregory A. Wills, "Sounds from Baptist History," in Schreiner and Crawford, *The Lord's Supper*, 285–312. Ray Van Neste, on the other hand, strongly advocates open Communion in "The Lord's Supper in the Context of the Local Church," in Schreiner and Crawford, *The Lord's Supper*, 378–86. "By the late twentieth century, most conservative Southern Baptist pastors practiced open Communion" (Wills, "Sounds from Baptist History," in Schreiner and Crawford, *The Lord's Supper*, 311). See also Bobby Jamieson's forthcoming book on baptism and membership.
[35] See Wayne Grudem, *Systematic Theology: An Introduction to Biblical Doctrine* (Grand Rapids: Zondervan, 1994), 989–91, and Peter Gentry, "Baptist Faith and Message: Article 7b: The Lord's Supper," http://www.bpnews.net/BPnews.asp?ID=14088.
[36] Unless otherwise indicated, all Scripture passages are taken from the ESV.

Additionally, the Supper beckons us to put our trust in Jesus now. The gospel calls us to continue trusting Jesus; so does the Supper. Just as another person cannot eat for us, so in the Supper we eat the bread and drink the cup for ourselves. At our Lord's last supper he told his disciples, "Take, eat; this is my body" (Matt 26:26). Although we don't believe the bread actually *is* or *becomes* the body of Christ, we do think it represents the body of Christ broken for us. When we eat the bread and when we drink the cup, we are reminded that, as we must eat food for physical nourishment, so we also derive our spiritual strength from Christ who died as our substitute and redeemed us. It calls us to exercise faith in Jesus.

In the third place, the Eucharist vividly portrays our Father's gracious character and his steadfast love for those who believe. It shows that God has initiated a relationship with his people that will never end since the Supper represents "the new covenant" to us (1 Cor 11:25). The new covenant is "new" because God initiates the relationship and God guarantees that the conditions of the covenant will be met in us, unlike in the old covenant. That is why the new covenant is both "new" and "better" than the previous one (Heb 8:8–13). In portraying this covenant to us, the Supper recounts God's faithfulness to save us by his grace, to raise us to new life with Christ, to grant us faith, to give us hearts that love him. "The Lord's Supper testifies that God keeps His promises."[37] This is what we celebrate at the Lord's Table. God initiates the Table just as he initiated and accomplished our salvation.

Fourth, the Eucharist acts as a visible symbol of the unity every believer present shares. As we look around and see brothers and sisters eating the Supper with us, we are reminded that we are part of the family of the church.[38] We are not on our own but are members of a body of other believers whom Christ has also redeemed. This is what Paul meant when he said, "Because there is one bread, we who are many are one body, for we all partake of the one bread" (1 Cor 10:17).

The Supper, in the fifth place, powerfully proclaims the gospel. It demonstrates that the blessings of salvation are reserved for those who believe the gospel. Unbelievers present will hear the gospel preached as they listen to the explanation of the Supper. They should be struck by the solemnity and joy of those partaking of the Eucharist as they examine themselves before receiving the Supper. Most of all, they

---

[37] Brian J. Vickers, "The Lord's Supper: Celebrating the Past and Future in the Present," in Schreiner and Crawford, *The Lord's Supper*, 323.

[38] Vickers insists on this point in ibid., 327–29.

should be shocked into realizing that they don't belong to the group called "Christians" as they watch the bread and the cup pass them by. What a powerful and loving way to differentiate between the sheep and the goats! Whether they are children of adult church members or visitors, they will hear and see the gospel clearly through the practice of the Lord's Supper. By it they will be called to faith in Jesus.

In the last place, Communion is a tremendous, hope-filled celebration. It is an expression of our certain future hope in Christ. In 1 Corinthians 11 Paul tells the believers to continue having the Supper, thus proclaiming "the Lord's death *until he comes*" (v. 26). When we eat at the Lord's Table, we remind one another that Jesus will certainly come again. Every knee will bow before him at that time; every tongue will confess that he is Lord (Phil 2:10–11). We might not see that reality now as millions live in rebellion against him. But as we celebrate Christ's death for us in the Supper, we remind ourselves and one another that he will vindicate himself when he returns in glory. We will soon be with the risen, victorious Lamb, celebrating his wedding feast in heaven forever.

The Lord's Supper, then, is a rich, meaningful practice for Christians to participate in regularly. We need Jesus. In the Supper we have a visible reminder that by faith we do have Jesus. We have him dying for us. We have him caring for us now. And we will have him forever. We do not believe Jesus is bodily or spiritually present in the elements as we take them. But we do not for a moment believe this enervates the Supper from the blessing it is to the church. The Supper is a wonderful blessing to us because it calls us to remember.

Following Augustine's lead, Brian Vickers has cogently described the power that remembering has in the life of God's people. Memory impacts both the present and the future:

> We give little thought to memory. . . . Memory, however, is anything but casual. Through memory we know things, judge actions, and make decisions and future plans. For better or worse, we rely on memory. We remember the past but memory itself is not in the past because in the act of remembering the past is brought up to the present. When we remember a past action or event (and whether we experienced it personally is often inconsequential) we remember it *now* in the present and on that basis we consider the future, a future also known (to us)

only in the present. In this way memory is a kind of cross-roads
of past and future in the present.[39]

God constantly called his people to remember his rescuing of his people throughout the Old Testament by means of the Passover meal.[40]
Observing this, Vickers comments, "The biblical pattern of remembering, established in the OT, means actively calling God's grace and salvation to mind, to bring the past into the present with hope for the future.
It is anything but a casual reminiscence about the past, or casting a few
wistful thoughts to what happened 'back there' somewhere."[41]

The same meaning and power of remembering continues in the New
Testament through the Lord's Supper. "When we take the bread and the
cup, we relive (not reenact) and take part in what God has done, is doing,
and is yet to do for us."[42] We actively take hold of Christ in the Supper
by faith, not because he is somehow uniquely present there.[43] Vickers,
though, argues that this doesn't detract from the force of Communion
because it calls us to what we desperately need—Christ. And it tells us
to seek him by faith continually.[44] This is a vivid, soul-satisfying, and
necessary practice of the church.

The Supper, in other words, is a present practice that brings the
church into contact with the past and has an unbreakable connection
to the future. This is the way to understand how Christ is present in the
Supper.[45] It tells us that remembering Christ's death for us should not
be divorced from asserting that Christ is still actively with us. Again,
Vickers says this strikingly:

---

[39] Ibid., 315.

[40] Ibid., 316–21.

[41] Ibid., 321.

[42] Ibid., 322.

[43] "As with the gospel, the only requisite for coming to the Table is faith—faith that
confesses sin and lays hold of forgiveness through the sacrifice of Christ" (ibid., 333).

[44] Ibid., 336.

[45] Gregg Allison also helpfully spells out that Christ is present in the Supper for his
people. His view is close to Calvin's understanding of "spiritual presence" although
Allison prefers the nomenclature of "covenantal presence":
"From my perspective, the God-man Jesus Christ, who reigns from heaven, is ontologically present everywhere and spiritually present either to bless or to judge the church's
celebration of his new covenant ordinance of the Supper. And where this covenantal
presence is, so is Christ's sacrificial work and its manifold benefits. Specifically, Jesus
Christ as the once-humiliated-and-crucified-but-now-resurrected-and-ascended God-
man, the exalted Lord foreknown from the foundation of the world as the Lamb who
would be slain (1 Pet. 1:20)—it is this person, marked forever by his one act of giving
his body to be broken for our sins and the shedding of his blood for the forgiveness of
our sins, who is present with all his salvific benefits to his church in its celebration of the
Lord's Supper" (Allison, *Sojourners and Strangers*, 397).

The gospel that proclaims Jesus' death also proclaims his resurrection, making the Supper not a memorial service in remembrance of the dead, but a remembrance of the dead and buried
Jesus who rose from the grave and who is coming again. The
constant interaction of the past, present, and future is nowhere
more evident than in the Lord's Supper. The death and resurrection of Christ guarantees the future and transforms the present
as believers are reminded through the interpreted symbols that
their lives are not just an endless loop of days; the One who gave
himself for his people abides with them and is coming again for
them.[46]

The Lord's Supper in the Church

Turning finally to life in the congregation, churches and their leaders
need to answer several practical questions: Who can administrate the
Supper? Where should it be given? How often should the Supper be
observed?

These simple questions have divided denominations and continue
to serve as a point of contention between different churches. As such,
we need to exercise biblical wisdom in these areas, following the Bible
when it speaks but willing to be silent when it is silent. Let's take each
question in turn.

Who Can Administrate the Supper?

In fact, who can rightly administrate both the ordinances in the church?
To answer, we have recourse to church tradition, Baptist precedent,
missiological concerns, a Reformation insight, and, most importantly, a
desire that the ordinances clearly symbolize the gospel to those watching.

Church tradition is uniform that only properly ordained clergy can
administrate baptism and the Eucharist. In the Catholic Church two
unbiblical notions fostered this position: the idea that sacramental grace
was given through these rites and the idea that a priest was endowed with
a special grace at his ordination. As such, only he could rightly administrate the ordinances so that grace would be conveyed to the recipients.

Allison rightly cautions against the speculative nature of Calvin's notion that in the
Supper the Spirit is active in uniting the church to the risen and ascended Christ. See
Sojourners and Strangers, 397, n155.

[46] Vickers, "The Lord's Supper," in Schreiner and Crawford, *The Lord's Supper*,
338–39.

In many Protestant evangelical churches, only ordained ministers administrate the sacraments both for the sake of maintaining "orderly practice" and because the ministry of the sacraments is tied to the ministry of the Word. This has been the case among Baptists as seen, for example, in the Second London Confession (1689). The confession states, "These holy ordinances are to be administered by those alone who are qualified and called to do so, according to the commission of Christ."[47] This point is driven home in the discussion of Communion:

> In this ordinance the Lord Jesus has directed his ministers to pray, and to bless the elements of bread and wine, and in this way to set them apart from a common to a holy use. They are to take and break the bread, then to take the cup, and to give both to the communicants, they themselves at the same time participating in the communion.[48]

Baptists have thus followed the church historically in believing that only pastors should administrate the ordinances.

One reason Baptists and other evangelicals have believed that only pastors should administrate the ordinances is because of a Reformational insight of tremendous importance. Against the Roman Catholic teaching that the sacraments conveyed grace *ex opere operato*, Luther and Calvin argued that the Spirit acts to bring grace in tandem with the word of the gospel. Because the ordinances are visible signs of the gospel, the practice only makes sense when the gospel is simultaneously explained. The ordinances have no inherent power; their strength derives from the gospel. And so the gospel has to be explained so that those participating in the ordinances understand that it's Jesus and his finished work on the cross, brought into the present by the Spirit, that make the ordinances significant. The word and the Spirit must act in unison.[49]

In our estimation the historic Baptist position offers biblically sound wisdom churches should follow. Before baptism or the Lord's Supper occurs, a recognized male teacher in the congregation should explain what's about to occur—and what's not occurring. And then he should call the congregants to use the ordinance as a means of entrusting themselves

---

47 Second London Confession 28.2.

48 Second London Confession 30.3. No biblical prooftexts are offered for the position that Jesus "appointed his ministers to pray, and to bless" the bread and the cup. This is telling. As I argue below, good reasons may exist to have someone other than a pastor preside over the Table.

49 See Calvin, *Institutes* 4.14; Ronald S. Wallace, *Calvin's Doctrine of the Word and Sacrament* (Edinburgh: Oliver and Boyd, 1953).

once again to Christ. Does this man have to be a pastor? Not necessarily. We know of instances on the mission field, for instance, where it would be culturally insensitive to have a man baptize a woman who was not his close relative. In those cases, by all means, a spiritually mature woman should perform the ordinance. Yet we think ordinarily a pastor should preside over the ordinances given the premium placed on rightly explaining the gospel and its relation to the ordinances.[50]

Where Should the Supper Be Given?

Given what we have argued above, we also believe the Supper should only be practiced when the congregation is gathered. Like baptism it is an ordinance of the church, not of a subset of the church. We derive this from the following truths. In the first place, the Lord's Supper is a covenantal meal enacted by the Lord to signify the new covenant he has made with the church. This meal is to be eaten by the covenant community, the church, under the authority of Christ.

Also, the bread signifies the body, that is, the entire fellowship of the church. One of the purposes of Communion, then, is to commune not only with Christ but also with brothers and sisters in the fellowship. We need to be with them when we take the meal, not only with a few friends from the church.

Finally, given what we've said about the importance of pastors explaining the significance of the Communion meal, the gathered church needs pastors present to be reminded of the purpose of the Supper.

For these reasons we think the church should celebrate the Supper together under the authority of the church's leadership at whichever gathering the most members are typically present. Most often this will be the main worship service on Sunday morning. Given the manner in which the Lord's Supper highlights and visualizes the gospel, we think the pastors should set out the requirements for those who can take the elements, even if this risks offending those who cannot. In our church we typically fence the table by saying something like, "If you are a member

---

[50] Two further comments need to be made. First, we want to open up ministry to the body as much as we can to women and men who are not pastors. So we allow women to serve the elements during the Supper, for instance, not seeing that as being a role reserved only for a diaconal position. We rotate who serves the elements each month, opening it up to female and male members, thinking that this visualizes well the picture of all the body serving all the body. Second, having only pastors do baptisms frees the church from the potential sentimentalism attached to having parents or the ones who led an individual to Christ be the ones who baptize. Jesus and his work in the person's life, not their attachment to the one doing the baptism, should be highlighted.

here, or if you're a baptized believer and a member in good standing of some other congregation where the same gospel you heard preached here today is preached, you're welcome to join us. If not, or if for some other reason you don't think you should partake, feel no embarrassment in letting the elements pass you by, but use the time to reflect on what Christ has done for sinners like us." Actually, the Supper provides another opportunity for nonbelievers and nonmembers to reflect on the meaning of the gospel and the call of Christ to commit themselves to a local church.[51] Special services like Christmas Eve or Maundy Thursday may be useful occasions to celebrate the Supper, but we think the bulk of the times the church celebrates Communion should be "when you come together" (1 Cor 11:17)—in your main weekly gathering.

This means there are illegitimate times to celebrate the Supper. Given its communal nature, we do not think churches should serve Communion at small group meetings, weddings of Christian couples when the elements are only given to the bride and groom,[52] gatherings of individual families at homes, or among some other subset of the church (e.g., youth groups or women's fellowships on retreat). Parachurch gatherings of different varieties also seem invalid arenas for the Supper.

Special consideration must be given to whether to give the Supper to church members who are "shut-ins," say, elderly individuals who are physically unable to attend church. It's our opinion that bringing the elements of the Supper to them is *not* the way to encourage them. Giving them the elements apart from the communion of the whole fellowship and apart from the teaching of the pastors actually may weaken, not strengthen, their faith. It could tempt them to look to the Supper for their comfort, when we should be calling them to seek Christ and find their hope in him for the present and for eternity. For these reasons we think the Supper should be celebrated in the main worship service of the church.[53]

How Often Should the Church Take the Supper?

The frequency of Communion has varied in the church over the centuries. The early church may well have practiced weekly Communion. During

---

[51] Speaking to our nonbaptized children about the meaning of the Supper and having them observe the plates passing by them has been a means the Lord has used to convict them of their sin and their need of trusting in Christ.

[52] I don't know when evangelicals began doing this, but the parallels with the Catholic doctrines of the Eucharist and marriage seem blatant. Because I'm not a sacramentalist, I strongly urge churches to avoid this practice.

[53] See Van Neste, "The Lord's Supper in the Context of the Local Church," in Schreiner and Crawford, *The Lord's Supper*, 375–77.

the middle ages, when the Roman Catholic Church was developing its sacramental system, complete with the preparation required before taking the Eucharist, the practice became less common. On the eve of the Reformation, it was common for laypeople to receive the Eucharist once annually, usually at Easter after having observed Lent.[54] Luther and Calvin wanted more frequent observance. Luther had it weekly; Calvin urged for it to be practiced weekly but was prevented from doing so by the Genevan city council. He conceded to monthly observance. Zwingli, with a more memorial view, advocated less regular practice in order to highlight its significance.[55]

Some recent Baptists have advocated weekly Communion,[56] but Scripture is not clear on this point. Paul certainly instructed the Corinthians about their practice of the Eucharist "when you come together" (1 Cor 11:17). It's not clear, however, whether Paul was saying the church in Corinth should have Communion every week or should do certain things *when* they had Communion. The frequency is not clear, even if the pattern in Acts, as we've already seen, was to break bread together weekly. It may be that the church in Jerusalem celebrated the Supper weekly in the first chapters of Acts, but I'm not convinced this is normative for churches today because it's a unique occurrence and the Scriptures do not decisively command this elsewhere, when they easily could have.

Churches have the freedom to exercise wisdom about how often they should have the Supper. Our own congregation practices it monthly, which has worked well.[57] Since the Supper does not communicate any special, divine grace that the church lacks in other ways, it is no disadvantage to church members to have the Supper twelve times a year.

---

[54] On the Catholic doctrine and practice of the Eucharist, see Oberman, ed., *Forerunners of the Reformation*, 243–55; Rudolph W. Heinze, *Reform and Conflict: From the Medieval World to the Wars of Religion, A.D. 1350–1648*, The Baker History of the Church (Grand Rapids: Baker, 2005), 38–39.

[55] George, *Theology of the Reformers*, 144–58. Euan Cameron, *The European Reformation* (Oxford: Oxford University Press, 1991), 161–66; Brian A. Gerrish, "Eucharist," *The Oxford Encyclopedia of the Reformation*, ed. Hans J. Hillerbrand (New York and Oxford: Oxford University Press, 1996), 2:71–80; Wright, "The Reformed View of the Lord's Supper," 248–53.

[56] Those advocating weekly communion include Hamilton, "The Lord's Supper in Paul," in Schreiner and Crawford, *The Lord's Supper*, 100–101, and Van Neste, "The Lord's Supper in the Context of the Local Church," in Schreiner and Crawford, *The Lord's Supper*, 370–74.

[57] See a similar argument in Hammett, *Biblical Foundations for Baptist Churches*, 292.

The Ordinances: Concluding Reflections

"This is my body which is for you."

"This cup is the new covenant in my blood."

"Repent and be baptized every one of you in the name of Jesus Christ for the forgiveness of your sins."

We end where we began—with Christ and the gospel. Our Lord Jesus Christ is the head of the church. He has inaugurated a new covenant and established a new covenant people. He has authority to regulate how his people will celebrate the gospel by which they are saved.

In baptism his people remember Christ's death and conquering resurrection on their behalf. They rejoice that they have died and are now risen with their Lord. At the Lord's Table they reflect on the broken body and shed blood of Jesus—for them. These visible signs of the gospel implore them to love Christ and wait eagerly for his return.

Far from being bare memorials, both baptism and the Supper are rich means of encouragement and blessing ordained by Christ. They visualize his victorious gospel and give his people hope. May Jesus be honored, and may his people find rich satisfaction in him, as we observe baptisms and partake of the Eucharist.

PART 3

CHURCH MEMBERSHIP
AND DISCIPLINE

John Hammett
Thomas White

The twin topics of church membership and discipline are essential aspects of any discussion of ecclesiology and church polity. Both are related to the nature of the church;[1] a proper understanding and practice of both is necessary for the health of a church. By membership a church establishes itself, for as many have recognized, a church does not so much have members as it is its members.[2] Church discipline regulates the boundaries of membership, primarily by warning and restoring those in danger of wandering beyond those boundaries or, when restoration is rejected, by recognizing that some have wandered so far they can no longer be recognized as members.

Together membership and discipline enable a church to identify itself. They enable members and pastors to know those to whom they have a special relationship and for whom they bear special responsibilities.

---

[1] See the argument for this in John S. Hammett, "Church Membership, Church Discipline, and the Nature of the Church," in *Those Who Must Give an Account: A Study of Church Membership and Church Discipline*, ed. John S. Hammett and Benjamin L. Merkle (Nashville: B&H Academic, 2012), 7–28.

[2] Most confessions of faith define the church in terms of the members who compose and constitute it. The Westminster Confession of Faith states that the universal church "consists of the whole number of the elect." Baptists, focusing more on local churches, have historically defined such a church as "a body of baptized believers" (see The Baptist Faith and Message 2000). Jonathan Leeman says explicitly, "A church is its membership" (Jonathan Leeman, *Church Membership: How the World Knows Who Represents Jesus* [Wheaton: Crossway, 2012], 46).

CHAPTER 8

The Why and Who of Church Membership

John Hammett

T he whole idea of membership has fallen on hard times in contemporary North American life. In *Bowling Alone*, Robert Putnam has shown the overall decline of membership in all types of societies, including churches.[1] The individualism and consumerism so characteristic of American life seem to be two of the key reasons behind this trend. In the case of church membership, an additional reason for the decline may be the widespread failure of churches to help their members grow as disciples of Christ[2] or the perceived harshness, hypocrisy, homophobia, and judgmental spirit in churches (particularly in evangelical churches), especially as seen by those in the under-thirty generation.[3]

---

[1] Robert Putnam, *Bowling Alone: The Collapse and Revival of American Community* (New York: Simon & Schuster, 2000), 70–71. Drawing on multiple sources, Putnam sees a long, slow decline of about 10 percent in church membership from the 1960s to the 1990s. The decline is most pronounced in the "younger generations," among whom he includes the "boomers" (79).

[2] This is the contention of George Barna, *Revolution* (Wheaton: Tyndale House, 2005). He projects a movement from 70 percent of people looking to a local church as the "primary means" of their spiritual experience and expression in 2000, to only 30–35 percent by 2025, with those in an "alternative faith-based community" rising from 5 percent to 30–35 percent by 2025 (49).

[3] See Dan Kimball, *They Like Jesus but Not the Church: Insights from Emerging Generations* (Grand Rapids: Zondervan, 2007). The major part of the book (73–209) is devoted to six problems emerging generations have with churches, including what is perceived as their political agenda, judgmental spirit, oppression of females, homophobia, arrogance and ignorance concerning other religions, and fundamentalist interpretations of the Bible.

Josh Harris looks at the case of those who go to church but avoid joining or becoming deeply involved. He calls such individuals "church-daters." They have some type of relationship with the church, but they are
unwilling to make a deep commitment, or fall in love with the church.
Such church-daters have absorbed three attitudes from the culture that
keep them from loving the church. First, they approach the church with
a self-centered consumer's attitude. They ask, "What's in it for me?"
Second, they have prideful independence that denies the need for others.
Third, they have an excessively critical eye on the admitted problems
and imperfections of all churches.[4]

Churches often encourage such attitudes by the way they treat membership. In many Baptist churches, one can attend on a Sunday morning,
walk forward during an invitation, answer a few perfunctory questions,
be presented to the congregation, and be voted in as a member without anyone knowing more than the most basic information about this
new "member." Should this person cease to attend, they would join the
majority of members, many of whom have not attended for years and
yet remain in good standing.[5] When membership is treated so carelessly
and cavalierly by the churches themselves, why should attenders think it
matters much at all whether they become members or not?

In spite of these obstacles, I will argue that the call to church membership for Christians is still strong and persuasive, with a basis in Scripture,
history, theology, and Christian practice. This basis implies the requirements for church membership, which will be the second topic discussed.
Third, both the responsibilities and the benefits of church membership
deserve mention. Finally, I will discuss the practical issues involved in
recovering and implementing a healthy practice of membership. To put
it in the form of questions, this chapter and the next will look at the why,
the who, the what, and the how of church membership.

---

[4] Josh Harris, *Stop Dating the Church* (Colorado Springs: Multnomah, 2004), 58–59.
Jonathan Leeman agrees that "consumerism," "commitment phobia," and commitment
phobia" and "hatred of authority" are some of the "cultural baggage" keeping many
from church membership. See Jonathan Leeman, *The Church and the Surprising Offense
of God's Love: Reintroducing the Doctrines of Church Membership and Discipline*
(Wheaton: Crossway, 2010), 357.

[5] In 2012, average attendance at morning worship in Southern Baptist Churches
was 37.6 percent of the total membership of the churches. See Marty King,
"Number of SBC Churches Increased Last Year; Members, Attendance and
Baptisms Declined," accessed June 19, 2014, http://www.lifeway.com/Article/
news-2012-southern-baptist-annual-church-profile-report.

Why Church Membership?

The case for church membership is nowhere argued in the New Testament but everywhere assumed. It is seen in the nature of salvation, in the commands given to Christians, in the relationship between Christians and their leaders, and in the nature of the church itself.

First, the call to salvation is also a call to church membership. In 1 Peter 2:5, we find that coming to Jesus is coupled with "being built into a spiritual house,"[6] one of many images for the church. Jesus desires to place everyone who comes to him in connection with other believers in the church. In the same way, baptism in the Spirit is seen as simultaneous with salvation, which is also seen as simultaneous with being placed in the church: "For we were all baptized by one Spirit into one body" (1 Cor 12:13 HCSB). This shows, as Joseph Hellerman puts it, that "salvation is a community-creating event," such that "salvation includes membership in God's group."[7] This understanding of salvation is reflected in the famous statement by Cyprian of Carthage: "You cannot have God for your father unless you have the Church for your mother,"[8] as well as the less famous statement of Calvin: "There is no other way to enter into life unless this mother [the church] conceive us in her womb, give us birth, nourish us at her breast, and lastly, unless she keep us under her care and guidance until, putting off mortal flesh, we become like the angels."[9]

Church membership is also implied in the commands given to Christians. We are told to "not give up meeting together" with other Christians (Heb 10:25), to use our spiritual gifts "for the common good" (1 Cor 12:7) with the goal being "that the body of Christ may be built up" (Eph 4:12). There are literally dozens of "one another" commands (love one another, pray for, teach, admonish, build up, etc.).[10] Living a

---

6 Unless otherwise indicated, all Scripture passages are taken from the NIV, 1984.

7 Joseph Hellerman, *When the Church Was a Family: Recapturing Jesus' Vision for Authentic Christian Community* (Nashville: B&H Academic, 2009), 124.

8 Cyprian, "The Unity of the Catholic Church," in *Early Latin Theology: Selections from Tertullian, Cyprian, Ambrose, and Jerome*, ed. and trans. S. L. Greenslade, Library of Christian Classics (London: SCM, 1956; paperback, Louisville and London: WJK, 2006), 127–28.

9 John Calvin, *Institutes of the Christian Religion*, ed. John T. McNeill, trans. and indexed F. L. Battles, Library of Christian Classics (Philadelphia: Westminster, 1960), 21:1016 (4.1.4).

10 In an unpublished paper a former student of mine catalogued thirty-one different one-another commands, many of which appear multiple times throughout the New Testament. See Jeremy Oddy, "Christian Fellowship: A Theological Study of *Koinonia*

life of obedience to these commands seems to require a relational body similar to the church.

But one final responsibility requires a fairly official church membership: believers are commanded to hold one another accountable and, when necessary, discipline someone who is "inside" the church (1 Cor 5:11–12). The only Christians who can obey this command are church members who recognize other people as fellow church members.[11]

Likewise, the necessity of church membership is seen in the reciprocal relationships of believers and their leaders. Paul instructed the Christians in Thessalonica to "respect" and "hold them in the highest regard" the leaders who are over them in the Lord (1 Thess 5:12–13). In Hebrews 13:17, believers are told, "Obey your leaders and submit to their authority" because one day those leaders will have to "give an account" of those under their care. The only context for such leadership and accountability in the New Testament is the church.[12]

Some may acknowledge that these verses imply the necessity of some involvement in a local church but may still object to the idea of membership, seeing it as a modern, formal, institutional matter that is foreign to the New Testament world. It is true that some approaches to church membership may be inappropriate, but the biblical idea of church membership is rooted in the image of the church as a body. This image, along with others, gives us insight into the meaning of church membership in the New Testament.

Members of the Body

Membership in the New Testament is not a dry, institutional, formal matter of paperwork. It comes explicitly from the image of the church as a body and individuals as its members. Membership in a physical body is vital and organic, life giving and essential. Severing a member

---

in the Local Church" (Guided Research Report, Southeastern Baptist Theological Seminary, 2004), 23, n75.

[11] Church discipline will be discussed in more detail in chap. 11, but it forms one basis of church membership, as argued by Ben Merkle, "The Biblical Basis for Church Membership," in John S. Hammett and Benjamin L. Merkle, eds., *Those Who Must Give an Account: A Study of Church Membership and Church Discipline* (Nashville: B&H Academic, 2012), 40–43.

[12] Most books on church membership highlight these relationships as one of the biblical bases for church membership. See, e.g., Merkle, "Biblical Basis," in Hammett and Merkle, *Those Who Must Give an Account*, 33–40; Mark Dever, *The Church: The Gospel Made Visible* (Nashville: B&H Academic, 2012), 41–44; and Wayne Mack and Dave Swavely, *Life in the Father's House: A Member's Guide to the Local Church*, rev. and expanded ed. (Phillipsburg, NJ: P&R, 2006), 73–94.

of one's body involves intense pain, and the whole body suffers when a member suffers.[13] In the New Testament the body-member image is used to highlight the church's unity in diversity (one body, many members); the mutuality of members' care for one another; and the connection of members to the head, Christ.[14] Membership in the body in 1 Corinthians 6:15–17 and Ephesians 5:30 is associated with union with Christ and the image of marriage, suggesting that church membership, like marriage, involves a covenantal commitment. It is worth noting that historically, Baptist churches developed hundreds of local church covenants to express their commitment to live out the mutuality of care implied in the image of a body. In the most complete study of these covenants, Charles Deweese comments, "Baptists have stated forcefully and repeatedly that the covenant idea is essential to the nature, definition, and constitution of a church."[15] The covenant idea is similarly essential to the meaning of church membership when understood in light of the image of the body.

Members of the Kingdom

A second way of understanding church membership is in light of the church as an outpost or embassy of the kingdom of God.[16] Jonathan Leeman says, "A local church is a real-life embassy, set in the present, that represents Christ's future kingdom and his coming universal church."[17] This recognizes that Christians are citizens of the kingdom of heaven, living in exile on earth (see Phil 3:20; 1 Pet 2:11). In the church we are "no longer foreigners and aliens, but fellow citizens with God's people" (Eph 2:19). Leeman recognizes that the meaning of church membership is also derived from other images, such as body and family, but he starts with the "embassy of a kingdom" idea "because it represents the kingdom authority that Christ has given not to us as

---

13 In fact, one test of the genuineness of membership is the pain one feels if departure is necessary. Put informally, "If you leave a church and don't feel the pain of being severed, you never really joined in the first place."

14 See Rom 12:4–5; 1 Cor 12:20, 26; Col 2:19–20.

15 Charles Deweese, *Baptist Church Covenants* (Nashville: Broadman, 1990), 97. See also the discussion of the meaning of the body image in John S. Hammett, *Biblical Foundations for Baptist Churches: A Contemporary Ecclesiology* (Grand Rapids: Kregel Academic & Professional, 2005), 37–43.

16 For a fuller discussion of the relationship between the church and the kingdom of God, see Gregg Allison, *Sojourners and Strangers: The Doctrine of the Church*, Foundations of Evangelical Theology, ed. John Feinberg (Wheaton: Crossway, 2012), 89–100.

17 Jonathan Leeman, *Church Membership: How the World Knows Who Represents Jesus* (Wheaton: Crossway, 2012), 28.

individual Christians but to us as local church members."[18] That authority is derived from the gift of the keys that Jesus gave initially to Peter and the apostles (Matt 16:19) and then to the church (Matt 18:18), the authority "to assess a person's gospel words and deeds and to render a judgment."[19] Thus, seen in the light of the church's authority to assess and render judgment, church membership is the church's declaration that an individual is "an official, licensed, card-carrying, *bona fide* Jesus representative."[20] Membership is essential to the church because recognizing members is what the church has been authorized to do; it is not all the church is called to do and be, but it is specifically what the church as church is authorized to do.

Members of the Family

Perhaps familiarity with biblical language has dulled us to the pervasiveness of the family image for the church, but when Paul referred to a fellow believer as "brother" or "sister," the underlying assumption is that the church is a family. The even more widespread New Testament use of "Father" to refer to the first person of the Godhead conceives of our relationship with God as a family relationship. So while no verse explicitly calls the church a family, and only a few refer to the church as a "household" (Gal 6:10 HCSB; Eph 2:19; 1 Tim 3:15), family imagery is nonetheless "the most significant metaphorical" reference to the church and thus should have "pride of place" in any discussion.[21] Seen in this light, church membership is unavoidable for any who come to God, for they must come to God as Father. Any who know God as Father are adopted into his family, which is the church. Some may recognize the intrinsic connection between being a child of God the Father and belonging to the church, his family, but try to restrict their involvement to membership in the universal church. But to do so is to ignore the overwhelming

---

[18] Ibid., 29.

[19] Ibid., 59. For further discussion of the meaning of the keys, see Leeman, *The Church and the Surprising Offense of God's Love*, 174–227.

[20] Leeman, *Church Membership*, 64. This is the idea in the book's subtitle: *How the World Knows Who Represents Jesus*.

[21] Robert Banks, *Paul's Idea of Community: The Early House Churches in Their Historical Setting* (Grand Rapids: Eerdmans, 1980), 53–54. See Hellerman, *When the Church Was a Family*, 77, for the number of times family terminology is used for the church by Paul (for example, there are 139 occurrences of the words for "brother" and "sister," 63 references to God as "Father," 39 places where Christians are referred to as "children," and 17 times where Christians are called "sons").

emphasis of the New Testament, which is on local churches, and the nature of the church, which demands visible manifestation.[22]

So, why church membership? It is inescapable for anyone claiming to be a Christian. Salvation itself plunges a believer into God's community, under God's Fatherhood of his family, the church. Believers are called to relate in numerous ways to "one another," including gathering. Some of the others they are to recognize as leaders; others they are called upon to hold accountable, and, if necessary, discipline and restore. They cannot fulfill these commands apart from membership in a local church. The propriety of referring to one's relationship with the church as membership is sustained by recognizing the church as body, kingdom outpost, and family. The New Testament leaves no room for anyone to claim to be a follower of Jesus and avoid church membership.

Who Is Called to Church Membership?

In one sense the answer to this question is obvious: everyone is called to faith and repentance, everyone is called to Christ, and thus everyone is called to church membership. Yet Christians disagree on the requirements for church membership, so the question must be narrowed. What type of response to Christ is required of those who would become church members, or, more generally, what are the requirements for church membership?

The Importance of Regenerate Church Membership

The requirements for church membership should be somewhat self-evident by what has already been said. Church membership is for Christians. It is in fact the way their claim to being Christians is affirmed, or publicly authorized. It is Christians to whom the link of salvation and church membership applies; Christians are commanded to obey the "one another" commands, to recognize and obey leaders and participate in the authorizing and disciplining of other believers. It is inconsistent with the body of Christ image for any member not to be united to Christ; it is inconsistent for churches to affirm the claim of some to be citizens

---

22 See Hammett, *Biblical Foundations for Baptist Churches*, 31, for the overwhelming use of *ekklēsia* for local churches in the New Testament. See also Matt Jenson and David Wilhite, *The Church: A Guide for the Perplexed* (London and New York: T&T Clark, 2010), 52, who say, "Every manifestation of the visible church is a local manifestation, and so to somehow ignore this fact to shift the focus to universal terms is to ignore how church is always defined in such a way as to be manifested locally."

of Christ's kingdom if in fact they are not; and only those who have received Christ are adopted into God's family (John 1:12). This is the principle of regenerate church membership—members of the church should be those who have experienced new birth. This seems so obvious and self-evident that it would not need to be mentioned had it not been for a mistaken path the church took for a long time in this regard.

In the early centuries of Christianity, persecution largely assured that none but genuine believers sought to be associated with churches, but churches also had their own check. Most employed a time of training for those seeking baptism and church membership. The training was called catechesis and the period of time the catechumenate. Baptism was administered only once a year, on Easter morning, and so the catechumenate could last many months, in some cases up to three years.[23] But gradually infant baptism began to be practiced, and baptism as a whole became much more widespread and was practiced much less cautiously after the conversion of Constantine. Armies marched by in rank to be baptized into church membership, with little regard for whether they had faith in Christ or not. Rodney Stark says of the fourth-century church, "The Church made it easy to become a Christian—so easy that actual conversion seldom occurred."[24]

By the end of the fourth century, infant baptism was the norm in areas where the church was established; mass baptisms incorporated whole tribes into the church in pioneer areas. Obviously, many of these new church members were not genuine believers. Augustine gave theological justification for this, appealing to the parable of the wheat and tares in Matthew 13. The church is like the field in which the wheat (believers) and tares (nonbelievers) must be allowed to grow together (overlooking the fact that Jesus tells us in Matthew 13:38 that the field in the parable is the world, not the church). Only at the judgment will God separate them. For now the church is a mixed body (*corpus permixtum*).[25]

This acceptance of the church as a mixed body of believers and nonbelievers endured for more than a thousand years. Luther, Calvin, and Zwingli all retained infant baptism and a territorial church, in which

---

[23] See the fascinating comparison of this early church practice to contemporary new Christian or new member classes in evangelical churches in Clinton Arnold, "Early Church Catechesis and New Christians' Classes in Contemporary Evangelicalism," *Journal of the Evangelical Theological Society* 47, no. 1 (March 2004): 39–54.

[24] Rodney Stark, *For the Glory of God: How Monotheism Led to Reformations, Science, Witch-Hunts, and the End of Slavery* (Princeton, NJ, and Oxford, UK: Princeton University Press, 2003), 40.

[25] For more on these developments and Augustine's influence, see G. G. Willis, *Saint Augustine and the Donatist Controversy* (London: SPCK, 1950).

every member of the state was baptized into the church, without requiring personal faith. It was left to Anabaptists, and later to Baptists, to issue a call for a pure church, composed of believers alone, gathered around the practice of believer's baptism. They reclaimed the principle of regenerate church membership. The Somerset Confession of 1656 reflects the care Baptists exercised in preserving this principle: "In admitting of members into the church of Christ, it is the duty of the church, and ministers whom it concerns, in faithfulness to God, that they be careful they receive none but such as do make forth evident demonstration of the new birth, and the work of faith with power."[26] From their early days to the twentieth century, Baptist churches exercised care in who they baptized into church membership and removed through discipline those whose lives contradicted their professions of faith. As late as 1905, J. D. Freeman could say of Baptists at the first Baptist World Congress, "This principle of a regenerated Church membership, more than anything else, marks our distinctiveness in the Christian world today."[27]

But even then changes were underway that eventually undermined regenerate church membership in most Baptist churches. To simplify a long and sad story, Baptists began to baptize those whose conversion was questionable at best, and we refused to discipline those whose lives gave clear evidence of nonconversion.[28] Today an average of less than 40 percent of members are present at the Sunday morning worship services of Southern Baptist churches.[29] Church members are about as likely as the general population to suffer a failed marriage, to experience alcohol and pornography addiction, to indulge in greed and materialism, and to experience almost any other symptom of a nonregenerate status that one can suggest. It seems evident that many of our churches are full of members who show no evidence of genuine spiritual life. Fortunately, some

---

26 The Somerset Confession can be found in W. L. Lumpkin, *Baptist Confessions of Faith*, rev. ed. (Valley Forge, PA: Judson Press, 1969), 211.

27 J. D. Freeman, "The Place of Baptists in the Christian Church," in *The Baptist World Congress: London, July 11–19, 1905, Authorised Record of Proceedings* (London: Baptist Union Publication Department, 1905), 27.

28 For a longer discussion of the rise, fall, and possible restoration of regenerate church membership in Baptist life, see Hammett, *Biblical Foundations for Baptist Churches*, 81–131, and Greg Wills, *Democratic Religion: Freedom, Authority, and Church Discipline in the Baptist South, 1785–1900* (New York and Oxford, UK: Oxford University Press, 1997).

29 See King, "Number of SBC Churches Increased Last Year; Members, Attendance and Baptisms Declined."

have begun to recognize and address this problem, as we will discuss later in this section.[30]

Baptism as the Rite of Entry into Church Membership

Though no explicit verse says as much, and while exceptions exist,[31] there is a strong cumulative case for baptism as a second requirement for church membership.[32] In fact, it appears to be the rite of entry into church membership. In Christian history this has been widely held among most Protestants and Catholics.[33] It is supported by the order of events in Acts 2:41 (where people are baptized and "added" to the church) and by the inclusion of baptism as one of the marks of church unity in Ephesians 4:3–6. Indeed, the idea of an unbaptized Christian is foreign to the New Testament.[34] So if, as argued above, church members must be Christians, and, as argued here, Christians must be baptized, there seems to be a link between church membership and baptism. Mark Dever finds further support for seeing baptism as a requirement for church membership in the fact that baptism is a command of Jesus. He observes:

> Baptism, then, is essential for membership in a church because if one were admitted by a church, only to refuse such a clear command of Christ, then such an unbaptized person claiming to follow Christ would simply be immediately disciplined until they either decided to follow Christ's commands, or stopped having the church's endorsement of their claim to follow Him. There will never be anything that Jesus calls you to do that will be easier than baptism.[35]

---

[30] Books such as this one, ministries such as 9Marks, and even a June 2008 Southern Baptist Convention resolution have highlighted this problem and suggested some responses.

[31] For example, the baptism of the Ethiopian eunuch in Acts 8:38 seems unrelated to church membership.

[32] For an extended discussion on this topic, see Bobby Jamieson, *Going Public: Why Baptism Is Required for Church Membership* (Nashville: B&H Academic, 2015).

[33] See Millard Erickson, *Christian Theology*, 2nd ed. (Grand Rapids: Baker, 1998), 1,099.

[34] See the argument of Robert Stein, "Baptism in Luke–Acts," in *Believer's Baptism: Sign of the New Covenant in Christ*, ed. Thomas Schreiner and Shawn Wright, NAC Studies in Bible & Theology (Nashville: B&H Academic, 2006), 35–66, that repentance, faith, confession, receiving the gift of the Holy Spirit, and baptism were all part of becoming a Christian in the book of Acts.

[35] Mark Dever, *A Display of God's Glory* (Washington, DC: Center for Church Reform, 2001), 52–53.

Requiring baptism for church membership is standard among virtually all denominations. For those groups that baptize infants, the connection between baptism and membership would seem to lead to infants becoming members of the church before they experience regeneration.[36] But this conflicts with the requirement that church members be regenerate persons. It would go beyond the scope of this essay to review the arguments for and against infant baptism,[37] but historically the strength of the biblical case for believer's baptism has been one of the principle reasons non-Baptists have became Baptists. The point to be made here is simply that if baptism is the rite of initiation into church membership, and church membership is limited to regenerate persons (believers), then baptism should be limited to believers. Baptists traditionally have followed the logic of this argument and required believer's baptism as a prerequisite to church membership, seeing the sprinkling of infants as something less than a valid, biblical baptism. It is true that there has been some resistance to this argument by some contemporary Baptists (most widely known is John Piper's objection). But despite diversity in baptismal practices, most Baptists still find compelling the argument for requiring believer's baptism for church membership, seeming to "most closely match New Testament practice."[38]

A Covenantal Type Commitment

New Testament teaching on church membership indicates that there is a third requirement for church membership. Church members must accept the responsibilities that come with a covenantal type of commitment to

---

[36] This would not apply to groups who believe infant baptism accomplishes regeneration of the infant. See Robert Kolb, "Lutheran View: God's Baptismal Act as Regenerative," in *Understanding Four Views on Baptism*, ed. Paul Engle (Grand Rapids: Zondervan, 2007), 91–109. But the lack of visible faith and repentance on the part of baptized infants has made this a minority opinion, even among those who support infant baptism.

[37] For such a presentation, see the contributions of Bruce Ware and Sinclair Ferguson to *Baptism: Three Views*, ed. David Wright (Downers Grove: IVP Academic, 2009).

[38] Nathan Finn, "A Historical Analysis of Church Membership," in Hammett and Merkle, *Those Who Must Give an Account*, 75. Finn, 73–74, notes that British Baptists have dropped the requirement for believer's baptism and sees a similar move among some "theologically progressive Baptists" in North America, such as Curtis Freeman ("Opinion: Should Baptists Adopt Open Membership? Yes," Associated Baptist Press [April 10, 2010], accessed July 29, 2010, http://www.abpnews.com/content/view/5077/53). John Piper has argued against the requirement because he sees the unity he shares with Reformed friends around the gospel as more important than their disagreements over baptism. For Piper's advocacy of dropping the believer's baptism requirement, see the relevant documents accessed July 29, 2010, http://desiringgod.org/ResourceLibrary/TopicIndex/70.

one another.[39] As the New Testament portrays it, church membership is an active role. In Acts 2:42–47 and 4:32, believers instinctively began to accept responsibility for one another's welfare and to gravitate toward spending time with one another. Time together was necessary to fulfill all the responsibilities placed on church members in the New Testament epistles. In Romans 12:9–16, Paul commanded the church members at Rome to be devoted to, honor, and live in harmony with "one another." That last phrase refers to the scope of the command and seems most naturally to refer to those to whom the letter was addressed, the members of the church in Rome. Similar "one another" responsibilities are found in Ephesians 4:25, 32; Colossians 3:13–16; 1 Thessalonians 5:11–15; Hebrews 10:24–25, and numerous other places in the New Testament. Moreover, a degree of care and commitment to one another seems inherent in some of the images the New Testament uses to reference the church. Paul took it as axiomatic that members of a body care for one another, such that all suffer and rejoice together (1 Cor 12:25–26). As a family, church members have a certain priority in the time and attention given to one another (see Gal 6:10).[40]

The failure of churches to require such a commitment from their members today is painfully evident. As noted above, a majority of Southern Baptist church members do not even attend the main worship services of the church. How then can they obey the command to avoid "giving up meeting together," but rather "spur one another on to love and good deeds" (Heb 10:24–25), not to mention all the other commands requiring personal interaction? For this reason some churches are returning to the practice which formerly was constitutive for Baptist churches in North America—formalizing the commitment to one another in a church covenant. Becoming a member of the church required "owning

[39] See the careful discussion in Allison, *Sojourners and Strangers*, 124–32. He notes that no specific biblical imperative or explicit example uses covenantal language for the relationship of members one to another, but argues that the New Testament does provide a "covenantal framework" for the church and sees the covenantal relationship of members with one another as grounded in the prior new covenant relationship of believers with God through Christ.

[40] Hellerman, *When the Church Was a Family*, 78–79, sees four themes emerging from the family terminology for the church in the New Testament. They experienced an "emotional bond" (he calls this "affective solidarity"); they were expected to live with "interpersonal harmony and absence of discord" ("family unity"); they were to share resources with brothers and sisters ("material solidarity"); and they were to show an "undivided commitment" to one another ("family loyalty").

the covenant," or pledging to live it out.[41] Some even see a covenant-type commitment to the other members as the essence of a local church.[42] While that may go too far, I do think it would be accurate to say at least that one requirement for church membership is a covenant-like commitment, especially if we see the covenant-like relationship of members with one another as grounded in their prior new covenant relationship with God through Christ.[43] As Stanley Grenz says of members, "Their shared commitment to be disciples of the Lord entails a commitment to one another. The church-constituting covenant is a mutual agreement to walk together as the people of God."[44] The only way for believers to live out the commitment to one another mandated by their Lord and Father is by living in a covenant-like relationship with other believers.

---

[41] See the discussion in Hammett, *Biblical Foundations for Baptist Churches*, 117–20. For historical background and dozens of examples of such church covenants, see Deweese, *Baptist Church Covenants*.

[42] J. D. Greear, "A Pastor Defends His Multi-Site Church," *9Marks Journal 6* (May–June 2009), 21, says flatly, "The essence of a local church is a covenant, not a manner of assembly." Alan Hirsch calls "a covenantal community" one of the two "irreducible minimums of a true expression of *ecclesia*" (Alan Hirsch, *The Forgotten Ways: Reactivating the Missional Church* [Grand Rapids: Baker, 2007], 40).

[43] Allison, *Sojourners and Strangers*, 128, emphasizes this, to distinguish his understanding of the covenantal nature of the church from "Presbyterian/Reformed covenantalism," which understands the covenant as one by which a person may enter through "family or church associations." He insists on "conversionistic covenantalism."

[44] Stanley Grenz, *Theology for the Community of God* (Nashville: B&H, 1994), 613–14.

CHAPTER 9

_____

The What and How of Church Membership

John Hammett

In the last chapter we entered somewhat into the question of responsibilities incumbent on church members. We saw that acceptance of such responsibilities is one of the requirements for church membership. Here we examine those responsibilities as part of the matter of church membership—the "what."

Church membership consists largely of fulfilling certain responsibilities and enjoying certain benefits. Because it is in fulfilling the responsibilities that the benefits are given, we will consider them together, looking first at the responsibilities and benefits church members have as individuals; then the responsibilities and benefits of church members as they act corporately; and finally, the responsibilities and benefits church members have in relationship to their leaders.

Individual Responsibilities and Benefits

While each individual Christian is called to obey all that Scripture commands regarding every area of life (as a citizen, worker, family member, etc.), our concern here is the commands that pertain to the responsibilities of church members in relationship to one another. Such responsibilities are found largely in the dozens of one-another commands noted in chapter 8. Church members are to love, forgive, bear with, pray for, watch over, encourage, teach, admonish, build up, and serve one another in a variety of ways.[1] Obviously, such responsibilities cannot be carried out apart from regular interaction, so church members must be present when the body gathers. In relationships with one another, they carry out these commands in dozens if not hundreds of specific ways,[2] but it could be argued that all the one-another commands are simply expansions on or expressions of the command to love one another. Love, Paul told us, is "the greatest of these" (1 Cor 13:13)[3] and "the most excellent way" (1 Cor 12:31). Above the virtues of compassion, kindness, humility, gentleness, and patience, Paul placed love, which "binds them all together in perfect unity" (Col 3:14). Jesus saw love for one another as the distinguishing mark of his disciples (John 13:35). Reflecting this emphasis, Jonathan Leeman develops an extensive treatment of church membership and discipline around the theme of love and sees the commitment members make to one another as a "covenant of love."[4] Thabiti Anyabwile is even more explicit, citing "committed love" as "the essence of membership."[5]

One resource God gives us to use in expressing love for fellow church members is spiritual gifts. Such gifts, Paul said, are given "for the common good" (1 Cor 12:7). The responsibility is thus placed on members to discover and utilize their spiritual gifts for the good of fellow members. In Romans 12, Paul directly linked being members of the body to the use of our gifts (Rom 12:4–8). Ben Merkle argues that the use of spiritual gifts forms part of the biblical basis for church membership: "All of these gifts require a community. Without being joined to a local body, a Christian is not able to use properly the gifts God has generously given."[6]

It is in the carrying out of these mutual responsibilities that church members benefit each other. While church leaders are also gifted and

---

[1] Biblical texts reflecting such responsibilities could be multiplied. Readers are encouraged to use concordances or Bible software and make personal study to grasp the pervasive nature of such "one-another" commands, but they can also see the dozens of verses cited by Mark Dever, *The Church: The Gospel Made Visible* (Nashville: B&H Academic, 2012), 41–43, especially nn8–26.

[2] For examples, see the detailed discussion in Wayne Mack and Dave Swavely, *Life in the Father's House: A Member's Guide to the Local Church*, rev. and expanded ed. (Phillipsburg, NJ: P&R, 2006), 95–232, or Thabiti Anyabwile, *What Is a Healthy Church Member?* (Wheaton: Crossway, 2008), especially 67–71.

[3] Unless otherwise indicated, all Scripture passages are taken from the NIV, 1984.

[4] Jonathan Leeman, *The Church and the Surprising Offense of God's Love: Reintroducing the Doctrines of Church Membership and Discipline* (Wheaton: Crossway, 2010), 229. The word *love* is found in the title of every chapter of Leeman's book.

[5] Anyabwile, *What Is a Healthy Church Member?*, 67.

[6] Benjamin L. Merkle, "The Biblical Basis for Church Membership," in *Those Who Must Give an Account: A Study of Church Membership and Church Discipline*, ed. John S. Hammett and Benjamin L. Merkle (Nashville: B&H Academic, 2012), 44.

play a crucial role in equipping church members for service in the world and to one another, it is as church members minister to one another that the body of Christ is built up and grows to maturity in faith and knowledge. Indeed, the body "grows and builds itself up in love, as each part does its work" (Eph 4:16). Among the conclusions James Samra reaches after a thorough study of "the undisputed Pauline epistles" is that "Paul expected that believers' participation in their local church would be beneficial to them with regard to the process of maturation." He continues: "The way the local community facilitates the process of maturation is by facilitating the five components of the process of maturation," which he identifies as "1) identifying with Christ; 2) enduring suffering; 3) experiencing the presence of God; 4) receiving and living out wisdom from God and 5) imitating a godly example."[7] Joseph Hellerman elaborates on the fourth of these components as one of the benefits of covenantal, committed membership. Church members get the benefit of the wisdom of others in making key personal decisions. From twenty-five years of experience, he offers this general principle: "The closer a Christian group approximates the strong-group, church family model that characterized early Christianity, the better the decisions that are made by the group's individual members and nuclear family units."[8] Thus, one strong incentive to church membership should be the manifold benefits members enjoy by their mutual ministry, one to another.

Corporate Responsibilities and Benefits

Some responsibilities begin as individual but can become corporate. The clearest example is discipline. Because other sections of this book are devoted to church discipline, it will not be necessary to develop it in detail here; but it is related to our discussion because it begins when church members take seriously the command to watch over one another and hold one another accountable.[9] Church leaders are especially called to watch over the members under their care (Heb 13:17), but the call to care for fellow church members in this way is also unmistakable: "See to it that no one misses the grace of God and that no bitter root grows up to

---

[7] James Samra, *Being Conformed to Christ in Community: A Study of Maturity, Maturation and the Local Church in the Undisputed Pauline Epistles*, Library of New Testament Studies 320 (New York and London: T&T Clark, 2006), 169, 168.

[8] Joseph Hellerman, *When the Church Was a Family: Recapturing Jesus' Vision for Authentic Christian Community* (Nashville: B&H Academic, 2009), 170. He relates this especially to vocational and marital decisions.

[9] See for example Matt 18:15; 1 Cor 5:12–13; Gal 6:1–2; 2 Thess 3:15.

cause trouble and defile many" (Heb 12:15). In this verse the verb translated "see to it," is plural, placing the responsibility on all the members of the community to watch over one another. The process for warning, restoring, and, if necessary, excluding members is given to the church as a whole (Matt 18:17; 1 Cor 5:12–13).

Similarly, the benefits related to discipline apply first to the individual and then to the corporate body. The individual receives the benefit of warning, accountability, and restoration. In a world where tolerance is the only virtue recognized by some, having people who love you enough to warn you if they see danger in your life is a rich treasure indeed. The corporate benefit comes in the effect of discipline upon the body's integrity and health. In some instances the family is spared the pain of grieving over a brother gone astray (1 Cor 5:2), and in all instances the purity of their testimony before the world is preserved. When the "root of bitterness" is dealt with in a timely manner, the body is preserved from the danger of its spreading and defiling many. F. F. Bruce observes, "If some incipient sin manifests itself in their midst, it must be eradicated at once; if it is tolerated, this is a sure way of falling short of God's grace, for the whole community will then be contaminated."[10] This responsibility of the church for watching over its members is usually connected to the authority granted to the church in the gift of "the keys of the kingdom" (Matt 16:19; cf. 18:18).[11]

Another corporate responsibility given to church members is to assemble in Christ's name, to offer him worship, and to encourage one another. This is inherent in the church's nature as a "holy priesthood." As such, they are to be "offering spiritual sacrifices acceptable to God through Jesus Christ" (1 Pet 2:5). Among such sacrifices are worship, praise, and being transformed by God's Word (Heb 13:15; Rom 12:1–2). When church members fulfill their responsibility and gather in his name, the benefits are amazing. Christ promises to be present with them in a special way (Matt 18:20). Paul even said that "the power of our Lord Jesus is present" (1 Cor 5:4) when they gather. Samra says that, for Paul, when believers assemble, Christ becomes present among them "in a unique way" and for their benefit. Since participation in Christ brings believers to maturity, and because Christ is uniquely present when they assemble, assembling brings maturity. Samra concludes,

---

[10] F. F. Bruce, *The Epistle to the Hebrews*, New International Commentary on the New Testament (Grand Rapids: Eerdmans, 1964), 365.

[11] For a thorough discussion of "the keys of the kingdom" and their relationship to church membership and discipline, see Leeman, *The Church and the Surprising Offense of God's Love*, especially 177–95.

"When believers assemble together their 'being-in-Christ' is uniquely actualized and maturation is made 'uniquely possible.'"[12] According to 1 Corinthians 14:24–25, even unbelievers will be able to recognize the unique presence of God among believers when the believers assemble in Christ's name. To be specific, when church members gather for worship, the hearing of God's Word, prayer, and the observance of baptism and the Lord's Supper, they may expect the transforming power of Christ in a way they cannot expect in personal, individual times of worship. We might also make a more contemporary application and affirm that Christ is present among his assembled people in a manner different than that experienced by a believer who "attends" via podcast, DVD, or any other media assisted fashion.

A third corporate responsibility and benefit relates to the practice of congregational government.[13] That responsibility is to serve as the final human authority in the church, though the specific duties reserved for entire congregations differ from church to church. Some of the responsibilities given to congregations in Scripture include admitting and disciplining members, choosing leaders, and guarding the purity of doctrine.[14] These responsibilities require church members corporately to pray and seek God's guidance. They are also required to listen to, respect, and obey their leaders, but not in a slavish manner because even elders can come under the discipline of a congregation.[15]

Congregations that take seriously the responsibility to admit and discipline members show that the covenant-like commitment they ask of new members is matched by the commitment of the existing members to them. The covenant relationship is lived out from the beginning. Such churches also get the benefit of being congregations of regenerate persons. Congregations that have a voice in choosing their leaders enjoy the benefits of their collective wisdom. After all, it is easier to follow leaders that they chose to lead them. In terms of taking responsibility for

---

12 Samra, *Being Conformed to Christ in Community*, 135.

13 For a more thorough discussion of congregational polity, see John S. Hammett, *Biblical Foundations for Baptist Churches: A Contemporary Ecclesiology* (Grand Rapids: Kregel Academic & Professional, 2005), 135–57; Gregg Allison, *Sojourners and Strangers: The Doctrine of the Church*, Foundations of Evangelical Theology, ed. John Feinberg (Wheaton: Crossway, 2012), 277–95; and chaps. 1–3 of this book.

14 On congregational involvement in admission and discipline of members, see 1 Cor. 5:9–13 and 2 Cor 2:5–8; on congregational involvement in choosing leaders, see Acts 6:3–6; on congregational involvement in preservation of doctrine, note that most of Paul's letters were addressed to churches, including Galatians, where the apostle is calling on the church to reform its doctrine.

15 On the responsibilities to listen to, respect, and obey leaders, see 1 Thess 5:12–13 and Heb 13:7, 17. On the discipline of elders, see 1 Tim 5:19–20.

doctrinal fidelity, Mark Dever observes that congregations have historically proven to be better guardians of sound doctrine than leaders have: "Friends, the verdict of history is in. While it is clear that no certain polity prevents churches from error, from declension, and from sterility, the more centralized polities seem to have a worse track record than does congregationalism in maintaining a faithful, vital, evangelical witness."[16] The maintenance of sound doctrine is a significant benefit.

In general, churches in which members play a role in setting the overall direction of the body benefit in the development of greater loyalty and support among members. People are naturally more committed to decisions they helped make. James Leo Garrett says that expecting more of members in terms of responsibilities for guidance is "very likely to produce stronger, more mature Christians than other polities."[17]

One final benefit is simply the peace that comes with providing what human nature inevitably wants. People want a say in decisions affecting them; they will express their thoughts and feelings. They will either do so openly if leaders value and seek their input or indirectly, through their support (or lack of support) of the decisions made. The challenge is to develop congregations that will fulfill their responsibilities and do so well. Only then can they reap the benefits.

Responsibilities of Members to Leaders and Associated Benefits

Many passages in the New Testament instruct church members about their responsibilities to the leaders of their churches. Paul exhorted the Thessalonian Christians to "respect" their leaders and "hold them in the highest regard in love because of their work" (1 Thess 5:12–13). This respect makes members slow to entertain accusations against their leaders (1 Tim 5:19). It also makes them consider carefully the example leaders set and imitate them, particularly their faith (Heb 13:7; 1 Pet 5:3). One mark of members' love and respect for their leaders is the provision of material support (1 Cor 9:14; Gal 6:6; 1 Tim. 5:17). Even

---

[16] Mark E. Dever, *A Display of God's Glory* (Washington, DC: Center for Church Reform, 2001), 38–39.

[17] James Leo Garrett Jr., "The Congregation-Led Church," in *Perspectives on Church Government: Five Views of Church Polity*, ed. Chad Brand and R. Stanton Norman (Nashville: B&H, 2004), 193. Earlier Baptists made the same point; see J. L. Reynolds, "Church Polity or the Kingdom of Christ" (1849), in *Polity: Biblical Arguments on How to Conduct Church Life*, ed. Mark Dever (Washington, DC: Center for Church Reform, 2001), 395–99.

more often cited, especially by Paul, is the importance of prayer support (e.g., Eph 6:19; Col 3:4; 2 Thess 3:1; Heb 13:18).

Most striking of all is the command to "obey your leaders and submit to their authority" (Heb 13:17). This command raises a point of tension for Baptists and all advocates of congregational polity between pastoral authority and congregational governance. The authority of leaders cannot be absolute; God's authority is always supreme (Acts 4:19), and leaders may be subject to congregational discipline (1 Tim 5:19–20). Moreover, Baptists believe the authority granted to leaders should be limited both by the precise terms used to describe that authority and by what the New Testament teaches about the authority granted to congregations.[18] Thus Baptists have balanced pastoral authority for leadership with final congregational governance. But congregations choose leaders and thus should choose those whom they are willing to follow and grant them the authority to lead. They are commanded to follow that leadership, unless it is clearly contrary to the teaching of Scripture. In that case the first allegiance of all Christians is to God, and he must be obeyed above any human authority.

As Daniel Akin observes, a command to obey leaders and submit to their authority is "foreign to our radically autonomous, democratic, and egalitarian culture."[19] But like all divine commands, it is for our good. Congregations benefit from fulfilling their responsibilities to their leaders. They receive the ministry and watch care of their leaders. They receive from their leaders "instruction in the word" (Gal 6:6) and protection from false doctrine (Acts 20:28–31). Leaders serve as examples to the flock (1 Pet 5:3) and have the awesome responsibility of watching over those under their care "as men who must give an account" (Heb 13:17).[20] When leaders take these responsibilities seriously, members benefit from obeying and submitting to them.[21]

---

18 The key term in deciding the scope of pastoral authority is *prohistēmi*, used for the authority of leaders in Rom 12:8; 1 Thess 5:12; 1 Tim 3:4–5, 12; 5:17. See the discussion in Hammett, *Biblical Foundations for Baptist Churches*, 164–65. For New Testament teaching on the final governing authority granted to congregations, see Hammett, 146–48. For a similar but slightly different understanding of the authority of leaders and the congregation, see Allison, *Sojourners and Strangers*, 304–10.

19 Daniel Akin, "The Single Elder-Led Church," in Brand and Norman, *Perspectives on Church Government*, 72.

20 For a pastor's reflection on the meaning of these words, see Andrew Davis, "Those Who Must Give an Account: A Pastoral Reflection," in Hammett and Merkle, *Those Who Must Give an Account*, 205–21.

21 Is this good timing, since Driscoll has left Mars Hill over his leadership failings?

How Can We Practice Meaningful Membership?

Another question to consider concerning church membership is "how?" In view of how far most churches have fallen from the principles and practices of membership reflected in Scripture, how can we go about recovering and then maintaining in practice meaningful or, better, biblical, church membership? We want to offer some personal prerequisites to biblical membership and then some practical suggestions for getting there.

Personal Prerequisites

1. Understanding What Meaningful Membership Is

Most of the matters discussed thus far might be foreign to many churches. They may never have seen membership practiced in a meaningful way. Mark Dever rightly says, "To practice membership well, we must teach it clearly. And to teach it clearly, we must understand it well."[22] So when preaching on the texts and themes discussed above, pastors should draw out the implications for our understanding of church membership. Until members see how far their practice of membership is from Scripture, they will not see the need for changes.

2. Understanding the Importance of Meaningful Membership

Anyone working for the recovery and practice of meaningful membership in their local church must be deeply convinced of its importance because doing so will involve challenging long-standing practices in most churches. Most Protestant and Catholic churches surrendered the principle of regenerate church membership centuries ago with the acceptance of infant baptism. Baptist churches never surrendered the principle but undermined it in practice during the past hundred years. They increasingly baptized into church membership people whose lives gave no credible evidence of regeneration, and they allowed many individuals to continue in membership whose lives no longer gave any credible evidence of regeneration.[23]

---

[22] Mark Dever, "The Practical Issues of Church Membership," in Hammett and Merkle, *Those Who Must Give an Account*, 83. Dever's essay provides numerous practical suggestions, including "12 Practical Steps to Meaningful Membership" (96–100).

[23] On historical and theological developments that led to the loss of regenerate church membership among Catholics and Protestants, see Hammett, *Biblical Foundations for*

Despite the difficulty, the importance of recovering meaningful membership can be easily seen by considering the effects such a recovery has. First, it allows churches to give a credible corporate witness and make the common complaint "The church is full of hypocrites" less warranted. With members in whom Christ really lives, the church can serve as the window through which the world can see God and the gospel on display.[24]

Second, meaningful membership strengthens a church's corporate health. If, as we argued above, numerous benefits come to members through responsible membership, churches that practice such membership will have healthier, growing, maturing members.

Third, it shows love to those involved in meaningless church membership. Many of them may be trusting in their church membership to get them to heaven, with no evidence of any transforming encounter with Christ. It is not loving to leave these people with such false hopes. Warning them that they are not living as genuine followers of Christ is a loving warning. And taking the final step of removing from membership those who do not respond to our warnings is the strongest way we can express our concern for their eternal destiny. Such a course of action is far more loving than allowing such members to continue in an apparently lost state without a word of warning.

Finally, the most important effect of restoring meaningful membership is honoring Christ. Christ died for the church to make her holy, radiant, and without stain or wrinkle or blemish (Eph 5:25–27). Christ is honored when his bride is holy, but that cannot happen when membership is meaningless.

Such effects are well worth working for, but they will not come easily. What James Leo Garrett Jr. said of recovering church discipline a generation ago applies as well to the larger task of recovering meaningful membership: "Those who would lead in the renewal of discipline must be thoroughly convinced of its terrible urgency."[25]

Baptist Churches, 87–91; on developments in Baptist life that undermined regenerate church membership, see Hammett, 109–14.

[24] Bruce Ashford and Danny Akin, "The Missional Implications of Church Membership and Church Discipline," in Hammett and Merkle, *Those Who Must Give an Account*, 197, cite the numerous theologians and missiologists who have seen the church as a window for God and the gospel. They see the development of meaningful membership as one of God's "chosen arms for 'cleaning the glass' so that the window provides a clear picture of God, His gospel, and His kingdom."

[25] James Leo Garrett Jr., *Baptist Church Discipline* (Nashville: Broadman, 1962), 25.

3. Believing in the Possibility of Recovering Meaningful Membership

Some may be convinced of the importance of meaningful membership but feel overwhelmed by the difficulties they see standing in the way. Such concerns are justifiable and should not be minimized. Indeed, anyone working for such a recovery should think in terms of a multiyear process, perhaps three to five years or longer. But for those willing to patiently and lovingly work, we want to offer some words of encouragement. We think the time is ripe for change in this area. There has been a rash of books dealing with church membership in the last decade;[26] there is anecdotal but growing evidence of churches recovering practices like new member classes, church covenants, and redemptive church discipline;[27] and the Southern Baptist Convention in 2008 officially adopted a resolution calling for churches to work toward a recovery of regenerate church membership.[28]

Moreover, in calling for a recovery, we acknowledge that we are not the first to walk this path. We are following what earlier Baptists practiced. Their documents reflect what may be called a doctrine of church competence, the idea that Christ gifts his churches with the ability to rightly govern themselves and practice meaningful membership.[29] One of the fullest statements of this idea is found in the Second London Confession of 1677/1689, which was adopted by Philadelphia Baptists in 1742 as the Philadelphia Confession, the most popular Baptist confession of faith throughout the nineteenth century. It states,

---

[26] Many of them have been cited earlier in this chapter, such as Mack and Swavely, *Life in the Father's House*; Hammett, *Biblical Foundations for Baptist Churches*; Anyabwile, *What Is a Healthy Church Member?*; Leeman, *The Church and the Surprising Offense of God's Love*; Hammett and Merkle, *Those Who Must Give an Account*; and Jonathan Leeman, *Church Membership: How the World Knows Who Represents Jesus* (Wheaton: Crossway, 2012). Also helpful on many issues related to membership is Thomas White, Jason Duesing, and Malcolm Yarnell III, eds., *Restoring Integrity in Baptist Churches* (Grand Rapids: Kregel Academic & Professional, 2008).

[27] Perhaps the leader in this regard is Capitol Hill Baptist Church in Washington, DC, and 9Marks, which grew out of it. Through their online resources, publication of books and journals, and sponsorship of conferences, including one in which they invite guests to come and see how Capitol Hill practices meaningful membership, they have sparked renewal in many churches.

[28] See "On Regenerate Church Membership and Church Member Restoration," accessed June 13, 2008, http://www.sbc.net/Resolutions/amResolution.asp?ID=1189.

[29] A number of these documents are reprinted and made available in Mark Dever, ed., *Polity: Biblical Arguments on How to Conduct Church Life* (Washington, DC: Center for Church Reform, 2001). The bulk of the book consists of reprints of articles from Baptists dating from 1697 to 1874, all reflecting a high view and practice of church membership.

> To each of these Churches thus gathered, according to his [Christ's] mind, declared in his word, he hath given all that power and authority, which is in any way needful, for their carrying on that order in worship and discipline, which he hath instituted for them to observe; with commands, and rules for the due and right exerting, and executing of that power.[30]

This statement affirms that Christ gives a church all the "power and authority" it needs to carry out his purposes, which certainly include the practice of meaningful membership. Thus, Christ makes churches competent to make accurate decisions on matters like admitting and disciplining members. Admittedly, many of our churches, as presently constituted, are not gathered according to Christ's mind. But when we seek to restore them, we are working toward what Christ desires and equips churches to be. We are not working toward some impossible ideal but toward something taught in the pages of the New Testament, something reflected, albeit imperfectly, among our Baptist forbears, and something Christ gifts churches to accomplish today.

Practical Suggestions

Once convinced of the importance and possibility of change, what concrete steps should a local church take to develop meaningful membership? In short, a church should develop a process for church membership that properly reflects its importance. Most Baptist churches routinely vote in new members who come forward and request membership at the close of a worship service. Yet such votes are mere formalities, and the fact that they are cast so casually reflects a casual attitude toward membership.

What processes for membership would more properly reflect its importance? While there is certainly room for some variation among churches of different sizes, and while churches in different cultures should carefully consider their contexts,[31] here are six elements of a

---

30 Second London Confession, chap. XXVI, 7, in William Lumpkin, *Baptist Confessions of Faith*, rev. ed. (Valley Forge, PA: Judson Press, 1969), 286–87. For a fuller discussion of church competence, see John Hammett, "From Church Competence to Soul Competence: The Devolution of Baptist Ecclesiology," *Journal for Baptist Theology and Ministry* 3, no. 1 (Spring 2005), 145–63, available at http://www.baptist-center.com.

31 For example, what is helpful for a typical American church may be foreign and out of place in an Asian house church. The goals of having members who are regenerate, who have been baptized upon a credible profession of faith, who understand and commit to all that biblical membership asks of them, and who are accepted by the congregation

process that could be adapted in a variety of circumstances to develop meaningful membership.[32]

1. Develop a Church Covenant

Once a pastor leads his congregation to understand the meaning of biblical church membership, it will be equipped to state some of the essential aspects of that commitment in a formal written statement. Developing such a statement allows the church members to reflect on the commitment they believe Scripture calls them to make to one another. The church could then decide to limit its membership to those who are willing to affirm the covenant. Those not willing to sign would be allowed to opt out.

A covenant also makes concrete the commitment the church asks of prospective members. And it provides a basis for accountability and a rationale for the exercise of church discipline, should discipline become necessary.[33]

While many excellent models may serve as a guide,[34] the covenant may be more fully "owned" by the church if the members develop it themselves.

2. Reform the Practice of Baptism

While this is not the place for a full discussion of baptism, baptism is widely accepted as the rite of entrance into church membership. As such it is inescapably related to meaningful membership. Put simply, we need a process that will ensure that, as far as humanly possible, those we baptize into membership are regenerate. Thus, when someone requests baptism and church membership, the church needs to provide a class.

Such classes—whether they go by the name of New Member Class, New Convert Class, Prebaptismal Class, or Membership 101—are

---

as members, are goals all churches should embrace. The means used to pursue such goals may vary. Jonathan Leeman examines how these kinds of principles work in churches in four different international contexts in *The Church and the Surprising Offense of God's Love*, 275–92.

[32] Some of these suggestions are developed more fully in Hammett, *Biblical Foundations for Baptist Churches*, 114–26.

[33] In view of the legal challenges raised against the practice of church discipline by some, it seems wise and prudent for the church to have a clear statement in which members agree to come under the discipline of the church as a condition of membership.

[34] See three examples in Hammett, *Biblical Foundations for Baptist Churches*, 127–29, and dozens of additional examples in Charles Deweese, *Baptist Church Covenants* (Nashville: Broadman, 1990).

becoming common in evangelical churches today and with good reason. They allow a church to examine prospective members to see if they meet the requirements for baptism. For those who advocate believer's baptism, the most important requirement for baptism is a credible profession of faith.

This can be difficult to discern, especially in young children. The class should help with that. It should equip parents to discuss the meaning of conversion and baptism with their children and also provide opportunities for church leaders to interact with the children, ask them questions to check their understanding of conversion, and look for credible evidence to support their professions of faith. Only then can a decision be made on whether to recommend baptism for a child.

How old must a child be to make a credible profession of faith? The Bible gives no explicit help. Historically, Baptists treated believer's baptism as normally belonging to adults, and rarely did they baptize children. That remains the case among Baptists in many countries, but in the United States the acceptable age for baptism of children has gone steadily down. Today suggestions of a minimum age for baptism among Baptists range from seven, to nine, eleven, twelve, and even eighteen— and some suggest no minimum age. I think some evidence points to twelve as a good minimum age,[35] but even that is somewhat arbitrary.

One way to approach the question is to ask at what age a child can begin to live out the commitments of the church covenant. Because affirming the covenant is a requirement for membership, baptism should occur at an age at which one can fulfill the covenantal commitments. Moreover, a genuine, living faith is the primary element that will enable a child to fulfill the covenant requirements, and churches are called and enabled by Christ to assess the credibility of a child's profession. Whatever policies a church adopts for baptism, it should baptize and bring into church membership only believers because only they can live out meaningful membership.

3. Require a New Member Class and Interview of All Prospective Members

Prospective members should be required to take new member classes whether they are coming as new converts requesting baptism or transferring their membership from another church. Separately, a pastor should

---

[35] See Hammett, *Biblical Foundations for Baptist Churches*, 123, for that evidence.

sit down with each prospective member for a conversation about the gospel and the person's testimony.

Sadly, many may be coming from existing churches who are not new creatures in Christ. Again, the first order of business is discerning whether the applicant for membership credibly professes faith in Christ. This can begin in the class through a time for discussing the gospel, where applicants ask and answer questions. It should also occur through a personal interview with a prospective member, in which he is asked if he has come to a saving relationship with Christ. Those who claim a relationship with Christ should be asked to explain what that means, both in terms of the content of the gospel and how they personally have responded to the gospel.

The new member class should also cover the second requirement for church membership, believer's baptism. There should be a time where the prospective member tells whether she has been baptized as a believer and, if so, her understanding of that baptism.[36] If the person has not been baptized, or severely misunderstands baptism's meaning, there needs to be further conversation about baptism as a command of Christ that the church expects its members to obey. If the applicant does show credible evidence of regeneration, she should be baptized as part of the process of church membership.

Third, churches should discuss the covenantal expectations associated with membership. What can members expect from the church, and what does the church ask of them? This involves some explanation of the doctrine and ministries of the church because new members would be expected to support both. It may be helpful to explain other practical aspects of the church's life, history, structures, philosophy, and practices.[37]

4. Publicly Enter into Covenant with One Another

One way people show the importance of covenant commitments like marriage is by celebrating them formally and publicly. While the

---

[36] Most Baptist churches specify believer's baptism by immersion. Because in the language of the New Testament to be baptized is to be immersed, I include the issue of immersion under a proper understanding of the meaning of baptism.

[37] Dever, "The Practical Issues of Church Membership," in Hammett and Merkle, *Those Who Must Give an Account*, 97, calls such things the "nuts and bolts of how your own local church works" and suggests several items that might be helpful for prospective new members to know. A statement of the church's doctrine would be important, especially since many church covenants include a commitment to support the doctrine of the church.

covenant-like commitment of church membership is not as serious as marriage, celebrating it formally and publicly does rightly show its importance. At a time when the largest number of church members gather (the main worship service or a members-only meeting), the prospective new members should be formally presented and introduced to the congregation. By this point they should have gone through the new member class, given evidence that their professions of faith are credible, experienced believer's baptism, and agreed to make the covenant commitment. Those who led the new member class or interviewed them should briefly introduce them, vouch for them, explain that they have completed all the requirements for membership, and recommend them for membership. The congregation should then have the opportunity to ask any questions they may have and then express by common consent whether they admit these applicants to membership. Finally, the covenant commitment should be read aloud and the prospective members asked to say something like "I do." Similarly, the church should signify their acceptance of them as new members by saying "I do" to the reading of the commitment the church makes to new members.

5. Provide Pastoral Oversight and Follow-up

Some churches, especially larger churches, assign new members to a deacon, elder, or pastoral staff member to make sure they are integrated into the life of the church and receive oversight. Others assign mature members as new member sponsors or require involvement in a small group as part of the covenant commitment.

Smaller churches may need less formal arrangements, but there should be some plan to live out the church's commitment to new members, to make sure they do not get overlooked or forgotten. If the church has genuinely made a covenantal commitment to the member, it must be expressed in concrete ways.

6. Practice Redemptive Church Discipline

Since this will be discussed more fully in the next chapter, the only thing to say here is that the accountability of discipline should be part of the commitment spelled out in the church covenant. It is a blessing to both the member and the church. It is designed to warn and reclaim the member who is in danger of wandering away and undermining the credibility of the claim to be a follower of Christ. In cases where a wandering member does not repent, church discipline is a blessing to the church in that it enables the church to protect itself from the spread of evil among members and to prevent the distortion of its witness to the gospel in its community.

This will probably be the most difficult aspect of the membership process to incorporate and the most demanding and painful to implement, but it is essential to maintaining meaningful membership in the long run.

A Final Question

One question seldom openly discussed but often faced by church members and pastors is, when is it proper to leave a church and terminate one's membership?

The most common situation will be when education, vocation, or some other call of God requires a geographical move. A geographical move prevents one from living out the covenant commitment. Therefore it should prompt a person to terminate his or her membership in that church and begin a membership in the new location. A helpful practice for such situations is an exit interview. This allows the leaders of the church to get contact information, encourage the person leaving to find a church of like faith and practice in their new location, and make plans to continue in contact until they transfer their membership to a new church. (Christians might be advised to ensure a healthy church exists in the new location *before* accepting the college offer of admission or job offer.) Until then, such members remain among those for whom the leaders will give an account (Heb 13:17).

In other situations the decision of whether to leave may not be clear-cut. No church is perfect, and people will differ over style of music, priorities in a church budget, or experience difficulties in relationships. This should be expected as part of life among finite and fallen people. For most such situations pastors should encourage members to practice the love that overlooks such minor irritations. The commitment made in church membership is not one that should be easily broken.

Some situations warrant departure. Teaching and preaching that obscure or miss the gospel render a church less than a church and are strong warrants for leaving. Moral failures among leaders that render them unfit to lead and yet go unaddressed are also grounds for departure. An overall toxic spiritual atmosphere can develop in a church that makes it dangerous to one's spiritual health or the health of one's family. Some diagnostic questions are, "Can I in good conscience bring my family and friends here? Will they hear the gospel? Will they be discipled and encouraged to grow in the Lord?" If not, it is difficult to see how one can have a God-honoring ministry among them. It may be time to leave.

Conclusion

My conviction is that recovering and maintaining meaningful, regenerate membership should be a top priority in Baptist churches today. Membership is the centerpiece of Baptist ecclesiology. It serves as part of the rationale for believer's baptism, is the indispensable prerequisite for responsible congregational polity, and is both prerequisite to church discipline and protected by church discipline.

More importantly, meaningful membership produces churches that honor Christ. They are not open to the charge of being full of hypocrites; rather, they are full of imperfect but growing disciples. Christ is not honored by membership rolls bloated with "members" who give no sign of genuine faith yet are trusting that their membership makes them acceptable before God. Churches should love such members enough to confront them, to tell them that their lives give no sign of the presence of Christ and that they are concerned for their eternal welfare. If the church cannot restore such individuals, it further loves them by removing them from membership, in the hopes of removing their source of false hope.

Churches that do this more closely resemble the church as it is one day destined to be—the church that he will one day present to himself "without stain or wrinkle or any other blemish, but holy and blameless" (Eph 5:27).

CHAPTER 10

The Why, How, and When
of Church Discipline

Thomas White

This chapter builds on the last two. Churches cannot maintain meaningful church membership without practicing biblical church discipline, and churches cannot regain biblical church discipline without establishing meaningful church membership. Unless you have meaningful membership, then neither will the offended take the time to walk prayerfully through the steps of redemptive church discipline, nor will an offender tolerate such steps before leaving or suing the church. The congregation likely will fire the pastor if he attempts biblical church discipline before establishing meaningful church membership.

Unfortunately, the concepts of meaningful church membership and biblical church discipline seem as foreign to most people as the rotary dial telephone. R. Albert Mohler Jr. comments, "The absence of church discipline is no longer remarkable—it is generally not even noticed."[1] Because few have restored the practice, perhaps the oft-used quote of J. L. Dagg on church discipline is also the most unobserved: "It has been remarked, that when discipline leaves a church, Christ goes with it."[2] If that statement

---

[1] R. Albert Mohler Jr. "Church Discipline: The Missing Mark," in *Polity: Biblical Arguments on How to Conduct Church Life*, ed. Mark E. Dever (Washington, DC: Center for Church Reform, 2001), 43.

[2] John L. Dagg, *A Treatise on Church Order* (Charleston, SC: The Southern Baptist Publication Society, 1858), 274.

is true, then Jonathan Leeman accurately describes the state of many churches: "An undisciplined church membership is an undiscipled church membership. It will be weak and flabby, foolish and unchaste."[3]

In an effort to encourage readers to embark on the bold mission to reestablish biblical church discipline, this chapter will begin with the most compelling evidence for the practice, which comes from the pages of Scripture itself. After demonstrating the biblical mandate and biblical steps for church discipline, I will describe its decline and offer thoughts on how to restore it. As in the last two chapters, the format here will be a series of questions—the why, how, and when of church discipline, followed by the discussion of how to restore it.

Why Practice Discipline: The Biblical Mandate

Jesus Commands It

The first reason to practice church discipline is that Jesus commands it. The Gospels use the word *ekklesia* ("church") only three times, all of which occur in two verses spoken by Jesus.[4] In both of these passages, he calls his disciples to bind and loose on earth what is bound and loosed in heaven. Among other things he means for them to practice church discipline.

> And I tell you, you are Peter, and on this rock I will build my church, and the gates of hell shall not prevail against it. I will give you the keys of the kingdom of heaven, and whatever you bind on earth shall be bound in heaven, and whatever you loose on earth shall be loosed in heaven. (Matt 16:18–19)
>
> Truly, I say to you, whatever you bind on earth shall be bound in heaven, and whatever you loose on earth shall be loosed in heaven. Again I say to you, if two of you agree on earth about anything they ask, it will be done for them by my Father in heaven. For where two or three are gathered in my name, there am I among them. (Matt 18:18–20)[5]

---

[3] Jonathan Leeman, *The Church and the Surprising Offense of God's Love: Reintroducing the Doctrines of Church Membership and Discipline* (Wheaton: Crossway, 2010), 220.

[4] The word *church* appears once in Matt 16:18 and twice in Matt 18:17.

[5] All Scripture in this chapter unless otherwise noted is from the ESV.

As I read these verses, the binding represents what continues to be held against an offender, and the loosing represents what is forgiven. If an offender refuses to repent after the efforts of the church, then he will be bound; however, if the offender truly repents, then he will be forgiven and loosed.[6] Jesus expects and encourages the binding and loosing of church discipline. As long as that discipline occurs with the proper attitude, steps, and goals, as Scripture outlines, then we can anticipate the same binding and loosing in heaven as in the church. Martin Luther summarized the meaning of the keys well:

> God's people or holy Christians are recognized by the office of the keys exercised publicly. That is, as Christ decrees in Matthew 18[:15–20], if a Christian sins, he should be reproved; if he does not mend his ways, he should be bound in his sin and cast out. If he does mend his ways, he should be absolved. That is the office of the keys.[7]

Discipline Demonstrates Godlike Love

A second reason to practice church discipline is that it demonstrates a Godlike love. After all, God disciplines those he loves.[8] A church

---

6 Debate exists over the meaning of the future perfect participle "shall have been," but that discussion does not affect the point we make here. The future tense leads to discussion of whether the binding and loosing have already occurred in heaven, occurs simultaneously, or will occur in heaven. R. T. France contends it has already been decided in *Matthew: Evangelist and Teacher* (Grand Rapids: Zondervan, 1989), 247–49. See also R. T. France, *Matthew*, New International Commentary on the New Testament (Grand Rapids: Eerdmans, 2007), 694–97. John Nolland believes it is simultaneous in *The Gospel of Matthew: A Commentary on the Greek Text*, New International Greek Testament Commentary (Grand Rapids: Eerdmans, 2005), 680–81. Joe Coker notes the change among Baptists from regarding it as a pronouncement ratified in heaven to regarding it as the preexisting condemnation of the sinner by God. See Joe L. Coker, "'Cast Out from among the Saints': Church Discipline among Anabaptists and English Separatists in Holland, 1590–1620," *Reformation* 11 (2006): 19. Mohler, "Church Discipline: The Missing Mark," in Dever, *Polity: Biblical Arguments on How to Conduct Church Life*, 52, writes, "He is not stating that the church has the power to determine what shall later be decided in heaven. The verb tense indicates that as the church functions on the authority of Scripture, what it determines shall have already been determined in heaven."

7 Martin Luther, "On the Councils of the Church," vol. 41 of *Luther's Works*, ed. Jaroslav Pelikan and Helmut T. Lehmann (Philadelphia: Fortress, 1966), 153.

8 Alexander Strauch, *A Christian Leader's Guide to Leading with Love* (Littleton, CO: Lewis and Roth, 2006), 152, writes, "A critical test of genuine love is whether we are willing to confront and discipline those we care for. Nothing is more difficult than disciplining a brother or sister in Christ who is trapped in sin. It is always agonizing work—messy, complicated, often unsuccessful, emotionally exhaustive, and potentially divisive. This is why most church leaders avoid discipline at all costs. But that is not

who claims to love its members without disciplining them contradicts Scripture and applies a different love than God's.[9] Revelation 3:19 states, "Those whom I love, I reprove and discipline, so be zealous and repent." Additionally, Hebrews 12:6–11 compares God's discipline to the discipline of earthly fathers, concluding that those who do not receive discipline are illegitimate children and not sons.

> "For the Lord disciplines the one he loves, and chastises every son whom he receives." It is for discipline that you have to endure. God is treating you as sons. For what son is there whom his father does not discipline? If you are left without discipline, in which all have participated, then you are illegitimate children and not sons. Besides this, we have had earthly fathers who disciplined us and we respected them. Shall we not much more be subject to the Father of spirits and live? For they disciplined us for a short time as it seemed best to them, but he disciplines us for our good, that we may share his holiness. For the moment all discipline seems painful rather than pleasant, but later it yields the peaceful fruit of righteousness to those who have been trained by it. (Heb 12:6–11)

Fatherly discipline, while painful, works for good.[10] Church discipline will also be painful for all parties while working for good in the life of the offender, as an example to the assembly, and to maintain the church's witness to Jesus Christ. Finally, Proverbs 3:12 states, "For the LORD reproves him whom he loves, as a father the son in whom he delights." Most churches would not claim to understand love better than God or to ignore the commands of Scripture, but our actions speak louder than words. The absence of church discipline demonstrates a lack of biblical love in churches.

Taking the analogy one step further, John Hammett discusses the church as family when he writes, "There are a number of related

---

love. It is a lack of courage and disobedience to the Lord Jesus Christ, who himself laid down instructions for the discipline of an unrepentant believer."

9 Leeman, *The Church and the Surprising Offense of God's Love*, 111, makes a similar argument. He states, "God, after all, 'disciplines the one he loves'; and 'he chastens everyone he accepts as his son' (Heb 12:6). By abstaining from discipline, we claim that we love better than God."

10 J. Carl Laney, *A Guide to Church Discipline* (Minneapolis: Bethany House, 1985), 29, writes, "The word used for discipline, *paideia* (Heb. 12:6), speaks of the upbringing, education and training of a child." He draws a correlation to Ephesians 6 and parents who train their children by acts of discipline and by words of instruction.

expressions, such as references to God as Father (about 250 times in the New Testament), Christians as His Children (20 times), fellow Christians as brothers and sisters (99 times), with a few more occurrences of terms like *adoption*, *Abba*, and *inheritance*, all of which are family terms."[11] Understanding the implications of the church as family and of God as Father refutes a harsh view of discipline. Discipline is not simply resolving conflict through punishment. Proverbs, for example, asserts that a father who loves his child demonstrates diligence in discipline.[12] A loving father rebukes for the purpose of shepherding the child's heart toward God and away from evil. Every step of biblical church discipline should display the same desire for growth and restoration. If Christians viewed the church as a family, "the offenses that call for church discipline would be seen not just as offense against God's law but as betrayals of family loyalty. Second, the manner in which church discipline is exercised could never be coldly objective or merely legal."[13]

Scripture Requires Us to Separate from Sin

Third, many passages throughout the New Testament require separating from brothers who blatantly and unrepentantly sin. This dividing constitutes one form of church discipline. The verses typically mentioned are Matthew 18:15–20; 1 Corinthians 5:1–13; and Galatians 6:1–4, which we will discuss later. Here are several other passages:

> I appeal to you, brothers, to watch out for those who cause divisions and create obstacles contrary to the doctrine that you have been taught; avoid them. For such persons do not serve our Lord Christ, but their own appetites, and by smooth talk and flattery they deceive the hearts of the naive. (Rom 16:17–18)
>
> Now we command you, brothers, in the name of our Lord Jesus Christ, that you keep away from any brother who is

---

[11] John Hammett, "Membership, Discipline, and the Nature of the Church," in *Those Who Must Give an Account: A Study of Church Membership and Church Discipline*, ed. John S. Hammett and Benjamin L. Merkle (Nashville: B&H Academic, 2012), 25. J. Carl Laney also makes the connection to the family relationship in *A Guide to Church Discipline*, 30–31.

[12] See for example, Prov 13:24, "Whoever spares the rod hates his son, but he who loves him is diligent to discipline him"; Prov 29:15, "The rod and reproof give wisdom, but a child left to himself brings shame to his mother"; Prov 23:13–14, "Do not withhold discipline from a child; if you strike him with a rod, he will not die. If you strike him with the rod, you will save his soul from Sheol"; and Prov 22:15, "Folly is bound up in the heart of a child, but the rod of discipline drives it far from him."

[13] Hammett, "Membership, Discipline, and the Nature of the Church," in Hammett and Merkle, *Those Who Must Give an Account*, 27.

walking in idleness and not in accord with the tradition that you received from us. . . .

If anyone does not obey what we say in this letter, take note of that person, and have nothing to do with him, that he may be ashamed. Do not regard him as an enemy, but warn him as a brother. (2 Thess 3:6; 14–15)

But understand this, that in the last days there will come times of difficulty. For people will be lovers of self, lovers of money, proud, arrogant, abusive, disobedient to their parents, ungrateful, unholy, heartless, unappeasable, slanderous, without self-control, brutal, not loving good, treacherous, reckless, swollen with conceit, lovers of pleasure rather than lovers of God, having the appearance of godliness, but denying its power. Avoid such people. (2 Tim 3:1–5)[14]

These passages require congregations to separate from those who call themselves brothers yet do not obey the Scriptures. This separation constitutes church discipline and is intended to produce shame that leads to repentance and ultimately restoration. Yet these verses sometimes are overlooked when considering the necessity of church discipline.

Pragmatic Arguments

Finally, pragmatic arguments supplement the biblical case already presented. For example, some have argued for the necessity of church discipline to protect the Lord's Supper.[15] Over a century ago Edward T. Hiscox noted that discipline helps preserve the reputation of the church: "When these regulations fall into disuse, and the good order of the body is neglected, it becomes weak and inefficient, neither commanding the confidence of its own members, nor the respect of the world."[16]

On a more popular level, Charles Finney used an analogy to emphasize that discipline shows concern for others: "If you see your neighbor

---

[14] Other verses could be listed in this section, such as Luke 17:3–4; Gal 1:6–9; 2:11–14; 5:7–12; 1 Tim. 5:19–20; and James 5:19.

[15] J. R. Graves wrote at least three books on the Lord's Supper and made the link between closed Communion and church discipline. His most detailed work is *Intercommunion: Inconsistent, Unscriptural, and Productive of Evil* (Memphis: Baptist Book House, 1881). His other works include *The Lord's Supper: A Church Ordinance, and So Observed by the Apostolic Churches* (Texarkana, TX: Baptist Sunday School Committee, 1881) and *What Is It to Eat and Drink Unworthily?* (Texarkana, TX: Baptist Sunday School Board, 1881).

[16] Edward T. Hiscox, *The New Directory for Baptist Churches* (Philadelphia: Judson Press, 1894), 161.

sin, and you pass by and neglect to reprove him, it is just as cruel as if you should see his house on fire, and pass by and not warn him of it."[17] While such pragmatic or popular arguments are not the basis for church discipline, they do highlight the wisdom and benefits of biblical church discipline.

How to Practice Discipline

How does a church biblically exercise church discipline? This discussion will distinguish between formative and corrective discipline and includes the different steps in disciplining for personal or private sin as opposed to public or general sin. Throughout the discussion the desire to bring about repentance and to do good to one another is at the forefront. Different sins may require different styles of confrontation. First Thessalonians 5:14–15 tells us to seek good for one another by admonishing, encouraging, helping, and being patient.[18]

Formative Church Discipline

Church discipline breaks down into two categories—formative and corrective.[19] Formative discipline means forming spiritually mature believers through teaching and training. It is an effort to fulfill the final mandate of the Great Commission in Matthew 28:20, "teaching them to observe all that I have commanded you."[20] Every church engages in formative discipline to one degree or another. Leeman states it this way: "Just as education involves both formation and correction, so church discipline involves both formation and corrections. Teachers teach and teachers correct. That's how students grow."[21] A steady practice of formative discipline will produce healthier followers of Christ.

---

[17] Charles Finney, *Lectures to Professing Christians* (New York: Fleming H. Revell Co., 1878), 61. The sermon was titled, "Reproof, a Christian Duty."

[18] "And we urge you, brothers, admonish the idle, encourage the fainthearted, help the weak, be patient with them all. See that no one repays anyone evil for evil, but always seek to do good to one another and to everyone."

[19] Formative discipline has also been called "positive" discipline. See Mark Dever, *Nine Marks of a Healthy Church* (Wheaton: Crossway, 2004), 169.

[20] James P. Boyce, "Church Discipline—Its Importance," *Baptist Courier*, February 18, 1852, 2, cited in Gregory A. Wills, "Southern Baptists and Church Discipline: Development and Decline" in *Restoring Integrity in Baptist Churches*, eds. Thomas White, Jason G. Duesing, and Malcolm B. Yarnell III (Grand Rapids: Kregel, 2008), 186. Boyce "argued additionally that unless the church exercised church discipline, it could not fulfill the Great Commission."

[21] Leeman, *The Church and the Surprising Offense of God's Love*, 220.

The New Testament expects that formative discipline will occur. Ephesians 2:21–22 notes the growth of the church and the individual members together, "into a holy temple in the Lord. In [Christ] you also are being built together into a dwelling place for God by the Spirit." Furthermore, the officers of the church possess the responsibility to equip the saints through formative discipline.

> And he gave the apostles, the prophets, the evangelists, the shepherds and teachers, to equip the saints for the work of ministry, for building up the body of Christ, until we all attain to the unity of the faith and of the knowledge of the Son of God, to mature manhood, to the measure of the stature of the fullness of Christ. (Eph 4:11–13)

James 3:2 reminds us that "we all stumble in many ways." So formative discipline should occur in personal conversations and the preached Word. We see an example of the former in Acts 18:26: "When Priscilla and Aquila heard him [Apollos], they took him aside and explained to him the way of God more accurately."

The church that does not intentionally engage in formative discipline will find itself without mature believers (Heb 5:12–14). Formative discipline is the positive training that mitigates the need for corrective discipline. Mark Dever compares formative discipline to "the stake that helps the tree grow in the right direction, the braces on the teeth, the extra set of wheels on the bicycle. It is the repeated comments on keeping your mouth closed when you're eating, or the regular exhortations to be careful about your words. It is the things that are simply shaping the person as he or she grows emotionally, physically, mentally, and spiritually."[22] The work of formative discipline consists of training in righteousness, as noted in 2 Timothy 3:16–17.[23]

Corrective Church Discipline

On the other hand, corrective church discipline occurs when an individual or church confronts a brother or sister for a violation of a law of Christ. It may end quickly in repentance or may result ultimately in excommunication. For this chapter we will use Leeman's definition of *corrective church discipline*:

---

[22] Dever, *Nine Marks of a Healthy Church*, 169.

[23] "All Scripture is breathed out by God and profitable for teaching, for reproof, for correction, and for training in righteousness, that the man of God may be complete, equipped for every good work."

To define it more specifically, corrective church discipline occurs any time sin is corrected within the church body, and it occurs most fully when the church body announces that the covenant between church and member is already broken because the member has proven to be unsubmissive in his or her discipleship to Christ. By this token, the church withdraws its affirmation of the individual's faith, announces that it will cease giving oversight, and releases the individual back into the world.[24]

In a perfect world, corrective discipline would be unnecessary because believers would be sufficiently sensitive to the Holy Spirit's conviction. They would respond as advised in passages like Matthew 5:23–24: "So if you are offering your gift at the altar and there remember that your brother has something against you, leave your gift there before the altar and go. First be reconciled to your brother, and then come and offer your gift." They would heed Paul's exhortation to test ourselves in 2 Corinthians 13:5: "Examine yourselves, to see whether you are in the faith. Test yourselves."

Unfortunately, believers sometimes succumb to the deceptive power of sin and reject the conviction of the Holy Spirit. In some cases people may not know that they have offended a brother. In other cases they refuse to seek reconciliation, which is when the process for corrective church discipline begins.

Cases of corrective church discipline typically occur in two categories, personal and general. Historically the divisions "private" and "public" have also been used. These categories inevitably overlap. A sin against a person may be private or public, and a sin against the church in general may also be done in private or in public.[25] For this reason I will use the categories of "personal" to refer to sin that primarily affects one person and "general" to indicate sin that primarily affects the church body.

---

[24] Leeman, *The Church and the Surprising Offense of God's Love*, 220. Italics removed for ease of reading.

[25] Hiscox, *The New Directory for Baptist Churches*, 171–72 writes, "Offenses are usually considered as of *two* kinds, *private* and *public*; or *personal* and *general*. These terms do not very accurately define the distinction, or indicate the nature of the offenses themselves. Nor are these classes of evils very clearly defined, since they often run into each other." J. M. Pendleton, *Baptist Church Manual* (Nashville: Broadman, 1966), 125, makes a similar statement: "By a *private* is meant a personal offence, but a *personal* offence may be publicly committed. Hence the word *private* is inadequate to express the full idea intended to be conveyed. A *public* offence as distinguished from a private one is an offence committed in public; but as distinguished from a *personal* offence it is committed against a church in its collective capacity. It may be committed too, in secret, or in comparative secrecy."

Equally important to the steps of discipline is the attitude and goal of discipline. Previous generations' abuse of church discipline led some to abandon the practice altogether. In an attempt to keep the pendulum from swinging too far back in the opposite direction, we will point out the proper goal and attitude that must remain at every step of corrective discipline.

The Goal and Attitude of Corrective Church Discipline

Corrective church discipline should seek restoration of the offender in a spirit of gentleness. Perhaps Galatians 6:1–2 best presents this goal: "Brothers, if anyone is caught in any transgression, you who are spiritual should restore him in a spirit of gentleness. Keep watch on yourself, lest you too be tempted. Bear one another's burdens, and so fulfill the law of Christ." Those administering discipline should be gentle and bear the burdens of the offender as they seek to restore him. This principle can also be seen in part of Matthew 18:15, "If he listens to you, you have gained your brother." The goal through every step should be the restoration and regaining of the offender.

The faithful practice of restorative church discipline carries the promise of covering a multitude of sins. James 5:19–20 states, "My brothers, if anyone among you wanders from the truth and someone brings him back, let him know that whoever brings back a sinner from his wandering will save his soul from death and will cover a multitude of sins." The idea of bringing back the erring member provides a good description of what redemptive church discipline should look like.[26] The path may at times be steep, treacherous, and long, but the rewards of restoring a sinner and regaining a brother make the journey worthwhile.

Consequently, we must remember that the desire to punish or inflict vengeance has no place in church discipline, no matter how great the wrongdoing. Romans 12:19 states, "Beloved, never avenge yourselves, but leave it to the wrath of God, for it is written, 'Vengeance is mine, I will repay, says the Lord.'" Instead we must constantly display the attitude of forgiveness noted in Luke 17:3–4: "Pay attention to yourselves! If your brother sins, rebuke him, and if he repents, forgive him, and if he sins against you

---

[26] Gerhard Kittel and Friedrich Gerhard, eds., "epistrepho," Theological Dictionary of the New Testament, Volume VII, trans. W. Bromiley (Grand Rapids: Eerdmans 1971), 727, says, "The verb is employed transitively in the direction to the community in Jm. 5:19 f. This refers to the bringing back of the erring member by the Christian brother. He who accomplishes this restoration has saved a soul from spiritual death and by his act made good his own sins (or those of the other?)."

seven times in the day, and turns to you seven times, saying, 'I repent,' you must forgive him." The parable of the unforgiving servant demonstrates that our motivation for this forgiveness stems from how much God has forgiven us (Matt 18:21–35). And we must remember the stern warning of Jesus in Matthew 18:35: "So also my heavenly Father will do to every one of you, if you do not forgive your brother from your heart."[27]

Corrective Church Discipline: Personal Offense

A personal offense is a wrong committed against an individual that, if repented of and forgiven, leaves the fellowship of the church unharmed. It is possible that the offender in such an instance does not even realize that they have offended the other person. As Jay Adams writes, "Anything that creates an unreconciled state between us and another must be brought up and dealt with."[28] Matthew 18:15–20[29] provides four steps for dealing with a personal offense.[30]

---

[27] J. Knox Chamblin, *Matthew*, Baker Commentary on the Bible, Walter A. Elwell, ed. (Grand Rapids: Baker, 2000), 745, writes: "Failure to forgive fellow believers (none of whose debts to each other could compare with those incalculable debts that God has canceled) shows that one has never really understood God's forgiveness. The judgment threatening such a person is just as real and final (v. 34) as that which threatens the offender (cf. vv. 14–20)—strong incentive for offering genuine, not just apparent, forgiveness (v. 35b)."

[28] Jay Edward Adams, *Handbook of Church Discipline* (Grand Rapids: Ministry Resources Library, 1986), 55.

[29] In his dissertation Jeremy Kimble does a good job of discussing a textual variant, "'That His Spirit May Be Saved': Church Discipline as a Means to Repentance and Perseverance" (PhD diss., Southeastern Baptist Theological Seminary, 2013), 54, n85: "One should take note of the textual variant in this verse, where the shorter reading simply says 'sins' (ἁμαρτήσῃ), while the longer reading adds 'against you' (ἁμαρτήσῃ εἰς σὲ)." Turner observes that the shorter reading is supported by ℵ, B, and 579, while the longer reading garners support from D, L, Δ, Θ, 078, Byzantine, and most Latin MSS. He continues, "A complicating factor is that the phrase in question, *eis se*, sounds much like the verb ending *–ēsē*, which could lead to accidental omission if the text was being dictated to the copyist by a reader." When one takes this into consideration, along with the context of the passage and Peter's use of the phrase "against you" in 18:21, it appears that the longer reading is plausibly authentic (David L. Turner, *Matthew*, Baker Exegetical Commentary on the New Testament [Grand Rapids: Baker, 2008], 444, 447; cf. W. D. Davies and D. C. Allison, *Commentary on Matthew 8–18*, International Critical Commentary [New York: T&T Clark, 1991, 2004], 782). Ultimately, according to White and Blue, "Although the phrase is missing in some early manuscripts, the fact is unimportant. Other passages urge us to go whether the sin is directed against us or not." John White and Ken Blue, *Church Discipline That Heals: Putting Costly Love into Action* (Downers Grove: IVP, 1992), 88.

[30] Gregory A. Wills states it this way: "For offenses of a 'personal' nature and for less serious offenses generally, church members ought to follow the 'gospel steps' delineated in Matthew 18. For 'public' offenses and for grave offenses generally, church members

The first step in addressing a personal offense is for the offended brother to tell the offense to the offending brother, "and him alone," in hope of prompting his repentance. Carson writes,

> The proper thing is to confront the brother privately and "show him his fault." The verb *elenchō* probably suggests "convict" the brother, not by passing judgment, but by convicting him of his sin. The aim is not to score points over him but to win him over (same verb as in 1 Cor 9:19–22; 1 Pet 3:1) because all discipline, even this private kind, must begin with redemptive purposes (cf. Luke 17:3–4; 2 Thess 3:14–15; James 5:19–20; cf. Ecclus 19:13–17).[31]

If the brother repents, the offended party must forgive him.

There are occasions when more individuals might be involved from the beginning of the discipline process, as when a woman feels inappropriate attention from a married man. But in general the first step of personal corrective church discipline should remain confidential until it has failed. Telling others about offenses creates division among even close friends (Prov 17:9).[32] The offended party should not share a "prayer request," post on social media, or inform others before going directly to the offender. A young believer might need pastoral counsel for complex situations, but even then one might present the story if at all possible without using names. The offended party should also go as quickly as possible lest a root of bitterness or the exaggeration of the imagination create further division.

This first step might involve repeated attempts, or it might take only one. It depends on the nature of the sin. Either way, once it is clear that this first step has failed and that reconciliation will not occur, a person should move to the second step by taking one or two others with him.

generally brought the matter directly to the church, as Paul commanded the Corinthian church to do in 1 Corinthians 5." See Gregory A. Wills, "Southern Baptists and Church Discipline," in White, Duesing, and Yarnell, *Restoring Integrity in Baptist Churches*, 182.

[31] D. A. Carson, *Matthew*, Expositor"s Bible Commentary, ed. Tremper Longman and Donald Garland, rev. ed. (Grand Rapids: Zondervan, 2006), 402. Chamblin concurs in, *Matthew*, 744. See also Pendleton, *Baptist Church Manual*, 126, "The object of the offended brother must be to *gain* the offender. If this is not his purpose, he violates the *spirit* of Christ's law though he may obey it in the *letter*. He must earnestly hope and pray, that he may be so successful in this first step as not to find it necessary to take the second."

[32] "Whoever covers an offense seeks love, but he who repeats a matter separates close friends."

Matthew 18:16 states, "But if he does not listen, take one or two others along with you, that every charge may be established by the evidence of two or three witnesses." Not all believe that the witnesses must have firsthand knowledge of the incident. Greg Allison notes that the word for "witnesses" in Matthew 18:16 is *martures*, whereas the words translated as "eyewitnesses" are *autoptai* in Luke 1:2 and *epoptai* in 2 Peter 1:16.[33] If, however, eyewitnesses exist, then they should accompany the offended party, and in every case the offense must be demonstrable, not one person's word against another. Schreiner states, "Jesus appeals to the Old Testament standard of two witnesses to support the accusations (Deut 19:15)."[34] Whether they have firsthand knowledge or not, witnesses should be impartial and fair. Should the offended brother not prove his case, the witnesses have an obligation to tell him to drop the matter. The point is, wrong must be clearly established before church discipline proceeds to the next step. Individuals and churches should not rush to judgment. These kinds of issues are complicated and require much wisdom, to say nothing of their emotional stress. And people should typically be given the benefit of the doubt. Yet once the offense has been established, the offended believer and the witnesses should plead with the offender to repent and reconcile. The witnesses should be trustworthy individuals so that, if the second step fails to secure repentance, they may establish before the church what has taken place (notice Gal 6:1's reference to the "spiritual" being involved).

Only after the first two steps fail should the matter be told to the church. Matthew 18:17 states, "If he refuses to listen to them, tell it to the church." Wisdom suggests that one or more pastors be involved in the second step of church discipline, although Scripture does not

---

[33] Greg Allison, *Sojourners and Strangers: The Doctrine of the Church* (Wheaton: Crossway, 2012), 185 n20. R. Stanton Norman agrees when he says, "They will serve as witnesses, not of the initial transgression, but of the failure to repent." See R. Stanton Norman, "The Reestablishment of Proper Church Discipline," in White, Duesing, and Yarnell, *Restoring Integrity in Baptist Churches*, 214. See also Carson who writes, "It is not at first clear whether the function of the witnesses is to support the one who confronts his erring brother by bringing additional testimony about the sin committed (which would require at least three people to have observed the offense) or to provide witnesses to the confrontation if the case were to go before the whole church. The latter is a bit more likely, because Deuteronomy 19:15 deals with judicial condemnation (a step taken only by the entire assembly), not with attempts to convince a brother of his fault." Carson, *Matthew*, 402–3.

[34] Thomas R. Schreiner, "The Biblical Basis for Church Discipline" in Hammett and Merkle, *Those Who Must Give an Account*, 108. Kimble agrees in "'That His Spirit May Be Saved'; Church Discipline as a Means to Repentance and Perseverance," 55.

demand it.[35] The parties involved should definitely notify a pastor before bringing the matter before the church. After all, other texts show us that pastors have "oversight" over the whole church. The pastor should make sure that the first two steps have occurred appropriately before bringing it to the assembly. Again, the purpose of the third step remains restoration. The accused party should have the opportunity to present his side before the church should he desire it. Because the New Testament does not specify whether this should be done at a business meeting, at the Lord's Supper, or at any normal gathering of the church, we must not be dogmatic on when discipline is made public. But prudence does suggest trying to keep it among members only for the sake of keeping the matter in house, at least until a final decision is made.

Typically some time will pass before the church moves to the fourth step, whether a week or a couple of months. If the first three steps of corrective church discipline fail, then exclusion from membership and the Lord's Table occurs. The second half of Matthew 18:17 states, "And if he refuses to listen even to the church, let him be to you as a Gentile and a tax collector." William B. Johnson said this concerning exclusion: "The exclusion of a delinquent by the church should be regarded by both as a solemn and awful measure, having for its object the recovery of the former from his error, and the firmer establishment of the latter in the ways of righteousness."[36] Even the offended brother who has won his case should not rejoice but should experience the suffering referenced in 1 Corinthians 12:26: "If one member suffers, all suffer together." The entire congregation should be heartbroken over the exclusion and should ask God to bring repentance and restoration.

Exclusion has been formally called "excommunication," which means to withdraw or withhold communion. The word is "derived from the Latin *ex* ('out') and *communicare* ('share, communicate'). This refers to cutting off a person from church membership, fellowship and communion."[37] In 1 Corinthians 5:11 Paul instructed the church not to associate or eat with the unrepentant offender, which includes the Lord's Supper:

---

35 Kimble "'That His Spirit May Be Saved'; Church Discipline as a Means to Repentance and Perseverance," 55, writes, "However, it seems wise to involve one or two people who have at least some kind of knowledge of the sin that has been committed, and that at least one of these witnesses be a church leader (i.e. elder), though this is not dictated by the text itself."

36 William Bullein Johnson, *The Gospel Developed Through the Government and Order of the Churches of Jesus Christ* (Richmond, VA: H. K. Ellyson, 1846), in Dever, *Polity: Biblical Arguments on How to Conduct Church Life*, 222.

37 J. Carl Laney, "The Biblical Practice of Church Discipline," *Bibliotheca Sacra* (October-December 1986): 362.

"But now I am writing to you not to associate with anyone who bears the name of brother if he is guilty of sexual immorality or greed, or is an idolater, reviler, drunkard, or swindler—not even to eat with such a one."

Much confusion exists over exactly how to treat an excluded member. Some Anabaptists went too far, advocating the shunning of family members and employers who were under discipline.[38] They did so in an effort to "shame" the offender into repentance. However, in the end they treated them worse than an unbeliever. Jesus associated with Gentiles and tax collectors for the purpose of reaching them with the gospel. So even those excommunicated should be welcomed to services to hear the Word preached, and church members should make an effort to reconcile them to Christ. We must be careful not to "demand more for restoration than for baptism, to make the conditions for restoration more rigorous than for joining the body of Christ originally."[39] We must both withdraw fellowship from the person and exhort them to repent. Andrew Fuller notes the harm done if church members' relationships to the individual do not change after the individual is excommunicated:

> If individual members act contrary to this rule, and carry it freely toward an offender, as if nothing had taken place, it will render the censure of the church of none effect. Those persons also who behave in this manner will be considered by the party as his friends, and others who stand aloof as his enemies, or at least as being unreasonably severe; which will work confusion, and render void the best and most wholesome discipline. We must act in concert, or we may as well do nothing. Members who violate this rule are partakers of other men's sins, and deserve the rebukes of the church for counteracting its measures.[40]

---

[38] Joe L. Coker, "'Cast Out from Among the Saints': Church Discipline Among Anabaptists and English Separatists in Holland, 1590–1620," *Reformation* 11 (2006): 9, states, "They also taught that shunning applied to every person in all dealings with an expelled individual. This included spouses, children, and workers, who had to suspend all interaction with a spouse, parent or employer who was excommunicated." See also Menno Simons, "On the Ban: Questions and Answers" in *Spiritual and Anabaptist Writers*, ed. George H. Williams and Angel M. Mergal (Louisville: WJK, 1957): 261–71. There is even discussion of whether conjugal rights should be forbidden—this type of shunning takes discipline beyond healthy measures (Matt 19:9). See Coker, "'Cast Out from Among the Saints,'" 20.

[39] Marlin Jeschke, *Discipling in the Church: Recovering a Ministry of the Gospel*, 3rd ed. (Scottdale, PA: Herald, 1988), 101. See also Kimble, "'That His Spirit May Be Saved'; Church Discipline as a Means to Repentance and Perseverance," 179–81.

[40] Andrew Fuller, *Andrew Fuller Works*, vol. 3, 334–35 as in Pendleton, *Baptist Church Manual*, 142–43. Pendleton writes, "Social intercourse with the excluded is not to be entirely suspended; for then many opportunities of doing them good will be lost; neither

Second Thessalonians 3:14–15 provides some additional guidance by stating, "If anyone does not obey what we say in this letter, take note of that person, and have nothing to do with him, that he may be ashamed. Do not regard him as an enemy, but warn him as a brother." Biblical scholar Carl Laney argues that the Greek word *entrepo* translated as "ashamed or put to shame" (v. 14) is "derived from the word *trepo*, meaning 'to turn or direct someone or something.' With the preposition *en* ('in'), *entrepo* means 'to turn about' or 'to turn in,'" emphasizing the goal of repentance.[41] Paul used a similar idea in 1 Corinthians 5:11 (HCSB) when he said, "Do not even eat" with a professing believer who refuses to repent of sin.[42] The relationship must change, but we must also warn him as a brother. Summarily, Scripture suggests that casual friendships with excluded members should cease yet intentional efforts at reconciliation continue.[43]

Corrective Church Discipline: General Offense

Sometimes an offense affects the entire church collectively. Even if that offense occurs against one member in particular, the effects may be felt by all members, as the case is in 1 Corinthians 5:1–13. In verse 1, Paul stated that a member of the Corinthian church was committing sexual immorality with his father's wife. Paul likely would have said "mother" if it was the offender's mother, so we assume that the inappropriate relationship occurred with a stepmother. "In either case what had been forbidden by all the ancients, both Jewish and pagans, is the cohabiting of father and son with the same woman."[44] The offense in this case was

---

is it to be just as before the exclusion; for that would impair the efficacy of discipline," 141–42.

[41] Laney, *A Guide to Church Discipline*, 80. See also Simon J. Kistemaker, "'Deliver This Man to Satan' (1 Cor 5:5): A Case Study in Church Discipline," *The Master's Seminary Journal* (Spring 1992): 42, who provides two biblical examples where letting a sinner go resulted in restoration: Gomer in Hosea 2:7 ("I will go back to my husband as at first, for then I was better off than now") and the prodigal son who repented and returned home (Luke 15:24, 32).

[42] Andrew M. Davis, "The Practical Issues of Church Discipline," in Hammett and Merkle, *Those Who Must Give an Account*, 177.

[43] Jonathan Leeman, *Church Membership: How the World Knows Who Represents Jesus* (Wheaton: Crossway, 2012), 115, puts it this way: "The basic counsel the elders of my own church give is that the general tenor of one's relationship with the disciplined individual should markedly change. Interactions should not be characterized by casualness but by deliberate conversations about repentance. Certainly family members should continue to fulfill family obligations (see Eph. 6:1-3; 1 Tim. 5:8; 1 Pet. 3:1–2)."

[44] Gordon D. Fee, *The First Epistle to the Corinthians*, New International Commentary on the New Testament (Grand Rapids: Eerdmans, 1987), 200.

not only against a single person. It affected the witness and integrity of the entire Corinthian congregation, in part because they knew about the sin but failed to address it. With such a gross offense, the steps of going privately to the offender and of taking one or two witnesses were not mentioned because everyone already knew and because the man was characteristically unrepentant. The gross public nature of the sin demanded swift and public response to protect the honor of God and the witness of the church. Benjamin Keach states that "*Paul* takes no notice in this case of the *Incestuous* Person of his immediate Repentance; or if he repent not, &c. But says he, *deliver such a one to Satan.*"[45]

Paul wasted no words, immediately stating in verse 2, "And you are arrogant! Ought you not rather to mourn? Let him who has done this be removed from among you." Much like Matthew 18, Paul instructed the action to be taken "when you are assembled" (v. 4). Although Paul bypassed steps one to three and expelled the man immediately based on the public and unrepentant nature of his actions, that does not mean all public sins require bypassing the steps of Matthew 18.[46]

What cannot be overlooked, though, is the concern demonstrated in verse 5 where Paul said, "So that his spirit may be saved in the day of the Lord." Some commentators believe that in 2 Corinthians 2:5–11 Paul requested this same repentant offender be allowed back into the fellowship of the church.[47] Laney states, "Until recently, it was practically the universal conclusion of the church that the incident of incest in 1 Corinthians 5 provides the background for Paul's words in 2 Cor 2:5–11."[48] Paul wrote in verses 6–8, "For such a one, this punishment by the majority is enough, so you should rather turn to forgive and comfort him, or he may be overwhelmed by excessive sorrow. So I beg you to reaffirm your love for him." Despite the fact that not all commentators

---

45 Benjamin Keach, *The Glory of a True Church, and Its Discipline Display'd* (London: John Robinson, 1697), in Dever, *Polity: Biblical Arguments on How to Conduct Church Life*, 75. Pendleton agrees when he writes: "Offences of an infamous or scandalous character must have a peculiar treatment. The church must express its reprobation of them by an immediate act of exclusion. No preliminary steps are necessary. No penitence must prevent the withdrawal of fellowship. The honor of Christ and the purity of his religion are especially involved in these cases" (*Baptist Church Manual*, 140).

46 Leeman, *Church Discipline*, 55–61.

47 For support see, Laney, *A Guide to Church Discipline*, 91–93. Thomas R. Schreiner says, "I slightly favor the notion that the person in view in 2 Corinthians is the same man guilty of incest," "The Biblical Basis for Church Discipline" in Hammett and Merkle, *Those Who Must Give an Account*, 119–21. Greg Allison, *Sojourners and Strangers*, 190, links 1 Corinthians 5 with 2 Corinthians 2 in a major heading.

48 Laney, *A Guide to Church Discipline*, 92.

link 1 Corinthians 5 with 2 Corinthians 2, both instances demonstrate an ultimate concern for the offender to be spiritually helped.[49]

In 1 Corinthians 5:5, Paul commanded the assembly to "deliver this man to Satan for the destruction of the flesh." The phrase "deliver this man to Satan" is similar to 1 Timothy 1:20, where Paul wrote, "Among whom are Hymenaeus and Alexander, whom I have handed over to Satan that they may learn not to blaspheme." Handing over to Satan simply means that they are no longer under the authority of the church but have been turned over to the world of which Satan is ruler (John 12:31). Because Satan is described as "the god of this age" (2 Cor 4:4 HCSB), perhaps turning the person over to Satan will correct any false assumptions of salvation and cause the offender to seek the forgiveness of God, ultimately saving his soul on the day of judgment.[50] Kistemaker writes, "The destruction of the flesh serves the purpose of making possible the restoring of the sinner's soul before he dies."[51]

Paul continued to argue for the necessity of corrective church discipline in this case (and in general) when he asked in verse 6, "Do you not know that a little leaven leavens the whole lump?" Schreiner correctly notes that "Paul draws upon the Old Testament Passover traditions where leaven (or yeast) was to be removed for the feast of Unleavened Bread that immediately followed Passover (Exodus 12:15–20; 13:6–7)."[52] Paul developed the reference to the Passover in verse 7 when he wrote, "Christ, our Passover lamb, has been sacrificed." In Scripture leaven generally represents sin, and Paul told them that even a little sin will permeate the entire congregation. Paul wanted them to "cleanse out the old leaven" (1 Cor 5:7) and to "purge the evil person" (1 Cor 5:13).

---

[49] Some commentators do not think 1 Corinthians 5 and 2 Corinthians 2 are related. D. E. Garland provides a good discussion in *2 Corinthians*, New American Commentary 29 (Nashville: Broadman, 1999), 117–22; and Ralph P. Martin argues the connection is virtually excluded in *2 Corinthians*, Word Biblical Commentary 40 (Waco: Word, 1986), 31–34.

[50] Others take this as a reference to 1 Cor. 11:30, "That is why many of you are weak and ill, and some have died." See Hans Conzelmann, *1 Corinthians: A Commentary on the First Epistle to the Corinthians*, Hermeneia (Philadelphia: Fortress, 1975), 97. Kistemaker, "'Deliver This Man to Satan' (1 Cor 5:5): A Case Study in Church Discipline," 42, states, "This text does not warrant the interpretation that destruction of the flesh results in immediate death because, in a subsequent verse, Paul forbids the Corinthians to have table fellowship with such a man (v. 11)."

[51] Kistemaker, "'Deliver this Man to Satan' (1 Cor 5:5): A Case Study in Church Discipline," 44.

[52] Schreiner, "The Biblical Basis for Church Discipline," in Hammett and Merkle, *Those Who Must Give an Account*, 122.

Lastly, Paul clarified that corrective church discipline applies only to those who call themselves "brothers" and belong to the church: "I am writing to you not to associate with anyone who bears the name of brother" (v. 11). A person should not be allowed to withdraw from membership during the discipline process because the covenant entered upon membership involved two parties, and the dissolution of that membership covenant requires the agreement of both parties. As Benjamin Griffith states, "It is unreasonable also to grant a dismission to such a member, who should demand a dismission in a peremptory manner."[53] If, however, a person renounces the faith entirely, then the church should not continue the discipline process but simply remove them from membership.[54]

The New Testament presents other cases of general corrective church discipline. For instance, Titus 3:9–11 states: "But avoid foolish controversies, genealogies, dissensions, and quarrels about the law, for they are unprofitable and worthless. As for a person who stirs up division, after warning him once and then twice, have nothing more to do with him, knowing that such a person is warped and sinful; he is self-condemned." This general offense of causing division in the church warrants multiple warnings before withdrawal of fellowship.

An extremely unusual case of church discipline may be found in Acts 5. The offense here was lying to God, and God exacted his own discipline by striking down Ananias and his wife Sapphira. An important point to note is the effect on the congregation. Acts 5:11 states, "And great fear came upon the whole church and upon all who heard of these things." Corrective church discipline handled publicly serves as a warning and a deterrent to other members.

Corrective Church Discipline: Leaders

The discipline of church leaders deserves separate consideration. Because of the public nature of their ministry, leaders often experience unfair criticism. For this reason a charge against a leader should not be considered unless it can be clearly proven. Paul stated it this way in 1 Timothy 5:19–20: "Do not admit a charge against an elder except on the evidence of two or three witnesses. As for those who persist in sin, rebuke them in the presence of all, so that the rest may stand in fear." Schreiner writes, "The language of two or three witnesses must not be

---

53 Benjamin Griffith, "A Short Treatise," in Dever, *Polity: Biblical Arguments on How to Conduct Church Life*, 102.

54 Leeman, *The Church and the Surprising Offense of God's Love*, 321.

interpreted literally. Paul means that the evidence to support a charge against an elder must be clear enough to warrant a charge."[55] Once the case is clearly proven, then the confrontation comes into the presence of all. This serves to protect the witness of the church, communicate disapproval of the sinful action to those who have sat under the influence of that leader, and deter the listeners from sin in their own lives.

The New Testament provides little in the way of example of this type of public rebuke, with the possible exception of Paul's rebuke of Peter in Galatians 2:11–14:

> But when Cephas came to Antioch, I opposed him to his face, because he stood condemned. For before certain men came from James, he was eating with the Gentiles; but when they came he drew back and separated himself, fearing the circumcision party. And the rest of the Jews acted hypocritically along with him, so that even Barnabas was led astray by their hypocrisy. But when I saw that their conduct was not in step with the truth of the gospel, I said to Cephas before them all, "If you, though a Jew, live like a Gentile and not like a Jew, how can you force the Gentiles to live like Jews?"

Paul believed Peter's error was inconsistent with the gospel, and this error had even led Barnabas astray. Because of the public nature of the sin, Paul rebuked Peter "before them all."

The moral failures of leaders may require swift, public rebuke. A pastor clearly caught in sexual sin, embezzlement, or other significant moral failures must be confronted publicly. The motivation for a public form of rebuke is to minimize the harm to the testimony of Christ and to maintain the holiness of the church.

When Should Churches Practice Discipline?

A pastor must use wisdom to determine when and how a church should practice discipline. Scripture never provides a complete list of doctrinal or moral offenses that warrant discipline. History also demonstrates that one reason for the decline in corrective church discipline was that churches enforced rules that went beyond the biblical witness. Members

---

[55] Schreiner, "The Biblical Basis for Church Discipline," in Hammett and Merkle, *Those Who Must Give an Account*, 127.

rebelled against such legalism and threw the proverbial baby out with the bathwater.

Sometimes church discipline is warranted for offenses not listed in Scripture such as hacking into a government computer or snorting cocaine. The problem occurs when churches enact discipline for behaviors that are not obviously sins, like dancing. Wisdom must be used in determining what behaviors require discipline.[56]

Scripture does provide a few lists of sins that warrant discipline, although none of these lists is exhaustive. Combining Mark 7:21–23; 1 Corinthians 5:11; 6:9–10; and 2 Timothy 3:1–5 provides the following sins: sexual immorality, adultery, homosexuality, theft, greed, coveting, wickedness, deceit, envy, slander, pride, murder, idolatry, reviling, drunkenness, swindling, divisiveness, arrogance, abusiveness, ungratefulness, and blasphemy. Other sins could be added. The point is not to create a legalistic set of sins but rather to help fellow believers overcome temptation. Leeman includes absenteeism when he writes: "Prolonged and unrepentant nonattendance is grounds for formal church discipline. In line with Matthew 18 and Hebrews 10, someone who refuses to gather with the church should be warned several times and then excluded."[57] On the general question of which sins warrant discipline, Leeman provides a useful rubric: "Formal church discipline should occur with sins that are *outward*, *serious*, and *unrepentant*," and "All three of these factors should be present before a church moves toward excommunication."[58]

Because church discipline rightly practiced aims at repentance and growth, the key element for determining how far one should go is the attitude of the offender. A person genuinely struggling to overcome sin and heartbroken over wrong actions does not warrant discipline unless the sin is so severe that it undermines the credibility of their claim to have faith in Christ. Many members will find themselves at some point coveting the newest gadget, puffed up with pride, struggling with arrogance, or stuck in many other sins. If, when convicted by the Holy Spirit or confronted by a brother, they demonstrate a repentant attitude and

---

[56] Laney discusses this subject in *A Guide to Church Discipline*, 45–47, and he quotes Daniel E. Wray, *Biblical Church Discipline* (Edinburgh: The Banner of Truth Trust, 1978), 8–9, who writes, "The sins which necessitate church discipline can be divided into four major categories: *violations of Christian love, unity, law, and truth*." Schreiner also provides a brief discussion on the sins for discipline. See Thomas R. Schreiner, "The Biblical Basis for Church Discipline," in Hammett and Merkle, *Those Who Must Give an Account*, 123.

[57] Leeman, *The Church and the Surprising Offense of God's Love*, 316.

[58] Jonathan Leeman, *Church Discipline: How the Church Protects the Name of Jesus* (Wheaton: Crossway, 2012), 54.

genuine desire to change, then church discipline should not continue. Someone displaying habitual sinfulness and rebelling against confrontation needs to be disciplined for two reasons. First, such a person may not be saved. Discipline demonstrates love in prompting the offender to consider whether he or she has truly followed Christ. Second, such a person causes harm to the testimony of the church by living a life that looks like the world and is devoid of the fruit of the Spirit. Discipline protects the witness of the assembly.

So when and how should restoration occur? Restoration occurs when a person genuinely repents. Unfortunately, Scripture does not provide step-by-step guidelines on restoration, and we cannot see into someone's heart so leaders must apply godly wisdom to each scenario. Second Corinthians 2:5–8 provides the closest example of restoration in Scripture. In this passage Paul urged the congregation to reaffirm its love to the repentant sinner so sorrow does not become excessive. How quickly this reaffirmation comes may vary in each situation. If a man demonstrates repentance by returning to the wife he left, then restoration may come quickly. Someone struggling with addiction, however, has a more difficult time demonstrating genuine repentance and improved victory over temptation. The elders may choose to wait longer in more difficult scenarios.

Once church leaders believe genuine repentance has occurred, they should restore and celebrate as the Father does with the returning prodigal son (Luke 15:11–32). Such restoration would typically but not necessarily include membership and participation in the Lord's Supper. In some cases the offender may have relocated before requesting forgiveness so the two are not necessarily connected. The celebration should be as public as the discipline, demonstrate genuine forgiveness, and thank God for his grace in this restoration, which is the goal of all discipline (Gal 6:1).[59]

The Decline of Church Discipline and How to Restore It

Church discipline has historically been seen as important to the life and health of local churches.[60] In some settings it has been called the third mark of the church in addition to the gospel and the ordinances.

---

[59] Leeman provides a helpful and practical discussion in *Church Discipline*, 79–86.

[60] Gregory A. Wills discusses discipline in the early church in his chapter "A Historical Analysis of Church Discipline," in Hammett and Merkle, *Those Who Must Give an Account*, 132–39.

In 1561, the Belgic Confession stated, "If the pure doctrine of the gospel is preached therein; if she maintains the pure administration of the sacraments as instituted by Christ; if church discipline is exercised in punishing of sin . . . hereby the true Church may certainly be known, from which no man has a right to separate himself."[61]

Church discipline was a fixture historically in Baptist life. The *Abstract of Principles*, which governs two Southern Baptist seminaries alongside the Baptist Faith and Message, mentions the role of discipline in the local church. Greg Wills, commenting on antebellum Baptists, stated, "A church without discipline would hardly have counted as a church."[62] He notes that "southern Baptists excommunicated nearly 2 percent of their membership every year."[63]

The situation has changed so much that R. Albert Mohler Jr. now calls church discipline "The Missing Mark."[64] Perhaps the abuse of church discipline took its toll on members. Hiscox wrote in 1894, "Our churches do not have too much discipline—indeed, they have too little—but it is often so unwisely administered as to produce more evil by the method than is removed by the act."[65]

Hiscox had a valid point as he lived through the time of one of the messiest cases of church discipline in Baptist history—the Graves-Howell Controversy. The controversy began with a disagreement between J. R. Graves and his pastor R. B. C. Howell over the Southern Baptist Convention Bible Board and the formation of the Southern Baptist Sunday School Union under Landmark control.[66] Howell wrote a harsh letter to the editor of the *Christian Index* paper criticizing the Landmark movement. This sparked a series of attacks on Howell by Graves in the

---

[61] Philip Schaff, ed., "The Belgic Confession," in *The Creeds of Christendom*, rev. David S. Schaff, vol. 3 (New York: Harper and Row, 1931), 419–20.

[62] Gregory A. Wills, *Democratic Religion: Freedom, Authority, and Church Discipline in the Baptist South, 1785–1900* (New York: Oxford University Press, 1997), 12, 33.

[63] Ibid., 22.

[64] R. Albert Mohler Jr., "Church Discipline: The Missing Mark," in Dever, *Polity: Biblical Arguments on How to Conduct Church Life*, 43. George B. Davis, "Whatever Happened to Church Discipline?" *Criswell Theological Review* 1.2 (1987): 346, provides seven reasons for the neglect of church discipline: "(1) a denial of the biblical mandate, (2) the demand for perfection, (3) the wrong interpretation of some passages of scripture, (4) the abuse of church discipline in the past, (5) the appearance of a non-loving spirit, (6) the lack of 'models,' and (7) the difficulty of the task."

[65] Hiscox, *The New Directory for Baptist Churches*, 193.

[66] J. R. Graves, J. M. Pendleton, and A. C. Dayton formed the Landmark triumvirate. Landmarkism denied that Pedobaptist ministers were gospel ministers because their churches were not true churches. The churches were not true churches because they did not exhibit the mark of rightly administering the ordinances—particularly the ordinance of baptism. Landmarkism reached its height during the mid-1800s.

pages of the *Tennessee Baptist* paper.[67] Howell responded by bringing Graves before the church for discipline in a trial that lasted from October 12 to October 18, 1858, and concluded with Graves's exclusion from church membership at the First Baptist Church of Nashville.[68] Graves appealed to the Baptist General Association of Tennessee, claiming that his group now constituted the true First Baptist Church, and won his appeal by a vote of 164 to 27.[69] This controversy continued to be fought in print[70] and came to a public confrontation at the Southern Baptist Convention in 1859, where Howell was elected president but immediately declined to serve in an effort to avoid division.[71] The politicizing of church discipline hindered its proper usage and harmed its perception.

Commenting on the abuse of church discipline, H. E. Dana wrote in 1944:

> The abuse of discipline is reprehensible and destructive, but not more than the abandonment of discipline. Two generations ago the churches were applying discipline in a vindictive and

[67] For a complete study, see Kenneth Vaughn Weatherford, "The Graves-Howell Controversy" (PhD diss., Baylor University, 1991). For a summary, see chap. 11 on "Landmarkism," Albert W. Wardin, *Tennessee Baptists: A Comprehensive History, 1779–1999* (Brentwood: Tennessee Baptist Convention, 1999). For Howell's article and Graves's response, see *Tennessee Baptist*, February 28, 1858. Part of this section is adapted from Thomas White, "James Madison Pendleton and His Contributions to Baptist Ecclesiology" (PhD diss., Southeastern Baptist Theological Seminary, 2005).

[68] The church found Graves guilty and excluded him. However, Graves's followers declared that they were the true First Baptist Church because the disciplinary proceedings had not been handled correctly. In February 1859, Dayton and seven other men, including three deacons, were also excluded for supporting Graves. Before it was over, forty-seven were excluded over this issue. See Wardin, *Tennessee Baptists: A Comprehensive History, 1779–1999*, 187.

[69] Ibid.

[70] Unsigned article, "The Baptist Watchman," *Tennessee Baptist*, February 27, 1858; unsigned article, "The Baptist Church in Murfreesboro to the First Baptist Church in Nashville, Tennessee," *Tennessee Baptist*, October 23, 1858; James Madison Pendleton, "The South Western Baptist," *Tennessee Baptist*, March 20, 1858; "Startling Disclosures," *Tennessee Baptist*, March 27, 1858; and "The Charges Against J. R. Graves," *Tennessee Baptist*, September 18, 1858. For the other viewpoint of the controversy, see R. B. C. Howell et al., *Both Sides* (Nashville: Southwestern Publishing House, 1859).

[71] Jesse C. Fletcher, *The Southern Baptist Convention: A Sesquicentennial History* (Nashville: B&H, 1994), states on p. 65 that it took two ballots before Howell received a majority. After Howell declined to serve, it took four more ballots before Richard Fuller was elected. However, the 1859 *Proceedings of the Southern Baptist Convention* state on p. 13 that Howell won on the first ballot and that Fuller was elected after Howell's resignation. It appears Fletcher has made an error as he cites these same proceedings. For a full discussion of Howell's election, consult James Hilton, "Robert Boyte Crawford Howell's Contribution to Baptist Ecclesiology: Nineteenth Century Baptist Ecclesiology in Controversy" (PhD diss., Southeastern Baptist Theological Seminary, 2005), 201–14.

arbitrary fashion that justly brought it into disrepute; today the pendulum has swung to the other extreme—discipline is almost wholly neglected. It is time for a new generation of pastors to restore this important function of the church to its rightful significance and place in church life.[72]

Marlin Jeschke rightly comments, "The answer to bad church discipline is good church discipline, not no church discipline."[73]

Added to this historic abuse was church discipline's perceived inefficiency in an age of industrialization and streamlining. Gaines S. Dobbins's 1923 book *The Efficient Church* included a section called "The Problem with Discipline" in which he wrote: "Put on a commanding program, refuse to listen to tale-bearers, and difficulties will often disappear."[74] As churches began to focus more on numbers and finances, they found less room for discipline. William L. Bennett wrote: "There is a problem of our success. How can we discipline if our foremost motive is numbers? I contend that we shall never come to grips with discipline until our first concern is to make disciples rather than to amass numbers."[75] His words still ring true. Greg Wills summarizes this historical trajectory well when he writes, "It [church discipline] simply faded away, as if Baptists had grown weary of holding one another accountable."[76] Laney comments: "God snuffed out the candle of the church at Thyatira because of moral compromise (Rev 2:20–24). Churches today are in danger of following this first-century precedent."[77]

Fortunately, the story has not ended. There has been a revival of writing on this topic. Wills serves as the dean of the School of Theology at The Southern Baptist Theological Seminary and is perhaps the foremost

---

[72] H. E. Dana, *A Manual of Ecclesiology*, 2nd ed., rev. L. M. Sipes (Kansas City: Central Seminary Press, 1944), 244.

[73] Marlin Jeschke, *Discipline the Brother* (Scottdale, PA: Herald, 1972), 14.

[74] Gaines S. Dobbins, *The Efficient Church* (Nashville: Sunday School Board of the Southern Baptist Convention, 1923), 194. Dobbin served as the first professor of church efficiency at Southern Baptist Theological Seminary in Louisville, Kentucky.

[75] William L. Bennett, "Discipline in the Church," in *Church Training* (November 1971): 25.

[76] Wills, *Democratic Religion*, 9. Wills writes in "A Historical Analysis of Church Discipline," 153: "The causes were complex. Such factors as urbanization, faith in moral and social progress, civil religion, activism, and the search for church efficiency contributed. Commitment to an expansive individualism grew in response to such trends and undermined the commitment to the authority of the congregation. Pragmatism and pietism bolstered these trends."

[77] J. Carl Laney, "The Biblical Practice of Church Discipline," 354.

scholar on the history of church discipline among Southern Baptists.[78] Southwestern Baptist Theological Seminary held a conference that resulted in a book entitled *Restoring Integrity in Baptist Churches*. Contributors included professors and pastors, with two chapters devoted to church discipline and two chapters on membership.[79] More recently two professors at Southeastern Baptist Theological Seminary edited a book focused on the subject of membership and church discipline.[80] For years Mark Dever, pastor of Capitol Hill Baptist Church in Washington, DC, and founder of 9Marks, has promoted biblical church discipline as a mark of a healthy church.[81] Finally, Jonathan Leeman has recently written both a 375-page book entitled, *The Church and the Surprising Offense of God's Love: Reintroducing the Doctrines of Church Membership and Discipline* as well as a much shorter guide, *Church Discipline: How the Church Protects the Name of Jesus*. These resources, along with dissertations, conferences, sermons, classroom emphasis, and a resurgent focus on the inerrancy and sufficiency of Scripture, have generated greater awareness of this issue.

What happens next is up to you. We need a generation committed to the long and challenging road of restoring meaningful church membership and then carefully implementing redemptive church discipline.[82] Wills writes, "Recovery will not be easy should it ever occur. Powerful trends run counter to all that discipline entails. Our ecclesiology is weak in theory and practice; that is, we cannot find a scriptural ecclesiology so we substitute whatever seems to promote conversion and denominational loyalty. We lack spirituality; we fear man more than God."[83] Wills is right.

---

[78] See Wills, *Democratic Religion*; also Gregory A. Wills, "Southern Baptists and Church Discipline," *Southern Baptist Journal of Theology*, 4:4 (Winter 2000): 4–14; "Southern Baptists and Church Discipline: Development and Decline" in White, Duesing, and Yarnell, *Restoring Integrity in Baptist Churches*; and "A Historical Analysis of Church Discipline," in Hammett and Merkle, *Those Who Must Give an Account*.

[79] White, Duesing, and Yarnell, *Restoring Integrity in Baptist Churches*.

[80] Hammett and Merkle, *Those Who Must Give an Account*.

[81] I can remember Mark Dever coming to speak at Southeastern Seminary while I was a student there in the 1990s. His emphasis on redemptive church discipline has helped the subject gain ground.

[82] Andrew M. Davis has written a helpful chapter on the practical considerations of restoring church discipline. See "The Practical Issues of Church Discipline," in Hammett and Merkle, *Those Who Must Give an Account*, 157–85. See also Norman, "The Reestablishment of Proper Church Discipline," in White, Duesing, and Yarnell, *Restoring Integrity in Baptist Churches*, 199–219.

[83] Wills, "A Historical Analysis of Church Discipline," in Hammett and Merkle, *Those Who Must Give an Account*, 154.

If we want to restore meaningful membership and biblical church discipline, we must determine in our hearts that the reputation of Christ and the genuineness of church members' faith matter more than any difficulty the steps of discipline may bring. We must remember that when we water down our membership, we weaken our testimony and our faithfulness to Christ. No program, no plan, no human creativity will bring glory to God or an awakening to our nations like a movement of the Holy Spirit. "We must keep in mind that corrective church discipline is a small act of judgment on earth that dimly points to God's final judgment in heaven."[84]

Once a pastor makes up his mind that restoring meaningful church membership and discipline is worth the cost, then he should begin teaching and shepherding his congregation in this direction. The process will be slow because it entails cultivating a whole new culture. It can take a while for Christians who have grown up in individualistic church environments to understand their biblical obligations for one another and what it means to live together as a church. A pastor's attempt to lead his church toward discipline simply will not make sense in a congregation where the gospel has been poorly taught, where people are not accustomed to helping one another fight for the holiness of the faith.

That said, there are steps that will help a pastor lead his church toward a meaningful practice of membership and discipline. First, "lay a biblical foundation for church discipline by preaching and teaching on the texts dealing with church discipline and illustrate the teaching with examples of traditional Baptist support for this practice. These actions should spark some discussion of the issue. That discussion should lead to incorporating some official statements about church discipline in key documents such as the bylaws and church covenant."[85] Second, develop a church covenant and bylaws that spell out the steps of church discipline.[86] Third, make sure the new members class or prospective members class

---

84 Leeman, *The Church and the Surprising Offense of God's Love*, 322.

85 John Hammett, *Biblical Foundations for Baptist Churches: A Contemporary Ecclesiology* (Grand Rapids: Kregel, 2005), 125.

86 Laney provides a helpful section on avoiding lawsuits in his work *A Guide to Church Discipline*, 136–39. Norman, "The Reestablishment of Proper Church Discipline," in White, Duesing, and Yarnell, *Restoring Integrity in Baptist Churches*, 212, wisely encourages a careful examination of the legal documents in order to avoid lawsuits. He writes on p. 213, "A critical examination of the bylaws of a church in its statements about church discipline will not only ensure that a congregation acts appropriately and legally when it exercises church discipline, but also will remind the members that church discipline is an essential part of its biblical and ministerial identity. The theology and methodology regarding discipline should be stated clearly in the constitution and other legal documents of the church."

clearly explains that members submit to discipline, follow the biblical steps of discipline, and waive the right to go to court. Fourth, publicly have members enter into the covenant relationship with one another and agree to hold one another accountable with biblical church discipline, without gossip or slander. Fifth, the pastor and leaders must continue to cast the vision, lead the people, teach on biblical church discipline, and follow up to make sure it occurs according to Scripture.

We must begin to establish meaningful membership, and while we work toward that goal, we must lay the groundwork for the practice of biblical church discipline. Without meaningful membership, discipline will do more harm than good. Without the proper execution of discipline, meaningful membership can never be maintained. Without both of these practices, our churches will not properly reflect the glory of God or bear a strong testimony for the gospel. And our members will not take the church seriously. We must do what is difficult and not grow weary because Christ commands us and love compels us. Anything less demonstrates that we do not truly love our brothers and sisters as Christ has loved us.

PART 4

ELDERS AND DEACONS

Andrew Davis
Mark Dever
Benjamin L. Merkle

Despite the tendency to ignore it, biblical leadership is crucial to building a church that glorifies God. The exercise of leadership in the church relates to God's nature and character. When Christians exercise proper authority through the law, around the family table, in our jobs, in the scout troop, in our homes, and especially in the church, we help to display God's image to his creation. This is a Christian and a church's calling and privilege.

While some Presbyterians and Baptists alike view congregationalism and a plurality of elder leadership as being at odds, we do not. We believe they complement each other and that churches should aspire to practicing both. The two leadership offices in the local church are elder and deacon, and the subjects of the following chapters. We should always be careful to maintain a distinction between the ministry of deacons and the ministry of elders. In one sense both elders and deacons are involved in "deaconing," which means serving. Jesus even presented himself as a type of deacon (e.g., Matt 20:28; Mark 10:45; Luke 22:26–27; cf. John 13; Luke 12:37; Rom 15:8). But the "deaconing" of elders and deacons takes on two different forms. One is a service of practical matters; the other is a service of the Word. And churches should neglect neither the Word nor practically caring for one another. Both lead us toward Christ, foster unity, and teach us to love one another.

Our treatment of these two offices begins with a history of elders and deacons. Then we will turn to Scripture's treatment of each, as well as a number of practical applications for the life of the church.

CHAPTER 11

Elders and Deacons in History

Mark Dever

During the time of the apostles, the organization of churches was somewhat fluid. That said, a plurality of elders and a plurality of deacons were constant. The New Testament church universally employed the plural-elder model, as coming chapters will argue.

But that raises the question, how and when did the model change? Few if any Protestants would deny that the immediate postapostolic church changed rapidly and radically. In everything from the rise of infant baptism to the belief in the efficacy of the sacraments and the role of works in salvation, the fledgling churches experienced rapid doctrinal decay in the centuries following the departure of Christ's apostles. It is no surprise, then, that changes occurred in church organization and governance as well. The goal of this chapter is briefly to explore that history, first for the office of deacon and then for the office of elder.

A crucial question, particularly for this volume, is whether elders belong to Baptist history. I will argue that they do, even if many Baptist churches lost sight of this in the twentieth century. Not only that, more and more Baptists are recovering a vision for elders in Baptist life today.

A Brief History of Deacons

Immediately following New Testament times, the separate offices of elder and deacon persisted. Then the church began to distinguish between two types of elders—bishops and priests—while deacons continued to be regarded as those tasked with assisting the bishops or overseers.

In the early church the office of deacon generally seems to have been held for life. The functions of the office, however, varied from place to place. Diaconal duties might include:

- reading or singing Scripture in church;
- receiving the offerings and keeping records of who gave;
- distributing the offerings to the bishops, presbyters, and themselves; to the unmarried women and widows; and to the poor;
- distributing Communion;
- leading prayers during gatherings, and giving a signal for those who were not to take Communion to leave before the ordinance was administered.

This summarizes deacons' work from the second through the sixth centuries. As the monarchical episcopate developed, so did a kind of monarchical diaconate beneath it. As the role of bishop developed, so did the role of archdeacon. The archdeacon was the chief deacon of a particular place and might be described as a deputy concerned with material matters. It is not surprising that the archdeacon in Rome became particularly important. Sad to say, abuses crept in, and deacons—especially archdeacons—became wealthy, an irony in light of the fact that the title of deacon indicated they were to serve others, not their own desires. For a number of reasons, the deacon's influence declined in the Middle Ages. Caring for the poor became a vehicle for contributors to gain credit with God and lessen their time in purgatory.

The Eastern Orthodox church has always kept separate deacons—laymen who served in that capacity. In the West, though, by the late Middle Ages, being a deacon had become a step on the way to being ordained as a priest, that is, an elder. Deacons in the Roman Catholic and the Episcopalian churches are still that—trainee ministers who serve as deacons for one year before becoming full-fledged priests. However, the Second Vatican Council reopened the possibility of a different, permanent, more biblical kind of deacon in the Roman Catholic Church.

Luther recovered the church's responsibility to care physically for its members and especially for the poor ones, though Lutheran churches didn't recover the idea of the New Testament deacon. In the Lutheran churches today, practice varies. In some places deacons are nonordained, but in other places any ordained assistant minister is called a deacon, particularly those with responsibilities for pastoral care and evangelism.

In many of the more evangelical Protestant churches during the Reformation, the biblical practice of having deacons distinct from elders or pastors was recognized. Some Protestants, like Martin Bucer at Cambridge, urged that the duties of deacons should be reestablished. In each church, they said, the deacons should distinguish between the deserving and the undeserving poor, discreetly investigating and quietly caring for the needs of the one and expelling the other from the church. They should also keep written records, as they were able, of funds given by church members.

In the Presbyterian church deacons are those who administer the alms and care for the poor and sick (though we might argue that these functions have largely been taken over by the secular state). The deacons are a separate body from the elders and are responsible to them. This is how many Baptist and Congregational churches were once organized, and some still are organized in this way.

In many Baptist and Congregational churches, however, a number of spiritual functions, typically the domain of elders, have been assigned to the deacons. They assist the pastor in various ways, especially in distributing the elements at the Lord's Supper, and have evolved into a kind of executive and financial board for the church, particularly in congregations that no longer have boards of elders. Deacons often serve actively for limited periods of time, though the recognition of a person as a deacon is generally considered permanent.

A Brief History of Elders

As important as deacons have been in the life of the church, even more fundamental to the church is the ministry of elders. Yet with the close of the New Testament era, the office of elder did not remain the same for long.

The Early Church and the Monarchical Episcopate

The shift from the local elder leadership described in the New Testament to the full-blown episcopacy of the Roman Catholic Church occurred over several centuries. In an early church document called the *Didache*, written in the late first or the early second century, the only church officers are elders and deacons.[1] Yet as early as the second century, Ignatius of Antioch, a pastor, refers to a council of elders called to give counsel

---

[1] *Didache* 15:1: "Appoint, therefore, for yourselves, bishops and deacons worthy of

to a chief pastor, or bishop. Ignatius uses the words *presbyter* (elder) and *bishop* distinctly from each other. This distinction is crucial for understanding the centralization of authority that occurred in the church of the second and third centuries.

During this time leading pastors/elders of churches in the urban centers that experienced early evangelization seem to have become the informal arbiters of orthodoxy. This development took place more slowly in some places than in others. Egypt, for instance, was notably slower in moving beyond its more informal associations and decentralized structures of authority. But generally, competent and noted pastors like Ignatius were gradually recognized not only as the first among equals, as Timothy at Ephesus or James at Jerusalem might have been. Instead, they came to assume a formal office that was distinguishable from local church eldership. And such bishops seem to have accrued authority not only in their own congregations but among congregations in their general area and sometimes even in wider regions, as in the case of the "metropolitan sees" of Jerusalem, Antioch, Alexandria, Rome, and, by the fourth century, Constantinople. These larger metropolitan sees eventually began vying for position against one another until finally the see of Rome became dissatisfied with its own informal authority over the other metropolitan bishops and insisted on its exclusive preeminence. As the bishop of Rome increasingly staked this claim to be the sole arbiter of matters of truth in the faith, the transition from congregational elder leadership to a centralized authority was complete.

It is not difficult to see how, in an era of vigorous church planting, rapid geographical expansion, ever-looming heresy, and celebrated martyrdoms, certain central locations and their noteworthy bishops began to acquire a respect and deference that would be extended to their successors. Cyprian of Carthage, one century after Ignatius, insisted that the recognition of a single bishop in a church was closely linked with the unity of the church in the world through the college of bishops. Jerome, writing in the fourth century, admitted the equivalence of bishop and elder in the New Testament but argued for the historical need to commit oversight to one person. In the struggle to identify orthodoxy amid a sea of heresy, one can understand such centralizing tendencies in order to ensure conformity, even uniformity.[2]

---

the Lord, men meek, and not lovers of money, and truthful and proved; for they also render to you the service of prophets and teachers."

[2] For more on this, see Cyprian's famous *On the Unity of the Catholic Church*. For some of the earliest references, see ed. Henry Bettenson and Chris Maunder, *Documents of the Christian Church*, 3rd ed. (London: Oxford, 1999), 68–90. A classic study of this

Reformation Recoveries

Following this centralization, the bishop of Rome managed to maintain ecclesiological hegemony in the West for the better part of a millennium. This centralized authority was finally questioned at the time of the Protestant Reformation when a number of thinkers and churchmen recovered the conviction that Scripture, rather than the mere antiquity of traditions, is sufficient for determining the doctrines of the church. As the critical gaze of the Reformers began to fall across their churches, they required some word of Scripture—at least some intimation or implication—to justify their doctrines and practices.

For early Anabaptist, Reformed, Congregationalist, and Baptist Christians in the sixteenth and seventeenth centuries, offices in the church entered a state of flux. Even some of the magisterial reformers began to recover the equivalence of bishop and elder. The discovery that no biblical basis existed for an episcopacy not only destabilized the authority of Rome in western Europe; it also threatened the monarchs who had for centuries leaned upon the structures of the church for supplying everything from order to education to income. Thus the Reformers' movements away from episcopal structures were piecemeal at first.

While Martin Luther declined to interfere with the distinct extracongregational role of the bishop, he repeatedly emphasized in his sermons and writings that bishops and elders or pastors were all the same office in Scripture. He denounced the bishop of Rome as a false prophet with whom no bishop should be in communion. He furthermore denied that the pope had unique authority given him through succession from Peter, as the Catholic interpretation of Matthew 16 had long claimed. But for Luther and his successors, as long as the office of bishop or pastor was recognized, other aspects of church organization within and among congregations were understood to be matters appropriately settled by human law, normally at the discretion of the state.

John Calvin, who was less encumbered by interprincely politics than Luther, pushed even harder for Scripture to define the church's polity. Calvin was zealously committed to what has been called the regulative principle, the idea that both a church's polity and everything done during

topic is Hans von Campenhausen, *Ecclesiastical Authority and Spiritual Power in the Church of the First Three Centuries* (Stanford: Stanford University Press, 1969). Though von Campenhausen denies that the New Testament provides a full church structure and would not seem to adhere to a Protestant understanding of the sufficiency of Scripture, the historical aspects of his work are careful and well repay time spent in the reading.

its weekly gatherings should be explicitly or implicitly commanded in Scripture. He also recovered the identity of the bishop and the elder, thus removing a level of authority above and apart from the local church. Calvin called for ministers of the Word, or what the New Testament describes as elders or pastors, in every congregation. But he drew a distinction between "elders" (what Presbyterian churches today call "ruling elders," that is, nonordained elders) and "ministers of the Word and the Sacraments" (what Presbyterians call "teaching elders").

Calvin's careful scholarship of the early patristic period is rehearsed in book IV, chapter 4, of his *Institutes of the Christian Religion:* "In each city," he wrote, "these [elders] chose one of their number whom they specially gave the title 'bishop' in order that dissensions might not arise (as commonly happens) from equality of rank. . . . The ancients themselves admit that this was introduced by human agreement to meet the need of the times."[3] Following this example, the Reformed churches in Geneva, Germany, the Netherlands, and Scotland developed a series of interlocking courts that would settle disputes of doctrine and discipline between congregations and foster the unity of the churches in an area with a reformed magistrate.

Anabaptists' polity was fluid. They were "radically de-centralized," as James Stayer puts it, "most of them making exclusivist claims and condemning the other [groups of Anabaptists]."[4] Various offices, including elder, proliferated among them. In the 1529 *Discipline of the Believers; How a Christian Is to Live*, we find the statement, "The elders [*Vorsteher*] and preachers chosen for the brotherhood shall with zeal look after the needs of the poor, and with zeal in the Lord according to the command of the Lord extend what is needed for the sake of and instead of the brotherhood."[5] A basic pattern of delegated leadership within a congregational pattern emerged.

---

[3] John Calvin, *The Institutes of the Christian Religion*, ed. John T. McNeill, trans. Ford Lewis Battles, in *Library of Christian Classics* (Philadelphia: Westminster Press, 1977, 8th printing), IV.iv.2. Cf. Elsie Anne McKee, "Calvin's Teaching on the Elder Illuminated by Exegetical History," in *John Calvin & the Church: A Prism of Reform*, ed. Timothy George (Louisville: WJK, 1990), 147–55. John Owen, an early champion of congregationalism, defended the separate office of ruling elder. See John Owen, *The Works of John Owen*, vol. 16, ed. William Goold (London: Johnstone and Hunter, 1853), 42.

[4] James Stayer, "Anabaptists," in *Oxford Encyclopedia of the Reformation*, vol. 1, ed. Hans Hillerbrand (New York: Oxford, 1996), 32.

[5] Werner O. Packull, *Hutterite Beginnings* (Baltimore: Johns Hopkins University Press, 1995), 312. Cf. Emir Caner's summary of Anabaptist polity, "Ecclesiology in the Free Churches (1525–1608)," in *Who Rules the Church? Examining Congregational*

In the Reformation period, then, a return to ancient patterns followed on the heels of an affirmation of the sufficiency of Scripture. Protestant churches began to give nonordained members more responsibility, and many churches returned to the congregational election of officers. At the same time Reformed groups and some Anabaptists recovered the idea of a plural eldership. The Church of Scotland, reformed through the preaching of John Knox and others, established the office of elder. In England the Presbyterians, the Congregationalists, and the Baptists also recovered the office from the New Testament. And to the Baptists we now turn.

Baptist Elders in the Past

"It's not Baptist," the lady protested when I advocated adopting elders in Baptist churches. Strictly speaking, she was incorrect, though I understand what she meant: in the churches she had known in the second half of the twentieth century, *she* had never seen or even heard of Baptist elders. But *other* Baptists had.

The word *elder* was frequently used in historic Baptist statements of faith. But was the word simply used synonymously with our modern word *pastor*, or even *senior pastor*? Did Baptists in the past understand that the New Testament recognized a plurality of leaders called "elders" in one local congregation?[6] Let me present a sampling.

Throughout seventeenth-century England, Baptists affirmed the office of elder. In 1697, Benjamin Keach wrote of "Bishops, Overseers, or Elders," clearly implying that these New Testament titles referred to one office.[7] Keach presented it as essential that a church have one or more pastors but not that it have a plurality of them. He rejected the Presbyterian practice of having a separate group of ruling elders who do not teach, saying that if that practice was in the apostolic church, it was only temporary because neither the qualifications nor the duties of the so-called ruling elder are laid out in the New Testament.[8]

Leadership and Church Government, ed. Gerald Cowen (Nashville: B&H, 2003), 117–32.

  6 See Greg Wills's succinct summary of this in his article "The Church: Baptists and Their Churches in the Eighteenth and Nineteenth Centuries," in *Polity*, 2nd ed., ed. Mark Dever (Washington, DC: 9Marks, 2004), 33–34.

  7 Benjamin Keach, *The Glory of a True Church*, in Dever, *Polity*, 65.

  8 Ibid., 68–69. Cf. James Renihan, "The Practical Ecclesiology of the English Particular Baptists, 1675–1705: The Doctrine of the Church in the Second London

In the eighteenth century Benjamin Griffith wrote in favor of distinguishing ruling elders from the pastors or teaching elders.[9] Citing Exodus 18; Deuteronomy 1; Romans 12:8; 1 Corinthians 12:28; and 1 Timothy 5:17 as the basis for his argument, Griffith asserted that the distinction between the two offices is shown by the fact that the ruling elder would have to be ordained to become a teaching elder. The demarcation between ruling and teaching elders was common in the Philadelphia Baptist Association in the eighteenth century, but in this practice Griffith and his contemporaries disagreed with their English counterparts of the previous decades.[10] The Charleston Association's 1774 *Summary of Church Discipline* did not recognize a distinction between the two offices, but it did affirm that ministers of the gospel in the New Testament are "frequently called elders, bishops, pastors and teachers." The *Summary* also implied that there is sometimes within one local congregation a "presbytery," or plurality of elders.[11]

In the nineteenth century Samuel Jones of the Philadelphia Association wrote, "Concerning the divine right of the office of ruling elders there has been considerable doubt and much disputation." Jones then summarized the arguments for and against ruling elders and essentially conceded that Griffith's defense of ruling elders is weak. But he still argued the office was beneficial and not forbidden and left congregations free to keep ruling elders if they found them useful for assisting the pastor.[12]

Turning to the South, the first president of the Southern Baptist Convention, W. B. Johnson of South Carolina, wrote of the New Testament churches that "each church had a plurality of elders" in his book *The Gospel Developed*.[13] Johnson wrote, "A plurality in the bishopric is of great importance for mutual counsel and aid, that the government and edification of the flock may be promoted in the best manner."[14] For several pages Johnson then delineated the duties and benefits of a plurality of elders in a local congregation.[15]

Baptist Confession as Implemented in the Subscribing Churches" (PhD diss., Trinity Evangelical Divinity School, 1997).

[9] Benjamin Griffith, *A Short Treatise*, in Dever, *Polity*, 98.

[10] Renihan writes, "The majority of the writers and churches did not recognize a distinct office of ruling elder" (200). Also, "The majority of particular Baptists were committed to a plurality and a parity of elders in their churches" (205). Renihan, "The Practical Ecclesiology."

[11] *Summary of Church Discipline*, in Dever, *Polity*, 120.

[12] Samuel Jones, *Treatise of Church Discipline*, in Dever, *Polity*, 145–46.

[13] W. B. Johnson, *The Gospel Developed*, in Dever, *Polity*, 192.

[14] Ibid., 193.

[15] See ibid., 189–95.

In 1849 J. L. Reynolds, pastor of the Second Baptist Church of Richmond, Virginia, wrote that "the apostolic churches seem, in general, to have had a plurality of elders as well as deacons."[16] Nevertheless, Reynolds maintained that "the number of officers, whether elders or deacons, necessary to the completeness of a church, is not determined in Scripture. This must be decided by the circumstances of the case, of which the party interested is the most competent judge."[17] Reynolds competently and carefully dissected the arguments in favor of a distinct class of ruling elders.[18] And he devoted a whole chapter to defending the interchangeability of the terms *bishop* and *elder*.

In 1874 William Williams, part of the founding faculty of The Southern Baptist Theological Seminary, wrote, "In most, if not all the apostolic churches, there was a plurality of elders."[19] Williams then speculated that this was true perhaps because the early Christians could only meet in small groups, and each small group needed an elder to instruct them. Therefore, a plurality of elders was a product of temporary circumstances and should not be perceived as a continuing requirement for churches. Williams also disagreed with any idea of a separate office of ruling elder. In short, he placed the plurality of elders in the same category as deaconesses, the holy kiss, and the frequency of the Lord's Supper. All are matters that should be left up to the "pious discretion of the churches."[20]

We could point to many more examples. C. H. Spurgeon had a plurality of elders at the Metropolitan Tabernacle in nineteenth-century London.[21] J. L. Burrows, pastor of First Baptist Church, Richmond, for

---

16 J. L. Reynolds, *Church Polity or the Kingdom of Christ*, in Dever, *Polity*, 349.

17 Ibid., 350.

18 Ibid.

19 William Williams, *Apostolical Church Polity*, in Dever, *Polity*, 531.

20 Ibid., 537. Without citing Williams, Gerald Cowen has more recently rehearsed this same argument in his book *Who Rules the Church?*

21 "To our minds, the Scripture seems very explicit as to how this Church should be ordered. We believe that every Church member should have equal rights and privileges; that there is no power in Church officers to execute anything unless they have the full authorization of the members of the Church. We believe, however, that the Church should choose its pastor, and having chosen him, that they should love him and respect him for his work's sake; that with him should be associated the deacons of the Church to take the oversight of pecuniary matters; and the elders of the Church to assist in all the works of the pastorate in the fear of God, being overseers of the flock. Such a Church we believe to be scripturally ordered; and if it abide in the faith, rooted, and grounded, and settled, such a Church may expect the benediction of heaven, and so it shall become the pillar and ground of the truth." C. H. Spurgeon, "The Church Conservative and Aggressive," in *The Metropolitan Tabernacle Pulpit*, vol. 7 (1862; repr. Pasadena, TX: Pilgrim Press, 1969), 658–59.

twenty years and chairman of the Foreign Mission Board for six years, wrote in his book *What Baptists Believe*, "Elders and deacons are the only officers [Christ] has instituted."[22] It is indisputable that at the beginning of the twentieth century, Baptists either had or advocated elders in local churches—and often a plurality of elders. They had done so for centuries. A. H. Strong, president of Rochester Theological Seminary and author of the influential 1907 *Systematic Theology*, summarized the position perhaps most Baptists in America held at the beginning of the twentieth century:

> In certain of the N. T. churches there appears to have been a plurality of elders. . . . There is, however, no evidence that the number of elders was uniform, or that the plurality which frequently existed was due to any other cause than the size of the churches for which these elders cared. The N. T. example, while it permits the multiplication of assistant pastors according to need, does not require a plural eldership in every case. . . . There are indications, moreover, that, at least in certain churches, the pastor was one, while the deacons were more than one, in number.[23]

Yet throughout the twentieth century, both the practice of plural eldership and the use of the title "elder" grew increasingly scarce in Baptist life. To mention elders in many Baptist churches today would raise suspicions of being a crypto-Presbyterian. But in the past few decades, the office of elder has seen a significant revival among Southern Baptists.

Influences in the Revival of Elders in Baptist Churches

Why has this office of elder been revived among some Southern Baptists in recent history? I have no extensive research for the comments that follow, only anecdotal experience and my own reflections. The "whys" are difficult questions to answer not only for historians; even those living in the midst of change can have difficulty discerning causation. I have been an elder at a Baptist church in England, and I have preached in Baptist churches in South Africa that had elders. But here in America, what is causing the reevaluation that is indisputably occurring?

Let me suggest two factors unrelated to the inerrancy controversy in the SBC, and three factors related to the controversy, all of which may

---

[22] J. L. Burrows, *What Baptists Believe* (1888), 14, cf. 12 and 16.

[23] A. H. Strong, *Systematic Theology* (Valley Forge, PA: Judson, 1907), 915–16.

partly explain an otherwise surprising surge of interest in this ancient office.

Causes Unrelated to the Inerrancy Controversy

First, prominent advocates outside the Southern Baptist constituency have raised the idea of elders in local churches. John MacArthur, pastor of Grace Community Church in Sun Valley, California, has for many years advocated and practiced having a plurality of elders (of which he is one) lead the congregation. MacArthur has published a variety of writings that touch on this issue, but perhaps most widely read is his thirty-two-page booklet *Answering the Key Questions About Elders* (1984). In 1991, John Piper, who for thirty-three years pastored Bethlehem Baptist Church, a Baptist General Conference church in Minneapolis, Minnesota, also led his church to adopt a plural-elder model of leadership. He has written a sixty-three-page booklet, *Biblical Eldership* (1999).

Even more broadly, a number of widely used contemporary systematic theologies testify to the New Testament evidence for a plurality of elders. Since its completion in 1985, Millard Erickson's *Christian Theology* has been perhaps the most widely used systematic textbook in Southern Baptist seminaries, and in many other evangelical schools as well. At its publication in the mid-1980s, few systematic theologies had gained such wide usage since Louis Berkhof's Dutch Reformed work in the 1930s. In Erickson's section on the church, he carefully lays out episcopalian, presbyterian, and congregational polities, showing the strengths and weaknesses of each. He gingerly advocates congregationalism, though not with the vigor of earlier divine-right congregationalists like John Owen and Thomas Goodwin, nor even with the mildness that characterized writers in the American South in the nineteenth century, like W. B. Johnson and J. L. Reynolds. Erickson also makes two qualifying provisos: a more presbyterian form of government will probably be needed when the congregation becomes large or when it is filled with more immature Christians.

Wayne Grudem's popular 1994 *Systematic Theology*, also used in many Southern Baptist and evangelical seminaries, states, "There is quite a consistent pattern of *plural elders* as the main governing group in the New Testament churches."[24] Grudem points to two main conclusions from the New Testament evidence: "First, no passage suggests that any church, no matter how small, had only one elder. The consistent New

---

24 Wayne Grudem, *Systematic Theology* (Grand Rapids: Zondervan, 1994), 912.

Testament pattern is a plurality of elders 'in every church' (Acts 14:23)." And, "Second, we do not see a diversity of forms of government in the New Testament church, but a unified and consistent pattern in which every church had elders governing it and keeping watch over it (Acts 20:28; Heb. 13:17; 1 Pet. 5:2–3)."[25] When Grudem wrote his *Systematic Theology*, he was a member of a Southern Baptist church in Chicago with elders.

Second, the idea of elders in local churches has been raised recently because of more internal and pragmatic considerations, namely, a frustration with current structures in our congregations. Many Southern Baptist churches increasingly sense that the present structures are simply not working. Some churches led by a single pastor suffer under an authoritarian rule too much like the Gentile leadership Jesus forbade in Mark 10:42.[26] Other times young pastors have gone into churches and found them ossified, effectively ruled by deacons, a nominating committee, a personnel committee, or some other group that has no biblical standard of maturity in understanding and teaching the Scriptures. And for those churches where our congregational heritage is still rightly valued, that congregationalism is too often wrongly exercised with an anti-Christian individualism, rather than as part of the corporate responsibility we bear before the Lord. Furthermore, where baptismal and membership ages plunge lower than driver's license, elementary-school, or even preschool ages; where church membership generally requires nothing other than a one-time decision; and where regular attendance is not even required for membership, it cannot be surprising that meetings of members for church business become more and more ineffective. As John Hammett has argued, "Many Baptist churches have strayed so far from regenerate membership that they are incapable of responsible church government at the present time."[27] Congregationalism fades as membership expectations evaporate.

Causes Related to the Inerrancy Controversy

I believe the SBC's inerrancy controversy also produced some echoes, or unintended results, leading to a reevaluation of church government and the prominence of the topic of elders in recent discussions. The least

---

[25] Ibid., 913.

[26] Mark 10:42: "Jesus called them together and said, 'You know that those who are regarded as rulers of the Gentiles lord it over them, and their high officials exercise authority over them'" (NIV).

[27] John Hammett, "Elder Rule in Baptist Churches" (working paper, 2003), 11.

important of these echoes is related to the accelerated larger cultural trend of being less attached to particular denominations. Brand loyalty is down everywhere. Throughout much of the past century, Southern Baptists assumed such loyalty would continue and did not work to create or cultivate it. The inerrancy controversy led to a rupturing of the denominational womb that many Southern Baptists had lived in their entire lives. As a result of the intramural fighting, conservative Southern Baptists began looking outside the fold in a way their more liberal counterparts had done for decades. There they found a wide world that stretched from southern California megachurches to Chicago-based schools and publishers. Many of us in the 1970s learned that we could not depend on our Baptist Student Unions—mine had a female minister who denied the bodily resurrection. The books we read from "our" people sorely disappointed us. Dale Moody's *The Word of Truth*, for instance, not only served as a poor guard against liberal mainline Protestantism; it sometimes even advocated liberalism's tenets.[28] And the seminaries were increasingly untrustworthy. So John Hammett, one of the authors of this volume, went to Trinity Evangelical Divinity School, and I went to Gordon-Conwell. Many others of our generation have similar stories.

All of this interaction with broader evangelicalism was multiplied by the rise of the Bible churches and Dallas Theological Seminary's influence among conservatives. Gene Getz, longtime Dallas professor, advocated a plurality of elders. Interestingly, a 1977 paper from the Conservative Baptist Association of Oregon attempts to address the growing problem of elders in Baptist churches—and ascribes it entirely to the growth of the Bible churches.

Other denominations, too, became more familiar to us. Though the churches of Christ and the Brethren had long had elders, we never talked much with them. By the 1970s and 1980s, many of the fastest growing churches around us were—of all things—Presbyterian! The Presbyterian Church in America (PCA), born in 1973, quickly began to raise questions about the old canard among some Baptists that Calvinism is antievangelistic. Now, forty years later, PCA churches are full of former Southern Baptists, and it is not because these former Baptists have all been convinced of the validity of infant baptism. Many of those churches—even with their unbiblical practices of infant baptism and extracongregational government—were out-evangelizing, out-teaching, and even out-disciplining our Southern Baptist congregations.

---

28 Dale Moody, *The Word of Truth: A Summary of Christian Doctrine Based on Biblical Revelation* (Grand Rapids: Eerdmans, 1981).

Through all of this, we were finding allies—even Anglicans like John Stott and J. I. Packer—with whom we had more in common than we had with many of those whose salaries we paid to teach in our institutions. As these outside voices gained fresh respect, we gave more consideration to their arguments and practices. Subjects we had not discussed for a century or more once again became topics of conversation—like church government and the role of elders. This renewal of interdenominational conversation was new for many in the more conservative circles of the SBC.

A second unintended consequence of the SBC's inerrancy controversy was that conservative Southern Baptists were forced to reconsider our denominational identity, and that inevitably included studying our Baptist past. And what we found in our past, among many larger issues like inerrancy, confessions, slavery, and Calvinism, were elders aplenty! I am just old enough to remember that across from my grandmother's house in Kentucky lived an old, retired Southern Baptist minister who was called by the title of "elder."

A final explanation for this renewed emphasis on elders emerging from the inerrancy controversy is simply the renewed emphasis on the inerrancy of the Bible itself. In defending the inerrancy of the Bible—fighting for it, and even firing over it—it is not surprising that people opened the revered book, began studying it afresh, and asked questions about the plain meaning of texts. In the context of loosened loyalties and openness to redefinition, we can easily imagine that if none of these other factors had obtained—outside influences, inner frustrations—we still might find ourselves scratching our heads today, staring at the Bible, and saying, "Why don't we see elders in our churches like the ones in the early church?"

CHAPTER 12

The Scriptural Basis for Elders[1]

Benjamin L. Merkle

With the history of the conversation covered, this chapter turns to consider the Bible's teaching on elders, beginning with the question of the office's origin. Did the early church consciously borrow the title *elder* from a previously existing model of eldership? In other words, why were some leaders in the early church referred to as elders?

Elders in the Old Testament and Synagogue

Today, many scholars simply assume that the origin of the New Testament elder is found in the Old Testament elder. Certainly the Old Testament usage of the term *elders* had some influence on why the early church referred to its leaders as elders. Yet it would be wrong to say the New Testament church patterned its leaders on these ancient predecessors. Although their functions overlap at times, there is not a one-to-one parallel. A. E. Harvey rightly concludes that there was no "*institution* in the Old Testament times which could be regarded as the forerunner . . . of the Christian presbyterate."[2]

---

[1] For a more detailed treatment of this topic, see Benjamin L. Merkle, *The Elder and Overseer: One Office in the Early Church* (New York: Peter Lang, 2003), 44–56, 62–65; idem, *40 Questions About Elders and Deacons* (Grand Rapids: Kregel, 2008), 54–88.

[2] A. E. Harvey, "Elders," *Journal of Theological Studies* 25 (1974): 320.

A second view is that the New Testament church adapted the structure of the synagogue and with it came the office of elder. The assumption is that because most of the early Christians were Jews who formerly worshipped in the synagogue, it would be natural for them to adopt its form of government. For example, J. B. Lightfoot states, "With the synagogue itself [the Christian congregations in Palestine] would naturally, if not necessarily, adopt the normal government of a synagogue, and a body of elders or presbyters would be chosen to direct the religious worship and partly also to watch over the temporal well-being of the society."[3] There are, however, noticeable differences between elders in the Jewish and Christian contexts. For example, the elders did not lead the synagogue meeting. The "ruler of the synagogue" (*archisunagōgos*) was the officeholder of the synagogue who was responsible for the specifics of the meeting. "Elder" was not technically an office in the synagogue but was a title of someone respected in the community. This is not to say, however, that the elders had no influence in the synagogue. In Jewish society there was not a separation between the civil and the religious. Just as the elders had a great influence over civil affairs, so they also exercised authority over the religious life of the community, of which the synagogue was a major part. As leaders of the community they were also leaders of the synagogue but only in a general sense. Therefore, because synagogue elders "had no responsibility for the worship of the synagogue (this belonged to the [*archisunagōgos*]) nor for the custody of right doctrine or the exposition of scripture . . . synagogue elders provide at best a shadowy model for the Christian presbyters."[4]

It is difficult to determine the precise relationship between Christian elders and elders of the Old Testament and the synagogue. From the outset one must acknowledge both similarities and differences. Yet in each case the differences are substantial enough to reject any direct correlation. It appears, therefore, that the Christian office of elder was not directly borrowed from Judaism. The New Testament church borrowed the title, and the official status that came along with that title, more than the specific duties that those who held this title performed.

---

[3] J. B. Lightfoot, *St. Paul's Epistle to the Philippians* (London: Macmillan, 1881), 192. Earlier Lightfoot writes, "It was not unnatural therefore that, when the Christian synagogue took its place by the side of the Jewish, a similar organization should be adopted with such modifications as circumstances required; and thus the name familiar under the old dispensation was retained under the new" (96). See also James T. Burtchaell, *From Synagogue to Church: Public Services and Offices in the Earliest Christian Communities* (Cambridge: Cambridge University Press, 1992), 190.

[4] Harvey, "Elders," 325–26; see also Thomas M. Lindsay, *The Church and the Ministry in the Early Centuries* (London: Hodder & Stoughton, 1902), 131, 153.

Elders in the New Testament

A major question regarding elders in the New Testament concerns the relationship of the term *elders* to other terms referencing church leaders such as *overseers* and *pastors*. What makes matters even more difficult is that sometimes leaders are mentioned but no title is given. This phenomenon seems to have been especially prevalent during the earliest years of the church. In Galatians 6:6, for example, Paul stated, "The one who is taught the message must share all his good things with the teacher."[5] This verse suggests that there was a class of instructors or catechizers who taught the Word to such an extent that they needed to be financially supported for their work. But if such people held a particular office, we are not told what the name of that office was.

In 1 Thessalonians 5:12–13, Paul exhorted the congregation: "Now we ask you, brothers, to give recognition to those who labor among you and lead you in the Lord and admonish you, and to regard them very highly in love because of their work." Here, Paul made a distinction between the "brothers" and those to whom they are "to give recognition" or respect because of the work they do in teaching the congregation. No formal title is used, but some were clearly given positions of leadership in the church.

The author of Hebrews likewise distinguished between the leaders and those who should obey them: "Obey your leaders and submit to them, for they keep watch over your souls as those who will give an account" (Heb 13:17; cf. 13:7). If a leader must give an account, he needs to know not only that he is a leader (which implies some formal position recognized by the church) but also who he is accountable to lead (which implies a distinction between the leaders and the followers). Although we do not know what particular "office" these leaders may have held, we do know that the author had in mind a distinct group of individuals.

By the time the Pastoral Epistles (1–2 Timothy, Titus) were written, it appears two established offices were in the church: elders (or overseers) and deacons—though elders (or overseers) and deacons were also mentioned in Paul's earlier letter to the Philippians, where in his opening greeting, he addressed "all the saints in Christ Jesus who are in Philippi, including the overseers and deacons" (Phil 1:1). In 1 Timothy 3, Paul gave qualifications for the two offices. In verse 1 he wrote, "If anyone aspires to be an overseer, he desires a noble work." The following verses

---

5 Unless otherwise indicated, all Scripture passages are taken from the HCSB.

give the qualifications for those who might hold the office. Then, in verse 8, Paul shifted to the office of deacon: "Deacons, likewise, should be . . ." Paul's letter to Titus, however, refers only to overseers, making no mention of deacons (Titus 1:5–9). This omission possibly indicates that the church in Crete was less developed than the church in Ephesus.

It should also be noted that "elder" (*presbuteros*), "overseer" (*episkopos*), and "pastor" (*poimēn*) refer to the same office. Although "pastor" (or "shepherd") is commonly used in our modern church context, it is used only one time in the New Testament as a reference to a church leader (although the verb "to shepherd" and the noun "flock" are occasionally found).[6] In Ephesians 4:11, we are told, "And He personally gave some to be apostles, some prophets, some evangelists, some pastors and teachers." The term *pastors* is coupled with the term *teachers*, which together denote one order of ministry. In other words the Greek construction favors interpreting this phrase as one office: the pastor/teacher—not one office of pastor and a separate office of teacher.[7]

What are the reasons for interpreting "elder," "overseer," and "pastor" as representing the same office?

"Elder," "Overseer," and "Pastor" Are Used Interchangeably

The first indication that the terms *elder*, *overseer*, and *pastor* represent the same office is that they are used interchangeably. Three texts clearly demonstrate this synonymous usage (Acts 20:17, 28; Titus 1:5, 7; 1 Pet 5:1–2). Upon returning from his third missionary journey, Paul's ship harbored at Miletus for a few days. Knowing that he might not return to the region again, Paul decided to contact the leaders of the church at Ephesus. Luke informs us that Paul "sent to Ephesus and called for the elders [*presbuterous*] of the church" (Acts 20:17). After the elders arrived, Paul gave them a sort of farewell speech. He exhorted them, "Be on guard for yourselves and for all the flock, among whom the Holy Spirit has appointed you as overseers [*episkopous*], to shepherd [or 'pastor,' *poimainein*] the church of God" (v. 28, author's translation). Thus,

---

6 The verb "to shepherd" (*poimainō*) occurs in Matt 2:6; John 21:16; Acts 20:28; 1 Cor 9:7 (refers to shepherding animals); 1 Pet 5:2; Jude 1:12; Rev 2:27; 7:17; 12:5; 19:15. The noun "flock" (*poimēn*) occurs in Matt 26:31 and John 10:16. The diminutive form (*poimnion*) is used in Luke 12:32; Acts 20:28–29; and 1 Pet 5:2–3.

7 In the Greek one article governs the two nouns that indicate one group of people (*tous de poimenas kai didaskalous*, "and the prophets and teachers"). Although the Granville Sharp rule does not apply here because we are dealing with plural nouns, it is best to take this as a twofold designation referring to one group (the pastor-teachers).

in verse 17 Paul summoned the "elders," but in verse 28 we read that the Holy Spirit gave them the tasks of overseeing and shepherding (or pastoring) God's church.

Perhaps the most convincing passage which demonstrates that the terms *elder* and *overseer* are interchangeable is Titus 1:5–7. In verse 5, Paul wrote to Titus, "The reason I left you in Crete was to set right what was left undone and, as I directed you, to appoint elders [*presbuterous*] in every town." When Paul gave the qualifications in verse 7, however, he replaced the term *elder* with *overseer*. He continued, "For an overseer [*episkopon*] . . . must be. . . ."

A similar usage is found in 1 Peter 5:1–2. Peter, as a fellow elder, exhorted the elders of the churches. He wrote, "I exhort the elders [*presbuterous*] among you, as a fellow elder . . . shepherd [*poimanate*] the flock of God that is among you, serving as overseers [*episkopountes*]."[8] Although this example uses the verb forms ("shepherd" and "serving as overseers"; cf. Acts 20:28), it still emphasizes that the duty or function of the elders was to shepherd and oversee the congregation. It would be strange if the elders were not the same people as those who were called "pastors" or "overseers" since they both performed the same duties.

Elders and Pastors Are Never Given Separate Qualifications

A second indication these terms refer to the same office is that Paul never mentioned the qualifications for "elders" or "pastors." If elder, overseer, and pastor are separate offices, then it would seem reasonable to expect Paul to give the qualifications for each office. In both 1 Timothy 3:1–7 and Titus 1:7–9, Paul gave the qualifications for anyone who aspires to the office of "overseer." But 1 Timothy 5:17–25 and Titus 1:5 mention elders, and Ephesians 4:11 mentions pastors. If the offices are distinct, then what are the qualifications for someone to become an elder as opposed to an overseer?

This omission is especially telling because in 1 Timothy 5:22–25 Paul warned Timothy not to appoint someone to the office of elder hastily because that position is to be filled only by qualified individuals (cf. 1 Tim 4:14; 2 Tim 1:6). If elder is a distinct office from overseer, we would expect the qualifications to be clearly stated for such an important position. What guidelines was Timothy to use in determining the moral and spiritual readiness of elder candidates? Was Timothy left to find his

---

8 Author's translation.

own way? No, Paul had already given Timothy the qualifications needed for someone to become an overseer (or elder or pastor) in the church. Although such arguments from silence are never conclusive, one wonders if Paul would have ignored the requirements given the importance he attributes to the office.

Elders, Overseers, and Pastors Have the Same Function

A third reason for equating these terms is that elders, overseers, and pastors have the same function: ruling/leading and teaching. For example, 1 Timothy 3:4–5 states that an *overseer* must "manage" or "rule" (*proistemi*) his own house before he is fit to "take care of" the church (cf. Rom 12:8; 1 Thess 5:12). Likewise, 1 Timothy 5:17 speaks of *elders* who "rule" (ESV, *proistemi*) well, indicating that all elders are involved in ruling or leading the church. In Acts 20:28, Paul charged the Ephesian *elders* or *overseers* to "shepherd" the church of God. Thus, both elders and overseers are given the task of ruling/leading the church.

In a similar manner all three are given the duty of teaching the congregation. In Ephesians 4:11, the term *pastor* is linked with the term *teacher*, indicating that the primary means by which a pastor shepherds his flock is teaching them God's Word. In 1 Timothy 3:2, every overseer must be "an able teacher," and in Titus 1:9 an elder/overseer must "be able both to encourage with sound teaching and to refute those who contradict it." Likewise, elders who rule well should be considered worthy of double honor, "especially those who work hard at preaching and teaching" (1 Tim 5:17). It is probably best to interpret this text as teaching, that all elders teach but that some work harder at it than others.[9] Because elders, overseers, and pastors are given the same tasks of ruling/leading and teaching, the terms should be viewed as describing the same office.

Elders, Overseers, and Pastors Are Never Listed as Separate Offices

A final reason for equating the terms *elder*, *overseer*, and *pastor* is that the New Testament nowhere mentions the three offices together. This usage suggests that the three-tiered ecclesiastical system of bishop (overseer), elder, and deacon that later developed in many churches is

---

[9] David Mappes rightly comments, "While all elder-overseer-pastors must be able to teach (1 Tim. 3:2) and exhort and refute with sound doctrine (Titus 1:9), they may not all have the spiritual gifts of teaching and exhorting (Rom. 12:7)" ("The New Testament Elder, Overseer, and Pastor," *Bibliotheca Sacra* 154 [1997]: 174).

foreign to the New Testament. Not until the second century—in the epistles of Ignatius—do we see a distinction between the overseer (i.e., the monarchical bishop) and the elders (i.e., presbytery). Indeed, Ignatius provides us with the first example of a three-tiered system with a bishop, a presbytery, and deacons. For example, Ignatius exhorts his readers, "Be eager to do everything in godly harmony, the bishop presiding in the place of God and the presbyters in the place of the council of the apostles and the deacons, who are most dear to me, having been entrusted with the service of Jesus Christ" (*Magn.* 6:1).[10] For Ignatius the overseer is clearly distinct from the council of elders and is the sole head of the city-church. This later development, however, is not found in other writings of the postapostolic era. For example, *1 Clement* (44:4–5) and the *Didache*, both probably written at the end of the first century, use the terms *elder* and *overseer* interchangeably.[11]

If these terms represent the same office, then why was it necessary to employ different terms? The reason could be that *elder* is more a description of character, whereas *overseer* and *pastor* are more descriptions of function.[12] *Elder* conveyed the idea of a wise, mature leader who was honored and respected by the community. *Overseer* and *pastor* spoke more to the work of the individual whose duty it was to "oversee" and "shepherd" those under his care.

The Question of Distinctions Between Elders

Though the Bible uses the terms *elder, overseer,* and *pastor* to represent the same office, various denominations and churches have adopted the practice of making distinctions between different classes of elders, some more formal, some less formal. What do we think of this?

---

10 This quotation from Ignatius is from J. B. Lightfoot, J. R. Harmer, and Michael W. Holmes, ed., *The Apostolic Fathers: Greek Text and English Translations of Their Writings*, 2nd ed. (Grand Rapids: Baker, 1992). Also see Ignatius *Eph.* 2:2; 4:1; *Magn.* 2:1; 13:1; *Trall.* 2:2–3; 7:2; *Phld.* 4:1; 7:1; *Smyrn.* 8:1; 12:2; *Pol.* 6:1.

11 See Eric G. Jay, "From Presbyter-Bishops to Bishops and Presbyters," *Second Century* 1 (1981): 136. Jay also asserts that the monoepiscopacy is not found in the *Didache*, Polycarp, and Hermas (128, 142–43).

12 Schaff states that "the terms PRESBYTER (or Elder) and BISHOP (or Overseer, Superintendent) denote in the New Testament one and the same office, with this difference . . . that the one signifies the dignity, the other the duty" (Philip Schaff, *History of the Christian Church*, vol. 1, *Apostolic Christianity*, 3rd rev. ed. [Peabody, MA: Hendrickson, 1996; originally published in 1858], 491–92).

Senior Pastors?

For instance, is it appropriate to use the term *senior pastor*, which might imply that he holds a different office than "elder"? This question is raised primarily because the idea of having a "senior" pastor is so common today that many assume it has a scriptural basis. The senior pastor is usually the professional "clergyman" who has the most authority, does most of the preaching, and is the driving force behind the direction of the church. But if "pastor" refers to the same office as "elder," making a hard distinction between an elder and a pastor or senior pastor is unwarranted. That is, it can be unhelpful and misleading to speak of someone being a pastor *and* an elder. By creating a "professional" class of elders (i.e., pastors or senior pastors), we can create an unhealthy and unbiblical distinction. Nowhere in the Bible are elders who work "full time" for the church given a different title than those elders who also hold a "secular" job. It is possible for such a distinction to create an unhealthy dichotomy between the full-time and part-time elders as well as the clergy and laity. Consequently, a church might understandably use the title of "senior pastor" for prudential reasons, but caution must be given so that we do not create a third office, similar to what took place in the second century with the development of the monarchical bishop.[13]

From a New Testament perspective, a distinct office of "senior pastor" is a foreign concept. The early churches were not governed by one person but were led by a group of leaders. For example, in every instance the term *elder* is used in the New Testament, it occurs in the plural form (*elders*), except when it is used generically (1 Tim 5:19) or when it refers to a specific elder (such as Peter [1 Pet 5:1] or John [2 John 1; 3 John 1]). There is no instance of anyone ever being called "the pastor" of a local church, much less being called "the senior pastor." Actually, there is one reference of someone being called "senior pastor." In 1 Peter 5:4, Jesus is called the "chief Shepherd" (i.e., Senior Pastor). Perhaps it is best to reserve this title for Jesus because all other shepherds are "undershepherds," though certainly Christians may disagree on this as a matter of prudence.

---

[13] L. Roy Taylor, himself a Presbyterian, rightly criticizes churches that "originate with congregational church government" but "develop a *de facto* episcopal government whereby the senior pastor is the primary decision-maker on major issues." He then adds, "While some may regard this as novel, it is actually a replication of the older monoepiscopacy of the second century" ("Presbyterianism," in *Who Runs the Church? 4 Views on Church Government*, ed. Paul E. Engle and Steven B. Cowan [Grand Rapids: Zondervan], 74).

Teaching Versus Ruling Elders?

The Presbyterian model of church government formally acknowledges only two church offices: elder and deacon. Yet a distinction is made between "teaching elders" and "ruling elders." Thus, within one *office* there are two *orders*.[14] The support for this twofold office is found in 1 Timothy 5:17, which states, "Let the elders who rule well be considered worthy of double honor, especially those who labor in preaching and teaching" (ESV). Roy Taylor explains, "All elders rule, but some elders also have special responsibilities in preaching and teaching. This is why, in some presbyterian circles, lay elders are called 'ruling elders' and ministers are referred to as 'teaching elders.'"[15]

Three interpretations of 1 Timothy 5:17 can be offered that make no formal distinction between "teaching elders" and "ruling elders." Paul could be making a distinction related to (1) time, (2) talent, or (3) type of teaching. First, it is possible that Paul was making a distinction between those who were currently spending much time in preaching and teaching and those who were not. Perhaps some were too busy with their "secular" professions or with their families and, as a result, they could not be as committed to the gospel ministry as others. According to Paul, every overseer/elder needed to be "an able teacher" (1 Tim 3:2), but maybe only some had enough time to do much or any actual teaching.[16]

Second, it is possible to take 1 Timothy 5:17 as making a distinction between talent and gifts. While every elder needs to be "an able teacher," apparently some were more gifted in teaching and preaching than others. Among those who held the same office, some were more gifted in particular areas. Consequently, they were often called upon to lead the church through exercising their gifts of teaching. "The division could be based on those who were able to teach and those who were especially gifted

---

14 For example, the *Book of Church Order* of the Presbyterian Church of America declares, "Within the class of Elder are two orders of Teaching Elders and Ruling Elders. The Elders jointly have the government and spiritual oversight of the Church, including teaching. Only those elders who are specially gifted, called and trained by God to preach may serve as Teaching Elders."

15 Taylor, "Presbyterianism," in Engle and Cowan, *Who Runs the Church?*, 81.

16 Mounce explains, "While asserting that all elders are able to teach, Paul could have based the division on those currently teaching and those who were not. Perhaps . . . [some] overseers would have had to vary the amount of time spent specifically on teaching because of other responsibilities, and this admonition would address those actively teaching" (William D. Mounce, *Pastoral Epistles*, Word Biblical Commentary [Nashville: Nelson, 2000], 308). Similarly, Waldron notes: "The contrast is not between no teaching and teaching. It is between some teaching and a greater degree of teaching" (Samuel E. Waldron, "Plural-Elder Congregationalism," in Engle and Cowan, *Who Runs the Church?*, 216).

to teach, dividing the elders on the basis of ability and giftedness and assuming that the more gifted did more of the corporate instruction."[17]

A third, but less likely, option is that the distinction made in 1 Timothy 5:17 primarily involves the type of preaching or teaching performed. That is, those who teach the church corporately were singled out for special respect and financial support. While some elders teach in the private or "small group" settings, others are given the more crucial task of instructing the entire gathered church during the worship service. As such, "elders who rule well" "could apply to gifted teachers who were currently leading in other ways (while still allowing for one-on-one teaching, both with the opponents and the other members of the church), and 'laboring hard at preaching and teaching' could apply to those currently teaching the church as a whole."[18]

There is also the possibility of translating the Greek word *malista* ("especially") as "namely" or "that is."[19] In this case Paul was not making a distinction between those who rule well and those who, in addition to ruling well, also preach and teach. Rather, those who rule well are precisely those who teach and preach; on this view Paul was stating that the elders rule well *by* their teaching and preaching. This interpretation seems to fit Paul's stress on the importance of teaching, and a threefold division of elders is hard to imagine (i.e., those who rule, those who rule well, and those who rule well and also preach and teach). Regardless of how this difficult verse is interpreted, it in no way demands one to see two offices involved. At most the text indicates a relative distinction of function within one office. The distinction Paul made should not be exaggerated so that, in essence, a new office is created.

---

[17] Mounce, *Pastoral Epistles*, 308. This is the position of Knight who writes, "Although all elders are to be able to teach (1 Tim 3:2) and thus to instruct the people of God and to communicate with those who oppose biblical teaching (Tit 1:9ff.), the 1 Timothy 5:17 passage recognizes that among the elders, all of whom are to be able to teach, there are those so gifted by God with the ability to teach the Word that they are called by God to give their life in such a calling or occupation and deserve therefore to be remunerated for such a calling and occupation" (George W. Knight, "Two Offices [Elders/Bishops and Deacons] and Two Orders of Elders [Preaching/Teaching Elders and Ruling Elders]: A New Testament Study," *Presbyterion* 11 [1985]: 6). Similarly, Mappes comments, "While all elder-overseer-pastors must be able to teach (1 Tim. 3:2) and exhort and refute with sound doctrine (Titus 1:9), they may not all have the spiritual gifts of teaching and exhorting (Rom. 12:7)" ("New Testament Elder," 174).

[18] Mounce, *Pastoral Epistles*, 308.

[19] See Skeat, who convincingly argues that *malista* is often best translated as "namely" (T. C. Skeat, "'Especially the Parchments': A Note on 2 Timothy IV. 13," *Journal of Theological Studies* 30 [1979]: 173–77).

CHAPTER 13

The Biblical Qualifications for Elders[1]

Benjamin L. Merkle

W hen reading the qualifications for an elder or overseer, one is
immediately struck by their relative simplicity. In fact, the qualifications to be an elder are basic characteristics all Christians should
have. The only exceptions are that an elder must not be a new convert
and must be able to teach. The focus of the qualifications is on who a
person is more than what he does.

For the most part the qualifications given seem to be listed in ran-
dom order. The one exception is that both lists begin with being "above
reproach" (or "blameless") and "the husband of one wife" (1 Tim 3:2;
Titus 1:6).[2] We will examine the qualifications under the subdivisions of
situational, family, and moral qualifications.

Situational Qualifications

These qualifications relate to one's situation in life. They are not so much
moral or spiritual qualifications but concern one's desire and ability to
serve as well as the time of one's conversion.

---

[1] For a more detailed treatment of this topic, see Benjamin L. Merkle, *40 Questions About Elders and Deacons* (Grand Rapids: Kregel, 2008), 109–34.

[2] Unless otherwise indicated, all Scripture passages are taken from the HCSB.

Desire to Serve (1 Tim 3:1)

Although not formally a qualification, Paul mentioned that it is a good thing ("a noble work") for someone to aspire to the office of overseer. "Noble" is translated from the Greek word *kalos*, which means "good," "excellent," or "worthwhile." Of course, some may desire this office from impure motives such as greed or pride. Yet Paul wanted to make clear that those who are chosen to serve should want to serve. Often churches nominate people to serve and then have to twist their arms to get them to reluctantly accept the position. These people may serve faithfully but never really experience joy and fulfillment in their service. It is better to select those people who are eager to serve. Indeed, it is best to select those people who are already joyfully serving in some capacity, although they may have no formal office in the church. Those who desire to serve God as elders desire a good thing, but desire alone is never enough. This desire must be accompanied by moral character and spiritual capability.

Able to Teach (1 Tim 3:2; Titus 1:9)

This is one of only two qualifications that directly relate to an elder's duties in the church (1 Tim 3:4–5 speaks of managing and caring for the church). Elders must be able to communicate God's Word in a way that is accurate and understandable. In Titus, Paul expanded on what he wrote in 1 Timothy. He added that an overseer must hold "to the faithful message as taught, so that he will be able both to encourage with sound teaching and to refute those who contradict it" (Titus 1:9). An elder must not only be "an able teacher," but he must also teach sound doctrine and correct those who are in error. He cannot merely have a cursory knowledge of the Bible but must be immersed in the teachings of Scripture so that he can both exhort in sound doctrine and rebuke those who reject sound doctrine.

If every elder must be "an able teacher," does that mean all elders must teach or preach publicly? Such an interpretation is probably more restrictive than what Paul had in mind. Certainly all elders should be involved in some kind of teaching. It would seem odd for Paul to require that all elders be able to teach and then some of them not be involved in any type of teaching ministry. All elders must be able to teach and should be using their teaching abilities or gifts in the church actively. But the type of teaching should not be limited to preaching on Sunday mornings or at other times when the entire congregation is gathered. Some elders may not be gifted in teaching or preaching to large groups but may have an incredible gift to teach or disciple in a small-group setting.[3]

Not a New Convert (1 Tim 3:6)

In 1 Timothy, Paul wrote that an elder must not be a new believer. He then gave the reason for this qualification: "Or he might become conceited and fall into the condemnation of the Devil" (1 Tim 3:6). Without the deep maturity that develops over time, when a new convert takes on an important and respected leadership role, he may become filled with pride and end up falling from grace just as the devil did (Ezek 28:11–19). A new convert does not truly understand his own weaknesses and the temptations that might ensnare him. As a result, he is more vulnerable to pride that will lead to his destruction (Prov 16:18). Time is therefore needed to let the new believer mature in his faith and gain the respect of others through faithful service in lesser roles. The difficulty is that Paul did not specify what constitutes a "new convert." Was he referring to six months, one year, or ten years? Perhaps the answer to this question depends on the congregation or circumstances involved. In some churches it might be unwise to let a person become an elder who has only been a Christian for five years. In other churches, however, it may be unwise to wait that long.

This conclusion is supported by the historical circumstances that surrounded the churches at Ephesus and Crete. The church at Ephesus was a somewhat well-established congregation when Paul wrote 1 Timothy. By that time the church had been in existence for about fifteen years and already had established leaders. In this circumstance Paul could write that elders should not be new converts because in that church others were more mature in their faith and could handle the respect and responsibilities given to such officeholders. Paul's letter to Titus, however, does not contain the restriction concerning new converts. Did Paul simply forget to add this qualification, or was it purposefully ignored? It is plausible that Paul ignored the restriction about new converts because the situation in Crete was different from that in Ephesus. The church in Crete

---

3 Grudem correctly writes, "Paul never says that all the elders are to be able to teach publicly or to preach sermons to the congregation, and it would be reasonable to think that an 'apt teacher' could be someone who is able to explain God's Word privately. So perhaps not all elders are called to do public teaching—perhaps not all have gifts for teaching in that specific way. What is clear here is that Paul wants to guarantee that elders have a mature and sound understanding of Scripture and can explain it to others" (Wayne Grudem, *Systematic Theology: An Introduction to Biblical Doctrine* [Leicester: IVP; Grand Rapids: Eerdmans, 1994], 915–16 n19).

was much younger, making nearly all the potential candidates for elder-ship "new converts." In this case, if new believers were not appointed as elders, there would be no elders. Consequently, this qualification is not absolute but depends somewhat on the situation of the congregation.[4]

Family Qualifications

The second area of qualifications relates to the family life of the candidate. He must be faithful to his wife and manage his children well before he can be considered fit to lead the church of God.

The Husband of One Wife (1 Tim 3:2; Titus 1:6)

This qualification appears at the forefront of both lists directly after the general qualification of being "above reproach." This placement suggests the importance of marital and sexual faithfulness and also highlights that this may have been a problem in the Ephesian and Cretean churches. The best interpretation of this difficult phrase is to understand it as referring to the faithfulness of a husband toward his wife. He must be a "one-woman man." That is, there must be no other woman in his life to whom he relates intimately, whether emotionally or physically. It is important for men to put a hedge of protection around their lives so they do not get into a position where they became emotionally or physically connected with another woman. As a general rule, it is best if a man is never alone with a woman who is not his wife. Unfortunately, many men have disqualified themselves from ministry because of unwise decisions regarding their contact with other women. The Bible is full of warnings about sexual unfaithfulness, but often these warnings go unheeded.

Should this office be restricted to men because only a man can be a "husband of one wife"? In order to answer this question, we also have to take into consideration 1 Timothy 2:12, where Paul stated, "I do not allow a woman to teach or to have authority over a man." Apparently some women were causing commotion in the church at Ephesus by their elaborate dress and their desire to teach (1 Tim 2:9–11). Paul, therefore, exhorted women to dress modestly and prohibited them from teaching and having authority over men. In 1 Timothy 2:13, Paul gave his first reason for not permitting women to teach or have authority over men in the context of the local church. He stated, "For Adam was created

---

4 For a more detailed discussion, see Benjamin L. Merkle, "Are the Qualifications for Elders or Overseers Negotiable?" *Bibliotheca Sacra* 171 (2014): 171–88.

first, then Eve." In this text Paul used an argument from the order of creation based on Genesis (Gen 2:7, 22). Why did Paul use the Genesis text to make his case? The fact that Adam was created before Eve signifies that he was the one with authority in their relationship. Paul's second reason (or, better, illustration) for prohibiting women from teaching or having authority over men was that Eve was deceived by the serpent in the garden (Gen 3:6, 13): "And Adam was not deceived, but the woman was deceived and transgressed" (1 Tim 2:14). Some claim that Eve's deception was caused by a lack of knowledge (and thus a lack of "education"). But this interpretation of 1 Timothy 2:13–14 does not fit with the Genesis account. Eve's deception was not based on her inferior knowledge or education but on her willingness to let the words of the serpent hold more sway over her decisions than the word of God. The lack of education among the women of Ephesus was not the problem that provoked Paul's prohibition. Rather, Paul was indicating in verse 14 what occurs when God's created order is reversed.

Paul's appeal to the creation of Adam before Eve demonstrates the different roles that God established in creation. The order of creation is the reason Paul prohibited women from teaching men or having authority over a man. The prohibition therefore transcends cultural differences. Throughout the New Testament, male leadership in the family is clearly established (see Eph 5:22–24; Col 3:18; Titus 2:4–5; 1 Pet 3:1, 4–6). There is no hint in the context of 1 Timothy 3 and Titus 1 that women are eligible to serve as elders. For these reasons eldership in the church should be limited to men.

Manage His Own Household Well (1 Tim 3:4–5; Titus 1:6)

The second family qualification relates to the man's role as father. Paul wrote that he must be "one who manages his own household competently, having his children under control with all dignity" (1 Tim 3:4). An elder must have respectful, obedient children. He must not be heavy-handed and authoritarian with his children but must deal with them "with all dignity." A godly father does not seek to crush the spirit of his children, forcing them into submission by harsh discipline. Rather, he relates to them with dignity and seeks to nurture their hearts. Paul wrote elsewhere, "Fathers, don't stir up anger in your children, but bring them up in the training and instruction of the Lord" (Eph 6:4).

Paul then gave the reason this qualification is important: "If anyone does not know how to manage his own household, how will he take care of God's church?" (1 Tim 3:5; cf. Titus 1:6). Paul made an important parallel between the family and the church. If a man is not able to lead his family so that his children are generally respectful and obedient, then he is not fit to lead the church, the family of God. The leadership of his family becomes tangible proof that he is either fit or unfit to lead in God's church. In addition, by neglecting his family—even for the sake of "the ministry"—a man can become disqualified to serve as an elder.

Moral Qualifications

Having briefly discussed an elder's situational and family qualifications, we will now discuss a potential elder's moral qualifications, which are more in number than the other qualifications. We will first consider the positive characteristics an elder is to possess and then the negative characteristics an elder is to avoid.

Positive Characteristics

Above Reproach (1 Tim 3:2; Titus 1:6)

The general or overarching qualification of an elder is that he must be "above reproach." This requirement does not call for perfection but for godliness. To be above reproach means to be free from any blemishes of character or conduct. His relationship with his wife and children is commendable, and he has no glaring moral weaknesses. Outsiders cannot point their finger and discredit his profession to be a faithful follower of Christ.

Self-Controlled (1 Tim 3:2)

This word is sometimes translated as "temperate" (e.g., NIV, NRSV, NASB) and is often used in connection with sobriety from alcohol (wine). In the context of 1 Timothy 3, however, it is best understood as referring to mental sobriety, a mind that can think clearly and spiritually about important matters. It is the ability to be self-controlled, having balanced judgment and being able to rationally make cool-headed decisions. Elders must be mentally and emotionally stable enough to make important decisions in the midst of problems and pressures they will face in their ministry.

Sensible (1 Tim 3:2; Titus 1:8)

Similar to the previous qualification, this characteristic refers to the need for disciplined exercise of good judgment. It speaks of being prudent, sound minded, and discreet. Such discretion is often needed by elders who have to make difficult decisions in the face of problems and disagreements.

Respectable (1 Tim 3:2)

An elder must also have character that is respectable. It is not enough to get his respect from his office. If others are to follow and emulate him, he must prove that his life is worth following. His character must therefore be well balanced and virtuous.

Hospitable (1 Tim 3:2; Titus 1:8)

An elder's life must be open so that others can be a part of it. Being hospitable means making time not only for one's family but also for others. Hospitality is an important biblical virtue (see Job 31:32; Rom 12:13; Heb 13:2; 1 Pet 4:9). If an elder is to get to know people and invest in their lives, he must take the time to build relationships with them. If he is to shepherd the flock of God effectively, his home must be open so that he can minister to them more than on Sunday mornings.

Gentle (1 Tim 3:3)

The word translated "gentle" can also mean "kind," "gracious," or "forbearing." In Philippians 4:5, Paul wrote, "Let your gentleness be made known to all" (author's translation). A gentle person is not overbearing but patient with others, especially when they have done wrong. He does not retaliate when wronged but returns love for evil.

A Good Reputation with Outsiders (1 Tim 3:7)

Oftentimes "outsiders" or non-Christians are better judges of character than those in the church. Neighbors, coworkers, or relatives may actually spend much more time with the person than his fellow church members. An elder must maintain a good reputation before a world of watching unbelievers. If the church allows a person who has a bad reputation with non-Christians to become an elder, they will scoff and mock the church for being hypocrites. A man who is unfaithful to his family, dishonest in his business, or rude to his neighbors will bring shame on himself and on the church. Paul warned that those who have a sinful or unfavorable reputation with outsiders can "fall into disgrace and the Devil's trap" (1 Tim 3:7). The world is waiting to point their fingers to criticize and disgrace the church. Thus, an elder must have a good reputation with non-Christians.

A Lover of Good (Titus 1:8)

This characteristic is closely related to hospitality. It involves willingly helping others and seeking their good.

Righteous (Titus 1:8)

The Greek word *dikaios* means "just" or "righteous." To be righteous or upright means living according to God's Word. First John 3:7 states, "The one who does what is right is righteous, just as he is righteous." Elders must abide by God's righteous standard revealed in his Word. An elder who is righteous will make fair, just, and upright decisions for the church. Job is described as a man who was "blameless and upright, one who feared God and turned away from evil" (Job 1:1 ESV).

Holy (Titus 1:8)

Sometimes translated "devout," this characteristic involves being wholly devoted to God and his Word. It entails being set apart to God in order to obey his will. A holy person is dedicated to glorifying the name of God regardless of what others may think.

Disciplined (Titus 1:8)

In the HCSB this qualification is translated "self-controlled" but is a different term than what is used in 1 Timothy 3:3. This characteristic involves self-discipline in every aspect of one's life, including physical desires. An undisciplined person yields easily to temptation, but a disciplined person fights against lust, anger, laziness, and other ungodly traits. Shepherding God's people is difficult work, and discipline is needed to fulfill this ministry faithfully and effectively.

Negative Characteristics

Not a Drunkard (1 Tim 3:3; Titus 1:7)

A man is disqualified for the office of elder if he is a drunkard (addicted to wine or other strong drink). Such a person lacks self-control and is undisciplined. The abuse of alcohol is a problem in most cultures and often results in ruined lives, marriages, and ministries. However, Paul did not say it is wrong to drink alcohol. He told Timothy to drink a little wine for his stomach problems (1 Tim 5:23). Rather, Paul was referring to the excesses of drinking too much alcohol and drinking it too often—that is, alcohol abuse. Christians who object to alcohol use usually do so because of other biblical texts and other reasons. Although many churches require their leaders and members to abstain from alcohol, we do not believe Scripture requires abstinence[5]—though it warns of the dangers of alcohol (e.g., Prov 20:1; 23:29–35). The real issue is the abuse of any substance that would bring shame on the person and reproach on the church.

Not a Bully (1 Tim 3:3; Titus 1:7)

Sometimes translated "violent" or "pugnacious," this characteristic describes someone who is easily irritated and has a bad temper. Such a person is often ready to fight rather than to calmly talk through a difficult situation. A violent man not only uses verbal abuse but is ready to physically assault those who anger him. On the contrary, an elder must be self-controlled and patient, willing to turn the other cheek when wronged. He must be able to calmly and rationally deal with heated arguments and tense situations that often find their way into the church.

Not Quarrelsome (1 Tim 3:3)

A man who is not quarrelsome is gentle and peaceful. People are constantly quarreling, even in the church. There are quarrels over doctrine, quarrels over the color of the carpet in the sanctuary, and quarrels over whether the church should sing hymns or choruses. An elder must be

---

5 John Piper warns against the dangers of adding requirements to Scripture: "By imposing a restriction which the New Testament never imposes, this . . . requirement, in principle, involves us in a legalism that has its roots in unbelief. It is a sign of a faded power and joy and heart righteousness that once was created by the power of Christ but cannot be preserved by laws" (*Brothers, We are NOT Professionals: A Plea to Pastors for Radical Ministry* [Nashville: B&H, 2002], 158).

able to address these tensions and not add to them. He must be a peace-maker and find a way to bring about reconciliation. If he is quarrelsome himself, he will not be able to effectively lead and may divide the congregation. As Paul later wrote, "The Lord's slave must not quarrel, but must be gentle to everyone, able to teach, and patient, instructing his opponents with gentleness" (2 Tim 2:24–25). Paul also reminded Titus to encourage the congregation "to slander no one, to avoid fighting, and to be kind, always showing gentleness to all people" (Titus 3:2).

Not Greedy (1 Tim 3:3; Titus 1:7)

Greed (or literally, "the love of money") is a serious problem in the church. It was in Paul's day, and it is in ours. Paul wrote, "But those who want to be rich fall into temptation, a trap, and many foolish and harmful desires, which plunge people into ruin and destruction" (1 Tim 6:9). Loving money can end in the destruction of one's soul. This is no small sin. Paul continued, "For the love of money is a root of all kinds of evil, and by craving it, some have wandered away from the faith and pierced themselves with many pains" (1 Tim 6:10). The Bible is full of warnings to the rich. Jesus himself said, "It is easier for a camel to go through the eye of a needle than for a rich person to enter the kingdom of God" (Mark 10:25). Consequently, it is not difficult to understand why Paul included this qualification in both 1 Timothy and Titus.

If a person is a lover of money, it is difficult for him also to be a lover of God. If our passions are divided, we become ineffective and distracted. Money itself is not the problem, however. It is the *love* of money. Whether we are considered rich or poor, the issue is what we desire. It is not those who *are* rich who fall into temptation but those who *desire* to be rich.

Paul's wording of the qualification in Titus is different from that in 1 Timothy. He stated that an elder must not be "greedy for money" (Titus 1:7). A greedy person is never content with God's provision but is constantly seeking ways to acquire more money—often in ways that are immoral and unethical. In 2 Corinthians, Paul warned of some ministers who peddle the Word of God for money (2 Cor 2:17; cf. Titus 1:11). Likewise, Peter stated that elders must shepherd the flock of God "not for the money but eagerly" (1 Pet 5:2).

Elders should be those who are free from the love and controlling influence of money. A pastor should not have unchecked control over the funds of a church. The elders must be accountable to one another and to the congregation as a whole. How many times have leaders fallen due to unethical practices with the church's finances? In contrast, we must heed the Word of God, which states, "Your life should be free from the love of money. Be satisfied with what you have, for He Himself has said, I will never leave you or forsake you" (Heb 13:5).

Not Arrogant (Titus 1:7)

An arrogant person is self-willed, constantly insisting that things be done his way. This is the opposite of being "gentle" (1 Tim 3:3). He is inconsiderate of other people's opinions and feelings and attempts to get what he wants regardless of the cost to others. Such a person does not make a good elder because the elders must work together as a team, seeking the best for others, not themselves. A shepherd must be gentle with the sheep and not seek to overpower them by his strong will.

Not Quick-Tempered (Titus 1:7)

David told us that God is "compassionate and gracious, slow to anger and rich in faithful love" (Ps 103:8; cf. Exod 34:6–7). Those who lead the church are to model the characteristics of their heavenly Father and be slow to anger. A quick-tempered man, however, is not only easily angered, but he is unable to control that anger. He quickly lashes out at others, not displaying the patience and self-control of Christ. Although not all anger is sin (Paul told us, "Be angry and do not sin," Eph 4:26; cf. Ps 4:4), James reminds us that "man's anger does not accomplish God's righteousness" (Jas 1:20). Furthermore, "An angry man stirs up conflict, and a hot-tempered man increases rebellion" (Prov 29:22). An elder must be able to deal with difficult and emotionally charged situations that arise in his personal life and in the context of the church.

The qualifications of an elder are generally the basic character traits expected of all believers. Elders are not superspiritual people but are those who are mature in their faith and live consistent, humble lives. They are not content to look spiritual on Sundays or Wednesdays, but their spirituality pervades their entire lives. An elder has a healthy and pure relationship with his wife, and he is a godly leader in his home. His character has no glaring blemishes, and his godliness is even recognized by those who are not Christians. He is not perfect, but his life is characterized by integrity.

Controversial Qualifications

We turn now to consider in greater depth two qualifications whose mean-ing has been disputed: the first relates to marriage, the other to children.

"The Husband of One Wife"

In both 1 Timothy 3:2 and Titus 1:6, Paul wrote that an elder must be "the husband of one wife" or, more literally, he must be a "one-woman man." Because there has been much debate and confusion over this qual-ification, we need to deal with it in detail. There are four main interpre-tations of this phrase: (1) an elder must be married; (2) an elder must not be a polygamist; (3) an elder must have only one wife his entire life; (4) an elder must be faithful to his wife.

An Elder Must Be Married

Many Christians today are convinced that a man cannot be an elder unless he is married. They hold this view for an obvious reason: it is what the Bible says—or, at least, appears to say. Paul wrote that an over-seer (elder/pastor) "must be . . . the husband of one wife" (1 Tim 3:2; cf. Titus 1:6).[6] If Paul, under the inspiration of the Holy Spirit, stated that an elder *must* be the husband of one wife, then the case is settled. The other qualifications, it is argued, are not negotiable. An elder *must* be above reproach, sober minded, self-controlled, respectable, hospitable, and able to teach (1 Tim 3:2). In the same way, if a man is not married, then he is not the "husband of one wife" and thus fails to meet this qual-ification. As a result, he is not qualified to serve as an elder.

But this interpretation should be rejected for the following reasons. First, the focus of the phrase is not that a man is married but that he is faithful to his "one" wife. The Greek literally reads, "one-woman man" (*mias gunaikos anēr*), with emphasis placed on the first word, "one" (*mias*). Second, Paul clearly taught that singleness has many advantages over being married. In Corinthians, Paul even encouraged singleness, explaining how those who are not married are able to serve the Lord with undivided attention (1 Cor 7:32–35). Third, Paul could have writ-ten that an elder must be a man who has a wife (which is different from saying he must be a "one-woman man"). Fourth, this qualification would eliminate Paul, probably Timothy, and the Lord Jesus himself from

---

6 The same argument can be made for deacons because Paul likewise stated, "Deacons must be husbands of one wife" (1 Tim 3:12).

being eligible to serve as elders. Fifth, to be consistent, we would have to require men to have more than one child because Paul indicated that a potential elder must manage his "children" (plural) well. Rather, the phrase "husband of one wife" should be understood as merely reflecting the common situation of the time because most people were married. It was simply the norm that men married, and there was no need to highlight the exception.

An Elder Must Not Be a Polygamist

This view maintains that an elder cannot be married to more than one woman at the same time. In many cultures it is not only permissible but also a sign of blessing to have more than one wife. According to the Bible, however, Christians are to be monogamous. The dangers of polygamy can be seen in the life of Solomon. Although God granted him wisdom beyond that of any other person, Solomon unwisely married foreign women who introduced other gods to the king. As a result Solomon was led astray, and his kingdom was later divided.

Although polygamy is to be avoided, it is probably not what Paul had in mind when he specified that an elder must be the "husband of one wife." We know this because Paul used a similar phrase in 1 Timothy 5:9 where he gives qualifications for widows who are eligible to receive financial support from the church. Paul indicated that a widow must be "the wife of one husband" (literally, "a one-man woman"). It is unlikely that Paul meant a widow must not have been married to more than one man at the same time. For, although polygamy (having more than one wife) was somewhat common in the Greco-Roman and Jewish culture, polyandry (having more than one husband) was strongly rejected by both the Jews and the Romans. Further, "even if polygamy existed among the Jews, evidence is lacking that it was practiced by Christians, and therefore 'Christian polygamy' most likely is not in view."[7] If polygamy was rare among Christians, it does not seem likely that it would be singled out in all three lists (1 Tim 3:2, 12; Titus 1:6) and put at the head of both lists dealing with elders. Consequently, it is unlikely that the phrase "husband of one wife" was intended to address polygamy.

---

7 William D. Mounce, *Pastoral Epistles*, Word Biblical Commentary (Nashville: Nelson, 2000), 171.

An Elder Must Have Only One Wife His Entire Life

Another possible interpretation is that to be eligible for service as an elder, a man is not permitted to remarry under any circumstance. If his wife dies or divorces him, he is to remain unmarried. If he remarries, he is no longer qualified to be an elder because he is no longer "the husband of one wife." This view has several strengths. First, it takes the phrase "husband of one wife" seriously and offers a plausible interpretation. Second, this was the view of the early church, which valued celibacy after the divorce or death of a spouse. Third, the apostle Paul, while allowing remarriage in some cases, favored singleness and celibacy (1 Cor 7:9, 39). Thus, it may be that Paul was emphasizing the need for divorced men or men whose spouses have died to remain unmarried in order to be eligible for eldership. Others may be permitted to remarry, but the high calling of being an elder requires men in that office to remain single and celibate.

However, there are several reasons to reject this view. First, it is doubtful that Paul was holding elders to a higher standard of morality than he required of all believers. All of the moral and spiritual qualifications given to the elders are what is expected of all believers. Second, Paul seemed to indicate that sometimes remarriage is a viable option. He stated, "I say to the unmarried and to *widows*: It is good for them if they remain as I am. But if they do not have self-control, *they should marry*" (1 Cor 7:8–9, emphasis added). Later he wrote, "A wife is bound as long as her husband is living. But if her husband dies, she is free to be married to anyone she wants—only in the Lord" (1 Cor 7:39). These verses permit remarriage if a spouse has died. Paul also used the principle of a spouse's freedom (after the other spouse has died) to illustrate the believer's freedom from the law (Rom 7:1–3). Third, it is wrong to treat divorce and remarriage as the unpardonable sin. If a former murderer is able to be forgiven and later serve as a spiritual leader (like the apostle Paul, who was guilty of murder; Acts 9:1, 26), then it would seem rather arbitrary that a person who remarries cannot serve in such a capacity. Of course, if Scripture indicates that a remarried man cannot serve as elder, we must obey. It is unlikely, however, that this was Paul's intent.

Fourth, in 1 Timothy 5:14, Paul stated that it is better for younger widows to remarry than to become idle or gossips. Earlier, Paul indicated that if a widow is to be officially enrolled to receive financial assistance, she must be the "wife of one husband" (1 Tim 5:9). It seems unlikely that by encouraging younger widows to remarry, Paul was effectively disqualifying them from ever being able to receive assistance from the church should they be widowed again. We must assume that those who remarried and were later widowed again would still be considered the "woman of one man" and would still qualify to be enrolled for financial aid from the church.[8] As a result, the phrase "wife of one husband" most likely does not refer to a woman who only has one husband her entire lifetime but who is faithful to her husband while he is alive. Similarly, the "husband of one wife" should not be taken to mean that an elder can never remarry but that he must be faithful to his wife.

An Elder Must Be Faithful to His Wife

This final interpretation, and the one favored by this author, is that an elder must be faithful to his wife in a monogamous relationship. This view includes the prohibition of polygamy, promiscuity, and homosexuality. A potential elder must be a "one-woman man," meaning he must honor, love, and be devoted to his wife and her alone. This view allows for the possibility of an elder being remarried after the death of his wife or after a divorce, although the phrase in question does not directly address that situation. The emphasis of the qualifications given in 1 Timothy and Titus stresses the present situation of a man's moral and spiritual character. The real issue is not so much where he has come from but who he is now by God's grace. If a man is currently faithful to his wife, being above reproach, and has proven himself in that relationship, then it is possible for him to become an elder.

Must an Elder Have Children Who Are Believers?

This question is really composed of two separate questions: (1) Must an elder have children? and (2) Must his children be believers? If we insist that all elders be married, then, to be consistent, we would have to require them to have more than one child. After all Paul indicated that a potential elder must manage "his own household competently, having his children under control" (1 Tim 3:4). Paul did not say he must keep his child (singular) submissive but that he must keep his children (plural) under control or submissive. The point, of course, is not that a man must

---

[8] Mounce writes, "It seems doubtful that Paul would encourage the remarriage of 'younger widows' if this meant that they could never later be enrolled if they were again widowed. For such widows, it could be presumed that remarriage would not be inconsistent with being a 'one-man' woman, and hence the phrase in 1 Tim. 5:9 would not be a call for a single marriage" (*Pastoral Epistles*, 173; also see George W. Knight, *The Pastoral Epistles*, New International Greek Testament Commentary [Grand Rapids: Eerdmans, 1992], 158).

have a child or more than one child but that whether he has one child or many children, he leads them well and they are submissive to him. George Knight rightly comments,

> It is exceedingly doubtful that Paul intended that . . . the words about "children" (plural, vv. 4, 12) be understood as mandating that only a married man with at least two children could be an officer in the church. Probably he wrote in terms of the common situation, i.e., of being married and having children, and then spoke of what should be the case when this most common situation exists in an officer's life.[9]

So it is typical that an elder will have children. And he must manage those children well. Yet, just as we saw with marriage above, having children is not an absolute requirement for being an elder.

Further, if we press Paul's words beyond his original intention, we could not only argue that a potential elder must have at least two children but that his children must still live at home with him. Paul's reason for mentioning children was that a man's home life and his relationship with his children are the testing grounds for his ability to lead the church. Paul stated, "If anyone does not know how to manage his own household, how will he take care of God's church?" (1 Tim 3:5). Thus, we might (wrongly) infer that if a man's children are grown up and no longer live at home, this qualification cannot be met. The point, however, is not that his children must be living at home but that if his children are living at home he must manage them well and they must be respectful and obedient.

In addition, Paul stated in Titus 1 that an elder's children must be "believers [*pistos*] and not open to the charge of debauchery or insubordination" (Titus 1:6 ESV). Does this text indicate that for a man to be qualified as an elder all of his children must be professing believers? This interpretation is favored by some commentators and many Bible translations (ESV, NIV, NASB, NRSV, RSV, and NLT). A few translations, however, opt for a different interpretation, which states that a man's children must be faithful (HCSB, NKJV, and KJV). For example, the Holman Christian Standard Bible states that an elder must be the husband of one wife "having faithful children not accused of wildness or rebellion." There are at least four reasons this translation is to be favored.

---

9 Knight, *The Pastoral Epistles*, 157. Mounce agrees, "This is not a requirement that an overseer have children, but if he does have children, they should be faithful" (*Pastoral Epistles*, 388).

First, the interpretation that an elder's children must be "faithful" and not necessarily "believing" is a possible use of the Greek term *pistos* (see 1 Tim 3:11; 2 Tim 2:2).[10] In the following phrase, Paul stated that an elder's children must not be "accused of wildness or rebellion." This phrase qualifies the type of faithfulness Paul had in mind. Paul was referring to the behavior of the child ("faithful"), not the inner state of the child ("believing"). Thus, the content of a child's faithfulness primarily involves living a moral life and being obedient to his parents.

Second, the comparison with 1 Timothy 3:4 favors the meaning of "faithful" as opposed to "believing." Paul wrote to Timothy that an elder must manage "his own household competently, having his children under control with all dignity." Notice that Paul did not include that an elder's children must be believers. He simply stated that a potential elder must keep his children submissive. Again the focus is not on the child's inner state but on his behavior. The child does not have to be a Christian, but he must be obedient and respectful. It seems unlikely that Paul would require elders' children in Crete to be believers but have a lower standard in Ephesus, requiring them only to be faithful or obedient. This apparent distinction seems even more unlikely in light of the fact that Ephesus was the more established church. The churches in Crete were still young compared to the more mature church in Ephesus. Would Paul place a more restrictive requirement on the less mature church? In other qualifications we find just the opposite. When writing to the church at Ephesus, Paul included that an elder must not be a new convert (1 Tim 3:6) but did not mention this requirement to the churches in Crete. It is better to see the requirement in Titus 1:6 as virtually identical to that found in 1 Timothy 3:4—an elder's children must be faithful and submissive.

Third, the view that all of an elder's children must be professing Christians raises a series of difficult questions: What if a child is not old enough to understand the gospel and make a credible profession of faith? Is that father temporarily disqualified to serve as an elder? Does he have to wait until his child professes faith in Christ? Or should all the children of believers be considered Christians unless they renounce the faith? What if an elder has seven believing children, but his eighth child

---

10 W. Bauer, F. W. Danker, W. F. Arndt, and F. W. Gingrich, eds., *Greek-English Lexicon of the New Testament and Other Early Christian Literature*, 3rd ed. (Chicago: University of Chicago Press, 2000), 820–21; *Theological Dictionary of the New Testament* 6:175, 204. Paul often stressed the quality of "faithfulness" in his coworkers. He referred to Timothy (1 Cor 4:17), Tychicus (Eph 6:21; Col 4:7), Epaphras (Col 1:7), and Onesimus (Col 4:9) as being "faithful" in the ministry. Also see Matt 24:45; 25:21, 23; 1 Cor 4:2; Heb 3:5; 1 Pet 5:12.

forsakes the faith? This view is probably much more complicated than Paul was intending. It is more likely Paul intended the children of elders to be faithful and not necessarily be professing Christians.

Fourth, it seems unlikely that Paul would require something a father cannot control. This argument is not based on anything in the immediate context of the requirement in Titus 1:6 but is a larger theological and practical argument. The Bible teaches that salvation is of the Lord and that those who believe in Jesus are those who have been predestined, called, and justified (Rom 8:30). Even if a father brings up his children "in the training and instruction of the Lord" (Eph 6:4), there is no guarantee that his children will become Christians. Some may quote Proverbs 22:6, which states, "Teach a youth about the way he should go; even when he is old he will not depart from it." It is simply poor hermeneutics, however, to interpret the Proverbs as promises from God. Rather, the Proverbs are given to provide us with wisdom in life. Each proverb should be viewed *not* as a promise but as a general principle. That is, generally speaking, when children are trained correctly, they will not depart from that training but will remain faithful to what they have been taught. But this does not mean such will always be the case. Many good parents have faithfully raised their children in the discipline and instruction of the Lord only to see them reject their parents' teaching and go down their own path. Consequently, it seems unlikely that Paul would place a requirement on candidates for eldership that is simply beyond their control.[11]

The qualification that an elder must manage "his own household competently" should not be taken to mean that all elders must have children. In addition, an elder's children, if he has them, must be faithful and obedient but not necessarily believers.

---

[11] Strauch rightly comments, "Those who interpret this qualification to mean that an elder must have believing, Christian children place an impossible burden upon the father. Even the best Christian fathers cannot guarantee that their children will believe. Salvation is a supernatural act of God. God, not good parents (although they are certainly used of God), ultimately brings salvation (John 1:12,13)" (Alexander Strauch, *Biblical Eldership: An Urgent Call to Restore Biblical Church Leadership*, 3rd ed., rev. and exp. [Littleton, CO: Lewis & Roth, 1995], 229).

CHAPTER 14

The Biblical Role of Elders

Benjamin L. Merkle

In the contemporary church, elders or pastors are busier than ever. With so many programs, committees, and events, it is often difficult to find time to meet the needs of the congregation. Some view the pastor as the CEO, while others view him as an employee. Still others view the pastor as their personal therapist who has the answers to all their problems. With so many responsibilities vying for a pastor's time, what should take precedence? In other words, what are the main duties of an elder? And what authority does an elder have? These are the two main questions this chapter will try to answer. It will conclude by considering the biblical mandate for a plurality of elders.

The Duty of Elders

An elder has at least four duties. The elder is called to be (1) a leader, (2) a shepherd, (3) a teacher, and (4) an equipper.

Elder as Leader

First of all, an elder is called to lead the church. Paul wrote that an elder must be "one who manages his own household competently" and then adds the reason, "If anyone does not know how to manage his own household, how will he take care of God's church?" (1 Tim 3:4–5).[1] The analogy Paul made is between the role of the husband and the role of the elder. If an elder cannot manage (that is, rule, lead, care for) his own family, then how can he be expected to take on the additional responsibilities and challenges of leading the church? Later, Paul wrote, "The elders who are good leaders should be considered worthy of an ample honorarium" (1 Tim 5:17). It is evident, then, that one of the main functions of an elder is to lead the church (cf. Rom 12:8).

The author of Hebrews instructed the congregation, "Obey your leaders and submit to them" (Heb 13:17; cf. 1 Thess 5:12). The leaders, probably the elders, thus had a certain authority. Authority in the church is not equally divided among the members. And yet nowhere are the leaders told to force the congregation to submit to them. That is because leaders in the church must lead humbly and by example. A pastor should not ask people to do something he is not willing to do. Peter exhorted the elders to lead the people in a way that is not domineering, "but being examples to the flock" (1 Pet 5:3). The author of Hebrews wrote, "Remember your leaders who have spoken God's word to you. As you carefully observe the outcome of their lives, imitate their faith" (Heb 13:7).

Biblical leadership is humble, servant leadership. Jesus gave the perfect example of humility when he washed the feet of his disciples (John 13:1–20). What does a humble leader look like? First of all, a humble leader does not demand respect. He realizes that his position in the church is a gift from God and that the church itself is God's church. A humble leader is also teachable. He admits he does not have all the answers but is willing to listen and learn from others. Furthermore, he is willing to work with others because he realizes the importance of teamwork and accountability. A humble leader is a servant. When James and John asked if they could sit at Jesus' right- and left-hand side in heaven, Jesus said to his disciples, "You know that those who are regarded as rulers of the Gentiles dominate them, and their men of high positions exercise power over them. But it must not be like that among you. On the contrary, whoever wants to become great among you must be your servant, and whoever wants to be first among you must be a slave to all" (Mark 10:42–44). Finally, and most importantly, a humble leader does all to the glory of God (1 Cor 10:31).

---

[1] Unless otherwise indicated, all Scripture passages are taken from the HCSB.

Elder as Shepherd

As we have already demonstrated, the title "pastor" (Eph 4:11) is simply another term used to describe an elder or overseer, and the word *pastor* means "shepherd." Because the people of God are referred to figuratively as "sheep," those who tend to their needs and exercise leadership over them are figuratively called "shepherds." Peter exhorted the elders to "shepherd God's flock among you" (1 Pet 5:2). Thus, elders lead the people of God as a shepherd leads a flock of sheep. This is a significant analogy. Church leaders are not cowboys who drive the sheep. Rather, they are caring shepherds who lead and protect the sheep. Furthermore, the shepherd's primary task is not to run an organization but to care for people's souls. A pastor is not primarily a motivator, administrator, or program facilitator but a shepherd.

In the Old Testament the Lord rebuked the leaders of Israel for not being good shepherds. The basic charge against them was that they looked after their own interests and ignored the needs of the sheep (Ezek 34:2–4). Jesus, of course, is the perfect Shepherd. He is the good Shepherd who "lays down his life for the sheep" (John 10:11; cf. John 15:13). He is the one who always feeds his sheep. He strengthens them, heals them, binds their wounds, and brings back those who are straying. Peter therefore described Jesus as "the Shepherd and Overseer" of our souls (1 Pet 2:25 ESV). He is the "chief Shepherd" (1 Pet 5:4) who is the perfect example for undershepherds.

The shepherd must be willing to protect the sheep. Paul warned the Ephesian elders in his farewell speech, "Be on guard for yourselves and for all the flock, among whom the Holy Spirit has appointed you as overseers, to shepherd the church of God, which He purchased with His own blood. I know that after my departure savage wolves will come in among you, not sparing the flock" (Acts 20:28–29). A good shepherd will pay close attention to the flock so that they are protected from wolves who would seek to harm them spiritually.

Despite the shepherd's efforts, however, sheep get injured and need assistance. It is therefore important for the elders to attend to the needs of those in the congregation. They need to visit those who are not only spiritually sick or weak but also physically sick. James raised the question, "Is anyone among you sick?" His answer for this problem is, "He should call for the elders of the church, and they should pray over him" (Jas 5:14). Isaiah gave us a picture of a good shepherd as he explained how the Lord God shepherds his people: "He protects His flock like a shepherd; He gathers the lambs in His arms and carries them in the fold of His garment. He gently leads those that are nursing" (Isa 40:11). In giving the qualifications for an elder, Paul stated that he must be able to manage his own household well or else he will not be able to "care for" God's church. The Greek word translated "care for" (*epimeleomai*) is found only two other times in the New Testament, both in the parable of the Good Samaritan. We are told that the Good Samaritan had compassion on the injured Jew, cleaning and binding his wounds. He then set the dying man on his animal and brought him to the inn and "took care of him" (Luke 10:34). The Samaritan then commanded the innkeeper, "Take care of him" (Luke 10:35). It is this type of care that the shepherds of God's church are called to display in their ministries.

Shepherding carries with it a great responsibility before God. The sheep are placed under the shepherd's care. The sheep have a responsibility to follow the shepherd, but the shepherd has to be diligent in keeping watch over the sheep. The author of Hebrews exhorted his readers, "Obey your leaders and submit to them, for they keep watch over your souls as those who will give an account" (Heb 13:17). The reason the congregation is to follow the leadership of the elders is because they are given the task of watching over the congregation's souls—a responsibility for which they will be held accountable.

Elder as Teacher

It is clear from the New Testament that an elder is primarily a teacher. The elders' calling to lead the church through their teaching is what distinguishes them from the deacons because one of the qualifications given for an elder is that he must be "an able teacher" (1 Tim 3:2). A few chapters later Paul mentioned that those who rule well are worthy of double honor, that is, those who work hard at "preaching and teaching" (1 Tim 5:17). In Titus, Paul described this role in more detail. He explained that an elder must hold "to the faithful message as taught, so that he will be able both to encourage with sound teaching and to refute those who contradict it" (Titus 1:9). Paul indicated that the goal of teaching is not only to encourage believers by giving them biblical instruction but also to firmly rebuke those who oppose the truth of the gospel. The teaching role is inseparably connected to the function of the pastor when Paul stated that God has gifted the church with "pastors and teachers" or pastor-teachers (Eph 4:11).

Other texts associate the role of church leaders with teaching. Although the term *elder* or *overseer* is not actually used, in the following examples it is likely that those who were doing the teaching were in fact elders.

Paul reminded the church in Galatia that the "one who is taught the message must share his goods with the teacher" (Gal 6:6). Two things should be observed from this verse. First, that which was being taught was the Word. This emphasis on the Word of God was evident from the beginning of the church. We read that the first believers in Jerusalem "devoted themselves to the apostles' teaching" (Acts 2:42). Second, some leaders were so dedicated to the task of teaching that they required financial support. Though not named elders here, these people were performing the function of elders among the congregation. In 1 Thessalonians 5:12, Paul exhorted the congregation "to give recognition to those who labor among you and lead you in the Lord and admonish you." These leaders who are to be given recognition, or respected, are described as those who "labor," "lead," and "admonish" the Thessalonian Christians. Most likely, those who had the role of leading, teaching, and admonishing the congregation were the elders. Likewise, in Hebrews 13:7, the leaders are defined as those "who have spoken God's word" to the church. This text is most likely referring to the teaching ministry of the elders.

Paul also stressed the importance of the teaching ministry to his associate Timothy. Although it is incorrect to view Timothy as the "pastor" of the church at Ephesus because he carried more authority as Paul's apostolic delegate, it is clear that his role overlapped with that of the elders. Paul reminded his protégé Timothy, "Give your attention to public reading, exhortation, and teaching" (1 Tim 4:13). The reading and subsequent exposition of the Bible was at the heart of the worship service. For Timothy to neglect this task would be a colossal failure on his part. In 2 Timothy, probably Paul's last surviving letter, Paul realized that his death was imminent and sensed the urgency to once again encourage his son in the faith, Timothy. With the utmost solemnity and seriousness, Paul wrote, "Before God and Christ Jesus, who is going to judge the living and the dead, and by His appearing and His kingdom, I solemnly charge you: proclaim the message; persist in it whether convenient or not; rebuke, correct, and encourage with great patience and teaching" (2 Tim 4:1–2). Solid, gospel teaching in the church is vital to the church's existence. The Word must be preached, and it is the task of elders to preach it.

Elder as Equipper

It is not enough for elders to be teachers; they must also purposefully equip the next generation of elders to minister alongside of them or to plant new churches in the community. Too often pastors preach and teach year after year, but, when all is said and done, they have not effectively trained and equipped anybody to take their place. It is a sign of an unhealthy church when the pastor is gone and no one in the congregation can step in and fill the pulpit. Biblical eldership includes training others to do the task of preaching and teaching.

Again, Paul's words to Timothy were instructive. He told Timothy, "And what you have heard from me in the presence of many witnesses, commit to faithful men who will be able to teach others also" (2 Tim 2:2). As Paul's faithful coworker, Timothy was entrusted with the task of passing on the pure gospel as preached by Paul. He had been equipped by Paul and was now to become an equipper. Thus, he was to entrust what he had learned to "faithful men," which is probably another way of describing the elders of the church. But this task of equipping does not stop with the elders. They are likewise to become equippers "who will be able to teach others also." The task of raising up new leaders in the church does not belong primarily to Bible colleges or seminaries. It is the task of elders to identify young (or not so young) men who will be faithful to carry on the gospel message. Unfortunately, many pastors are either too busy or too insecure to mentor and disciple other gifted men in the church. Thus, this role of the elder is perhaps the most neglected and therefore one that must be emphasized in churches today.

The office of elder is important because of the role elders perform. Their primary task is not merely to run the church but to care for the spiritual lives of the congregation. As leaders, shepherds, teachers, and equippers, elders have the immense responsibility and privilege of helping God's people become more holy and more Christlike.

The Authority of Elders

Elders Have (Limited) Authority

The New Testament does not explicitly spell out how much authority the elders of a local congregation should have. We have to take relevant texts from the New Testament and attempt to synthesize the principles that are taught in them. As a result, we must be cautious of conclusions that are too rigid or dogmatic. The principles we gather from Scripture are binding, but the outworking of these principles can be applied in different ways.

In the first place, the Bible is clear that elders have authority. Paul wrote to the congregation in Thessalonica, "Now we ask you, brothers, to give recognition to those who labor among you and lead you in the Lord and admonish you" (1 Thess 5:12). This text demonstrates that in the earliest stage of the church, some were set apart as leaders and, as such, were to be respected because of their important work in the church. Paul made a distinction between the "brothers" and those whom they are to respect. Apparently not every believer was to be honored and respected in the same way. Some, because of their gifts and function in the community, were to be considered worthy of special recognition. This text is similar to 1 Timothy 5:17, where Paul stated, "The elders who are good leaders should be considered worthy of an ample honorarium, especially those who work hard at preaching and teaching." Just as men have authority in their homes, so elders have authority in the church (1 Tim 3:4–5).

Another text that demonstrates the authority of elders is found at the end of Hebrews. The author urged the congregation, "Obey your leaders and submit to them, for they keep watch over your souls as those who will give an account" (Heb 13:17). Although elders are not mentioned but merely "leaders," it is safe to assume that those who possessed this type of authority were indeed elders.[2] The first word, "obey" (*peithō*), can also mean "to be persuaded." The normal word for "obey" or "to subject oneself" is *hupotassō*, which is a stronger word. Although the verb *peithō* demands obedience, it is "the obedience that is won through persuasive conversation."[3] The second command, "submit" (*hupeikō*), is found only here in the New Testament and means "to submit to one's authority." Similarly, Paul encouraged the Corinthian believers to submit (*hupotassō*) to the household of Stephanas, as well as other workers (1 Cor 16:15–16; cf. 1 Pet 5:5). But those who lead the church must be servant leaders.[4]

The duties of elders communicate that their office carries a certain amount of authority. As teachers, they are charged with the task of

---

[2] Grudem affirms this position: "Since the New Testament gives no indication of any other officers in the church with this kind of authority, it is reasonable to conclude that the congregation is to submit to and obey its elders" (Wayne Grudem, *Systematic Theology: An Introduction to Biblical Doctrine* [Leicester: IVP; Grand Rapids: Eerdmans, 1994], 915).

[3] William L. Lane, *Hebrews 9–13*, Word Biblical Commentary, vol. 47b (Dallas: Word, 1991), 554.

[4] Schreiner notes: "Paul does not say that the leaders are to compel the congregation to submit. He urges the congregation to submit voluntarily and gladly to leadership. The congregation takes it upon itself to follow the leadership. Paul does not instruct leaders to compel the congregation to submit" (Thomas R. Schreiner, *Paul, Apostle of God's Glory in Christ* [Downers Grove: IVP, 2001], 386).

authoritatively proclaiming God's Word. They are not merely offering suggestions or voicing their own opinions but are declaring, "Thus says the Lord." Consequently, the congregation has a duty to obey not merely the words of the preacher but the words of God, insomuch as the preacher accurately and faithfully conveys the gospel message.

As shepherds, elders are given the task of leading God's people (Acts 20:28; Eph 4:11; 1 Pet 5:2). If some are leading as shepherds, the assumption is that others are following their leadership. Of course, with the authority given to a shepherd comes added responsibility. They must guide, watch over, and protect those in their flock. They are even called to go after wandering sheep and bring them back into the fold. Elders are accountable before God for their role as shepherds (Heb 13:17). In the same way the sheep are accountable before God to obey and follow the shepherds so that they can fulfill their responsibilities with joy (Heb 13:17).

As representatives the elders speak and act on behalf of the entire congregation. When Barnabas and Paul brought famine relief money on behalf of the church in Antioch, it was received by the elders of the Jerusalem church (Acts 11:30). Later in Acts, as Paul was journeying to Jerusalem from Greece, he briefly harbored at Miletus. There he called for the elders of the Ephesian church to come so that he might encourage them (Acts 20:17). Although his concern was for the whole church, he called the elders because they served as the leaders and representatives of the church.

The authority of eldership comes from God, not the congregation. Although the congregation affirms elders' calling and authority, their authority has a divine origin. Paul told the Ephesian elders that the Holy Spirit made them overseers (Acts 20:28). They were called and given authority by God and not by man. Yet it was probably the Ephesian congregation that endorsed them. Then Paul may have appointed them publicly to their office. Similarly in the letter to the Ephesians, Paul stated that Christ has given gifts to the church, including pastor-teachers (Eph 4:11). Therefore, the office of elder "does not derive its existence, or authority, from the congregation. The elder's authority comes from Christ, and the congregation's role is that of recognition of God's gifting and calling."[5]

---

5 James R. White, "The Congregation-Led Church: Response by James R. White," in *Perspectives on Church Government: Five Views of Church Polity* (Nashville: B&H, 2004), 205.

It must be pointed out, however, that the elders' authority is not absolute; it is *limited*. They derive their authority from the Word of God, and when they stray from that Word, they abandon their God-given authority. As an apostle of Jesus Christ, Paul possessed nearly unmatched authority. Yet, Luke tells us that the Bereans were more noble than others because they not only received the preached word with eagerness, but they examined the Scriptures daily to see if Paul indeed spoke the truth. Paul himself stated that if he or even an angel preached a gospel other than the true gospel, "let him be accursed" (Gal 1:8 ESV). The authority that elders possess is not so much derived from their office but from the duties they perform. That is, the elders are not to be obeyed simply because they are elders. Rather, they are to be obeyed because they have the responsibility of shepherding and teaching the congregation. They shepherd because the Word calls upon elders to shepherd. They teach because the Word calls upon elders to teach. But when their shepherding and teaching stray from Scripture, their authority as shepherds and teachers is no longer binding on the congregation.

Some may regard Timothy and Titus as elders and conclude that elders possess significantly more authority than we have just described. However, although Timothy and Titus performed pastoral or elderlike duties in their respective ministries in Ephesus and Crete, it would be wrong to assume that the authority they possessed is the same authority pastors have today. The reason for this distinction is because Timothy and Titus were not pastors but were Paul's apostolic delegates.[6]

There are at least three reasons to make a distinction between the roles of Timothy and Titus and the role of the elder or overseer. First, both Timothy and Titus held temporary positions (see 2 Tim 4:9–10; Titus 3:12). Second, it was their task to appoint elders in the churches (see 1 Tim 5:22; Titus 1:5; cf. Acts 14:23). Third, a single leadership

---

6 William D. Mounce rightly acknowledges the uniqueness of their position: "Timothy and Titus stand outside the church structure. They are not bishops or elders, and are not members of the local church. They are itinerant, apostolic delegates sent with Paul's authority to deal with local problems, just as they do in Acts. Timothy and Titus are never told to rely on their institutional position in the local church for authority; rather they rely on the authority of Paul and the gospel" (*Pastoral Epistles*, Word Biblical Commentary [Nashville: Nelson, 2000], lxxxviii). Others who hold that Timothy and Titus did not possess any office in the church but were sent as Paul's apostolic delegates with temporary authority include George W. Knight, *The Pastoral Epistles*, New International Greek Testament Commentary (Grand Rapids: Eerdmans, 1992), 29; J. N. D. Kelly, *A Commentary on the Pastoral Epistles*, Black's New Testament Commentaries (London: Adam & Charles Black, 1963), 13–14; Donald Guthrie, *The Pastoral Epistles*, rev. ed., Tyndale New Testament Commentaries, vol. 14 (Leicester, England: IVP; Grand Rapids: Eerdmans, 1990), 38–39.

position with the authority they possessed is not found in the New Testament. Based on these facts, it is best to view Timothy and Titus *not* as pastors or elders but as Paul's apostolic delegates. As delegates under Paul's authority, they were sent to their respective places of ministry to help establish the churches in the gospel as well as to protect the churches from false gospels. They had a specific task to accomplish, and when that task was complete, they would move on to another ministry. Because Paul sent them and they functioned as an extension of Paul's own ministry, they carried with them an authority that surpassed that of an elder or overseer. They were not elders but were given the unique task of appointing elders so that the church would be healthy and could function without them. Thus, although many of the commands given to Timothy and Titus are applicable for pastors, it is wrong to equate the ministries of Timothy and Titus with the modern-day ministry of an elder or pastor.

Another way elders' authority is limited is that it does not carry beyond the local church. No evidence is in the New Testament that elders exercised authority outside their congregation like the apostles. As shepherds they ministered to their flock, but once they ventured outside their community to another congregation, they no longer functioned authoritatively.

Furthermore, biblical church government should not be set up as an aristocracy or an oligarchy. The local congregation as a whole often took part in the governance of the church. They were involved in choosing new leaders (Acts 6:2–3), commissioning missionaries (Acts 13:3), making important theological decisions (Acts 15:22), and disciplining unrepentant church members (1 Cor 5:2; 2 Cor 2:6). In the New Testament there seems to be a balance between the authority of the elders and the authority of the congregation as a whole. To ignore either side of this equation will create an unhealthy and dangerous imbalance.

Thus, key decisions in the church should not be made only by the elders but should be brought before the entire congregation. Because the church is a body (and not merely a head or feet), all in the church are important and should be allowed to be a part of major decisions. In saying this, two items need to be stressed. First, the elders are the leaders in the church and should therefore be given freedom to lead. Every decision should not be brought before the church.[7] Important decisions, such

---

[7] Newton comments: "There is no evidence that the early church voted on every issue. Rather, the plural eldership competently and efficiently handled day-to-day matters" (Phil Newton, *Elders in Congregational Life: Rediscovering the Biblical Model for Church Leadership* [Grand Rapids: Kregel, 2005], 58).

as the addition of a new elder or deacon, the budget, and a change to the constitution or bylaws, are congregational matters. Most other areas of concern, however, should be left to the leadership of the elders and deacons. Second, if a church uses the democratic method of voting, then it *must* practice church discipline and keep a current record of its membership.[8] If church discipline is not practiced, then the church might allow members to vote who should no longer be members of the church.

We have been trying to balance the dual notions that elders have authority and that the congregation as a whole has the final authority on critical issues. The elders are not only accountable to the Lord Jesus Christ, but they are also accountable to each other and the entire congregation.[9] For a system like this to work, it requires people who are filled with the Holy Spirit and exhibit a spirit of humility in their relations with others.

Elders Have Equal Authority

There are a number of reasons all the elders should possess equal authority in a church. First, all the elders have to meet the same qualifications. The qualifications do not list certain degrees of fitness or rank, and no distinction should be made between teaching elders and ruling elders. Second, all elders share the same responsibilities—primarily teaching and shepherding. Although some may spend more time in these important tasks, all elders will be involved in them to some extent. There should also not be a hard distinction made between elders who serve only part-time and those who serve full-time or between elders who are paid and elders who are unpaid. Third, formally giving more authority to one

---

8 For a more detailed analysis of the importance of church membership, see John S. Hammett and Benjamin L. Merkle, ed., *Those Who Must Give an Account: A Study of Church Membership and Church Discipline* (Nashville: B&H, 2012), 7–101.

9 Schreiner comments: "Too much focus on leaders could obscure the equality of all believers in Christ. Paul maintained a delicate balance between the role of leadership and the contribution of each member in the church. Leaders were important in the Pauline churches, but they did not operate in such a way that individual members' contributions were quashed; they led mainly by example and persuasion, not by coercion" (*Paul*, 385). Samuel E. Waldron also rightly notes: "The Word of God has a tendency to put things together that we in our human wisdom tend to regard as contradictory. Thus, in spite of the apparently self-sufficient democracy suggested by the facts cited in connection with the Democratic principle, the Word of God appoints that the church should have a class of ruling officers" ("Plural-Elder Congregationalism," in *Who Runs the Church? 4 Views on Church Government*, ed. Paul E. Engle and Steven B. Cowan [Grand Rapids: Zondervan], 218). Later he adds, "The *consent of both* the church and its eldership (and, thus, the unity of the church) is required for every act where the church as a whole has a voice" (221).

elder implicitly creates a separate office. If the "pastor" (the full-time, paid staff member) receives more authority than the "elders" (the part-time, nonstaff), an unbiblical distinction results. Strauch is correct when he states, "To call one elder 'pastor' and the rest 'elders' . . . is to act without biblical precedence." He continues, "It will, at least in practice, *create a separate, superior office over the eldership, just as was done in the early second century when the division between 'the overseer' and 'elders' occurred.*"[10] Consequently, all elders are due the same respect and honor and should be equal in value, power, and rank.

We would be mistaken, however, to claim that all elders are equal in giftedness or leadership skills. Again, Strauch aptly comments, "Although elders act jointly as a council and share equal authority and responsibility for the leadership of the church, all are not equal in their giftedness, biblical knowledge, leadership ability, experience, or dedication."[11] This distinction is often referred to by designating one elder "first among equals" (*primus inter pares*). Jesus himself practiced this concept. Out of the twelve disciples, Peter, James, and John were chosen to receive special attention from their Master. And out of the three, Peter was often singled out and given special leadership. Because of his gifts and calling, he was the most prominent among the apostles. Yet, Peter was an apostle just like the rest of the Twelve. He was never given a special title. He did not wear different clothes or receive a higher salary. The others were not subordinate to him and did not function as his attendants or servants. He was equal in rank and authority to the rest of the apostles. At the same time, however, he was a natural leader and, as such, became the "first among equals." This concept is also illustrated in the roles of Philip and Stephen among the Seven and in the relationship between Paul and Barnabas (Acts 6:8; 13:13; 14:12).

The "first among equals" concept is expressed in the way congregations are to honor their elders. Paul wrote, "The elders who are good leaders should be considered worthy of an ample honorarium, especially those who work hard at preaching and teaching" (1 Tim 5:17). Thus, special honor and respect (including pay) is to be given to those who prove themselves faithful and effective in their ministry, especially in the area of communicating God's holy Word. We know from the qualifications in 1 Timothy 3 that every elder must be "an able teacher" (v. 2). Some, however, may be especially gifted in preaching or teaching. Because of

---

[10] Alexander Strauch, *Biblical Eldership: An Urgent Call to Restore Biblical Church Leadership*, 3rd ed., rev. and exp. [Littleton, CO: Lewis & Roth, 1995], 47–48 (emphasis original).
[11] Ibid., 45.

their training and giftedness, they may be asked to preach more often than the others.

The benefits of this principle are immediately evident. First, it allows those who are especially called and gifted to dedicate more of their time to pastoral ministry. Elders who have other full-time employment are, of course, extremely important and have been greatly used by God. Paul himself was a tent maker who often worked this trade to support his ministry, and he commended his own example in this to the Ephesian elders (Acts 20:33–35). But in today's society an elder who works a full-time job often has little time or energy to devote to the church. Sometimes it is more beneficial to the life and growth of the church if an elder is employed by the church. As a result, he is able to dedicate all his energy to the study and proclamation of God's Word, to shepherding, to counseling, and to other important tasks. A second benefit is that those who are exceptionally gifted as leaders or teachers are given greater responsibility and scope to exercise their gifts.

The Number of Elders

The Evidence of Plural Eldership

Shared leadership is a common theme in the Bible. In the Old Testament the elders of Israel shared leadership. In the New Testament Jesus chose twelve apostles to lead the church. In addition the early church appointed seven men to assist the apostles by caring for the church's widows (Acts 6:1–6). This pattern of plurality was continued with the establishment of the Christian eldership.

The first mention of Christian elders appears in Acts 11:30, where the church in Antioch sent Barnabas and Paul to the elders in Jerusalem with money to aid in famine relief. Later, in Acts 15, the elders are referenced along with the apostles in the context of the Jerusalem council. Similar to the apostles, the elders formed a collective body of leadership. On Paul's first missionary journey, he and Barnabas preached the gospel in Asia Minor, especially in the cities of Antioch, Iconium, Lystra, and Derbe. On their return trip, Luke records that they "appointed elders in every church" (Acts 14:23). In this verse we are specifically told that a plurality of elders was appointed in every church. Although the church was recently established, Paul and Barnabas believed it was important for each church to possess more than one spiritual leader. Even though Luke mentions Barnabas and Paul appointing "elders" only in Acts 14:23, it is likely that this was Paul's customary procedure.[12] At the end of his third missionary journey, Paul summoned "the elders of the church" in Ephesus (Acts 20:17). Together these elders were exhorted to "shepherd the church of God" (Acts 20:28). Many conclude that because the church of Ephesus is referred to in the singular (i.e., *not* as the church*es* of Ephesus), only one body of believers in Ephesus was governed by a plurality of leaders.[13]

Luke's record fits well with Paul's own account that each church was led by a plurality of elders. When Paul wrote to the church at Philippi, he specifically greeted the "overseers and deacons" (Phil 1:1). He wrote to young Timothy, "The elders who are good leaders should be considered worthy of an ample honorarium, especially those who work hard at preaching and teaching" (1 Tim 5:17). Although the term *elder* is not used in this context, we have already demonstrated that the terms *elder* and *overseer* referred to the same group of people. Later, Paul directed Titus to "appoint elders in every town" (Titus 1:5). At the end of his ministry, Paul still believed in the necessity of establishing a body of elders in the local church.

The practice of having a plurality of elders is consistently found in the other writings of the New Testament. James, the Lord's brother, raised the question, "Is anyone among you sick?" His answer was, "He should call for the elders of the church, and they should pray over him" (Jas 5:14). Again, we should note the sick person is to call for the "elders" (plural) of the "church" (singular). Finally, the apostle Peter exhorted the "elders" among the believers scattered throughout Pontus, Galatia, Cappadocia, Asia, and Bithynia (1 Pet 5:1).

---

[12] Ramsay comments: "It is clear, therefore, that Paul everywhere instituted Elders in his new Churches; and on our hypothesis as to the accurate and methodical expression of the historian [i.e., Luke], we are bound to infer that this first case is intended to be typical of the way of appointment followed in all later cases. When Paul directed Titus (I $_s$) to appoint Elders in each Cretan city, he was doubtless thinking of the same method which he followed here" (William M. Ramsay, *St. Paul the Traveller and the Roman Citizen*, 2nd ed. [New York: G. P. Putnam's Sons; London: Hodder & Stoughton, 1896], 121). Likewise, J. B. Lightfoot writes: "On their very first missionary journey the Apostles Paul and Barnabas are described as appointing presbyters in every church. The same rule was doubtless carried out in all the brotherhoods founded later; but it is mentioned here and here only, because the mode of procedure on this occasion would suffice as a type of the Apostles' dealings elsewhere under similar circumstances" (*St. Paul's Epistle to the Philippians* [London: Macmillan, 1881], 193).

[13] Strauch, for example, comments, "The natural reading of the passage, then, indicates that there is one church in Ephesus and one body of elders to oversee it" (*Biblical Eldership*, 143).

Other terms are used to describe the plurality of leaders in the church. Paul urged the Corinthians to "submit" to the household of Stephanas "and to everyone who works and labors with them" (1 Cor 16:15–16). In his first letter to the church at Thessalonica, Paul exhorted the believers "to give recognition to those who labor among you and lead you in the Lord and admonish you" (1 Thess 5:12). Although the term *elders* is not used, those to whom Paul was referring were clearly the spiritual leaders of the congregation, performing elderlike functions. Finally, the author of Hebrews indicated that a plurality of shepherds led the church to which he wrote. In Hebrews 13:7, the author stated: "Remember your leaders who have spoken God's word to you. As you carefully observe the outcome of their lives, imitate their faith." He then urged the congregation, "Obey your leaders and submit to them, for they keep watch over your souls as those who will give an account" (Heb 13:17). In the closing of his letter, he added, "Greet all your leaders and all the saints" (Heb 13:24). In each case the author referred to a plurality of leaders.

The New Testament evidence indicates that every church had a plurality of elders. There is no example in the New Testament of one elder or pastor leading a congregation as the sole or primary leader. A plurality of elders were at the churches in Jerusalem (Acts 11:30); Antioch of Pisidia, Lystra, Iconium, and Derbe (Acts 14:23); Ephesus (Acts 20:17; 1 Tim 5:17); Philippi (Phil 1:1); the cities of Crete (Titus 1:5); the dispersion of which James wrote (Jas 1:1); the Roman provinces of Pontus, Galatia, Cappadocia, Asia, and Bithynia (1 Pet 1:1); and possibly at the church(es) to which Hebrews was written (Heb 13:7, 17, 24).[14]

The Bible never identifies a specific number of elders that should lead each local congregation. Apart from having a plurality, we are left to use godly wisdom and common sense. There are at least three methods of determining the number of elders in a local congregation. In a *fixed-number system* a specific number of elders is determined. With

---

[14] Based on this evidence, Grudem notes: "First, no passage suggests that any church, no matter how small, had only one elder. The consistent New Testament pattern is a plurality of elders 'in every church' (Acts 14:23) and 'in every town' (Titus 1:5). Second, we do not see a diversity of forms of government in the New Testament church, but a unified and consistent pattern in which every church had elders governing it and keeping watch over it (Acts 20:28; Heb 13:17; 1 Peter 5:2–3)" (*Systematic Theology*, 913). Strauch similarly states: "On the local church level, the New Testament plainly witnesses to a consistent pattern of shared pastoral leadership. Therefore, leadership by a plurality of elders is a sound biblical practice" (*Biblical Eldership*, 37). Marshall likewise comments, "The picture that emerges from relevant passages (Phil 1.1; Acts 20.17, 28; 14.23; 16.4) suggests a plurality of leaders in a church" (I. Howard Marshall, *A Critical and Exegetical Commentary on the Pastoral Epistles*, in collaboration with Philip H. Towner [Edinburgh: T&T Clark, 1999], 153).

the *ratio system* the church determines an approximate ratio of elders to members. In the *open system* churches do not specify either the number of elders they should have or a certain ratio. If the church needs more elders, they pray that God will provide them with gifted and qualified men. An advantage to this approach is that it focuses more on letting God provide the correct people rather than seeking to fill an empty position. But there are several other important factors to consider.

First, it is important that every elder has a strong desire to serve in that capacity. Paul informed us that it is a noble task if someone aspires to the office of elder (1 Tim 3:1). Likewise, Peter informed us that elders should shepherd God's flock not from compulsion but willingly (1 Pet 5:2). An elder should not agree to serve out of guilt because he was nominated or because he received the most votes. To be effective, an elder must love and enjoy the hard work of being a shepherd. Second, we must remember that eldership is a calling. Paul told the elders of the Ephesian church, "Be on guard for yourselves and for all the flock, *among whom the Holy Spirit has appointed you as overseers*" (Acts 20:28, emphasis added). Paul may have appointed these men to their office, but ultimately God raised them up to serve in his church. Likewise, we read in Paul's letter to the Ephesian church that the ascended Christ "gave some to be . . . pastors and teachers" (Eph 4:11). Pastors or elders are a gift from Christ to his church. Therefore, from one perspective, a church should appoint as many elders as God gives to it. Third, being an elder does not have to be a full-time or even a paid position. An elder can have a secular job and still be effective in shepherding the congregation. Requirements include diligence, faithfulness, and a calling from God. Fourth, every candidate must meet the qualifications before he is eligible to serve as elder. *How many* elders a church has is not as important as *who* the elders are.

The Advantages of Plural Eldership

If having a plurality of elders is God's design, there will be many benefits of following his wisdom. Although having a plurality of elders does not eliminate all church problems or conflict, it does at least provide several safeguards against some problems and difficulties a single-pastor church often faces. Having a plurality of elders in each local congregation offers at least four advantages.

First, having a plurality of elders allows for biblical accountability. It helps protect a pastor from error. Pastors often possess too much authority with too little accountability. Such authority can cause one to believe that he is more important than others and thus become proud. Other pastors may act in ways that are insensitive or unscriptural but remain blind to their faults. Each person has certain blind spots and faults, which can distort his judgment. If a pastor has little or no accountability, these tendencies can go unchecked.[15] When a church has only one pastor, or a senior pastor with unmatched power, usually no accountability structure is built into the system—except for the congregation or the deacons firing the pastor, which is far too common.

Plural eldership helps ensure that one man does not dominate the church.[16] There must be others who are equal in status and authority who can face a fellow elder and confront him if he is being unreasonable or is living in sin—just as Paul confronted Peter (a fellow apostle) when Peter refused to eat with Gentiles (Gal 2:11–14). A pastor needs the constant reminder that he is not above the law but is subject to the other elders. Every pastor is prone to sin and must constantly be monitoring his spiritual walk. Paul warned the Ephesian elders, "Be on guard for yourselves and for all the flock" (Acts 20:28). Later he exhorted Timothy, "Keep a close watch on yourself and on the teaching" (1 Tim 4:16 ESV). But a pastor not only needs to keep watch over his own life; he also needs the help of others.

Biblical accountability is needed to help foster maturity and godliness among the elders. As the elders serve and lead together, they will often be challenged by the godly examples they see in each other. They will "stir up one another to love and good works" (Heb 10:24 ESV). The more mature elders can help train the younger ones in how to be effective shepherds. As the proverb says, "Iron sharpens iron, and one man sharpens another" (Prov 27:17).

Second, a plurality of elders provides the church with balance. No one person has all the gifts or the time necessary to minister faithfully to the congregation. As a result, most pastors are not able to adequately

---

15 Grudem notes: "A common practical problem with a 'single elder' system is either an excessive concentration of power in one person or excessive demands laid upon him. In either case, the temptations to sin are very great, and a lessened degree of accountability makes yielding to temptation more likely" (*Systematic Theology*, 931). Later he adds that a strength of the plural elder system "is seen in the fact that the pastor does not have authority on his own over the congregation, but that authority belongs collectively to the entire group of elders (what may be called the elder board)" (933).

16 Phil Newton stresses, *"Plural eldership serves to prevent one man from falling prey to the temptation of dominating a congregation"* (*Elders in Congregational Life*, 60, emphasis original). Similarly Strauch writes, "Only when there is genuine accountability between equals in leadership is there any hope for breaking down the terrible abuse of pastoral authority that plagues many churches" (*Biblical Eldership*, 43).

fulfill all the responsibilities set before them. They may be gifted in one area but lack in another. Some pastors are especially gifted at preaching and teaching. Others are more gifted in administration, counseling, or discipling. By having a team of elders, the deficiencies of one man are balanced by the other elders who complement his weaknesses. A plurality of elders also allows each elder to focus on his specific calling and gifting.

A third benefit of having a plurality of elders is that the burden of ministry is shared. Caring for the church is often too much for one man to handle and can lead to frustration and burnout.[17] Is it any wonder that so many pastorates are short lived? So many pastors are living and ministering under the burden of shepherding God's people alone. Often no one comes beside the pastor and encourages him when he is weary from doing good (see Eccl 4:9–12). It is difficult for a congregation to become mature and equipped for the work of the ministry through a single pastor. If one man attempts to do all the work himself, he will begin to neglect other important areas of his life, such as his own spirituality or his family.

A church is also better able to handle cases of church discipline when there is a plurality of elders. A lone pastor will tend to shy away from such confrontation or might be viewed by others as handling the situation too severely. It is usually too much responsibility for a single pastor to handle such a difficult situation. But with the wisdom that comes from a group of godly men, the situation will almost certainly be dealt with in a more God-honoring manner. During this difficult time the elders can encourage one another to do what is right instead of merely what is expedient. The criticisms that might be leveled against a single pastor do not fall as hard on a group of elders who can shoulder the weight together.

A final advantage of having a plurality of elders is that it better represents the nature of ministry and the church. When the church is led by a single pastor, it conveys the idea that only a select few can serve God in such a capacity. The gulf between the "clergy" and "laity" becomes widened and eventually uncrossable. A plurality of elders, however, demonstrates that the work of the ministry is not designated for only a select few. When ordinary members show themselves to be qualified and gifted to serve as elders, it opens a massive door of opportunity for

---

[17] Speaking from his experience, Strauch comments, "If the long hours, weighty responsibilities, and problems of shepherding a congregation of people are not enough to overwhelm a person, then dealing with people's sins and listening to seemingly endless complaints and bitter conflicts can crush a person" (ibid., 42).

others. They begin to think, *Perhaps someday I can become an elder too.* This encourages them to live godly lives and grow in serving the church. In this way plural eldership takes the focus off the paid staff and puts it on the average person, encouraging him to consider serving in a more committed capacity.[18]

Christ alone is the Head of the church (Col 1:18). He is the "Chief Shepherd," and those whom he calls to lead the church are merely under-shepherds. They shepherd the congregation under the authority and direction of the Word and the Spirit. But when each local church has only one pastor or a senior pastor, this distinction can become blurred. Plural eldership tends to keep the focus on Christ as the Head of the church.[19]

---

[18] Waldron notes that plural eldership "allows the development of younger leaders within the church by eliminating the sense that there is room for only one leader and one ministry in the church" ("Plural-Elder Congregationalism," in Engle and Cowan, *Who Runs the Church?*, 176).

[19] Again, Waldron aptly comments, "A church led by a plurality of elders will have in its very system of leadership a constant reminder that the head of the church is *not* the pastor or the bishop, but *the Lord Jesus Christ*" (ibid.).

CHAPTER 15

Practical Issues in Elder Ministry

Andrew Davis

In this chapter we will seek to address a variety of practical issues that will face elders in local church ministry. Because many resources already are available that address pastoral ministry broadly, we should focus here on how to face practical shepherding issues within the structure of plural eldership. Let's look at a series of topics through that lens. It is my prayer that God will use these insights to glorify himself in building the body of Christ to full maturity.

1. The Goal of Plural Eldership: Church Planting and Church Revitalization

The previous chapter made the case that a plurality of elders in every local church is the biblical norm. However, as with church discipline, it is sadly rarer than it should be to see local churches living in accord with this biblical standard. Quite a common form of Baptist polity usually involves a senior pastor with a paid staff that reports to him, a "deacon board" that frequently sees itself as a check and balance to the power of the senior pastor, committees chosen by expedience (the main requirement being willingness to serve), perhaps a church council (made up of the heads of the various committees and the pastor), and occasional church votes by democratic processes. Though this pattern has arisen out of tradition and not from biblical grounds, it can take on a powerful form of authority as "the way we've always done things around here."

However, convincing a church that plural eldership is truly the biblical standard is not the end of the battle. For both church planters and church revitalizers, there are significant practical obstacles to seeing this goal realized. After going through the patient doctrinal work of persuading the church that plural eldership is biblical, the two main issues are these: (1) the need to identify, train, and have the church install elders; and (2) the need to write and lead the church to formally embrace operating documents (constitution and bylaws) that require plural elders. Let us talk about the journey to attaining these two goals in two contexts: first a new church, then an existing church that a pastor is seeking to biblically revitalize.

Church planters should begin their praying and planning with this biblical pattern of plural eldership in mind. This is God's standard whether the church is planted in the planter's home culture or in a missions setting, so this should be clearly established from the beginning. In some cases a team of planters with men already qualified as elders can be sent out as the nucleus of a new church. This has the advantage of providing a ready-made team of preliminary elders, which may later be replaced by indigenous leadership. This pattern may be reflected in the example of Paul and Barnabas being sent out from the church at Antioch in Acts 13 to plant new churches. However, Paul and Barnabas were not called to settle down and be the elders for the churches they planted. Instead, they trained men to take their place and moved on (Acts 14:23).

Church planters should seek to evangelize their target community or people group with the goal in mind of training up gifted men to serve as elders. This seems to be what Paul had in mind in his command to Timothy in 2 Timothy 2:2. As the church plant develops, whether in a North American setting or in a cross-cultural missionary setting, the standards for being an elder will continue to rise. The filtering passages (1 Tim 3:1–7 and Titus 1:5–9) specify some attributes that are inflexible and absolute. That is, they either characterize elder candidates, or they do not characterize elder candidates—such as being "the husband of one wife" and "not given to drunkenness." But most of the attributes require continual development in the men's lives: blamelessness, hospitality, ability to teach, having a good reputation with outsiders, managing a family well, loving what is good, and holding firmly to the trustworthy message. These requirements stand over every elder and challenge him to grow into them by the power of the Spirit. As a church attains a greater and greater level of maturity among its male members, the expectations for elders will rise.

Therefore, at the beginning of a church's history, the church planters are faced with the challenge of interpreting and applying the biblical standards for elders charitably but faithfully. It is debatable whether the church should even be constituted as a church before the plurality is established. In other words, the early phase of church planting would very much be geared toward getting men ready to assume this vital role.

The same is true in church revitalization efforts. A new pastor coming to an older church often sees a polity like a garden overgrown with weeds, built on unbiblical traditions rather than the Word of God. In this situation he is likely to survey the men of the church with some dismay, not finding immediate candidates for the role of elder. Unlike the church planter, he will be operating under an existing church constitution and meeting weekly for public worship in the clear self-understanding, "We are a church." Indeed, they are a church but a church with a polity not sanctioned by the Word of God.

The pastor's immediate goal must be to begin preaching the Word of God faithfully in an expositional pattern. The church must learn to accept the "whole counsel" of God's Word and must learn to trust the pastor as a faithful expositor of the Bible. In due time, as part of that "whole counsel," he will begin to teach the biblical truths of a healthy church polity, including the need for plural elders. This is the public ministry of the pulpit, and the preaching elder must unfold it "with great patience and teaching" (2 Tim 4:2)[1] because the idea of plural elders may be new to some people who may oppose it.

In the meantime, like the church planter, the church revitalizer should seek to identify, instruct, and develop men for this vital role. As Jesus spent all night in prayer before choosing the twelve apostles (Luke 6:12–13), so the pastor should seek the face of God, asking, "Who might you be raising up to share in this ministry, O Lord?" He should look for men who desire to serve (1 Tim 3:1) and who are able to teach, if only in fledgling form. He should train to the standards of 1 Timothy 3 and Titus 1, laying plainly before them the goal that they should one day be ready to serve in this role. He should challenge them to carry out elder-like ministry before having actual elder authority. When the time comes to install them in office, the church will merely be assenting to a calling that God has already put on their lives.

---

[1] Unless otherwise indicated, all Scripture passages are taken from the HCSB.

For both church planters and church revitalizers, new elders cannot be installed in office unless the church's constitution and bylaws are written around this polity from the ground up because the leadership of plural elders is integral to everything the church does. Therefore, a church revitalizer should expect to write a new set of operating documents rather than merely amend the existing ones. To try to tack on plural eldership to another model of polity is akin to replacing all the structural girders from an office building one by one, hoping the building will not fall. Of course, it is much easier for a newly planted church to formally embrace plural elders than for a long-established church to adopt a new polity. From the beginning the members of the new church have all been attracted to the particular standard of the church planters, so planters will have far less pushback to this standard being established in the operating documents. The church revitalizer has a twin task of formulating the documents and patiently teaching the church so that it is ready to embrace them by formal church vote.

The goal of a church constitution and bylaws should be to establish and protect the biblical pattern of plural elders leading in the context of congregational polity. The documents should involve as few words as possible to avoid constantly getting in the way of the elders as they seek to lead the church.

A key practical issue related to elders is understanding the propriety of lay or unpaid elders serving with equal authority and responsibility as ordained or paid elders. Laymen can meet the criteria for eldership without a seminary degree. Yet there will be special challenges for lay elders, especially because they will have less time to give to ministry than paid elders will. So any division of labor in the elders should honor this limitation and ensure that lay elders do not get burned out. Many churches with plural elders have seen wisdom in mandating the rotation of elders from service after one or two terms, establishing a sabbatical of rest for these hardworking men.

Throughout the process both church planters and church revitalizers should saturate their efforts in prayer, asking God to raise up and install the correct men for this vital role and that the church will embrace this polity and delight in it.

2. Plural Elders and the Overall Purpose of the Church: The "Two Infinite Journeys"

The church exists for one central reason: to glorify God in everything it is and does (1 Cor 10:31). But *how* can the church glorify God? What are we left in this world to be and to do? Thankfully, Jesus has not left us as orphans, and therefore the Scripture has not left us in the dark. The Great Commission of Matthew 28:18–20 gives the church clear marching orders: "Then Jesus came near and said to them, 'All authority has been given to Me in heaven and on earth. Go, therefore, and make disciples of all nations, baptizing them in the name of the Father and of the Son and of the Holy Spirit, teaching them to observe everything I have commanded you. And remember, I am with you always, to the end of the age.'" From this famous passage it is possible to discern the two abiding central works of the church: evangelism/missions (making disciples of all nations) and discipleship ("disciples" are not merely converts, and they are to be taught to obey everything Christ has commanded). Because Jesus said the church would be doing this "to the end of the age," we should see both of these as lasting journeys that will stretch in front of every Christian and every local church until Christ returns.

We can also identify these "two infinite journeys" in Philippians 1:12 and 1:25. Common to both of these verses is the Greek word *prokopē* (usually translated "progress"). The word *progress* implies a journey toward a goal. In Philippians 1:12, Paul spoke of the progress of the gospel throughout the palace guard in the emperor's house because of his imprisonment. In verse 25, Paul spoke of his desire to live and be released from prison so that he could continue his ministry among the Philippians for their development (progress) in the faith.

The first of these could be called the "external journey": evangelism and missions. The second of these could be called the "internal journey": discipleship or spiritual maturity. Making continual progress in these two journeys is the work of every church member and every local church. The journeys are called "infinite" because they will continually stretch out before us until we die or until Jesus returns and because only by the infinite power of God can we make one step of progress. These two journeys are intertwined because no church member or local church can choose one and forsake the other.

The calling of the elders is to keep both of these intertwined journeys continually before the church. The elders must teach these journeys constantly and be certain the church, and each individual member, is making progress in both. Furthermore, the elders must be aware of the tendency of all churches to favor one over the other, and they must correct any eccentricity in ministry by constant evaluation, prayer, and shepherding.

The elders should be filled with this kind of zeal for both journeys to fuel the church's progress in the face of Satan's opposition. The elders should be role models of holiness. The greatness of God and of Jesus, not worldly things, should fill their hearts and their mouths. The elders should be continually active as role models in evangelism. They should take younger disciples with them to teach them how to witness. The elders should also lead the church in adopting an unreached people group for special emphasis in prayer and in mission trips.

Beyond the overarching vision of these two lasting journeys, the elders of each local church are to discern aspects of ministry that are specific to that local church's gifts and providential opportunities. Just as the church in Antioch was worshipping the Lord and fasting and heard the Holy Spirit say, "Set apart for Me Barnabas and Saul for the work I have called them to" (Acts 13:2), so every church will have specific ministries and missions to which the Lord calls them.

3. Plural Elders' Teaching Ministry Primes the Pump for All Practical Ministry

The central role of the elders is faithfully teaching the Bible and shepherding the people to obey God's Word. The Word of God primes the pump for everything. By the Bible alone God's people can know what they are called on to do for his glory. Perhaps no passage of Scripture unfolds this truth as powerfully as Ephesians 4:7–16. In this passage the apostle Paul spoke of the different gifts and roles the Lord Jesus Christ bestows on each and every member of the church: "But to each one of us grace was given according to the measure of Christ's gift" (Eph 4:7 NASB). Christ carefully measures out spiritual gifts to each and every member of his church body. It is a central duty and delight for elders to unleash these spiritual gifts in the church and in the world for the completion of God's purposes. As an example of those spiritual gifts, Paul listed five roles in verse 11: "[Christ] gave some to be apostles, some to be prophets, some to be evangelists, and some to be pastors and teachers" (NIV 1984). The verb translated "gave" leaves open the question of who receives what is given by Christ's grace: either the grace is given to the men who serve in these five roles, or the men are given to the church as a gift. Both are true.

Yet we should notice something vital about the roles Paul highlighted here. Apostles, prophets, evangelists, pastors, and teachers all have one thing in common: the ministry of the Word of God. Apostles and prophets gave the church the Scriptures to begin with; evangelists bring the Word to a new region and proclaim it to those who have never heard it before; and pastors-teachers settle in and unfold the Word long-term to the people.

See what follows from this powerful ministry of the Word: "to equip the saints for the work of ministry" (Eph 4:12 ESV). The Word is sufficient to prepare all of God's people to do their own ministries, as 2 Timothy 3:16–17 teaches, "All Scripture is God-breathed . . . so that the man of God may be thoroughly equipped for every good work" (NIV 1984). As the apostles, prophets, evangelists, pastors, and teachers do the work of Bible instruction, the people of God are unleashed to do multifaceted works of ministry, resulting in the growth of the church into Christlike maturity.

The "ministry of the Word" can take a variety of forms: preaching the gospel to lost people, preaching expositional sermons to saved people, teaching Sunday school classes, leading small groups, counseling based on the Bible, discipling new converts in biblical doctrine, defending the faith in a highly charged apologetic setting, and so on. Though any elder should be able to function as needed in each of those settings, spiritual gifts are not merely about functioning but flourishing. It is helpful to see spiritual gifts like setting the direction of a sailboat on a windy day: though a skillful sailor can sail a well-designed boat in any direction on the compass, one direction maximizes the power of the prevailing wind, allowing the sailboat to run free before the wind. So it is with spiritual gifts. The gifting of the Spirit lifts a normal Christian function (e.g., speaking God's Word, evangelizing, showing compassion to the hurting) to a much higher level of power and delight—not merely functioning but flourishing. So it is with the varieties of gifts of teaching. Though all elders are able to teach, some will flourish better in counseling than in the pulpit. Each elder should identify his teaching gift accurately and maximize his ministry time in his particular area of gifting.

Often in the context of plural elders, one elder is set apart for the pulpit ministry as a central calling. This is certainly acceptable and even beneficial for a variety of reasons. First, preaching requires more preparation than other forms of teaching. Second, the development of a preacher's gifts requires a good deal of experience in the pulpit. This is in part what Paul meant when he urged Timothy to "keep ablaze the gift of God that is in you through the laying on of my hands" (2 Tim 1:6) and especially when he wrote:

> Until I come, give your attention to public reading, exhortation, and teaching. Do not neglect the gift that is in you; it was given to you through prophecy, with the laying on of hands by the council of elders. Practice these things; be committed to them, so that your progress may be evident to all. (1 Tim 4:13–15)

These words are best understood in the context of a consistent ministry of preaching, what we would call a "pulpit ministry." Paul urged Timothy to "devote himself" to the development of his preaching gifts, giving himself wholly to them so that the church may see his progress as a preacher of the Word. Applying this to a plurality of elders, it seems reasonable to have one individual, or perhaps a small number of elders, who regularly preach and who study the craft of preaching so they can constantly improve as preachers.

We might add a few caveats, however. First, such preacher-elders should not have more authority than other elders in the direction and leadership of the church. In elders' meetings they should be afforded one vote like all the other elders. They will likely have more influence in some matters because their hours of study in the Word should give them the ability to marshal biblical truth pointedly and skillfully, but this influence is really only that of the Word itself. Any elder can do the same, and God in his providence often hides certain insights from one elder and reveals them through other elders. This keeps the preacher-elders humble and dependent on their brothers. At the same time the elders who preach should be respected for their insights and their wisdom sought without any jealousy by their brother elders. Second, there is a tension between the necessity of a gifted preacher being the consistent pulpit voice of a local church and the danger of a church failing to develop other gifted men, especially for the goal of church planting.

4. Plural Elders and Congregational Polity

How can the congregation be both in authority over the elders (in appointing them to begin with and, if necessary, removing them by discipline) and also submit to their leadership day by day? How can the balance between congregationalism and plural eldership be achieved?

First, the elders must be established by a congregational vote; this is a clear implication of Scripture's teaching that a congregation is accountable to God for the teachers it chooses to listen to (Galatians 1; 2 Tim 4:3). The candidates must meet the requirements of 1 Timothy 3 and Titus 1. The existing elders should assess each candidate by the biblical criteria, including personal interviews covering doctrine and lifestyle. When the elders are satisfied that a man meets the biblical qualifications, they should recommend him to the congregation for their affirmation. The congregation should then have the opportunity to offer feedback or ask questions, perhaps over a period of weeks, before putting its final, authoritative stamp on each man by voting him into the position.

Having established the elders in their office, the congregation is instructed by Hebrews 13:17 to submit to their leadership: "Obey your leaders and submit to them" (cf. 1 Thess 5:12–13). The church must follow the leadership of its elders. It must submit to their instruction and counseling in life situations. And it should respond gladly and generously with time, energy, and money as the elders urge the church to move ahead in key ministry initiatives.

Yet, even as the church demonstrates godly, submissive "followship," it is the congregation's responsibility to ensure that the elders' teaching, modeling, and ministry leadership are plausibly biblical. The church is to be continually evaluating the leadership of the elders, such as the Bereans who were commended by Luke as noble in their scrutiny of the apostle Paul's teachings (Acts 17:11). In the same way the congregation should be watching the life and doctrine of the elders (see Acts 20:28) and comparing them with Scripture to see that all things are being done in a biblical fashion. But this ongoing assessment should be quiet and not "in the face" of the elders; rather, in the judgment of charity, the elders should receive the benefit of any doubt. That is why any accusation against an elder should only be entertained if two or more witnesses attest to it (1 Tim 5:19).

If members of the congregation disagree with the leadership of the elders on a controversial issue, they should respectfully bring their concerns and biblical arguments to the elders and patiently talk them through. But if it is at least plausible that the elders are hearing God more clearly on this issue than church members, the members should submit and follow humbly and gladly.

5. Plural Elders and the Ministry of Prayer

In Acts 6:4, the apostles said, "We will devote ourselves to prayer and to the preaching ministry." The elders should also follow Jesus' example of doing nothing but what the Father willed (John 8:28) and expressing total dependence on the Father by constant prayer.

The elders should follow biblical examples of prayer, learning from the apostle Paul what to pray for based on his own statements in the epistles.[2] They should pray for the people of their church to grow in their knowledge of God, of the greatness of their eternal reward in him, and of the immeasurable power of God to ensure all of the elect will survive Satan's attacks and make it safely to heavenly glory (Rom 8:38–39; Eph 1:17–19). They should pray for believers to know the scope and magnitude of God's love for them in Christ (Eph 3:17–19). They should pray for the holiness of the saints, that they would put sin to death by the power of the Spirit (Rom 8:13). They should pray consistently for the advance of the gospel of Jesus Christ to the ends of the earth (Ps 2:8; 2 Thess 3:1). Along with such biblical themes, they should target specific needs in the church body as they arise: counseling matters, medical issues, relational strains, ministry opportunities, and so on. The elders should frequently ask God for wisdom in specific providential circumstances, especially in venturing out in new ministries or handling difficult church discipline issues. God has promised to give wisdom to all who ask in faith (Jas 1:5–8). To fail to ask for wisdom and guidance from God is to show the arrogance of King Saul (1 Chr 10:13–14) and not the humility of David (1 Chr 14:10, 14).

6. Plural Elders and the Variety of Spiritual Gifts

As we already noted, God has given the body of Christ a marvelous array of spiritual gifts to further his eternal purpose—the total conformity of the elect to their Head, Jesus Christ. Christ gives spiritual gifts, or special abilities (Eph 4:7), through the Holy Spirit (1 Cor 12:11), which build up the body to full Christlike maturity (Eph 4:13). Every Christian has spiritual gifts: Ephesians 4:7 says Christ gives gifts to *each one* according to his own measure. The elders are, of course, no exception. Spiritual gifts are scattered abroad among Christ's people (2 Cor 9:9) so that no one may boast or feel excluded. No Christian is omnicompetent—God

---

[2] For an excellent treatment of this theme, see D. A. Carson, *A Call to Spiritual Reformation* (Grand Rapids: Baker, 1992).

has spread the gifts around so that we genuinely need one another. We are meant to be humbled by that and to learn to depend on one another's gifts. So it is within the body of elders. The elders are in some ways a microcosm of the body, with an array of gifts that, taken together, are essential for accomplishing the church's mission.

Of course every elder must have the gifts of teaching and of hospitality (1 Tim 3:2) because these are listed in the requirements for the office. One could also argue that the ability to manage both family and church well (1 Tim 3:4–5; cf. also 1 Tim 5:17) implies the gift of administration. Beyond that, however, the elders as a group will have a marvelous diversity of gifting. They will learn to discern one another's gifting and assign roles of instruction, shepherding, leadership, and oversight as is best suited to each man. Some elders will have an exceptionally developed sense of compassion for suffering people, and they may well be charged with more hospital and homebound visits than the other elders. In addition, such elders may have a passion for ministries of benevolence to the poor and needy in the church and in the surrounding community. Other elders may have the gift of faith, and they may be the strongest, most visionary leaders—able to discern how God is leading the church into uncharted waters for new ministries. Other elders may have the gift of giving, and by their insights and example, they may well be entrusted with the role of stimulating the financial generosity of the entire church. Though all elders have the gift of administration to some degree, some elders may shine in that area above all the others; and they would make excellent elder chairmen, entrusted with the task of organizing elders' meetings and keeping them running efficiently. Beyond that, such administratively gifted elders may play a fruitful role in ensuring that all the ministries of the church as a whole are well harmonized and are orderly down to small details. Other elders may have musical gifts to organize the corporate worship life of the church. The elders must learn to use their gifts within the context of the elders' whole pattern of ministry to the church.

It is also vital that the elders train the church as a whole to use their gifts. To this end elders should teach each member to assess his or her spiritual gifts by a faith-filled, humble process. Romans 12:1–8 is the key passage in the Bible for this self-analysis. The elders should focus a great deal of their attention on unleashing the church to do works of service that will help the body of Christ reach its full maturity (Eph 4:7–16). No matter how gifted and effective the elders are at leading people to Christ, or caring for the poor and needy, or counseling and encouraging the downcast or the struggling, their impact pales in comparison with what the church can do when unleashed by the power of the Spirit to exercise their spiritual gifts. In their ongoing shepherding of the flock, the elders should continually evaluate and challenge members to discover, develop, and use their spiritual gifts. And the elders as a whole should learn to rely on one another's gifts and assign ministry responsibilities to the elders best gifted for them.

7. Plural Elders and Friendship, Encouragement, and Accountability

One of the most delightful aspects of plural eldership is the marvelous camaraderie that develops when the group is functioning biblically. Created in the image of God, we were designed for fellowship with one another in the pattern of the Trinity, individual persons in perfect unity.

In his prayer of John 17, Jesus prayed for the church to be brought to "complete unity to let the world know" that the Father sent the Son (v. 23 NIV 1984). In other words, to the watching world the obvious growing unity in the church is a powerful witness of the truth of the gospel. Elders are set apart unto God to be role models for the church, and the obvious delight elders have in one another is a powerful example to the church first and then to a lost and dying world that is watching the church closely.

Therefore, quite practically, the elders should develop their relationships with one another, their sense of teamwork, their love for one another, and simply their conspicuous friendship. They may want to have team-building retreats and social times together. They should openly enjoy one another's company in public. They should expect to laugh a lot at elders' meetings, as well as cry together if any of them is suffering a trial.

Because the conspicuous unity of the elders is vital to the overall health of the church, the Devil will constantly seek to sow seeds of dissension among them. Because of this the elders should spare nothing to preserve their unity. Elders are living out Christianity in a mature way, so they should put into practice the "rules of the road" God has given us for loving one another, being quick to listen, slow to speak, and slow to become angry (Jas 1:19).

Beyond this, it is vital that the elders shepherd one another spiritually, holding one another accountable and protecting one another from besetting sins. Satan will come hard after each elder, seeking to disqualify him from ministry. Elders should help one another set positive spiritual goals for sanctification: growth in Bible intake and memorization, deeper prayer and worship life, more faithful and courageous witness, better marriage and parenting. Elders should also ask one another deep questions about struggles with sin so that they can protect one another from falling. And elders should hold one another accountable to achieve ministry goals: people met with for shepherding, Bible studies completed in a timely fashion, specific goals met in preparation for an outreach.

One of the primary Satanic attacks in ministry is discouragement. Martin Luther once was so discouraged with the slow progress of reformation in Wittenberg that he quit preaching in the parish church there for more than a year. (He was not the pastor of the church, but as a professor of theology and the leader of the Reformation, he was constantly asked to preach.)[3] Charles Spurgeon spoke in his *Lectures to My Students* of "the minister's fainting fits," times when discouragement so powerfully overwhelms a pastor that he does not want to continue in the ministry.[4] Elders should regularly confide in one another when discouragement grows because, in the kind providence of God, this condition will rarely hit all of the elders at once.

8. Plural Elders and Shepherding

Again and again throughout the Scriptures, God's people are likened to sheep: "For he is our God, and we are the people of his pasture, and the sheep of his hand" (Ps 95:7 ESV); "My sheep hear My voice, I know them, and they follow Me" (John 10:27). This recurring metaphor shows the frailty of God's people compared to the Satanic forces that oppose us, for at one time we were "harassed and helpless, like sheep without a shepherd" (Matt 9:36 NIV). Though the regenerate now have the Shepherd, the demonic powers have by no means given up their assault on their souls. For this reason each Christian is commanded to put on spiritual armor and be ready constantly for a fight against our true foes—the "spiritual forces of evil in the heavens" (Eph 6:12). Although Christ's sheep are guarded constantly by his perfect vigilance as our chief Shepherd (1 Pet 2:25; 5:4), he has entrusted a significant portion of

---

[3] Fred Meuser, *Luther the Preacher* (Philadelphia: Augsburg Fortress Press, 1983), 27–34.

[4] Charles Spurgeon, *Lectures to My Students* (Carlisle, PA: Banner of Truth Trust, 2008), 179–92.

care to the undershepherds, the elders of the church. This is probably the reason "overseer" (*episkopos*) is chosen as one of the titles for this role. The concept depicts a lofty perspective, as from a hillside, from which the shepherds can oversee the entire flock and see the dangers coming.

These dangers will most certainly come, as Satan tries to entice and destroy God's people. Making matters worse is the bent toward evil that resides in the heart of each of God's sheep. Truly we are "prone to wander . . . prone to leave the God [we] love."[5] Our indwelling sin rises in the middle of the night to unlock the gates and allow the encroaching enemy within the walls of the citadel. For Christ's glory the shepherds of his flock are called to "keep watch over your souls as those who will give an account" (Heb 13:17), which involves constant vigilance over the wanderings of God's people.

How can the elders of a church organize themselves for this ministry? First, we see again the wisdom of plural eldership as the polity the Lord has established. This task is so unrelenting and vital that it is best done by many godly men who are equally tasked for the responsibility but who have different perspectives and different relationships with various members of the flock and who together can provide more constant care for them.

The elders' shepherding will take two forms: (1) the shepherding each individual elder does as providence allows his path to cross that of various church members—fruitful conversations, prayer requests shared, observations made about life choices, and so on; (2) the systematic shepherding the elders organize for the entire flock so that each member may be cared for and protected spiritually.

The practical start of careful shepherding is an accurate list of the church members. In churches of any considerable size, this is a practical necessity, for how can anyone know who is "inside the church" (see 1 Cor 5:12) without an accurate list? The members list usually takes the forms of a church database and phone booklet, and care must be taken that the list the elders work with has only members on it (not regular attenders or children who have not yet joined). Each elder should pray through this list on a daily basis—perhaps dividing the congregation into reasonably sized groups for daily prayer.

Beyond that, the elders should go through the list regularly at their elders' meetings. A large portion of their time together should be spent carefully considering the spiritual condition of each member, name by name. As the next name is read, the elders should discuss that member

---

5 "Come Thou Fount of Every Blessing" by Robert Robinson (1757).

and categorize them generally into one of five categories: (1) regularly attending and apparently spiritually healthy, (2) not regularly attending and/or apparently not spiritually healthy, (3) physically unable to attend and needing some kind of increased care from the church (e.g., homebound members), (4) needing to be removed from membership at the next members' meeting, and (5) need more information about this member. The elders' discussion of the individual members should be respectful, careful, spiritually minded, and loving. The dual question in front of the elders in every case is, What shepherding needs to be done to bring this individual into a healthy pattern of involvement in church life or, if necessary, to protect the church from harm at the hands of this person? The health of the individual should always be considered side by side with the health of the church as a whole.

For members in all five categories, the elders can take a wide range of helpful actions. Even if someone is regularly attending and apparently spiritually healthy, the elders can still ask deeper questions of one another about the person and eventually of the person himself: Is this person growing in grace and in the knowledge of Jesus Christ (cf. 2 Pet 3:18)? Is this person using spiritual gifts in a regular pattern of ministry? Is this person in healthy relationships and meaningful friendships within the church body? Does this person have any spiritual accountability and dedicated discipleship relationships? Is this person married? If so, how healthy is the marriage? What struggles is this person facing? What are this person's goals and ambitions? In order to ask these questions of each member of the church, the elders may divide up the church and begin a systematic pattern of private interviews with each member. In this division it is best for the paid elders to have a greater burden than the unpaid elders because they will have more time to give to the ministry.

9. Plural Elders and Church Discipline

One of the most important responsibilities the elders have is to maintain the church's commitment to holiness. Part of that responsibility is to address the sins of the people as need arises. The New Testament describes the process of church discipline in two key passages: Matthew 18:15–20 and 1 Corinthians 5:1–13. Interestingly, the role of elders in overseeing the process of church discipline is nowhere spelled out in the New Testament. Yet it is reasonable to assume that elders must shepherd the church at such times.

Sadly, many churches neglect the New Testament's clear instruction regarding church discipline. Therefore, one of the key practical issues before the elders of any local body is how to prepare the church as a whole to do its duty in maintaining purity in its membership. If the church has not practiced church discipline in years or decades, the elders must patiently instruct the believers to understand key passages and to embrace their responsibilities.

Elders can go a long way in addressing sin in the local church by learning to nip it in the bud. Much of the elders' discipleship ministry is done in light of sin patterns they hope to train out of people before they become bigger issues down the road. Not every sin church members commit should even come close to the final step of excommunication, which both Matthew 18 and 1 Corinthians 5 reference. As the elders shepherd the flock, they will undoubtedly uncover sinful actions and attitudes in the people. Instruction, encouragement, exhortation, correction, admonishment, warning, and rebuke will, by God's grace, often result in repentance so that excommunication is only rarely necessary.

However, from time to time the usual means of discipleship will prove inadequate for addressing more stubborn and serious sins in the body. The stubbornness in which a sinner refuses to repent and be reconciled to his offended brother is addressed by taking along other witnesses (Matt 18:16). Though these do not have to be elders, it is a vital part of the ministry of oversight in the flock to be sure this process is carried out biblically and faithfully. Elders should train the flock to look after their own issues as much as possible and not feel they have to bring everything to the elders for resolution. A big part of that training comes in teaching patterns of conflict resolution to the body.[6] Perhaps the most important setting for such conflict resolution is the marriage relationship, cutting off divorce long before it ever gets to that stage. But a general pattern of instruction based on unity (Eph 4:3), humility (Phil 2:1–4), peace (2 Cor 13:11), forgiveness (Col 3:13), and love covering a multitude of sins (1 Pet 4:8) is vital to the health of the body.

If despite these efforts a sinner will not repent, it is reasonable for the elders to get involved and manage the church discipline case before it comes to the church as a whole. When issues of sin come up in the shepherding ministry of the elders, they should deputize two (or more) elders to address the situation with biblical truth and a Christlike demeanor.

---

6 Ken Sande's *The Peacemaker* is an excellent resource for balanced conflict resolution in the life of the church. See Ken Sande, *The Peacemaker: A Biblical Guide to Resolving Conflict* (Grand Rapids: Baker, 2004).

If the situation is not resolved through genuine repentance, the elders should then bring the matter to the church for consideration.

In presenting a case to the church, the elders should call the sin by its biblical name. They should give as many details as are necessary for establishing the pattern of behavior but should not go beyond what the church really needs to know. In discipline cases the church must learn to trust the judgment and character of the elders. This is one reason the elders must have unimpeachable character and a good reputation. At this stage in a church discipline case, the elders are "telling it to the church" (see Matt 18:17) and desiring that the hitherto unrepentant sinner will "listen to the church." Therefore, the elders must lead the church to give the unrepentant individual one final chance to repent. Hopefully this will occur during the period of time between members' meetings, during which time the church should pray for the person and encourage him or her to repent. The elders should carry on an ongoing ministry of counseling and biblical admonishment, seeking to bring the person to his or her senses (2 Tim 2:24; Luke 15:17; 1 Cor 15:34). If the person refuses to repent, the elders should lead the church to remove him or her from membership at a subsequent members' meeting.

In the same way, elders should also play a role in reestablishing a repentant sinner who was formerly removed. In 2 Corinthians 2:5–11 Paul commanded the church to gladly restore a repentant sinner. It should be the delight of elders to seek out and bring to repentance some who have been excommunicated and to seek from the church the necessary vote to make them members again.

Probably the most common issue in church discipline elders will need to address is church members' failure to fulfill the church covenant by not attending public worship regularly. If a member starts to drift away from involvement in church life, the elders should train the body to respond with care, concern, phone calls, and efforts to restore the wandering member to healthy involvement. Failing that, the elders will need to bring such people to the church for discipline. This will serve as an ongoing warning to current members not to forsake the assembling of themselves together for corporate worship (Heb 10:25). The goal of elders' ongoing shepherding of the church roll is that every member who is physically able will regularly attend and serve.

We should mention in closing how much superior the plurality of elders is to a single-elder model in leading out in church discipline. Whereas the single-elder model can result in a discipline case seeming like a personal vendetta, such a false charge cannot be made as easily with a group of godly men.

10. Plural Elders and Leadership Development

As Paul began his teaching on elders in 1 Timothy 3, he started with the godly ambition that should be in the heart of many young men in the church: "This saying is trustworthy: 'If anyone aspires to be an overseer, he desires a noble work'" (1 Tim 3:1). If a church is going to urge its young men to have such a desire, it is reasonable for that church to have a well-ordered and effective pattern of training by which that desire can be nurtured and come to fruition. One of the key responsibilities of a body of elders is to train their future colaborers and replacements.

Beyond training future elders, a wise pattern of general leadership development should exist for both men and women in the church. Not every leader in the church will be an elder, but the elders of the church should establish godly habits of leadership development that guide members from spiritual immaturity to powerful leadership in the body.

Two basic, and equally important, aspects of discipleship are in the New Testament. These two aspects are taught in two key passages, each of which uses the Greek word *tupos* ("pattern"):

> Hold on to the pattern [*tupos*] of sound teaching that you have heard from me, in the faith and love that are in Christ Jesus. (2 Tim 1:13)

> Join with others in following my example, brothers, and take note of those who live according to the pattern [*tupos*] we gave you. (Phil 3:17 NIV 1984)

This Greek word *tupos* refers to the image struck on a coin—such as the face of Caesar. The image was perfectly reproduced again and again on the soft silver coins being struck. This word speaks of the need to reproduce a pattern of godliness in the hearts and lives of disciples. Beyond general Christian discipleship, the training of future elders should include formal training in exegesis, theology, homiletics, counseling, evangelism, and leadership. The elders should think and pray about which men in the church show leadership potential and select candidates for this training.

Beyond training future elders, the present elders should consider how to train and prepare future church planters and cross-cultural missionaries. This is the highest level of specialized training a church should conduct, and though it is commonly left to seminaries, the local church is ultimately the best place for it because real ministry is constantly going on.

Summary

Elders have a high calling in the church. Their work is so comprehensive and strategic that it is no wonder the Lord appointed it for a godly group of men working together. The wisdom of God in this is evident to any who have had the privilege of serving with a healthy group of elders. And though the world, the flesh, and the Devil will constantly assault the elders, by the grace of God they will be more than conquerors together in fulfilling the ministry entrusted to them. And when they are finished, they will receive the "unfading crown of glory" (1 Pet 5:4).

CHAPTER 16

The Office of Deacon

Benjamin L. Merkle

M ost historic Baptist statements of faith recognize two offices in Scripture. They typically say "pastor and deacon" or "elder and deacon." In single-pastor churches deacons[1] are sometimes treated as de facto elders or something in between elders and deacons. But how does the Bible speak to this second office? What are the qualifications, and what role do deacons play in the church, particularly in relationship to the elders? This chapter will answer those questions.

The Scriptural Basis for Church Deacons

The word *deacon* is a transliteration of the Greek term *diakonos*, which normally means "servant" or "helper." Only context can determine whether the term is being used in its ordinary sense or it is being used more technically as a designation of a church officer (i.e., deacon). The Greek term is used twenty-nine times in the New Testament, but only three or four of those occurrences refer to an officeholder (Rom 16:1[?]; Phil 1:1; 1 Tim 3:8, 12). While there are some parallels between the Jewish elder and the Christian elder, there does not seem to be a parallel to the role of deacon in Jewish or Greek society.

---

[1] For a more detailed treatment of this topic, see Benjamin L. Merkle, *40 Questions About Elders and Deacons* (Grand Rapids: Kregel, 2008), 227–48.

Acts 6 as a Model for Deacons

The origin of deacons is not known for certain, but many scholars believe the Seven chosen in Acts 6 are the prototypes of the New Testament deacon. The reason many are hesitant to call the Seven the first deacons is because the noun "deacon" (*diakonos*) does not occur in the text. Only the related noun *diakonia* ("ministry" or "service") and verb *diakoneō* ("to serve") are found (Acts 6:1–2). Another issue is that the text mentions the apostles but not elders. Therefore, a direct correlation is difficult to make. Yet Acts 6 does provide a paradigm that seems to have continued in the early church. It is necessary, then, to investigate this passage in more detail.

> In those days, as the number of the disciples was multiplying, there arose a complaint by the Hellenistic Jews against the Hebraic Jews that their widows were being overlooked in the daily distribution. Then the Twelve summoned the whole company of the disciples and said, "It would not be right for us to give up preaching about God to handle financial matters. Therefore, brothers, select from among you seven men of good reputation, full of the Spirit and wisdom, whom we can appoint to this duty. But we will devote ourselves to prayer and to the preaching ministry." The proposal pleased the whole company. So they chose Stephen, a man full of faith and the Holy Spirit, and Philip, Prochorus, Nicanor, Timon, Parmenas, and Nicolaus, a proselyte from Antioch. They had them stand before the apostles, who prayed and laid their hands on them. (Acts 6:1–6)[2]

The need for the Seven to be chosen stemmed from growth in the church. As the church grew, more spiritual and physical needs arose among the new converts. Widows, for example, were usually dependent on others for their daily needs. One problem that emerged was that the Greek-speaking, Jewish widows were being neglected. When the twelve apostles received news of this problem, they knew something had to be done. They understood the importance of providing for the physical needs of the people. They understood that allowing this problem to continue could cause division in the church.

But there was another problem. Although the apostles realized the gravity of the situation before them, they also realized that serving tables would divert them from their primary calling of preaching the Word of

---

2 Unless otherwise indicated, all Scripture passages are taken from the HCSB.

God. The apostles were not indicating that it would be too humiliating for them to serve widows. Jesus had already taught them that being a leader in his kingdom is different from worldly leadership (Matt 20:25–27). He had already washed their feet to demonstrate servant leadership (John 13:1–18). Rather, they wanted to remain faithful to the calling and the gifts they received from God. For them to leave the preaching of the Word to serve tables would have been a mistake. Instead, they proposed a better solution to this problem.

The apostles decided to call all the disciples together and present a solution to the problem. The disciples were to appoint seven men to oversee the daily distribution of food. The congregation, however, was not simply to choose anyone who was willing to serve; they had to select men who had a good reputation and were Spirit filled. By appointing these men to help with the daily distribution of food, the apostles took this need seriously and, at the same time, did not get distracted from their primary calling. With the Seven appointed to take care of this problem, the apostles were able to devote themselves "to prayer and to the preaching ministry" (Acts 6:4).

This is similar to what we see with the offices of elder and deacon. Like the apostles the elders' primary role is preaching the Word of God (Eph 4:11; 1 Tim 3:2; Titus 1:9). Like the Seven, deacons are needed to serve the congregation in whatever needs may arise. Thus, although the term *deacon* does not occur in Acts 6, it provides a helpful model of how godly servants can assist those who are called to preach the Word of God.[3]

Deacons in the New Testament

Surprisingly, the Greek term *diakonos* only occurs three or four times as a designation of an officeholder. The first possible occurrence is in Romans 16:1 where Phoebe is called a *diakonos* "of the church in Cenchreae." It is debated whether Paul was using the term *diakonos* as a general term for "servant" here or as a more technical term for the church office of deacon. Most English Bible versions choose the more neutral term "servant"; but the RSV renders it "deaconess," and the NIV and NRSV render it "deacon."

The second occurrence of *diakonos* as a reference to a church office is found in the opening greeting of Paul's letter to the Philippians. He

---

3 Wayne Grudem comments, "It seems appropriate to think of these seven men as 'deacons' even though the name *deacon* had perhaps not yet come to be applied to them as they began this responsibility" (*Systematic Theology: An Introduction to Biblical Doctrine* [Leicester: IVP; Grand Rapids: Eerdmans, 1994], 919).

addressed "all the saints in Christ Jesus who are in Philippi, including the overseers and deacons" (Phil 1:1). This is the only place where Paul greeted church officers in the salutation of a letter and is perhaps the clearest indication of a distinction between church members and church leaders in Paul's early writings. Interestingly, apart from the introductory greeting in Philippians 1:1, we would have no indication of church leaders and an organized ministry in the Philippian church. The presence of such leaders did not change Paul's writing style of addressing the entire congregation. He linked the overseers and deacons with all the saints because they are not to be treated as believers on a higher level. Yet they were, for reasons unknown, distinguished within the greeting.[4]

The final two occurrences of *diakonos* as a reference to a church office are found in 1 Timothy 3, where Paul listed the requirements for "deacons." Paul did not explain the duties of this office, which suggests the Ephesian church already had experience with deacons. Paul simply listed the qualifications and assumed the church would use these officers in the appropriate manner. The fact that a deacon does not need to be "an able teacher" is a feature that sets deacons apart from elders (cf. 1 Tim 3:2; 5:17). Because Paul did not list any of the duties deacons should perform, the early church likely understood the Seven chosen in Acts 6 to be a model for deacon ministry. That is, deacons were responsible to care for the physical needs of the congregation and do whatever was needed so the elders could focus on their work of teaching and shepherding.

The Qualifications of Church Deacons

The only passage in Scripture that mentions the qualifications for deacons is 1 Timothy 3:8–13. Unlike elders, Paul did not mention deacons

---

[4] A. T. Robertson aptly comments: "Paul does not ignore the officers of the saints or church, though they occupy a secondary place in his mind. The officers are important, but not primary. The individual saint is primary. Church officers are made out of saints. . . . Paul does not draw a line of separation between clergy and laity. He rather emphasizes the bond of union by the use of 'together with'" (*Paul's Joy in Christ: Studies in Philippians* [New York: Revell, 1917], 42–43). Gerald F. Hawthorne likewise states: "Paul did not address himself to these 'officers' over the head of the congregation. Rather, as was his custom elsewhere in his letters, he addressed the congregation; he addressed the bishops and deacons second and only in conjunction with the congregation" (*Philippians*, Word Biblical Commentary, vol. 43 [Waco, TX: Word, 1983], 7–8). Similarly, Gordon D. Fee writes, "When they [i.e., overseers and deacons] are singled out, as here, the leaders are not 'over' the church, but are addressed 'alongside of' the church, as a distinguishable part of the whole, but as part of the whole, not above or outside it" (*Paul's Letter to the Philippians*, New International Commentary on the New Testament [Grand Rapids: Eerdmans, 1995], 67).

in his letter to Titus (Titus 1:5–9). In 1 Timothy 3, the similarities of
the qualifications for deacons and elders/overseers are striking. Like an
elder,[5] a deacon must not be addicted to much wine (cf. 1 Tim 3:3), not
greedy for money (cf. 1 Tim 3:3, not "greedy" or a lover of money),
blameless (cf. 1 Tim 3:2, "above reproach"), the husband of one wife,
and manage his household well (cf. 1 Tim 3:4–5). The focus of the qualifications is on the moral character of the person who is to fill the office.[6]
The main distinction between an elder and a deacon is a difference of
gifts and calling, not character.

In 1 Timothy 3, Paul gave an official, but not exhaustive, list of the
requirements for deacons. If a *moral* qualification is listed for elders
but not for deacons, that qualification still applies to deacons. The same
goes for qualifications listed for deacons but not for elders. For example,
even though it is not listed in the requirements for elders, they are not
permitted to be double-tongued (1 Tim 3:8). Likewise, Paul stated that
elders must be "above reproach," which implies this prohibition for deacons as well. Differences in the qualifications either signify a trait that
is particularly fitting for an officeholder to possess in order to accomplish his duties or something that was a problem in the location to which
Paul wrote (in this case, Ephesus). Most likely Paul was describing a
character that stood in opposition to the character of false teachers in
Ephesus. Thus, his descriptions mostly involved personal characteristics, not duties. Because many of the requirements for deacons are the
same as those for elders, in this section we will focus our attention on
those requirements that are unique in the list for deacons.

Worthy of Respect (1 Tim 3:8)

The first requirement Paul listed for deacons is that they must be "worthy of respect" or "dignified." This word occurs only four times in the
New Testament (Phil 4:8; 1 Tim 3:8, 11; Titus 2:2). The term normally
refers to something that is honorable, respectable, esteemed, or worthy
and is closely related to "respectable" (*kosmios*), which is given as a
qualification for elders (1 Tim 3:2). In Philippians 4:8, Paul exhorted
the believers to meditate on things that are true, *honorable*, just, pure,
lovely, commendable, excellent, and worthy of praise. In Titus 2:2, Paul

---

5 See discussion above in chap. 13.

6 William D. Mounce comments, "Both the office of a church leader and the office
of church worker require the same type of person: a mature Christian whose behavior
is above reproach" (*Pastoral Epistles*, Word Biblical Commentary [Nashville: Thomas
Nelson, 2000], 195).

commanded the older men to be "worthy of respect." The other two occurrences are found in 1 Timothy 3—one as a requirement for deacons (v. 8) and the other for their wives or for female deacons (v. 11). Thus, a deacon and his wife (or a female deacon) must be people who are honored and respected by those who know them. The work of a deacon is service oriented. This does not mean, however, that the leadership a deacon provides is unimportant. Such work is often crucial to the life of the church and requires someone who is respected.

Not Hypocritical (1 Tim 3:8)

The second requirement is that a deacon must not be hypocritical, or double tongued. The Greek word (*dilogos*) literally means "something said twice" and only occurs here in the New Testament. Such people say one thing to certain people but then say something else to others, or they say one thing but mean another. They are two-faced and insincere. Their words cannot be trusted, and thus they lack credibility.[7] Instead, deacons must speak the truth in love. They cannot be slippery with their words, seeking to manipulate situations for their own personal gain.

Sound in Faith and Life (1 Tim 3:9)

Paul also indicated that a deacon must hold "the mystery of the faith with a clear conscience" (1 Tim 3:9). The reference to "the mystery of the faith" is another way Paul spoke of the gospel (cf. 1 Tim 3:16). Consequently, this statement refers to the doctrinal beliefs of a deacon. Unlike those who have suffered shipwreck regarding the faith (1 Tim 1:19) and whose consciences are seared (1 Tim 4:2), deacons are to hold firm to the true gospel without wavering.

    Yet this qualification does not merely involve the content of a deacon's beliefs, for he must also hold these beliefs "with a clear conscience." That is, the behavior of a deacon must be consistent with his beliefs. If it is not, his conscience will speak against him and condemn him. "It is not sufficient to have a grasp on the theological profession of the church; that knowledge must be accompanied with the appropriate behavior, in this case a conscience that is clear from any stain of sin."[8] Similarly, Paul instructed older men to be "sound in faith" (Titus 2:2). False teachings were rampant in Ephesus and were wreaking havoc in the church.

---

[7] Mounce writes, "Deacons thus must be the type of people who are careful with their tongues, not saying what they should not, being faithful to the truth in their speech" (ibid., 199).

[8] Ibid., 200.

Paul, therefore, stressed the need for deacons to be sound in their faith. One might think this requirement is not necessary because deacons are not responsible for teaching in the church. Yet, as church officers and leaders, they influence the lives and beliefs of others. Furthermore, that deacons are not required to teach does not mean they are not permitted to teach.

Tested (1 Tim 3:10)

Another qualification not specifically mentioned in the list for elders is the need for deacons to be tested before they can serve the church in an official capacity. Paul wrote, "And they must also be tested first; if they prove blameless, then they can serve as deacons" (1 Tim 3:10). Paul stated that those who prove themselves to be "blameless" are qualified to serve as deacons. This is a general term referring to the overall character of a person's life and is similar to a word used of elders in 1 Timothy 3:2 ("above reproach;" cf. Titus 1:6 where the same word is used).

Although Paul did not specify what type of testing is to take place, at a minimum the candidate's personal background, reputation, and theological positions should be examined. But not only should the prospective deacon's moral, spiritual, and doctrinal qualifications be tested; the congregation must also consider the person's actual service in the church. A person with a deacon's heart is one who looks for opportunities to serve. As a person is given more responsibilities in the church, his ability to serve responsibly and relate to others should be examined.

To allow someone to become a deacon who has not been tested can lead to many problems. As with the elders, time is needed to assess the candidate because the sins of some are not immediately apparent (1 Tim 3:6; 5:24). A hasty appointment to office is unwise and contradicts the intent of the qualifications. A specific length of time, however, is not given and should be left up to the local church to decide.

Woman Deacon or Godly Wife? (1 Tim 3:11)

It is debated whether 1 Timothy 3:11 refers to a deaconess or the wife of a deacon. Before we discuss the merits of each view, we will discuss qualifications for the position. Paul stated that the women in question must "be worthy of respect, not slanderers, self-controlled, faithful in everything." First, they must be worthy of respect, or dignified. Second, they must not be slanderers or people who go around spreading gossip. Later, Paul warned younger widows to remarry so that they do not become idle, "going from house to house." In general, younger widows "are not only idle, but are also gossips and busybodies, saying things they shouldn't say" (1 Tim 5:13; cf. 2 Tim 3:3; Titus 2:3). Third, deaconesses or deacons' wives must be sober minded or temperate, which is the same word used of elders in 1 Timothy 3:2. That is, they must be able to make good judgments and must not be involved in things that might hinder such judgments. Finally, they must be "faithful in everything" (cf. 1 Tim 5:10). This general requirement functions similarly to the requirement for elders to be "above reproach" (1 Tim 3:2) or for deacons to be "blameless" (1 Tim 3:10; cf. Titus 1:6). In other words, deaconesses or deacons' wives must be trustworthy people with godly character.

The question of whether women can be deacons must be considered independently of whether they can be elders. While many Christians believe the Bible forbids women to hold the office of elder, some of these same Christians are also convinced that women can hold the office of deacon, provided the role of deacon is primarily one of service and does not involve leading or ruling the church.

With that in mind, let's turn to the text. In 1 Timothy 3:8–13, Paul listed the qualifications needed for a man to become a deacon. In verse 11, however, he introduced the requirements needed for "women." According to the NRSV, Paul stated, "Women likewise must be. . . ." The ESV, on the other hand, reads, "Their wives likewise must be. . . ." The question is whether Paul was speaking of the requirements for the wife of a deacon or for a woman deacon.

Those in favor of allowing women to be deacons note first that the Greek term *gunaikas* (from the word *gunē*) can either refer to "women" or more specifically to "wives"—the distinction can only be determined by the context. Second, if Paul was referring to the wives of the deacons, he could have indicated his intention by adding the word "their" ("*Their* wives likewise . . ."), which is not found in the Greek. Third, Paul began verse 11 in a manner similar to verse 8, which introduces a new office with the use of the word *likewise*. Fourth, because the qualifications for overseers do not include any reference to their wives, it does not seem likely that Paul would add a special requirement for the wife of a deacon when the more important office of overseer has no such requirement. Fifth, in Romans 16:1–2 Paul commended Phoebe to the church at Rome and calls her a *diakonos* "of the church at Cenchreae," which many take as referring to the office of deacon.

Others, however, maintain that Paul was referring to the wife of the deacon. First, elsewhere in the immediate context the Greek term *gunē* is translated as "wife" (1 Tim 3:2, 12). Second, the possessive article "their" is not required to make the passage understandable as referring to the wives of deacons. Third, if Paul was referring to women deacons in verse 11, we would expect some reference to their marital status and fidelity since every other list of qualifications includes one (elders/overseers [1 Tim 3:2; Titus 1:6]; deacons [1 Tim 3:12]; widows [1 Tim 5:9]). Fourth, the argument that the "likewise" in verse 11 must introduce a new office is not compelling based on other uses of the same term in 1 Timothy (cf. 1 Tim 2:8–9). Fifth, it would be strange for Paul to give the qualifications for male deacons in verses 8–10, interrupt himself to introduce a new office of female deacon in verse 11, and then return to the qualifications for male deacons in verses 12–13.[9] Sixth, if Paul had intended to establish an additional office (female deacons), it is likely he would have done so explicitly rather than incidentally. In addition, in 1 Timothy 2:12, Paul forbade a woman "to teach or to have authority over a man." Because all offices in the church, including the office of deacon, possess an inherent authority (which is why they must meet certain qualifications), women are not permitted to hold such offices. Finally, that Phoebe was described as a *diakonos* "of the church at Cenchreae" does not prove the term is used as a designation for an office, but rather it indicates that Paul sent her on an official mission.

The Role of Church Deacons

Whereas the office of elder is often ignored in the modern church, the office of deacon is often misunderstood. In many churches the board of deacons provides spiritual leadership in partnership with, or sometimes in opposition to, the pastor. Deacons are involved in making the important decisions of the church and are often involved in teaching and shepherding. But based on the New Testament data, the role of the deacon is to serve. Deacons are needed in the church to provide logistical and material support so that the elders can concentrate their effort on the Word of God and prayer.

Duties of Deacons

We have already indicated that deacons are not responsible to teach or lead the congregation. They are not the spiritual leaders of the church. Instead, based on the pattern established in Acts 6 with the apostles and

---

9 For similar arguments, see Grudem, *Systematic Theology*, 919 n25.

the Seven, it seems best to view the deacons as servants who do whatever is necessary to allow the elders to accomplish their God-given calling of shepherding and teaching the church.[10] Just as the apostles delegated administrative responsibilities to the Seven, the elders are to delegate responsibilities to the deacons so the elders can focus their efforts elsewhere.[11] Each local church is free to define the tasks of deacons based on their particular needs.

Some clues about the function of deacons are in the requirements of 1 Timothy 3. Grudem offers some possibilities:

> [Deacons] seem to have had some responsibility in caring for the finances of the church, since they had to be people who were "not greedy for gain" (v. 8). They perhaps had some administrative responsibilities in other activities of the church as well, because they were to manage their children and their households well (v. 12). They may also have ministered to the physical needs of those in the church or community who needed help [Acts 6]. . . . Moreover, if verse 11 speaks of their wives (as I think it does), then it would also be likely that they were involved in some house-to-house visitation and counseling, because the wives are to be "no slanderers."[12]

We must note, however, that some of the requirements could have been given to counter the characteristics of false teachers and were not so much directed toward deacons' duties. Mounce says the requirements suggest that a deacon has substantial contact with people: not be double-tongued, a dignified wife, faithful in marriage, a well-managed family.[13] Again, although such a conclusion is possible, it cannot be given too much weight.

What are some duties deacons might be responsible for today? Basically they could be responsible for any item not related to teaching and ruling the church, such as facilities, benevolence, finances, ushering,

---

[10] The role of the Seven should not be compared too closely with the role of deacons since Steven was also a miracle-worker (Acts 6:8) and preacher (6:8–10) and Philip was an evangelist (Acts 21:8).

[11] Phil A. Newton rightly concludes: "In the servant role, deacons take care of those mundane and temporal matters of church life so that elders are freed to concentrate upon spiritual matters. Deacons provide much needed wisdom and energy to the ample physical needs in the church, often using such provision as opportunities to minister as well to the spiritual needs of others" (*Elders in Congregational Life: Rediscovering the Biblical Model for Church Leadership* [Grand Rapids: Kregel, 2005], 41).

[12] Grudem, *Systematic Theology*, 919.

[13] Mounce, *Pastoral Epistles*, 195.

and other matters related to the practical logistics of operating a church. The role of a deacon is different from the role of an elder. Whereas elders are charged with teaching and ruling or leading the church, deacons are given a more service-oriented function. That is, they take care of matters related to the physical or temporal concerns of the church.

Relationship Between the Offices of Elder and Deacon

The relationship between the office of elder and the office of deacon is often assumed and rarely articulated. In this section we will analyze the New Testament data and seek to answer the question of whether deacons hold a lower office than elders and, if so, how the two offices should relate to each other.

1. The Office of Deacon Is, in Some Respects, a Lower Office

First, the function of the deacons is to provide support for the elders so they can continue their work without being distracted. Just as the apostles appointed seven men to tend to the physical needs of the congregation in the daily distribution of food (Acts 6:1–6), deacons are needed so elders can attend to the spiritual needs of the congregation. The title *deacon* also suggests one who has a secondary role of coming beside and assisting others. Deacons are not involved in the important tasks of teaching (cf. 1 Tim 3:2; 5:17; Titus 1:9) and shepherding (cf. Acts 20:28; Eph 4:11; 1 Pet 5:1–2). These tasks are reserved mainly for elders. Rather, the deacons are needed to provide assistance and support so the work of the church can continue effectively and smoothly.

Second, the office of deacon is mentioned after the office of elder/ overseer. Two examples of this are in the New Testament. In Philippians 1:1, Paul not only greeted the entire congregation (as was his normal practice), but he also greeted the "overseers and deacons." Later, when Paul listed the qualifications for overseers and deacons in 1 Timothy 3, he listed the qualifications for overseers first. Although such ordering does not necessarily indicate order of priority, it likely emphasizes the importance of those who teach and lead the church.

Third, references to the office of deacon are far less frequent than references to the office of elder. Although the Greek term *diakonos* occurs frequently, its specific use as a reference of an officeholder is only found three or four times in the New Testament (Rom 16:1[?]; Phil 1:1; 1 Tim 3:8, 12). On the other hand, the terms *elder* and *overseer* as a reference to an officeholder occur more than twenty times.[14] Again, these numbers are not conclusive by themselves, but they add to the evidence that deacons held a lesser office.

Fourth, elders were appointed to new churches before deacons were. The early church in Jerusalem had elders before they had deacons—assuming the Seven appointed in Acts 6 could not technically be considered "deacons." During Paul's first missionary journey, he and Barnabas appointed elders in the churches of Asia Minor (Acts 14:23). Yet nowhere does Luke indicate that deacons were appointed. While this omission does not prove deacons did not exist in the churches at that time, the fact that they are not mentioned indicates they were not as important to the progress of the gospel in the mind of Luke. Later, Paul commanded Titus to appoint elders in every city on the island of Crete (Titus 1:5) but says nothing of deacons. If deacons were as important to the life of the church, it would seem that he would have also included instructions to appoint deacons and included the needed qualifications as he did in 1 Timothy.

2. Deacon Is a Distinct Office

Some danger exists in describing the office of deacon as a lower office than the office of elder. There is no indication in Scripture that the office of deacon is a lower office in the sense that one must become a deacon before he can serve as an elder. These offices are distinguished by their function in the church and the gifts of the individuals who hold them. Similar, yet distinct, qualifications are given for elders and for deacons. Paul did not indicate in his qualifications for elders that one must have first been a deacon. As a matter of fact, his comment that an elder must not be a recent convert (1 Tim 3:6) would make little sense if he expected a person to be a deacon before he could move up to the position of an elder. Furthermore, many churches likely did not have deacons at the beginning of their existence.

The distinction between elders and deacons is not as much a distinction of rank as a distinction of function. Unlike elders deacons do not teach and shepherd the congregation (1 Tim 3:2, 5). If a person is a gifted teacher and meets the qualifications listed in 1 Timothy 3:1–7, he should seek to become an elder. On the other hand, if someone does not have the gift of teaching but enjoys serving in other areas, he might

---

[14] Elder: Acts 11:30; 14:23; 15:2, 4, 6, 22–23; 16:4; 20:17; 21:18; 1 Tim 5:17, 19; Titus 1:5; Jas 5:14; 1 Pet 5:1, 5; 2 John 1; 3 John 1. Overseer: Acts 20:28; Phil 1:1; 1 Tim 3:2; Titus 1:7.

consider becoming a deacon. Becoming a deacon is not a stepping-stone to becoming an elder. The two offices are distinct in that they require different kinds of people.

Deacons are not merely the personal assistants of the elders. Deacons are not called to serve the elders. Rather, they are called to serve the church. The Seven in Acts 6 were not enlisted to serve the apostles. Instead, they were selected and appointed to help solve a critical issue in the life of the congregation. Although it is necessary for elders to work closely with deacons, deacons are not there simply to answer to the call of the elders but should be given freedom to serve the church. Moreover, it is inappropriate for the elders to elect the deacons. While the elders should take the lead in examining and then nominating deacon candidates, the congregation as a whole should make the final decision because deacons serve the congregation as a whole.

3. Deacon Is an Important Office

To say that the office of deacon is, in some senses, a lower office than the office of elder is not to minimize its importance in the life and health of the church. The appointing of the seven men in Acts 6 might have saved the church from disaster. Because the church was overlooking Hellenistic widows, some Hellenistic Jews may have been tempted to form their own congregations, which would have been devastating to the unity of the church. What began as a minor issue could have turned into a massive problem if left unchecked. The church could have experienced its first split and might have been stifled in its progress of proclaiming the gospel message to all nations. Wisely, however, the apostles appointed the Seven to solve this problem. In a similar manner, deacons are needed in the church to care for the "physical" life of the church with a view toward the church's spiritual health.

Deacons are also not less than elders in the sense that they are lesser Christians or are lesser in God's eyes. All gifts are from God and are given according to his will (1 Cor 12:11). Paul used the analogy of a body to illustrate the point that all members of a church are necessary. Although they have different functions, the foot, hand, eye, and ear are all integral parts of the body and cannot be ignored (1 Cor 12:12–25).

All members are needed, and this is especially true of deacons. Scripture seems to indicate that the office of deacon is a secondary office to that of elder. This distinction is due primarily to the ruling and teaching function of the elders. The deacons, on the other hand, are primarily servants who handle the details of the church, allowing the elders to do their work more effectively and efficiently. The role of the deacons is vital to the life and health of the church. Although deacons work closely with elders, they are not there to serve the elders but to serve the church. Also, a person does not need to become a deacon before he is qualified to become an elder.

CHAPTER 17

Practical Issues in Deacon Ministry

Andrew Davis

In mainstream Baptist polity, deacons have held a position somewhere between simple servants in the church and a power bloc acting as a "check and balance" against the authority of the senior pastor. But the previous chapter provided a biblical portrait of deacons' proper role. That done, we can turn in this chapter to considering several issues of practical significance in the life of a church concerning deacons.

Distinguishing Elders and Deacons

A significant step toward a biblical understanding of deacons is to define their relationship with the elders. We will discuss the job description of deacons in just a moment, but it is important to say from the outset that nowhere in Scripture do we see deacons taking a leadership role in the overall life of the church. That role is given exclusively to elders. The role of deacon needs to be redefined with this understanding in place: deacons serve under the leadership of elders to accomplish various ministries in the church. Elders should lead with grace and humility, respecting the gifting of deacons, seeking their input regarding ministries, and even ministering alongside them at times. With such leadership in place, following elders will be a joy for deacons and not a burden. Nonetheless, elders are the leaders.

Therefore, the church's operating documents (constitution and bylaws) should be clear in establishing the authority of elders over the ministry of deacons. The deacons serve as the elders see fit. When a ministry responsibility is entrusted to deacons, they should not feel as though that ministry is their "turf" to defend against the intrusion of elders. The turf mentality is based on pride of ownership and does not properly represent the relationship between elders and deacons at any point. Also, even the most rudimentary practical ministries in the church have some spiritual aspect and impact; all things are under the oversight and shepherding of elders.

It is vital for elders to do an excellent job of communicating with deacons. They should make plain what they expect from deacons in an area of ministry. If new issues arise that necessitate changes in ministry strategy, elders should shepherd deacons closely through those changes. And the communication needs to run freely and accurately both ways. As issues arise, deacons need to feel the freedom to pass those on to elders for guidance. A loving and honest relationship between elders and deacons is essential to the smooth running of the church.

The Selection and Installation of Deacons

Deacons must undergo a similar filtering process as elders, meeting the spiritual qualifications of 1 Timothy 3:8–13 and Acts 6:1–6. As with new elder candidates, the elders should assess deacon candidates. This should involve a formal interview process, along with time for elders to discuss each candidate carefully to be sure he meets the qualifications.

This filtering by spiritual criteria is vital and represents a major difference between the biblical pattern and the traditional "board of deacons/ church committees" polity. In the latter, people are selected based on skill set and willingness to serve, though they may not be growing in grace and in the knowledge of Christ. Because deacons exist to serve the elders and the church, humility and spiritual maturity are key factors in their selection.

The final step in the installation of deacons is the church vote, by which alone they are empowered to serve in this role. Some churches may wish to have an installation ceremony in which the elders lay their hands on the deacons and pray for their roles of service, but this is not essential.

A Possible Approach to Structure: Deacon Ministry Teams

So, how should deacons be organized for maximally fruitful service in the church? Ultimately, it is up to the elders in each local church. One approach, however, is to set up deacon ministry teams in which deacons are subdivided to focus their attention on key areas of ministry. An elder can oversee each team and report to the elders as a whole. Among the possible ministry teams in a church are: college, corporate worship, encouragement (including bereavement, event support, hospital visitations, and new births), building and grounds, finances, family and youth, hosting (including greeters, security, ushers, and visitor follow-up), new member assimilation, internationals (ministering to those who are in the community from other countries), men's ministry, women's ministry, missions (including evangelism support, missionary support, overseas trip support, and prison ministry), senior adult ministry, and urban outreach.

In each of these ministries, elders set the big-picture agenda for what the team is to address, and deacons are foot soldiers with the responsibility to "make things happen" in their assigned areas. So for example, the elders may decide to have a targeted outreach to international graduate students at a local university—a lunch welcoming new students and setting up adopt-a-student hospitality relationships with willing church members. The international and encouragement deacon ministry teams would work together to make the event a success: advertising, food, decorations and set-up, organization of host family sign-ups, and follow-up with interested students. These kinds of practical ministries should occur constantly and are essential to a church's ministry in the world.

Of course, one does not have to be a deacon to serve in the church, but deacons are responsible under the elders to make certain the necessary steps are carried out. They can and should recruit people to assist them in their labors. They can also make suggestions to the elders for improvements to the ministry or new avenues of ministry.

A Special Deacon Focus: Benevolence Ministry— Inside and Outside the Church

Of all the ministries deacons could be involved with, benevolence ministry (caring for the physical needs of people inside and outside the church) may most closely resonate with the original responsibility of the Seven in Acts 6. The church will have continual opportunities to show the compassion of Christ to those in challenging financial circumstances, and this ministry needs to be done with great wisdom. Though the elders must set the priorities and principles for the church's ministry to the needy, the deacons should be mobilized to carry it out on a continual basis.

It is beyond the scope of this chapter to go into detail about various aspects of mercy ministry. Many other books do that far better than we can do right now.[1] But every healthy congregation must be involved in mercy ministry, both inside and outside the church. A key verse that teaches this is Galatians 6:10 (HCSB): "Therefore, as we have opportunity, we must work for the good of all, especially for those who belong to the household of faith." The needs of people within the church must take precedence over those outside the church, as James 2:15–16; Matthew 25:31–46; and 1 John 3:15–18 make plain. All of these passages speak of the need for our faith in Christ and love for his people to overflow into meeting their physical needs. Many other passages speak of alleviating suffering in the world as a pressing issue, as well as an opportunity for the gospel to spread.

Deacons can and should be heavily involved in the benevolence ministry of the church. Together with the elders, they should make sure a steady stream of money is available from the members to care for benevolence needs as they arise. Deacons should also be aware of specific needs within the church and should wisely address those needs according to principles laid down by elders. First Timothy 5:3–16 speaks of caring for various types of widows based on their needs and their family support. These verses give a solid doctrinal basis for meeting ongoing food, clothing, and shelter needs of church members. The elders should study this and other passages and determine a wise policy for benevolence ministry. Deacons can administer and apply that policy on a case-by-case basis.

In the same way, the elders should develop a wise approach to the needs of outsiders who approach the church for assistance and then entrust to deacons the ongoing administration of this approach. In many

---

[1] Timothy Keller, *Ministries of Mercy: The Call of the Jericho Road* (Phillipsburg, NJ: P&R, 1997); idem, *Generous Justice: How God's Grace Makes Us Just* (New York: Dutton, 2010); Kevin DeYoung and Greg Gilbert, *What Is the Mission of the Church? Making Sense of Social Justice, Shalom, and the Great Commission* (Wheaton: Crossway, 2011); Steve Corbett and Brian Fikkert, *When Helping Hurts: How to Alleviate Poverty Without Hurting the Poor and Yourself* (Chicago: Moody, 2012).

places the needs of the community can be overwhelming. This calls for great wisdom among the elders and great compassion and endurance among the deacons. But if the Lord blesses them with his grace, mercy ministry can be an astonishingly powerful avenue of gospel advance. The deacons can have the joy of seeing many come to faith in Christ as they share the gospel message with the poor they are caring for.

The Eternal Reward for Faithful Deacons

Jesus made plain who will be rewarded most lavishly on the Day of the Lord, namely, those who are the most faithful servants:

> But Jesus called them over and said, "You know that the rulers of the Gentiles dominate them, and the men of high position exercise power over them. It must not be like that among you. On the contrary, whoever wants to become great among you must be your servant, and whoever wants to be first among you must be your slave; just as the Son of Man did not come to be served, but to serve, and to give His life—a ransom for many." (Matt 20:25–28 HCSB)

The elders should teach this principle to the entire church because it has the power to humble all members and teach them that even the smallest acts of service are eternally valuable.

In that spirit the deacons should be held in honor for their labor. In countless ways they act as the servants of all, and the Lord will certainly repay them for their works of love. As Paul wrote, "For those who have served well as deacons acquire a good standing for themselves, and great boldness in the faith that is in Christ Jesus" (1 Tim 3:13 HCSB).

PART 5

THE CHURCH AND CHURCHES

Jonathan Leeman

This book began with congregationalism. It then turned to the ordinances, membership practices, and leaders inside a congregation. The final two chapters now turn outward to ask how a church should relate to other churches. This means coming full circle to some of the questions that were originally raised by the topic of congregationalism but could not be addressed there at length. Specifically, what is a local church, and what is the relationship between one local church and every other church on earth? Do certain authoritative structures hold them together? If not, how should churches think about their independence and interdependence in light of the clear biblical concern with unity? These are the kinds of questions this final section will try to answer. Chapter 18 offers a more in-depth academic discussion. Chapter 19 applies the lessons of chapter 18 in a series of practical implications.

CHAPTER 18

A Congregational Approach to Unity, Holiness, and Apostolicity: Faith and Order

Jonathan Leeman

The conversation promised to be epic. To me, a young seminarian, it might as well have been the Jerusalem Council in Acts. Two of the bigger kids in our little neighborhood of American evangelicalism, Mark Dever and John Piper, were planning on going head-to-head on baptism and church membership. Should a Baptist church admit someone into membership who has been baptized as an infant but not as a believer? Piper believes Baptist churches should; Dever believes they should not. The conversation was to transpire inside a church van en route to Washington, DC, from North Carolina.

To our chagrin Dever's personal assistant and I ended up driving in the car that followed the van. It was like finding the council doors locked but being able to hear rowdy murmuring inside. At the first rest stop, everyone climbed out of our respective vehicles, and the two of us immediately accosted a van passenger. What happened? What did they say? "Not much," said our informer. "Piper kept repeating, 'How could I bar Jonathan Edwards or J. I. Packer or Sinclair Ferguson from membership in my church?!' And Dever kept replying, 'I agree, it's hard. I just don't have the authority to overrule Jesus.'"

The work of this chapter is not to resolve this debate between Dever and Piper,[1] but the episode offers one glance at the screen of a long-running drama: the 2,000-year-old conversation about the unity of the church. And two of the main interlocutors in this conversation are named Holiness and Apostolicity, or at least that claim will provide the starting point of this chapter.

Christians have professed to believe in the one, holy, catholic, and apostolic nature of the church at least since the Nicene Creed, but one might narrate the history of the church's quest for unity as a tussle between the two characters Holiness and Apostolicity. It's as if Holiness has sought the church's unity by asking the questions, "Who is holy, and what makes a person holy?" Apostolicity, meanwhile, has sought unity by asking, "Who or what possesses the apostles' authority, and what is it an authority to do?" Holiness has God's work as Redeemer in mind. Apostolicity has God's work as Ruler in mind. But in one fashion or another, these two parties, as well as a number of others, have been sitting at the negotiator's table for 2,000 years contending over who gets what.

The Piper and Dever conversation was only one more installment. Piper pushed the seemingly evident status of certain individuals as saints or "holy ones." Dever counterpushed by calling attention to the question of authority and what his local church had or had not been authorized to do. The kinds of unity available in this instance to the Christian credobaptist and the Christian paedobaptist differ depending on how those two matters are ordered and connected.

Church unity can occur on at least two levels: unity within the local church, which concerns how the individual is united to a congregation; and unity between separate churches, which concerns the unity of all Christians everywhere. In some formulations these forms of unity can overlap significantly. This was particularly the case in the early church with the growth of the episcopacy, especially from Cyprian onward. With Cyprian one was bound to a church through a bishop, who in turn was united to other churches through their bishops. This is how all Christians were united, yet there is no reason logically or theologically to assume *prima facie* that the bonds of union within a church and between churches are the same. The determinative matter is, what does Scripture say?

---

[1] See Bobby Jamieson, *Going Public: Why Baptism Is Required for Church Membership* (Nashville: B&H, 2015), to resolve this debate.

The basic thesis of this chapter, in a sentence, is that apostolic doctrine unites all Christians and all churches, but a local church is united by both apostolic doctrine and apostolic office. Notice, this thesis has two parts, based on two forms of unity. First, all gospel-believing churches and Christians are united by the apostolic gospel in the holiness of justification and faith. The universal church, in other words, possesses a new covenant unity created by apostolic doctrine. But second, local churches are united as more than members of the new covenant. They are united through the ordinances by their shared affirmation of one another as holy, or by what I am calling the apostolic office. This is the office new covenant members assume when gathered together as churches to exercise the keys of the kingdom given by Jesus in Matthew 16 and 18. If the first form of unity is a new covenant unity, the second form involves the public presentation of that unity. Churches publicly administer and ratify the new covenant through the ordinances. At the risk of oversimplification, we might say the local church possesses a new covenant unity *and* a visibly manifest kingdom unity. It displays God's redeeming *and* kingly work.

The whole discussion of unity in this chapter will occur through the rubric of apostolicity and holiness. Wrongly relating holiness and apostolicity leads to either nominal unity or oppressive unity. If nonconnectionalist or free churches (Baptist and non-Baptist) tend to err in one direction today, it is to emphasize the positional holiness of believers over and against the church's authority. As such, the accountability structures of local congregations are flabby and do little to promote lives of virtue and holiness. The solution is not to establish authority above the local church, instituting some form of connectionalism but to reinvigorate our understanding and practice of local church authority. In the next chapter I will then turn to consider the catholicity of churches and some practical implications for their independence and interdependence.

Unity, Holiness, and Apostolicity

Theologians and traditions have defined the marks of the church differently throughout the centuries, and, to be sure, there are no normative definitions of the marks because these are theological concepts, not exegetical ones. Two different definitions of any one concept might be equally useful for different purposes.

For instance, Justo González, painting with a brush broad enough to capture 2,000 years in a dictionary-length summary, locates patristic unity around acceptance at the Eucharist, medieval unity around the authority of the pope in the West or a patriarch in the East, and reformational unity around doctrine or statements of faith.[2] But dig a little deeper into any one of these eras, and complexity quickly emerges. Another historian, Roger Haight, highlights eight loci of unity in only the pre-Constantinian church: worship and cult, the bishop, the canon of Scripture, the rule of faith or creed, ordered ministries, patterns of behavior, the catechumenate, and reconciliation.[3] And within these categories are different conceptions of the Spirit's work and the nature of apostolic succession.

Our interest here is with the tussle between various conceptions of holiness and apostolic authority as they relate to defining the church's unity, both locally and universally. Several snapshots show us the pattern.

Tertullian (c. 160–c. 225)

Tertullian's own evolution from Catholic to Montanist captures something of this tussle. From the start Tertullian viewed the church as a Spirit-filled eschatological community called to live according to the rule of Christ. Members were to abstain from political responsibilities and various secular occupations, always concerned to live in contrast to a society thoroughly suffused with pagan idolatry.

> Today let God see you as he will see you then. . . . We are they upon whom the ends of the ages have fallen. We are those whom God predestined before creation to exist in the extreme end of time. And so God disciplines us by our reproving and (so to speak) castrating the world. We are the spiritual and fleshly circumcision of all things, for both in the spirit and in the flesh we circumcise the things of this age.[4]

Holiness, in Tertullian's understanding, was a Spirit-filled, eschatological moral rigorism belonging not only to the bishops but to the whole

---

2 Justo L. González, *Essential Theological Terms* (Louisville: WJK, 2005), 178.

3 Roger Haight, S. J., *Christian Community in History*, vol. 1, *Historical Ecclesiology* (New York: Continuum, 2004), 176–79.

4 In Robert F. Evans, *One and Holy: The Church in Latin Patristic Theology* (London: SPCK, 1972), 10.

body.[5] "The holiness of the community was the collection of the holiness of its individual members."[6]

Institutionally, Tertullian believed churches were governed by monarchical bishops and bound together by their acknowledgment of an authoritative "rule of faith," the basic doctrines of apostolic Christianity that might vary in their wording but that were unchanging in their theological substance. A true church was planted by the apostles or linked to the original churches by a succession of bishops. These were the agents who handed over the apostolic faith. In short, the unity of the apostolic church depended on both the ethical holiness of the congregation as well as its acknowledgment of the authoritative rule of faith as preserved by a succession of monarchical bishops. Or so believed Tertullian the Catholic.

The later Montanist Tertullian essentially affirmed all this, but his view of the Spirit as the vicar of Christ, who brought the redemptive work of Christ to fulfillment in the increasing purity of the church, began to drive a wedge between the Spirit-indwelt community and the institutional church as defined by its historical episcopacy.[7] He disagreed with Roman bishops like Callistus, who was willing to offer sexually immoral church members an opportunity to repent. Tertullian decided he was not. Callistus believed bishops had inherited Peter's keys of the kingdom for acting in such matters of discipline. But Tertullian believed Peter's key of loosing pertained to the forgiveness of sins, and it belonged not to the bishops since the apostles were not bishops (and the bishops were not apostles) but to all "spiritual" people. Tertullian did not write systematic treatises on the church, but increasingly he seemed to view the church as constituted simply by holy and spiritual people: "The Church itself, both in its present identity and in its origin, is the Spirit himself."[8] Where then is this church? Wherever there are two or three meeting together presenting evidences of the Spirit. In short, says historian Robert Evans, "The holding together of Law, Spirit, and purity this way means for Tertullian that the purity of the Church is the criterion for discovering its unity in the Spirit and is in fact the criterion for establishing the boundaries of the church."[9]

---

[5] Ibid., 24, 29, 33–34.
[6] Haight, *Christian Community in History*, 1:168.
[7] Evans, *One and Holy*, 26–30.
[8] Ibid., 33.
[9] Ibid., 35.

Cyprian (c. 200–258)

Cyprian, like Tertullian, viewed the church's holiness principally in terms of its moral rigor and eschatological orientation. And like Tertullian he was interested in the unity of the local congregation and every member in it, driven by the question of the *lapsi* who had fallen away during the Decian persecution and whether they could be restored to the church upon repentance. His answer (unlike Tertullian) was yes but only after an "exacting and prolonged" season of penance.[10]

Also like Tertullian the primary referent for Cyprian's concept of the church remained the local eucharistic community gathered around the bishop.[11] The emphasis he gave to the bishop's role in constituting a church, a bishop's unity with other bishops, and the apostolic nature of a bishop's authority are where Cyprian represented a significant break with Tertullian. His concept of the church began with Christ's commissioning of Peter and by extension the apostles. Cyprian quoted Jesus' famous charge to Peter concerning the keys of binding and loosing in Matthew 16:18–19 and then wrote:

> It is on one man that He builds the Church, and although He assigns a like power to all the Apostles after His resurrection . . . yet, in order that the oneness might be unmistakable, He established by His own authority a source for that oneness having its origin in one man alone. No doubt the other Apostles were all that Peter was, endowed with equal dignity and power, but the start comes from him alone, in order to show that the Church of Christ is unique.[12]

Cyprian then moved from the apostles to the bishops and from the bishops to the church around the globe:

> Now this oneness we must hold to firmly and insist on—especially we who are bishops and exercise authority in the Church—so as to demonstrate that the episcopal power is one and undivided too. . . . The authority of the bishops forms a unity, of

---

[10] Cyprian, "The Lapsed," in *The Lapsed, The Unity of the Catholic Church*, trans. Maurice Bévenot, Ancient Christian Writers, vol. 25 (New York: The Newman Press, 1956), sec. 35, p. 40.

[11] Haight, *Christian Community in History*, 1:170, 190.

[12] Cyprian, "The Unity of the Catholic Church," in *The Lapsed*, sec. 4, p. 46. I am quoting from the second edition of Cyprian's work. The first edition of the paragraph just quoted observes "a primacy is given to Peter," which Cyprian then removed for the second.

which each holds his part in its totality. And the Church forms a unity, however far she spreads and multiplies by the progeny of her fecundity; just as the sun's rays are many, yet the light is one, and a tree's branches are many, yet the strength deriving its sturdy root is one.[13]

In short, the apostles were the first bishops, and by constituting the episcopacy, Jesus constituted the church.[14] Hence, Cyprian observed elsewhere, "The bishop is in the Church and the Church in the bishop."[15] Where Tertullian presented a division between the Spirit and the historic episcopacy, Cyprian did not. The Spirit belonged to the historic episcopacy, such that a bishop who had broken off from the church, as with a Novatian bishop, could not offer baptism. Members of a Novatist church entering a Catholic Church, therefore, would be required to be not *rebaptized* but *baptized*:[16] "Those who come from heresy are not being rebaptized with us; they are being baptized."[17] For the schismatic, then, there is no salvation apart from the church:

> Whoever breaks with the Church and enters on an adulterous union, cuts himself off from the promises made to the Church; and he who has turned his back on the Church of Christ shall not come to the rewards of Christ: he is an alien, a worldling, an enemy. You cannot have God for your Father if you have not the Church for your mother. . . . If a man does not keep this unity, he is not keeping the law of God; he has lost his faith about Father and Son, he has lost his life and his soul.[18]

Unity with the church is unity with a bishop: "Does a man think he is with Christ when he acts in opposition to the bishops of Christ, when he cuts himself off from the society of His clergy and people?"[19] It's not surprising that Cyprian located holiness principally in the lives of the

---

[13] Ibid., sec. 5, p. 47.

[14] Evans, *One and Holy*, 49–50. Haight refers to the bishop as constituting the "centering presence and authority" within the church, *Christian Community in History*, 1:184.

[15] In Evans, *One and Holy*, 52; from Cyprian, "Epistle 68," in the *Anti-Nicene Fathers*, vol. 5, ed. Alexander Roberts and James Donaldson (Buffalo: The Christian Literature Company, 1886), sec. 8.

[16] Evans, *One and Holy*, 61–62; Haight, Christian Community in History, 1:175.

[17] Cyprian, "Letter 71.1," in *Ancient Christian Doctrine, 5: We Believe in One Holy Catholic and Apostolic Church*, ed. Angelo Di Berardino (Downers Grove: IVP Academic, 2010), 63.

[18] Cyprian, "The Unity of the Catholic Church," in *The Lapsed*, sec. 6, pp. 48–49.

[19] Ibid., sec. 17, p. 60.

bishops rather than the members.[20] Hence, a bishop tainted by schism, idolatry, or apostasy could be readmitted upon repentance as a member of the laity but not as a bishop.[21]

Cyprian's concept of the church's unity, in short, began with the unity of the bishops, who as a group could trace their authority back to the apostles, not just in matters of doctrine, as with Tertullian's rule of faith, but in discipline.[22] Tertullian, too, employed a concept of law and boundaries, but the church on earth was still viewed as made up of "bodies."[23] For Cyprian, Evans summarizes, "The Church's bishops are the essential organs of her unity and the essential bearers of her holiness."[24]

Augustine (354–430)

If the movement from Tertullian to Cyprian represents a movement from congregation to bishop—at least for understanding the church's unity, holiness, and apostolicity—then the movement from Cyprian to Augustine represents a movement from bishop to something even more transcendent and objective for grounding the church's holiness and unity, namely, both the institution as a whole and Christ: "The whole Christ (*totus Christus*), as Scripture presents him to us, is both head and body. Just as Christ is the head of the church, so the church is the body of Christ."[25] Christians experience unity through the Eucharist: "The apostle says, 'We who are many are one body.' That's how he explained the sacrament of the Lord's table; one loaf, one body, is what we all are, many though we be."[26]

Like Tertullian and Cyprian, Augustine conceived of God's spiritual people in juxtaposition and contrast to idolatrous Roman society. All humanity, he said, belongs to one of two societies—one city which "lifts up its head in its own glory" and "loves its own strength as displayed in its mighty men," and another city that "says to its God, 'Thou art my glory and the lifter up of mine head'" and "I will love Thee, O Lord, my strength."[27] Yet by Augustine's day Christianity had become the established religion of the Roman Empire: "In the early years of the

---

[20] Haight, *Christian Community in History*, 1:173, 189.

[21] J. Patout Burns Jr., *Cyprian the Bishop*, in Routledge Early Church Monographs (New York: Routledge, 2002), 132, 141.

[22] Evans, *One and Holy*, 55; Burns, *Cyprian*, 151, 157.

[23] Evans, *One and Holy*, 47.

[24] Ibid., 64.

[25] Augustine, Sermon 364.3, in *Ancient Christian Doctrine*, 27.

[26] Ibid., Sermon 227.1, 66.

[27] Augustine, *The City of God Against the Pagans*, ed. and trans. R. W. Dyson, in

fourth century the Church had passed from a situation in which leading and honoured bishops had been martyrs to one in which her leaders
were the emperor's table guests and court advisors."[28] For the first time,
"Christianity could be the religion of convenience."[29] Augustine's two
cities, therefore, were "mixed" or "intermingled"; and they were mixed
inside the church, which was essentially coterminous with the empire.
Only a couple of sentences after Augustine referred to the "whole
Christ," quoted a moment ago, he continued:

> I will add something else, which has to be admitted; in the very
> companionship of the sacraments, in fellowship of baptism, in
> the sharing at the altar, the church has just members and it has
> unjust ones. Now after all, the body of Christ, which you know
> about, is the threshing floor; later on it will be the granary. Still,
> as long as it is the threshing floor, it does not refuse to put up
> with straw. When the time comes for storing, it will separate the
> wheat from the straw.[30]

The parable from Matthew 13:24–30 alluded to here was an Augustinian
favorite for explaining the mixed nature of the church. Never mind the
fact that Jesus used that parable to describe the world and not the church.
Augustine believed the wheat and straw, now inside the church, will
only be separated at the end of time when heaven's angels come for
judgment. For now the wheat must bear patiently with the straw. Not
even a bishop can distinguish between wheat and straw.[31] Essentially,
Augustine transposed Old Testament remnant theology onto the church;
historians and theologians refer to this view as a distinction between the
visible and invisible church.[32] To borrow from Romans 9:6, not all the
church are the church.

Where the primary referent for "church" in Tertullian and Cyprian
remained the local congregation, Augustine moved back and forth
between three referents: church as the heavenly community encompassing

---

Cambridge Texts in the History of Political Thought (New York: Cambridge University
Press, 1998), book 15, chap. 1, p. 634; book 14, chap. 28, p. 632.

[28] Evans, *One and Holy*, 78.

[29] Haight, *Christian Community in History*, 1:206.

[30] Augustine, Sermon 364.3, in *Ancient Christian Doctrine*, 27.

[31] Evans, *One and Holy*, 85.

[32] The invisible/visible distinction is used differently by paedobaptists and credobap-
tists. The former, I believe, is problematic while the latter is not. See the discussion of
this in chap. 2, "The Biblical and Theological Case for Congregationalism," by Stephen
J. Wellum and Kirk Wellum.

all angels and saints, church as the empirical and institutional society on earth containing both wheat and straw, and church as the inner church or the elect within the empirical church.[33] The holiness of the church, then, is both a property of the whole institutional body insofar as it participates in the holiness of Christ, and it is the subjective holiness of this inner church, this group of pilgrims slowly traveling from imperfection toward perfection.[34] Holiness is not what we should expect in great measure of the congregation generally, as in the Tertullian's perspective (the members) or even Cyprian's view (the bishops).

For Augustine, the church's unity could be viewed in terms of its transcendent ground (Christ) as well as in something more visible, namely, the external signs of the sacraments and the communion of bishops.[35] Here is where Augustine's ecclesiology especially ran afoul of Donatism. The Donatists maintained something like the perfectionism of Cyprian, whereby the holiness of the church depended on its bishops. Donatists established their own churches in 312 following the Diocletianic persecutions in which numerous Christians and bishops handed over the Scriptures to their persecutors, a sin regarded as equivalent to idolatry. To the Donatist's mind, the bishops' participation meant sin had spread like a contagion throughout the whole Catholic Church, leading to the Donatists' withdrawal and insistence on a new, pure baptism.[36] Yet precisely this separation and rebaptism provoked Augustine to charge them with being schismatics, a sin all but equivalent to heresy. This separate baptism violated the unity of the Catholic and apostolic church, since it is the Catholic Church "which has been founded on a rock, which has received the keys of binding and loosing." And "the water of the Church is full of faith, and salvation, and holiness to those who use it rightly. No one, however, can use it well outside the Church."[37] Union with the church includes union with its historic episcopacy and its one baptism. Speaking of his own membership, Augustine observed, "The succession of priests keeps me, beginning from the very seat of the Apostle Peter . . . down to the present episcopate."[38]

---

[33] Haight, *Christian Community in History*, 1:226–27; cf. Evans's two-part division in *One and Holy*, 81.

[34] Evans, *One and Holy*, 83–86; Haight, *Christian Community in History*, 1:246.

[35] Evans, *One and Holy*, 88–89; Haight, *Christian Community in History*, 1:244.

[36] Evans, *One and Holy*, 66–69.

[37] Augustine, "On Baptism, Against the Donatists," in *St. Augustin: The Writings Against the Manichaens and Against the Donatists*, in The Nicene and Post-Nicene Fathers, vol. 4, ed. Philip Schaff (Kessinger Publishing Reprint, no date or location), 4.1–2, p. 447.

[38] Augustine, "Against the Epistle of Manichaeus," in Schaff, *St. Augustin*, 4.5, p. 130.

From Bottom Up to Top Down

By Augustine's day the bishop of Rome had begun to possess a primacy of juridical authority, at least in the West. That centralizing trend would be articulated most fully in the middle of the fifth century by Pope Leo I and at the end of the sixth century by Pope Gregory I. It is not necessary for our purposes to trace this discussion into their pontificates or to keep trudging through church history beyond them and into the present. These first three snapshots are sufficient for demonstrating the changing relationship between unity, holiness, and apostolicity in the movement from Tertullian to Cyprian to Augustine. For Tertullian all three qualities belonged to the local congregation: the church's unity consisted of the purity of its members' lives and their shared acknowledgment of the apostolic rule of faith as taught by a bishop. With Cyprian these qualities remained partially located in the congregation but were increasingly measured with respect to the bishop and the larger collection of bishops. By the time of Augustine, the unity, holiness, and apostolicity of the church were construed as objective qualities of the whole institutional catholic church.[39] As such, Augustine observed that his own faith was kept not only by the episcopacy, as observed above, but by "the name itself of Catholic, which, not without reason, amid so many heresies, the Church has thus retained."[40] It was the one global or catholic institution where the unity, holiness, and apostolicity of Christ's church could be found, unlike, say, in the Donatist church, which was largely restricted to North Africa. The general movement for defining unity, in short, was from bottom up to top down—from practical and subjective to objective, from individual to institutional. Local congregation members participated in these three marks in varying degrees, sometimes more, sometimes less.

The difficulty with this upward and outward movement, of course, is that "objective holiness with no holiness among the members is no holiness at all."[41] It might not be surprising then that the historical development that has been sketched above "entailed a lowering of the standards of Christian morality."[42] Nor is it surprising that, in this environment, the Christian world began emphasizing practices like monasticism and

---

[39] Haight makes this observation with regard to the church's holiness, *Christian Community in History*, 1:261. I am expanding it to include its unity and apostolicity.
[40] Augustine, "Against the Epistle of Manichaeus," in Schaff, *St. Augustin*, 4.5, p. 130.
[41] Haight, *Christian Community in History*, 1:261–62.
[42] Ibid., 253.

clerical celibacy as replacements for the moral rigorism once located in the congregation and in the celebration of the pre-Constantinian martyrs.

To put all this critically, the movement from Tertullian to Augustine might be characterized as a movement from an oppressive unity of moralism to a lackadaisical unity of nominalism (i.e., one in name only; there is no true saving faith), at least at the local level. On the level of the universal church, however, it might be characterized as a movement from the nominal unity of a shared creed to a slightly more coercive or forced unity that came with imposing objective signs (infant baptism, the Eucharist) on people apart from their will. In other words, I am suggesting that the Catholic Church of Augustine's day (and beyond) simultaneously combined a nominal unity at the local church level with a kind of coercive unity at the universal level. Those at least were the errors toward which these different models tended, even if healthy congregations could be found in each era.

John Calvin (1509–1564)

One last example is worth considering in order to bring this discussion into a Protestant context. For this John Calvin's ecclesiology works suitably. His doctrine of the church is Protestant, but it also represents something of an ecclesiological halfway point between the previous three authors and the free-church perspective recommended below. Indeed, Calvin located himself within the tradition of Cyprian and Augustine, while separating himself from the institution of the papacy.[43] (A major component of Calvin's view—interestingly, from a congregationalist's standpoint—is the right of a congregation to elect its own bishops, a position he ascribes to both himself and Cyprian.[44])

The first sentences of Calvin's ecclesiology section in the *Institutes* identify him as a Protestant: "It is by faith in the gospel that Christ becomes ours and we are made partakers of the salvation and eternal blessedness brought by him." A person does not procure salvation

---

[43] See Calvin's chapter, "The Ancient Form of Government Was Completely Overthrown by the Tyranny of the Papacy," in *Institutes of the Christian Religion*, ed. John T. McNeill and trans. Ford Lewis Battles, in The Library of Christian Classics, vol. 21 (Philadelphia: Westminster Press, 1960), 4.5, pp. 1,084f.

[44] Calvin, *Institutes*, 4.3.15 and 4.5.2. For an account of congregational election in Cyprian, see Haight, *Christian Community in History*, 1:183–84; and Paul J. Fitzgerald, S. J., "A Model for Dialogue: Cyprian of Carthage on Ecclesial Discernment," in *Theological Studies* 59 (1998): 236–53. Fitzgerald explains how Cyprian involved the whole congregation, perhaps even through a vote, not only in the affirming of a bishop but both in excommunication and in the receiving back into membership those who had lapsed before their persecutors.

through the church's sacraments but through faith.[45] Calvin views the church as the ordinary "external means" of salvation. He continues: "Since, however, in our ignorance and sloth (to which I add fickleness of disposition) we need outward helps to beget and increase faith within us, and advance it to its goal, God has also added these aides that he may provide for our weakness. And in order that the preaching of the gospel might flourish, he deposited this treasure in the church."[46] Later he invokes Cyprian by referring to the church as the "mother" of believers apart from whom "one cannot hope for any forgiveness of sin or any salvation."[47] Whatever Cyprian meant by the term "mother," Calvin surely intended it to describe the church's ordinary (but not necessary) instrumentality in salvation.

Like the authors above, especially Augustine, Calvin's concepts of the church's holiness and unity exhibited a number of tensions. Roger Haight characterizes the tension between Calvin's existential and objective concepts of the church's holiness thus:

> Calvin can be seen to dramatize this tension [between these two concepts of holiness] since he seems to want to maintain the church as a necessary society, to which all in a particular place belong, from birth with infant baptism, and at the same time retain the quality of existential uprightness typical of the Anabaptists, a voluntary association of people committed to moral discipline, but in this case encouraged through the institution of the consistory. In effect Calvin . . . makes the tension overt and palpable. A church holy only in its objective forms offers an empty claim; a church which claimed holiness only on the basis of its members' lives, given the reality of sin, will be judged fraudulent.[48]

In other words, Calvin, as a magisterial reformer, wanted to work within the Constantinian settlement whereby church and nation were essentially coterminous, an equation possible because of his reformulated concept of infant baptism. One author observes, "Calvin's ideal

---

45 Interestingly, Calvin leveraged Augustine earlier to argue that Christ alone can serve as a mediator for sinners, once again demonstrating why Augustine's ambiguity on justification allows both Roman Catholics and Protestants to claim him as their own. See Calvin, *Institutes*, 3.20.20, p. 877; see also, 3.12.3, p. 757.

46 Ibid., 4.1.1, pp. 1,011–12.

47 Ibid., 4.1.4, p. 1,016.

48 Haight, *Christian Community in History*, vol. 2, *Comparative Ecclesiology* (New York: Continuum, 2005), 145–46.

remained a society in which citizenship was equated with church membership."[49] Moreover, the citizens of Geneva, where Calvin spent much of his career, were legally required to attend sermons on Sundays.[50] Like Augustine's concept of the Eucharist enabled just and unjust Romans alike to participate in the holiness of Christ and even to be called holy, so Calvin's doctrine of imputed righteousness[51] attached righteousness, at least formally, to every citizen of Geneva in the church, both just and unjust. Calvin did not speak explicitly about the holiness of the church in these terms, but it is an inevitable implication. This being the case, Calvin found himself in the awkward position, like Augustine, of needing some way to say that not all the church were the church. Following Augustine, therefore, he borrowed the Old Testament's remnant theology and imposed it on the New Testament assembly (helped in no small part by adopting Augustine's doctrine of election): "Holy Scripture speaks of the church in two ways. Sometimes by the term 'church' it means that which is actually in God's presence," which would be God's elect. "Often, however, the name 'church' designates the whole multitude of men spread over the earth who profess to worship one God and Christ. . . . In this church are mingled many hypocrites who have nothing of Christ but the name and outward appearance." The former church is "invisible to us" and "visible to the eyes of God alone," while the latter church "is called 'church' in respect to men."[52] Calvin's reference to those who are church members in nothing "but the name and outward appearance" raises once more Augustine's problem of nominalism, even if we believe church members sitting in Calvin's pews would have heard the gospel articulated more clearly and consistently than those sitting under the bishop of Hippo.

The Anabaptists in the sixteenth century objected to the idea of a mixed church and called for regenerate church membership. Calvin responded with a bit of a sneer: "They claim that the church of Christ is holy [Eph. 5:26]." He then pointed to several parables—including Augustine's favorite concerning the wheat and straw (Matt 13:24–30)—to explain "the mixture of the wicked."[53] Calvin criticized the Anabaptists as "imbued with a false conviction of their own perfect sanctity" and

[49] G. S. M. Walker, "Calvin and the Church," in *Readings in Calvin's Theology*, ed. Donald K. McKim (Grand Rapids: Baker, 1984), 221.

[50] Harro Höpfl, *The Christian Polity of John Calvin* (New York: Cambridge University Press, 1982), 199.

[51] See Calvin, *Institutes*, 3.11.1–4.

[52] See John Calvin, *Institutes of the Christian Religion*, in McNeill and Battles, *The Library of Christian Classics*, vol. 21, 4.1.7, pp. 1,021–22.

[53] Calvin, *Institutes*, 4.1.13, pp. 1,027–28.

"vainly seeking a church besmirched with no blemish."[54] Certain communities of Anabaptists did push in a perfectionist direction, but the majority would have been content with the definition of the church's holiness that Calvin offered: "The church is holy, then, in the sense that it is daily advancing and is not yet perfect: it makes progress from day to day but has not yet reached its goal of holiness."[55]

The trouble for Calvin, of course, is that such a description of holiness could not really be predicated on the visible church because it only characterized the remnant inside the visible church. Therefore his Reformed successors defined churches as "more or less pure"—as the Westminster Confession eventually put it—"according as the doctrine of the Gospel is taught and embraced, ordinances administered, and public worship performed more or less purely in them."[56] Such a statement is no doubt accurate, but does it say everything that could be said? What it fails to acknowledge is that infant baptism and the political theology of Christendom functioned as pipelines for impurity. A more forthright statement might have read: churches are more or less pure according to the number of unregenerate infants baptized into membership, particularly when membership is equated with citizenship, placing a massive burden on the church to retain every child, adolescent, and adult as a member. How likely are pastors to remove adolescents from membership at the age of confirmation when doing so places in jeopardy their citizenship in the nation?

Writers like Calvin who emphasize the church's "mixed nature" tend to be ambiguous about whether they grant this point as a concession to the realities of fallenness, the sort of concession that even an advocate of regenerate church membership would make, or if they mean the church's "mixed nature" is by deliberate design, much like ancient Israel. In some passages, Calvin talks about the mixed nature of the church as if it were a concession.[57] The Westminster Confession, too, bears this tone: "The purest Churches under heaven are subject both to mixture and error; and some have so degenerated as to become no Churches of Christ, but synagogues of Satan." The subtext seems to be, "Such a mixture cannot be helped in this fallen world where evil abounds." The trouble is that it is not simply error that causes such a mixture but the practice of infant

---

[54] Ibid.

[55] Ibid., 4.1.17, p. 1,031.

[56] The Westminster Confession of Faith 25.4. See *The Evangelical Protestant Creeds*, vol 3 of *The Creeds of Christendom*, 6th ed., ed. Philip Schaff, rev., David S. Schaff (Grand Rapids: Baker, 1998), 658.

[57] See especially *Institutes*, 4.1.10–16, pp. 1,024–31.

baptism as well as the legal establishment of the church. The mixture in that sense is deliberate, not only a concession that anyone practicing regenerate church membership would grant. The deliberate nature of this mixture makes the practice of excommunication seem a little inconsistent, even if an explanation of excommunication can be given. Furthermore, sitting as we are at the tail end of centuries of Christian nominalism raises the question of whether Calvin was correct to criticize the "ill-advised zeal for righteousness" of the Anabaptists.[58]

In short, the Anabaptists sought to locate holiness in the entire local assembly. Calvin, like Augustine with a few adjustments, sought to locate holiness both "above" the local assembly in something more universal as well as "below" it in the lives of a subset of its members. What effect did this have on his conception of the church's unity?

Calvin offered two conceptions of unity, one for the invisible church and one for the visible church. Both emphasized the universal church rather than the local church. Calvin grounded an invisible concept of unity in God's election and the steadfastness of Christ. "To embrace the unity of the church in this way, we need not . . . see the church with the eyes or touch it with the hands. Rather, the fact that it belongs to the realm of faith should warn us to regard it no less since it passes our understanding than if it were clearly visible."[59] This invisible brand of unity is to be accepted on faith because it belongs to the elect, or the church within the church, whether in heaven or on earth. The visible brand of unity also belongs to the universal church but not Augustine's universal institutional church. Calvin's primary referent for the institutional church was a regional or city church.[60] Yet he remained concerned with the unity that existed between all such churches. As long as a church honors the ministry of the Word and the administration of the sacraments, "it deserves without doubt to be held and considered a church" and "[i]n this way we preserve for the universal church its unity."[61] Of course, he did not grant such charity of judgment to the Anabaptists, whose schisms he likened to the Donatists.[62] What is more, no hierarchy among these different churches is necessary to describe them as united, said Calvin, once again invoking Cyprian's precedent.[63]

---

[58] Ibid., 4.1.16, p. 1,030.
[59] Ibid., 4.1.3, p. 1,015.
[60] Haight, *Christian Community in History*, 2:102, 107.
[61] Calvin, *Institutes*, 4.1.9, pp. 1,023–24.
[62] Ibid., 4.1.13, p. 1,027.
[63] Ibid., 4.6.17, p. 1,117.

All true Christians are united in the faith, and all true churches are united by a shared ministry of the Word and ordinances. But, strangely, the local or city churches, where these two ministries occur, are not invisibly united in the faith since they are deliberately mixed assemblies. As with the church's holiness, Calvin placed its unity both above and below the local assembly. If his local church is going to err in one direction or another, it will most likely be toward a nominal unity—it will be composed of many who are Christians in name only. This, again, seems to be an inevitable consequence of *designing* the church on earth as a mixed assembly.

Finally, church authority for Calvin essentially rested with the leadership of the church, or even outside the church at higher levels: "The power of the church . . . resides partly in individual bishops, and partly in councils, either provincial or general."[64] In good Protestant fashion he made all such authority subservient to the Bible, whether the authority of bishops, apostles, tradition, or counsels.[65] Apostolic authority was unique only insofar as the apostles "were sure and genuine scribes of the Holy Spirit, and their writings are therefore to be considered oracles of God."[66] Otherwise, Calvin denied that the power of the keys uniquely rested with Peter or his fellow apostles.[67] He distinguished between the key of Matthew 16:18–19 and John 20:23, which he said is the authority given to ministers to preach the gospel since the gospel opens the doorway to heaven; and the key of Matthew 18:17–18, which he said is the authority given to the whole church to excommunicate.[68] The former key includes the authority "to lay down articles of faith, and authority to explain them." The latter key, which in one context Calvin said occurs "by vote of the believers,"[69] is in general to be exercised by "the tribunal of the church, that is, the assembly of the elders" because these men stand in for the church.[70] No doubt, Calvin intended the elders of a congregation to use their authority for maintaining its holiness, its internal unity, as well as various forms of unity at the regional and international levels.

---

64 Ibid., 4.8.1, p. 1,149.
65 Ibid., 4.8.4, 8, 9, 14 (pp. 1,152, 1,155–58, 1,163–64), and 4.9 (pp. 1,166–79).
66 Ibid., 4.8.9, p. 1,157.
67 Ibid., 4.6.1–5, pp. 1,102–7.
68 Ibid., 4.11.1–2, pp. 1,211–14.
69 Ibid., 4.11.2, p. 1,214.
70 Ibid., 4.12.2, p. 1,231.

The Reassertion of Scripture's Authority and a Protestant Concept of Apostolicity

Perhaps most noteworthy in Calvin ecclesiologically is the reassertion of scriptural authority as preeminent in the life of the church, which in turn gives a larger role to doctrine as the ultimate ground of the church's holiness, apostolicity, and unity. After criticizing the Anabaptists for their schismatic ways, Calvin said of his own separation from the Roman Catholic Church, "Now let them go and shout that we who have withdrawn from their church are heretics, since the sole cause of our separation is that they could in no way bear the pure profession of truth."[71] In Calvin's mind, and in the Protestant understanding generally, Scripture alone bears absolute authority, as we have said, not bishop, tradition, or counsel: "The Scriptures obtain full authority among believers."[72]

Therefore, the church's unity is predicated on fidelity to Scripture, somewhat like Tertullian's emphasis on the rule of faith. If the bishop has final authority, a person *must* be under him in order to be holy and united to the one and true church. To submit to him is to submit to God. If the Bible has final authority, a person *must* be under it in order to be holy and united to the one and true church. The question of apostolic authority in the Protestant mind, therefore, is typically reduced to a simple face-off between office and doctrine.[73] Does the bishop or the episcopacy possess apostolic authority? Or does the apostolic gospel and Scripture? As Calvin said: "A most pernicious error widely prevails that Scripture has only so much weight as is conceded to it by the consent of the church. As if the eternal and inviolable truth of God depended upon the decision of men!"[74] Paul testifies that the church was "built on the foundation of the apostles and prophets" (Eph 2:20),[75] and Calvin interpreted this as "the teaching of the prophets and apostles." He wrote, "If the teaching of the prophets and apostles is the foundation, this must have had authority before the church began to exist." Thus, Calvin continued, "While the church receives and gives its seal of approval to the Scriptures, it does not thereby render authentic what is otherwise doubtful and controversial."[76]

[71] Ibid., 4.2.6, pp. 1,047–48.
[72] Ibid., 1.7.1., p. 74.
[73] Matt Jenson and David Wilhite, *The Church: A Guide for the Perplexed* (New York: T&T Clark, 2010), 75–78.
[74] Calvin, *Institutes*, 1.7.1., p. 75.
[75] Unless otherwise indicated, all Scripture passages are from the HCSB.
[76] Ibid., 1.7.2., pp. 75–76.

In other words, the truth of Scripture, or right doctrine, or the gospel *constitutes the church, its unity, and its holiness.* To submit to the authority of Scripture is to submit to its king and the gospel word of its king. It is to repent, believe, and be saved. As such, "the church" can be alive and well on planet earth even though no ecclesial authority recognizes it as such. People hear the Word of God, repent, trust, and so become "the church" (see Rom 10:17). The Word precedes the church. Theologian Christoph Schwöbel observes, "As the creature of the divine Word the Church is constituted by divine action."[77] God's Word creates God's people.[78] This is a bedrock principle of Protestant ecclesiology.

Not surprisingly, a quick glance at recent Protestant writers on the church from connectionalist and nonconnectionalist traditions suggests that Protestants generally locate the church's apostolicity in the apostolic gospel or doctrine, not in an office.[79] The church's unity and holiness, as such, are attained and preserved through this apostolic gospel. After all, "what is certain about the church's apostolicity is that it is a mark of the church's connection to the original followers of Jesus."[80] What unites Christians and churches more clearly than a succession of bishops is the apostolic gospel. Even a classic book on church polity that attempts to ascertain which form of church government "is best entitled to be regarded as the *Apostolic Church*" points to "the modern Church which embodies in its government most apostolic *principles*."[81] In other words, right principles constitute apostolicity, not office.

One further matter is worth chasing down in this connection: Was Calvin inconsistent by criticizing the Anabaptists for standing on what they believed to be the truth about baptism and the nature of the church? After all, weren't they merely standing on truth too? Perhaps but not

---

[77] Christoph Schwöbel, "The Creature of the Word: Recovering the Ecclesiology of the Reformers," in *On Being the Church. Essays on the Christian Community*, ed. Colin E. Gunton and Daniel W. Hardy (Edinburgh: T&T Clark, 1989), 122.

[78] See my *Reverberation: How God's Word Brings Light, Freedom, and Action to His People* (Chicago: Moody, 2011), especially chaps. 1–4; Timothy Ward, *Words of Life: Scripture as the Living and Active Word of God* (Downers Grove: IVP, 2009); Michael Horton, *People and Place: A Covenantal Ecclesiology* (Louisville: WJK, 2008), 37–71.

[79] E.g., Philip G. Ryken, "An Apostolic Church," in *The Church: One, Holy, Catholic, and Apostolic*, Richard D. Phillips, Philip G. Ryken, and Mark E. Dever (Phillipsburg, NJ: P&R, 2004), 93–115; Edmund Clowney, *The Church, in Contours of Christian Theology* (Downers Grove: IVP, 1995); 73–78; John S. Hammett, *Biblical Foundations for Baptist Churches: A Contemporary Ecclesiology* (Grand Rapids: Kregel, 60–61); Gregg Allison, *Sojourners and Strangers: The Doctrine of the Church* (Wheaton: Crossway, 2012), 114, n32.

[80] Jenson and Wilhite, *The Church*, 78.

[81] Italics mine. Thomas Witherow, *The Apostolic Church—Which Is It?* (Skipton, North Yorkshire: Free Presbyterian Publications, 2001; orig. printed 1856), 20.

necessarily. Christian theologians, taking a cue from Jesus (Matt 23:23), have long conceded that some doctrines and truths are weightier than others. Calvin, no doubt correctly, adjudged a doctrine of the gospel to be weightier than a doctrine of baptism:

> What is more, some fault may creep into the administration of either doctrine or sacraments, but this ought not to estrange us from communion with the church. For not all the articles of true doctrine are of the same sort. Some are so necessary to know that they should be certain and unquestioned by all men as the proper principles of religion. Such are: God is one; Christ is God and the Son of God; our salvation rests in God's mercy, and the like. Among the churches there are other articles of doctrine disputed which still do not break the unity of faith.[82]

The Anabaptists, Calvin was saying, wrongly measured the weightiness of the sacraments relative to the weightiness of the saints' communion in the gospel.

To return then to the illustration with which this chapter began, we can surmise that John Piper stands squarely with John Calvin. Both Johns believe that sharing communion in the gospel trumps differences in how believers understand the ordinances, at least within the boundaries of a Protestant approach to the ordinances, whereby a word precedes and interprets the ordinances. Calvin again: "A sacrament is never without a preceding promise [word] but is joining to it as a sort of appendix, with the purpose of confirming and sealing the promise itself, and of making it more evident to us and in a sense ratifying it."[83]

A Complementary Concept of Apostolicity

Earlier I observed that two different definitions of any one concept such as apostolicity might be equally useful for different purposes. What I would like to do now is simultaneously affirm the standard Protestant concept of apostolicity as right doctrine, while also making matters complex by offering a complementary definition of apostolicity as right office—like Cyprian and Augustine. Assent to apostolic doctrine does create the universal church. Faith comes through hearing, which means that all gospel-believing churches are invisibly united in the holiness of

[82] Calvin, *Institutes*, 4.1.12, pp. 1,025–26.
[83] Ibid., 4.14.3, p. 1,278.

justification and faith. This far I agree with Calvin. But it takes more than apostolic doctrine to create a *local* church. It also takes apostolic office. Apostolic office, working together with apostolic doctrine, creates or constitutes the institution of the local church and the visible unity of the local church.

In fact, the Protestant failure to recognize the significance of apostolic *office* in the local church may be one contributor to the individualist nature of so much Protestant Christianity, including the churchlessness of so many evangelicals. I will not, however, take the time here to chase down that historical assertion.

What is critical for us to understand in order to come to terms with apostolic office and the unity of the local church can be drawn from my own work on the keys of the kingdom and Bobby Jamieson's work on the ordinances. Let's take each in turn.

Apostolicity Tied to the Keys of the Kingdom

For the remainder of this chapter, I will use the term *apostolic office* to mean "possessing the apostles' authority of the keys." To hold a set of keys is to possess the authority of an office. Yet here is where my interest in office sounds less like Cyprian and Augustine and more like Tertullian: in a congregationalist's perspective this apostolic office belongs to the entire congregation in its gathered capacity. The keys of the kingdom, which establish this apostolic office, do not belong to the pastors or some larger episcopal structure. They belong to every member of the new covenant who has been formally recognized as such through baptism into membership of a local church. Church membership is not only a status; it's an office, complete with a job description. And that job is to protect, preserve, and proclaim the gospel of the new covenant.

What Are the Keys?

Jesus first established the apostolic authority to exercise the keys of the kingdom in Matthew 16. He asked the apostles who he was, and Peter, answering on behalf of the group, replied, "You are the Messiah, the Son of the living God!" (v. 16). Jesus affirmed this answer, saying it came from the Father in heaven. He told Peter that he would build his church on him and this confession. To this end he handed Peter a set of office keys: "I will give you the keys of the kingdom of heaven, and whatever you bind on earth is already bound in heaven, and whatever you loose on earth is already loosed in heaven" (v. 19).

I am not going to take the time here to defend my interpretation of this highly contested passage. A more vigorous and footnoted argument can be found elsewhere.[84] The bottom line is that the keys of the kingdom authorize their holder to pronounce on heaven's behalf a judgment concerning the *who* and the *what* of the gospel: *what* is the right confession and practice of the gospel, and *who* is a right confessor. To bind or loose is to render a verdict in heaven's name.

The keys do not give their holder the power to shape the gospel or to make someone a kingdom citizen, like a judge neither makes the law nor makes a defendant innocent or guilty. After all, the gospel, the good news of Jesus' death and resurrection, is divinely given and fixed. A person becomes a kingdom citizen by the work of God and by faith, as stated a moment ago. Rather, the keys give the authority (1) to assess whether some confession, doctrine, or practice is in keeping with that gospel, as when the council of Jerusalem needed to determine whether circumcision was necessary for Gentiles (Acts 15). And the keys give the authority (2) to assess whether a certain person belongs to the gospel, as a church does anytime it baptizes someone into membership (e.g., Acts 2:41). Once the judicial assessment is made, the key holder then makes an official declaration on heaven's behalf, again, like a judge, or even like an ambassador who speaks on behalf of a king. The holder officially declares before the nations of the earth, "This doctrine is consistent with Jesus' gospel" or "This practice is not"; "He is a kingdom citizen" or "She is not." Whoever possesses the keys has an interpretive authority over the gospel word and gospel citizens and in that sense precedes the gospel word.

Strictly speaking, proclaiming the gospel is not the same as exercising the keys, but so closely are proclamation and the keys intertwined that the latter cannot occur without the former. If the keys are likened to speaking a verdict and pounding a gavel, proclaiming the gospel can be likened to reading the law upon which a verdict is based. For the judge to make a verdict, he must first read the law. That said, issuing a verdict also proclaims the law the verdict upholds. For that reason it is not too much of a stretch to say the keys not only authorize their holder to *protect* and *preserve* the gospel; they enable the holder to *proclaim* the

---

[84] My most up-to-date interpretation and argument can be found in *Political Church: The Local Assembly as Embassy of Christ's Rule* (Downers Grove: IVP Academic, 2016). A slightly older defense can be found in *The Church and the Surprising Offense of God's Love: Reintroducing the Doctrines of Church Membership and Discipline* (Wheaton: Crossway, 2010), 172–98. Both books offer the same account, but the new volume provides a slightly better articulation.

gospel. They present, again, a formal decision about *what* constitutes a right confession and *who* is a true confessor.

Practically speaking, the keys are put into practice whenever their holder

- decides upon or changes a confession of faith that will bind all church members;
- decides upon any other doctrinal or ethical standard that will be required of all members and that will become the standard of admittance or excommunication (e.g., the decision that a certain kind of divorce will lead to excommunication);
- admits or excludes a member based on these kinds of criteria.

The keys, in short, are the authority over a church's statements of faith and membership.

The supreme example of exercising the keys' authority occurred in Jesus' interchange with Peter: Jesus asked who the disciples thought he was, Peter made a confession, and then Jesus affirmed both the confession and Peter ("flesh and blood did not reveal *this* to you . . . *you* are Peter, and on this rock . . ." Matt 16:17–18). To jump ahead, the same kind of conversation transpired in Matthew 18, only in reverse. Jesus envisioned a situation in which a church gradually determined that the *what* of a gospel confession does not match the *who* of a gospel confessor.

The authority of the apostles may have gone beyond the authority of the keys, particularly in the apostles' capacity as witnesses of the resurrection and their role in establishing the foundation of the church (Acts 1:22; Eph 2:20). But surely the keys were central to their authority. By use of the keys, the apostles oversaw baptism (e.g., Matt 28:19; Acts 2:41; 10:48; 18:8). They regulated the Lord's Supper (1 Cor 11:17–34). They passed judgment on false professors (e.g., Acts 5:1–11; 8:18–24; 1 Cor 5:3). They participated in determining gospel ethics (e.g., Acts 15; cf. Gal 2:11–14). And through their Epistles they not only taught true doctrine, like elders; they clarified the boundaries of true doctrine (e.g., Gal 2:15f; 1 John 4:1–3).

Also, apostolic authority is effectual, not advisory (see Philemon 8–9). It can unilaterally effect what it commands in matters within its jurisdiction, as when Peter said to Simon the magician, "You have no part or share in this matter," effectively removing him from the fellowship (Acts 8:21). The completion of the action does not depend on the consent of any individual. The apostolic keys, in that sense, are like the sword of state. One way to answer the question of who holds the keys in the postapostolic age is simply to ask, who demonstrates unilateral, effectual authority? Congregations, elders, or bishops?

This much can be agreed upon across denominational traditions: the apostolic nature of the church is bound up with whomever possesses the authority of the keys. If the bishop of Rome or any other bishop possesses the keys, the church is apostolic by virtue of its connection to the bishop. If a presbytery or general assembly possesses the keys, the church is apostolic by virtue of being ruled by a presbytery. And if the congregation possesses the keys, the church's apostolicity is found in its self-governance and congregational rule.

Notice also, the concept of apostolic office I am using here does not depend on succession in some kind of mystical or sacramental sense. It depends on an authorization to exercise the keys.

Who Holds the Keys?

So, who holds the keys? The theological champions at the Westminster Assembly spent several days debating who in the postapostolic age holds the keys Jesus originally gave to Peter. They understood that the keys represent, at the very least, the power of excommunication. And whoever possesses the power of excommunication has the highest authority in a church, just as the power of the sword is the highest authority in a nation. There is no higher power than the power to remove, either by the sword or by the keys, and all power in a body politic derives from this.

The Presbyterian majority at the assembly argued that presbyteries hold the keys. The few Congregationalists present—the "dissenting brethren"—argued that the keys are held by the whole congregation together with the elders. And the Anglicans who were excluded from the assembly, had they been asked, would have surely contested that the bishops possess the keys.[85]

A fascinating passage for coming to grips with who holds the keys and with the location of the church's apostolic authority is Galatians 1. Paul accused the Galatian churches of "turning to a different gospel," and then said, "But even if we or an angel from heaven should preach to you a gospel other than what we have preached to you, a curse be on him!" (v. 8). Apostolic authority, in other words, was not inherent in the man. It was tied to the gospel message and his fidelity to it, which

---

[85] Hunter Powell, *The Crisis of British Protestantism: Church Power in the Puritan Revolution, 1638–44* (New York: Manchester University Press, 2015).

relativizes an apostle's authority, as Paul well knew since he had confronted Peter (2:11–14). An apostle's authority depends on both a *what* and a *who*. As such, Paul instructed the local churches of Galatia to repudiate any apostle who compromised the gospel. His exhortation did not demand a congregationalist reading, but it at least recommended it. If the bishop, or presbytery, or just the elders of the local congregation held the keys, wouldn't Paul have addressed them instead of the churches? What is absolutely clear is that Paul charged the Galatian congregations with protecting and preserving the gospel even against apostles like himself, which at least seems to imply they possessed the same authority of the keys that Paul did. Such a reading would also make sense of God's promise in the new covenant that "no longer shall each one teach his neighbor and each his brother, saying, 'Know the LORD,' for they shall all know me, from the least of them to the greatest" (Jer 31:34 ESV). Every member of the new covenant would have access to a true knowledge of God, which suggests that every member would have some responsibility to guard that knowledge.

A similar equivalence of Paul's authority and the church's authority seems to be in view in 1 Corinthians 5. In response to news that a member of the church was sleeping with his father's wife, Paul wrote, "For though absent in body, I am present in spirit; and as if present, I have already pronounced judgment on the one who did such a thing" (v. 3 ESV). The pronouncement of judgment suggests he was speaking from his apostolic chair. But then he called the church to act in an equivalent capacity, as if he were a father passing on the family business to his son: "When you are assembled in the name of the Lord Jesus and my spirit is present, with the power of our Lord Jesus, you are to deliver this man to Satan for the destruction of the flesh, so that his spirit may be saved in the day of the Lord" (vv. 4–5 ESV). As in Galatians 1, he did not address the elders or any external church structure. He instructed the assembled congregation to hand the man over to Satan.

The requisite setting for such an action is noteworthy. Paul envisioned (1) an assembly, (2) assembled in the name of Jesus, (3) with his apostolic spirit present, (4) together with the power of the Lord Jesus. The first criterion eliminated the possibility of doing this behind closed doors in a meeting of the session or across town at the regional presbytery. The second criterion suggested that the assembled church formally acts in Jesus' name, which brings us back to Matthew, as we will see in a moment. The third criterion suggested that Paul meant for the church to do exactly as he would have done, as if he were a father telling his son to "play the game as if I were there with you." It implied an informal transmission of his own authority. The fourth criterion suggested that the congregation actually possessed the power of Jesus, representatively, to excommunicate the man.

Both of these Pauline passages seem to build on the authority Jesus granted to the church in Matthew 18 and 28. The local church is "apostolic" most fundamentally because the keys Jesus handed to the apostle Peter in Matthew 16 he also handed to a local church in Matthew 18:15–20.

- According to verse 17, the church is the final court of appeal in a case of excommunication when the *what* and the *who* of the gospel are out of alignment.
- Verse 18 grounds the action of verse 17 by invoking the keys with a plural "you": "Whatever you bind on earth is already bound in heaven, and whatever you loose on earth is already loosed in heaven."
- Verse 19 likens exercise of the keys to asking the Father for something: "Again, I assure you: If two of you on earth agree about any matter that you pray for, it will be done for you by My Father in heaven."
- Verse 20 begins with an explanatory "For," as if verse 20 explains everything that has just been discussed. "For where two or three are gathered together in My name, I am there among them." Who are the two or three? Elders? Bishops? The witnesses of verse 16? The generic presentation suggests that they are any two or three believers who regularly gather in Jesus' name to exercise the keys. One person cannot be a church. Two or three can be. Churches are constituted by two or more people gathering together in Jesus' name to exercise the keys of the kingdom. And when believers gather in Jesus' name to exercise the keys, Jesus and his reputation are there. They represent him.

The same invocation of Jesus' authority and name occurs in Matthew 28:18–20. All authority in heaven and on earth belongs to him, Jesus began. Then he commanded the eleven disciples to go, make further disciples, and baptize them in the name of the Father, Son, and Spirit. Surely the apostles had the authority to make disciples and baptize. But does anyone else? The fairly easy answer must be, churches do—wherever two or three are gathered in his name to exercise those keys.

Later in the New Testament, we learn that elders should be set apart for teaching and oversight, which suggests they ordinarily lead the church in using those keys. We should even say that a church without elders is disorderly (see Titus 1:5 ESV), and that a church needs the elders to responsibly wield the keys. But finally the keys belong to the entire congregation. No text in the New Testament explicitly links the oversight of the elders with the keys of the kingdom in the manner Matthew 18 so clearly links the keys with the whole assembly. And no text in the New Testament presents elders making a unilateral and effectual decision concerning statements of faith or members. The apostle Peter did (see Acts 8:20–23). And churches do (see 1 Corinthians 5; 2 Cor 2:6–7). But nowhere does an elder. Elder authority is real, but it is a different kind of authority from this apostolic authority of the keys.

The Institutional Local Church

A local church, then, *is* its members. More specifically, a church is its members by virtue of the authority Jesus has given to believers who gather regularly in his name to constitute as a church. Cyprian, we saw, said, "The bishop is in the Church and the Church in the bishop." He was correct to pay attention to apostolic office for conceiving of the unity of the church, but we need to substitute "key-holding assembly of believers" for "bishop": the key-holding assembly of believers is in the church, and the church in the key-holding assembly of believers. Believers or members of the universal church, created by the Word, interpret the *what* and *who* of that Word and so establish a local church.

Here is another way to put it, which will lead us in a moment to Bobby Jamieson's work on the ordinances. Every body politic needs some way of publicly registering itself in the eyes of the world. For that reason nations use borders, border patrol stations, flags, immigration offices, and a whole host of institutional resources for marking off their "nation" or body politic from others. Ancient Israel did the same. Under the patriarchs and while in Egypt, they were marked off by circumcision. Then with the Mosaic covenant and habitation of Canaan, they added Sabbath laws, various cultic regulations, as well as national borders for publicly registering themselves as a bona fide nation in a manner the other nations of the earth would recognize.

The questions that face followers of Christ are: who publicly administers new covenant membership? How do the citizens of the new covenant get recognized? Notice that I am not asking, how does one *become* a member of the new covenant? God grants new covenant membership through the atoning work of Christ and the indwelling work of the Spirit. Rather, I am asking, how do these members or citizens become publicly recognized before the nations of the earth? Who exercises border patrol in a kingdom with no borders? Answer: whoever possesses the keys of the kingdom. The keys are the authority Christ gave to publicly administer the new covenant.

That public administration is critical precisely because God means to tie his name to some body of people, and he cares immensely about whom. "I will be your God and you will be my people," Yahweh repeatedly said to Israel. But when Israel brought shame on his name, he cast them out of the land (e.g., Ezek 36:22–23), and he promised a new covenant precisely so that he might vindicate his name (vv. 22–29). In Matthew 18, Jesus promised to dwell with two or three gathered in his name. And in Matthew 28, he spoke of being baptized into the name of the Father, Son, and Spirit.

What is the local church, these two or three baptized believers gathered in Christ's name to preach the gospel and exercise the keys? They are the people purchased by the new covenant in Christ's blood in order to represent him and his kingdom rule on planet earth. They are an embassy of his kingdom. Most embassies represent a kingdom across geographic space. The local church is an embassy representing Christ's rule across eschatological time. The individual Christian does not possess the keys of the kingdom by him or herself. He or she possesses them jointly with the entire congregation, as we saw with the four criteria Paul names in 1 Corinthians 5: "When you are [1] assembled [2] in the name of the Lord Jesus [3] and my spirit is present, [4] with the power of our Lord Jesus."

A moment ago we heard Calvin say, "As if the eternal and inviolable truth of God depended upon the decision of men!" Well, the truth does not depend on the decision of men, but the formally authorized public recognition and affirmation of that truth does. The apostolic gospel creates the universal church. The key-holding apostolic office of the local church then affirms and recognizes that gospel and everyone who belongs to that gospel.

The Ordinances

How does a church employ the keys? Through the ordinances. The keys represent the church's authority, and that authority is an authority to *identify* and to *publicly unite* members of the new covenant, which is precisely what the ordinances do. Baptism identifies a Christian with God: a Christian is baptized "in the name of the Father and of the Son and of the Holy Spirit" (Matt 28:19). And baptism unites a Christian with God's people: "So those who received his word were baptized, and there were added that day about three thousand souls" (Acts 2:41 ESV). The Lord's Supper, too, identifies us with Christ and unites us to his people. We "proclaim the Lord's death until he comes" (1 Cor 11:26), and we are "sharing in the body of Christ" (1 Cor 10:16–17). The ordinances proclaim the gospel and identify a people with the gospel. They are the raised flag of Christ's kingdom. They make the nation visible.

Theologian Oliver O'Donovan refers to the ordinances as the "abiding signs" and "marks of identification which will stamp a formal identity on the community."[86] Faith comes first, he says, but a "certain structuring of the church's life is a given with that life," which the ordinances present. He sums up the work of the ordinances or sacraments:

> The sacraments provide the primary way in which the church is "knit together," that is, given institutional form and order. Without them the church could be a "visible" society, without doubt, but only a rather intangible one, melting indeterminately like a delicate mist as we stretched out our arms to embrace it. In these forms we know where the church is and can attach ourselves to it. They are at once "signs" of the mystery of redemption wrought in Christ, and "effective signs" which give it a palpable presence in the participating church.[87]

Baptism, O'Donovan observes, "marks the gathering community" and is the sign by which "each new believer accepts Jesus as his or her representative, and accepts Jesus' people as his or her people."[88] The Lord's Supper should not be individualistically viewed as a "'sacramental grace' which affects the believer in a different way from other kinds of grace"; rather, its work has to do with "the formation of the body. The 'one loaf' binds 'many' into 'one body' (1 Cor. 10:17). It determines the identity of this society by reference to the Passion: it is the community of those who have not only gathered to God's Christ, but have died with him."[89]

---

[86] This paragraph is taken from *Political Church* (Downers Grove, IL: IVP Academic, forthcoming).

[87] Oliver O'Donovan, *Desire of the Nations: Rediscovering the Roots of Political Theology* (New York: Cambridge University Press, 1996), 172; see also, 177–78; 180.

[88] Ibid., 177–78.

[89] Ibid., 180.

Reflecting on this same passage in O'Donovan, Bobby Jamieson has observed what's pertinent: the local church is constituted as a public reality through the ordinances. In Jamieson's words:

> The sacraments—baptism and the Lord's Supper—are what "knit" the church together, giving it "institutional form and order." They make the church visible; they tell us where the church is and how we can join it. Because the sacraments make the church visible, they are effective signs. They give the gospel a "palpable presence in the participating church" and thereby make the church itself something palpable. Baptism and the Lord's Supper inscribe the gospel into the very shape and structure of the church.[90]

So, yes, the gospel word creates a believing people, but then the keys working through the ordinances create a public body politic. Jamieson again:

> God has appointed public, self-involving acts of witness to the gospel—baptism and the Lord's Supper—to craft this body's corporate existence. God constitutes the church not just by creating gospel persons, but by ordaining and enabling their social, institutional response to the gospel. In other words, baptism and the Lord's Supper make the church visible. They are the hinge between the "invisible" universal church and the "visible" local church. They draw a line around the church by drawing the church together. They gather many into one: baptism by adding one to many, the Lord's Supper by making many one.[91]

To return to the earlier conversation, the apostolic gospel creates a gospel people. People hear, believe, and are saved. They belong to Christ's heavenly and eschatological community, Christ's universal church. But at this point they are not yet *a* church. They are simply a bunch of Christians. For them to become a church, something more needs to occur. Someone needs to recognize someone else as believing in the same gospel, which presumes the ability to interpret and articulate the gospel. And those two people, presumably, would love for a third to join them in affirming, sharing, and declaring this same gospel. What the keys of the kingdom offer, then, is the authority for these two or three

---

[90] Jamieson, *Going Public*.
[91] Ibid.

to affirm one another in this shared gospel. The ordinances enact this public affirmation. The ordinances concretize, make real, give life to, constitute this public society called a local church. Jamieson again: "The ordinances themselves give a church its church-ness. . . . By drawing a line between the church and the world, the ordinances make it possible to point to something and say 'church' rather than only pointing to many somethings and saying 'Christians.'"[92]

What might we say now concerning Piper's (and Calvin's?) willingness to sideline the right practice of the ordinances for the sake of gospel unity? The first thing to realize, as Dever did, is that there is a question of authorization. Has a Christian or a church been authorized to overlook a right practice of the ordinances, say, by bringing into membership and the Lord's Table someone who has not been baptized? The second thing to realize is that a church is constituted in two steps. First is the invisible moment in which God constitutes someone to be a Christian. Yet this is not the "only constitutive moment for ecclesiology," observes John Webster.[93] A group of Christians, by right of the keys, must constitute themselves as a local church through the ordinances. "A church is born when gospel people form a gospel polity," says Jamieson.[94] To disregard the ordinances, in a sense, is to disregard the local church. No ordinances, no biblical local church.

From Apostolicity to Holiness to Unity

What then is the relationship between the church's apostolicity and holiness, and what can we conclude about the unity of the church?

Holiness

To be "holy" is to be *consecrated to God*. Something is holy if it is set apart *from* sin and set apart *to* or devoted *to* God. God is holy because he is set apart *from* sin and devoted *to* his own glory. He is consecrated to himself. The Scriptures are holy because they are consecrated to him and his message. And God's people throughout the Scriptures are holy because they are consecrated to God, his purposes, his name, his glory.

---

[92] Ibid.
[93] John Webster, "The Self-Organizing Power of the Gospel: Episcopacy and Community Formation," in *International Journal of Systematic Theology* 3, no. 1 (2001): 73.
[94] Jamieson, *Going Public*.

So with the church. Peter called the church, like Israel before it, a "holy nation" and "a people for his own possession" (1 Pet 2:9 ESV; cf. Exod 19:6). Paul characterized it as God's "chosen ones, holy and loved" (Col 3:12). Six of his letters greet his readers as saints, or "holy ones" (Rom 1:7; 1 Cor 1:2; 2 Cor 1:1; Eph 1:1; Phil 1:1; Col 1:2). And John anticipates the day when these saints will be gathered in the holy city that is the New Jerusalem (Rev 21:2, 10; 22:19). This indeed is Augustine's city of God.

The church is holy because it is consecrated to God. It has a holy *identity* (e.g., 1 Pet 2:9). It possesses a holy *calling* (e.g., 2 Tim 1:9; 1 Pet 2:5). And it is to practice holy *conduct* (e.g., 1 Thess 2:10; 2 Tim 2:21).

Notice, then, that the biblical concept of holiness contains both objective and subjective elements, as we saw in the discussion of church history from Tertullian to Calvin. The church's holiness involves a transcendent identity and calling, and it demands practical conduct. The indicative is followed by the imperative.

Notice, also, how these two ways of conceiving holiness intertwine with the apostolic gospel and apostolic office. The church's objective holiness is grounded in the apostolic gospel of the new covenant. Through the new covenant, God names a people as his own. He forgives their sin. Yet the new covenant also provides for the people's subjective holiness. God places his law on their hearts. And he establishes a basic equality of access to himself and the knowledge of him (Jer 31:31–34; Ezek 36:24–27). The indicative yields obedience to the imperative. Identity and activity are intertwined and inextricable. God's unilateral work in the new covenant produces both. The people are named holy so they might pursue holy callings and conduct.

The work of the apostolic office is to identify this objective holiness when it encounters a profession of holiness matched by some modicum of practical holiness. Here is where Tertullian and the Anabaptists were correct to insist on holy lives over and against the church as a mixed assembly. To baptize someone, which occurs by apostolic authority, is to identify them with the holy One. It is a declaration that a person is objectively holy in heaven's eyes, and, so far as the church can discern with earthly eyes, he or she is on the path of repentance and increasing practical holiness. Should a baptized person's life prove that he or she is not repentant and not on the path of practical holiness, excommunication should follow.

Surely we must concede that nonbelievers belong to churches. Nonetheless, God's purpose for the church is that visible churches represent invisible realities, and so leaders and members work toward this end. There is a difference between granting that churches are "mixed" as a concession to fallenness and finitude and structuring the church as "mixed" by design.

Unity

What then can we say about the church's unity? Jesus prayed, "May they all be one, as You, Father, are in Me and I am in You" (John 17:21). And Paul exhorted, "I . . . urge you to walk worthy of the calling you have received . . . diligently keeping the unity of the Spirit with the peace that binds us. There is one body and one Spirit—just as you were called to one hope at your calling—one Lord, one faith, one baptism, one God and Father of all, who is above all and through all and in all" (Eph 4:1, 3–6).

Unity, we observed, occurs at two levels: unity within the local church, which concerns how the individual is united to a congregation, and unity between separate churches, which concerns the unity between all Christians everywhere. With these two concepts of apostolicity and two concepts of holiness in place, we are ready to address both levels of unity. First, all gospel-believing churches and all Christians are invisibly united in the objective holiness of the apostolic gospel. And all churches and Christians have a united interest in seeing that objective holiness translate into practical holiness—for the indicative to follow through in the imperative. Paul explained both sides of this in Ephesians 4; he reminded believers of their unity in the gospel: one body, one Spirit, one Lord, one faith, one baptism. But then he urged the saints to walk in a manner worthy of this unity by "keeping the unity." This unity of the universal church, we might say, is a new covenant unity. It is grounded both in gospel identity and in the freely chosen activity of regenerate hearts, not in authoritative structures.

But there is a second kind of unity. Local churches, as eschatological embassies of Christ's kingdom, are visibly united by the apostolic authority of the keys of the kingdom. While the universal or catholic church on earth is bound together by objective holiness, the local congregation is bound together by objective holiness *and* apostolic authority. It possesses a new covenant *and* a kingdom unity (to slightly oversimplify). It specially displays God's redeeming *and* kingly work. The balance of these two kinds of unity, ideally, avoids an oppressive, coercive unity on one side or a nominal unity on the other side.

Apostolic doctrine unites Christians and churches. Both apostolic doctrine *and* office unite a local church.

Calvin, being a good Protestant, adamantly emphasizes that the apostolic gospel or word precedes and creates the church. But ironically, his (and Augustine's) "mixed assembly" conception of the local church means his local church is *not* constituted by an assent to the apostolic word. After all, infants are members. Calvin's local church members are united by apostolic office (the activity of binding and loosing) but not by apostolic doctrine. An advocate of a regenerate church says it is *both* office and doctrine.

Another way to understand the two forms of unity is by considering the relationship between two Christians who belong to the same church and two Christians who belong to different churches. What is the difference between those two relationships? No doubt many obligations of love and holiness and spiritual concern apply to both relationships. But the difference comes down to the fact that the keys are exercised among the two members of the same church. To put it bluntly, they can participate in the formal discipline of one another, whereas two Christians belonging to different churches cannot.

Christians united together in a local church live in relationships with one another, but those relationships are under constraint. They exist inside of an accountability structure afforded by the keys of the kingdom. This, when practiced wisely, helps saints pursue the "imperative" and, little by little, learn to live up to the "indicative"—to become what they are.

No doubt all this has practical implications for how we understand the independence and interdependence of churches. We will turn to that in the next chapter.

CHAPTER 19

A Congregational Approach to Catholicity: Independence and Interdependence

Jonathan Leeman

In the previous chapter I presented a case for two kinds of church unity. First, all churches and Christians are invisibly united by the apostolic gospel in the holiness of justification and faith. Second, local churches alone, as eschatological embassies of Christ's kingdom, are invisibly united by the apostolic gospel *and* visibly united by the apostolic authority of the keys of the kingdom. Christians possess the first type of unity by virtue of their membership in the new covenant. The second type occurs when the new covenant is publicly ratified and administered before the onlooking nations with kingdom authority. Apostolic doctrine unites Christians and churches. Apostolic doctrine and apostolic office unite a church.

With this heavy lifting done, we are in a position to explore the implications of these two forms of unity for both the local church and its relationship to other churches. In summary, the fact that the authority of the apostolic office belongs to the local church alone means churches are formally independent and Christians must be united to local churches. The New Testament never speaks of churches separating from one another at a denominational or larger structural level. It only speaks of individuals separating from specific local congregations. There is nothing such as a set of conservative-leaning Presbyterian churches breaking rank and dividing from the liberal-leaning Presbyterian denomination. There is nothing such

367

as a single Episcopal church splitting from its communion to join a different Anglican communion and losing its building in the process. There is not even a discussion of one church dividing from another church. The only discussion of separation in the New Testament occurs at the level of the sinning individual or the false teacher, which makes sense in a landscape of formally independent churches.

That said, the fact that all Christians and churches are united by apostolic doctrine places some obligation on all Christians and churches to cooperate with one another, as prudence dictates, for the advance of the gospel. As a new covenant unity, this unity depends on the freely chosen activity of regenerate hearts, not on authoritative structures. This is precisely the kind of cooperation and interdependence we observe being exercised among churches in the New Testament.

The structure of this chapter is simple. I will first offer practical implications of what it means for churches to be independent. Then I will offer practical implications of what it means for churches and Christians to be interdependent. All these implications emerge from the biblical and theological work done in the previous chapter.

Independence

The independence of the local church is grounded in the fact that it possesses the keys of the kingdom. Apostolic office is located *there*, among the two or three gathered in the name of Christ for preaching the gospel and exercising the keys through the ordinances. The keys, I argued in the last chapter, represent Jesus' authorization to build the church on earth by declaring *what* and *who* belong to the kingdom of heaven—*what* is a right confession of the gospel, and *who* is a right confessor. The keys are put into practice whenever a church decides on a confession of faith that will bind all church members or whenever it admits or excludes a member. A church effects these decisions through the ordinances.

In short, local churches are independent because they possess authority over their own members and statements of faith.

A Church Affirms Who Represents Christ

In the previous chapter I used the illustration of an embassy to describe the authority of a local church. An embassy does not *make* someone a citizen; it *affirms* someone as a citizen. It stamps the passport when it expires. An embassy, moreover, makes the rule of one nation visible inside of another nation. You can see the building, the flag, the passports, the ambassadorial staff, the soldiers with guns standing at the embassy gates. The authority of an embassy is independent from its host nation and formally independent from other embassies of its own nation.

In the same way, the independent authority of the local church affirms who represents Christ. It makes the rule of Christ's kingdom visible on planet earth. The ordinances make the authority of the keys *visible*. We might call the ordinances Christian passports. To baptize someone is to identify them with the name of the Father, Son, and Spirit. To give someone the Lord's Supper is to affirm their membership in the body of our Lord.

Practical Implication 1: The ordinances should be practiced in the context of the gathered assembly. If the gathered assembly holds the keys, and if the keys are exercised *through* the ordinances, then the ordinances should be practiced in the context of the assembly. Baptism and the Lord's Supper are not private mystical experiences in which a person shuts his or her eyes and *feels* Jesus' special presence. They are corporate and public proclamations of identification and belonging. Together a church declares that God's name is upon them (Matt 28:19); together they declare their union with Christ's death and resurrection (Rom 6:1–2); together they declare his death and membership in his body (1 Cor 11:18–19, 27–33). The ordinances are not for Christian families, youth camps, or even small groups. They are assembly activities.

Practical Implication 2: Baptism is ordinarily into membership. With the exception of settings in which a local church does not exist (e.g., the Ethiopian eunuch in Acts 8), it is irresponsible (and unbiblical) to baptize an individual—thereby affirming his profession of faith before the nations—and then leave him unaccounted for within a local body. Who will ensure that he remains faithful to his profession? How will this baptismally affirmed professor be excommunicated if he is not within a church?

Practical Implication 3: Christians should belong to local churches. Christians do not have the authority to declare themselves Jesus' representatives. The church has this authority, which it ordinarily exercises by dispensing the Lord's Supper to its members (which is not to say that a church cannot provide the Lord's Supper to visiting members of other churches for the sake of acknowledging the wider body of Christ). Maintaining the credibility of one's profession of faith requires a believer to remain under the oversight of a church.

Practical Implication 4: Churches should examine those whom they receive as members and maintain oversight of members for the sake of meaningful discipline. "Who do you say that I am?" Jesus asked Peter. In churches today, too, the elders should interview all prospective candidates for membership. A church should work hard to make sure it can give an account for the spiritual welfare of every member.

Practical Implication 5: Discipleship and pastoral care work best in the framework of accountability, which means they should primarily occur in the context of the local congregation. The local church possesses the keys and thereby represents something of Christ's authority, and the individual Christian has the opportunity to partake of instruction and fellowship under the umbrella of that authority. Christians grow best through their own church's formative and corrective discipline—teaching and correction. Also, the independent, geographically localized nature of the local church helps ensure that the exercise of gospel authority is conjoined with pastoral knowledge and care. Synods and presbyteries and general assemblies, on the other hand, exercise binding authority from afar without the benefit of personal and pastoral understanding.

Certainly Christians should form friendships with and seek instruction from believers in other congregations, as we will consider below. But as a father will care for his children before caring for other children, Christians should prioritize their own local churches in matters of friendship, physical and financial care, ethical accountability, and prayer. Paul observed that "the one who is taught the message must share all his good things with the teacher" (Gal 6:6 HCSB; cf. 1 Cor 9:15). A saint's first tithe dollars, in other words, should go to his or her own church. So with caring for the needy, demonstrating compassion and forgiveness, and influencing the culture—all of these should occur first in the context of a believer's local church. The *oneness* for which Jesus prayed, the oneness that would display the unity of the Father and Son, is not about a bureaucratic connection between a church in Naperville and denominational headquarters in Nashville (see John 17:21). It is about groups of people living their lives together in both Naperville and Nashville, loving the members of their own churches in the way Christ loved them, and so demonstrating to the nations that they are his disciples (John 13:34–35).

A Church Affirms a Right Confession

The independence of the local church is also seen in the fact that King Jesus has authorized each local assembly to affirm the faith that believers should confess.

Other bodies in church history have written confessions or creeds that were then used to bind churches—from the apostolically unique council in Jerusalem in Acts to the council of Nicaea to the Westminster Assembly. But biblically the legitimate body in a postapostolic age for exercising the keys that bind confessions on a group of Christians is the local church.

Practical Implication 6: Churches gather around correct preaching of the Word. As a church sits under the preaching of the Word, it learns to exercise the keys responsibly—assessing both the *who* and the *what* of the gospel.

Practical Implication 7: Churches should establish clear statements of faith. The thing that unites a church to all other churches—its confession of gospel faith—also makes each church independent. Because the gathered assembly has been given the keys, every member of the gathered assembly is responsible to affirm a single statement of faith, a responsibility that fits comfortably with the priesthood of all believers. In fact, by this act of corporately affirming a statement of faith (through the ordinances), a group of Christians constitute themselves as a local church.

On the flip side the fact that a statement of faith unites a church to every other Christian church suggests that it is wise to employ historical creeds or confessions in official statements of faith. A church must independently affirm a statement, but it should be a statement that is (or at least could be) broadly affirmed by Christians throughout the ages.

Practical Implication 8: Churches should choose their pastors. In Galatians 1, Paul rebuked the "churches of Galatia" for abandoning the gospel. He did not address the elders or pastors; he addressed the congregations. *They* are finally responsible for ensuring that correct doctrine is preached, which, by implication, suggests that the assembly should have final say in affirming who the teachers of the Word are.

Practical Implication 9: Local churches should separate from false confessions, false confessors, and false teachers. Such acts of separation will occur formally and informally. For instance, excommunication is a formal act of separation from someone who the church adjudges to be a false confessor. An informal act of separation occurs, for instance, when a pastor warns his congregation that a certain popular author or conference speaker teaches a "health and wealth" gospel and should not be trusted.

Practical Implication 10: One church is not bound by another's decision in a matter of discipline. Suppose, for instance, that an individual asks to join a church after having been excommunicated by another. The second church, if it is wise, will enquire into the circumstances of discipline. It should contact the first church in order to hear "the other side of the story." It should move slowly and deliberately and often may defer to the first church's decision, lest it undermine the good being done in the individual's life through the act of discipline. But in the final analysis, if the second church determines that the first church was mistaken or that the individual has truly repented, that second church possesses its own authority in the keys to receive the individual into membership, regardless of the first church's preference.

A Church Administers the Great Commission

Finally, the independence of the local church is seen in the fact that King Jesus has commissioned each local assembly to fulfill the Great Commission and to equip its saints for this task. Of course, this does not mean a church does this apart from cooperating with other churches, but the local church is the primary location where the work of the Great Commission gets done. It has the authority to baptize.

Practical Implication 11: Church membership should be treated as an office. It is a job. It is not a casual connection with a voluntary society like a country club, where a person comes for the benefits so long as the dues are not too high. It is a citizenship, and citizenship is an office of governance. Once a church has affirmed an individual as a Jesus representative and a member, that member becomes responsible for overseeing other confessors of the faith and proclaiming the gospel.

One might picture a person taking his passport to an embassy to be renewed but then, after standing in front of the desk to have his passport stamped, walking behind the desk in order to take part in the work of the embassy. In other words, part of fulfilling the Great Commission for an individual Christian is to take responsibility for other church members, that the keys might be exercised responsibly.

Practical Implication 12: Every member is responsible for declaring the gospel through evangelizing outsiders and discipling and counseling insiders. Speaking the truth in love, the body builds itself up in love (Eph 4:16). This is part of the office of member. Apostolic Christianity is not advanced Christianity. It is basic Christianity, and basic Christianity is nothing other than Membership 101.

Practical Implication 13: Pastoral authority in the church exists to equip the saints for the work of the ministry, the "office" work they possess in the keys (see Eph 4:11–12; Heb 13:17). If Christians are to guard the *what* of the gospel, they need pastors to train them in the gospel so they can recognize counterfeit gospels and counterfeit teachers. If

Christians are to guard the *who* of the gospel, they need pastors to exemplify the "above reproach" and Christ-imaging life so members know what gospel confessors should look like. It's not without reason that Paul commanded Timothy to guard his doctrine and his life (1 Tim 4:16). To oversimplify, there is a sense in which an elder's doctrine equips the saints to guard the *what*; an elder's life equips them to guard the *who*.

Practical Implication 14: Christians learn to guard the *what* and the *who* of the gospel by submitting to their pastors. Congregationalism is not about members leading the church. Ordinarily, leaders lead. The only time congregations should overrule their leaders is when those leaders explicitly depart from Scripture or implicitly demonstrate a significant departure from the path of biblical wisdom.

Integration

Though Christ has placed the apostolic authority of the keys into the hands of local assemblies, churches should work together to fulfill the Great Commission because they call upon the same Lord and share a common apostolic confession.

Again the embassy image is useful. One might imagine sitting inside the US embassy in Tehran on November 4, 1979, while angry Muslim students gathered just outside the embassy gates. The mob eventually broke into the compound, and fifty-two Americans spent 444 days as hostages in the Iran Hostage Crisis. But the question worth considering is, what would it have been like to be inside the embassy while the fury was still building? What would an embassy worker be thinking and doing in those moments before the mob broke through the gates? Presumably most would be on the phone in a frantic search for friends. The US State Department, the nearby Canadian embassy, the Swedish embassy in town—the occupants of the US embassy, presumably, were grabbing for whatever outside friends they could find to intervene. What a person in such circumstances presumably would *not* do is assume the little embassy compound, floating like a storm-embattled boat in the middle of the seething urban sea that was Tehran, would be fine all by itself. The inhabitants would not try to "go it alone" as if the fate of the US government's diplomatic mission in the world rested upon the embattled embassy's shoulders.

Strangely, this is the attitude many free or independent churches maintain as they seek to undertake God's mission in the world. Christians know they are sojourners and aliens. They know other embassies and friends are "out there." They know the world, the flesh, and the Devil oppose us like a bloodthirsty mob—"for your sake we are being killed all the day long" (Rom 8:36).[1] But too easily churches undertake Christ's mission by themselves. They go it alone. They don't cooperate with other local churches in evangelism and missions, in discipline, in counseling, in mercy ministry, and in prayer.

A Better Appreciation of Family Ties

The Bible offers a much more intimate picture of the relationship between local churches. One embassy quickly jumps in to help another. To switch to a family metaphor, the relationship between churches in the New Testament reveals close family ties.

Different churches shared love and greetings:

- "All the churches greet you" (Rom 16:16).
- "The churches of Asia send you greetings" (1 Cor 16:19).
- "All the saints greet you" (2 Cor 13:13).
- "I have heard of your faith in the Lord Jesus and your love toward all the saints" (Eph 1:15; also Col 1:4).

They shared preachers and missionaries:

- "With him we are sending the brother who is famous among all the churches for his preaching of the gospel" (2 Cor 8:18).
- "Beloved, it is a faithful thing you do in all your efforts for these brothers, strangers as they are, who testified to your love before the church" (3 John 5–6).

They supported one another financially with joy and thanksgiving:

- "At present, however, I am going to Jerusalem bringing aid to the saints. For Macedonia and Achaia have been pleased to make some contribution for the poor among the saints at Jerusalem" (Rom 15:25–26).
- "For the ministry of this service is not only supplying the needs of the saints but is also overflowing in many thanksgivings to God" (2 Cor 9:12; also 2 Cor 8:1–2).

They imitated one another in Christian living:

- "You became an example to all the believers in Macedonia and in Achaia" (1 Thess 1:7).

---

[1] Unless otherwise indicated, all Scripture passages are from the ESV.

- "For you, brothers, became imitators of the churches of God in Christ Jesus that are in Judea" (1 Thess 2:14).

These testimonies of shared love and support between the earliest churches are matched by exhortations. Churches were told to greet one another:

- "Greet also the church in their house" (Rom 16:5).

They were instructed to care for one another financially:

- "Now concerning the collection for the saints: as I directed the churches of Galatia, so you also are to do. On the first day of every week, each of you is to put something aside and store it up, as he may prosper, so that there will be no collecting when I come. And when I arrive, I will send those whom you accredit by letter to carry your gift to Jerusalem" (1 Cor 16:1–3).
- "So give proof before the churches of your love and of our boasting about you to these men" (2 Cor 8:24).

They were cautioned about whom to receive as teachers:

- "Do not believe every spirit, but test the spirits to see whether they are from God, for many false prophets have gone out into the world" (1 John 4:1).
- "For many deceivers have gone out into the world, those who do not confess the coming of Jesus Christ in the flesh. Such a one is the deceiver and the antichrist. Watch yourselves" (2 John 7–8a).

They were exhorted to pray for other churches and Christians:

- "To that end keep alert with all perseverance, making supplication for all the saints" (Eph 6:18).

They were exhorted to imitate other churches in steadfastness and faith:

- "Therefore we ourselves boast about you in the churches of God for your steadfastness and faith in all your persecutions and in the afflictions that you are enduring" (2 Thess. 1:4).

The point is impossible to evade: local congregations of the New Testament were very much integrated with one another. A church will best fulfill the Great Commission when it is connected in relationship, prayer, and work with other churches.

Local churches possess independence, we said a moment ago, because they possess authority for representing Christ, pronouncing a confession, and initiating the Great Commission. By a similar measure, the interdependence of local churches is founded in the fact that they share the same Christ, the same confession, and the same Commission.

Separate Churches Share the Same Christ

Christians and churches share the same Lord and Christ, which comes through in Paul's greeting to the church in Corinth: "To the church of God that is in Corinth . . . called to be saints together with all those who in every place call upon the name of our Lord Jesus Christ, both their Lord and ours" (1 Cor 1:2; cf. 2 Cor 1:1).

Members of different "embassies" share a kind of "political" unity, exemplified in Paul's description of the Ephesians as "fellow citizens with the saints and members of the household of God" (Eph 2:19). Fellow citizens in separate churches belong to a common nation, like the separate US embassies in Baghdad and Tehran. They are politically united, even if geographically separate, because they represent the same government. The shared government of separate churches, of course, is the eschatological lordship of Christ. His government has entered history through these embassies.

Practical Implication 1: Christians should care how other churches are structured because polity makes this political unity visible. And polity is how Christians are made accountable to our common Lord. Polity is the tool that disciplines Christians for righteousness.

Practical Implication 2: The names and reputations of all Christians in all churches are bound together, even when they belong to different denominations. The citizens of other nations sometimes make jokes about the "ugly American" because a few obnoxious Americans, it seems, have stained the nation's name with their loud-mouthed behavior. In the same way, when one Christian church presents a poor witness in a city (no matter the denomination), every Christian church in that city suffers. When one church presents a positive witness, every church benefits. Churches therefore share an interest in one another's spiritual welfare.

Practical Implication 3: Because churches share an interest in one another's spiritual welfare, they should pray for one another, encourage one another, financially support one another as opportunity allows, and generally do what they can to support one another's ministries. This means there should be openness to informal relationships among churches, particularly between church leaders. Having knowledgeable relationships facilitates specific prayer, encouragement, and aid. Such interaction and prayer matures congregations and helps them fight against "turfiness."

Andy Johnson, a pastor in Washington, DC, challenges fellow pastors to ask themselves whether, when praying for revival, they can rejoice if revival comes to a church down the street. Then he points to the tale of two leaders in 3 John as instructive: Gaius loved to welcome and support faithful missionaries sent out from other churches because he loved Jesus (vv. 5–8). Diotrephes refused to welcome these workers from other churches because he "loves to be first" (v. 9).[2]

Mark Dever similarly encourages pastors to dream bigger than the four walls of their churches and to strategize to help other pastors in their regions. He offers these practical pointers:

- "Pray privately for other local pastors and congregations.
- Set an example for our churches by publicly praying for God's blessing on other Bible-believing and Bible-preaching churches in your area.
- Encourage ministers of other evangelical denominations to preach from time to time in your pulpit. As occasion may arise, accept invitations to preach in theirs.
- Invite a fellow pastor to your church's prayer meeting. Interview him about the work in his congregation, and pray for him and his church.
- Discipline yourself to speak well of other churches. If a warning must be given, speak with great care.
- Be willing to encourage members who live a distance from your church to join likeminded congregations closer to their home."[3]

Practical Implication 4: Different levels of cooperation are possible based on different levels of doctrinal and ecclesial unity. Two Baptist churches can work together to share the gospel and plant churches (because they share the same gospel and the same polity). A Baptist and a Presbyterian church can work together to share the gospel but not plant churches (because they share the same gospel but not the same polity). A Baptist church and a gospel-denying "church," Baptist or otherwise, can work together to care for the poor (because they share a common concern for the poor though not the same gospel).

---

[2] Andy Johnson, "Pray for Revival—in the Other Guy's Church," accessed September 23, 2014, http://www.9marks.org/journal/pray-revival-other-guy's-church.

[3] Mark Dever, "Wanted: Apostolic Pastors," accessed September 23, 2014, http://www.9marks.org/journal/wanted-apostolic-pastors-0.

Separate Churches Share the Same Confession

Different Christian churches share the same gospel confession, even when they belong to different denominations. Think of how Paul exhorted "the *churches* of Galatia": "If anyone is preaching to you a gospel contrary to the one you received, let him be accursed" (Gal 1:2, 9). John expected every church to embrace a right doctrine of the incarnation (1 John 4:1–3).

Practical Implication 5: Churches should partner in learning from one another and teaching one another. The earliest churches did this in the sharing of preachers and guest missionaries, as we saw a moment ago. Today this can be done in several ways: attending or hosting conferences, supporting seminaries and the seminary educations of young aspiring pastors, subsidizing healthy Christian publishers, and starting local ministerial associations.[4]

Practical Implication 6: Churches should learn from other churches in different eras. The great creeds have much to teach, as do various controversies of the past. Churches can recite these creeds in their Sunday morning gatherings. Churches can learn from the practices and patterns of pastors in the past. Ministerial associations, for instance, played a large role in Baptist history, particularly in prompting the Baptist missions movement.[5] Generally, pastors should teach their people to read and be thoughtful. Pastors might even encourage their churches to care more about history than does the population at large because Christians know that Christ is Lord over all time.

Practical Implication 7: Churches should imitate one another in holiness, just as the apostolic churches imitated one another (1 Thess 1:7; 2:4; 2 Thess 1:4). Paul sought to "remind" the Corinthian church of his "ways in Christ," as he taught "them everywhere in every church" (1 Cor 4:7); and he often insisted on a common rule "in all the churches" (1 Cor 14:33b–34; also 7:17; 11:16, etc.).

This implication points to the value of multichurch conferences, books, and ministerial associations. But it particularly highlights the need for pastors to build relationships with one another beyond their own churches, as they seek to grow in pastoral wisdom. Such relationships

---

[4] See the two separate 9Marks Journals on how churches can care for one another (both accessed September 23, 2014): http://www.9marks.org/journal/church-and-churches and http://www.9marks.org/journal/wanted-apostolic-pastors.

[5] See Michael Haykin, "Baptists Reading Together and the Birth of Modern Missions," accessed September 23, 2014, http://www.9marks.org/journal/baptists-reading-together -and-birth-modern-missions.

can help pastors work through tough pastoral counseling or discipline situations.

Practical Implication 8: Churches should work to supply capable pastors or at least supply preachers to struggling churches who lack them. I know of several churches who, when they work to plant or revitalize another church, agree to pay the pastor's salary in that other church for the first couple of years. And they do so without asking to exercise any authority over that other congregation. It is a gift.

Separate Churches Share the Same Commission[6]

All churches are called to be holy (1 Cor 1:2). All of them are commissioned to make disciples (Matt 28:18–19). All of them are tasked with guarding the name and reputation of Christ through church discipline (see Matt 18:15–20).

Practical Implication 9: Churches should help one another with membership and discipline. As a congregationalist, I do not believe one church can exercise authority over another; but I have watched our church work well with other congregations in the transfer of members, as well as in the exercise of discipline. For instance, when one individual whom our church disciplined tried to join a nearby church with whom we have a relationship, that church turned to us for guidance. Our church did the same when individuals who were disciplined by other congregations tried to join us. Our church does not believe it is bound by the other church's decision, but we would be foolish not to make inquiries. Working together in matters of membership and discipline helps us make and oversee Christ's disciples and so fulfill the Great Commission.

Practical Implication 10: Churches should work together in missions and evangelism. This can happen locally, as when a church partners with nearby churches (from different denominations) to lead evangelistic Bible studies at lunchtime in the business district. Or it can happen nationally and globally, as when the churches of the Southern Baptist Convention pool their money to train and send missionaries overseas.

Practical Implication 11: Churches should partner together in their mercy ministry work. Paul's example of collecting from multiple churches to support the church in Jerusalem provides the most obvious biblical example. Churches today do well to look for ways to support sister churches with fewer resources at their disposal. This helps Christ's

---

6 See Bobby Jamieson, "The Great Commission Is Bigger than Your Church," accessed September 23, 2014, http://www.9marks.org/journal/great-commission-bigger -your-church.

kingdom and serves the Great Commission. Compiling and coordinating resources for mercy ministry among non-Christian neighbors can help churches fulfill the Great Commission and live as holy ones who are salt and light in the world.

Conclusion

It was not until 2:15 in the morning of December 18, 1944, that orders came for the 422nd and 423rd regiments of the 106th Division of the US Army to retreat westward toward Saint Vith, Belgium, from their position in the German forests of Schnee Eifel. By then it was too late. The German army had executed a pincer movement, surrounding and cutting off the two American regiments. By the next day more than 7,000 American soldiers found themselves German prisoners of war.

Once again we might imagine what the commanders in the two army regiments were doing in the moments leading up to the pincer movement before it succeeded. Were they trying to fight their way out alone, without contacting other regiments or the larger division or battalion? It seems unlikely. Presumably they had lieutenants screaming into their radios asking for backup.

The army analogy breaks down insofar as each church "division" or "battalion" is independent, commanded only by Christ in heaven. But every local church's formal independence hardly means churches do not depend on other churches, such as one regiment depending on another.

Healthy churches are churches with a vibrant gospel witness. And a healthy church is one that understands both its independence and its interdependence with other churches. Because it is independent, it works hard to equip itself for the work of apostolic office. It works to keep the line between church and world clear by carefully attending to its membership and discipline practices and by proclaiming the gospel. It works to present a picture of Christ's holy love in its life together for the sake of the onlooking nations. Because churches are interdependent, they work together for fulfilling the Great Commission. They pray for, encourage, challenge, and support one another because they know that the success of one is the success of all, and the defeat of one is the sorrow of all (see 1 Cor 12:26).

Name Index

Abbott, Cortez   *36*
Achtemeier, Paul J.   *103*
Adams, Jay   *209*
Adams, John Quincy   *87*
Akin, Daniel   *187, 189*
Alexander, Paul   *47*
Allison, D. C.   *209*
Allison, Gregg R.   *ix, 48–49, 63–65, 72,
   88, 117, 121, 123, 146–47, 149–50,
   157–58, 171, 178–79, 185, 187,
   211, 215, 351*
Anderson, Marvin   *86*
Anyabwile, Thabiti   *182, 190*
Aquinas, Thomas   *146*
Arndt, W. F.   *269*
Arnold, Clinton   *174*
Ashford, Bruce   *189*
Augustine   *86, 110, 156, 174, 340–46,
   348, 352–53, 364, 366*

Banks, Robert   *172*
Barber, Nick   *1*
Barker, S. K.   *28*
Barna, George   *167*
Barth, Karl   *113*
Bauer, W.   *269*
Beale, G. K.   *52–53, 59*
Beasley-Murray, G. R.   *99,
   101, 103, 105*
Bennett, Martyn   *35*
Bennett, William L.   *223*
Bettenson, Henry   *232*
Blaising, Craig A.   *50*
Blue, B. B.   *138*
Blue, Ken   *209*
Bock, Darrell L.   *50*
Booth, Randy   *116–17*
Boyce, James P.   *ix, 205*
Brinkel, K.   *111*
Bruce, F. F.   *184*
Buchan, John   *35*

Burns, J. Patout, Jr.   *340*
Burrage, Champlin   *41*
Burrows, J. L.   *237–38*
Burtchaell, James T.   *244*

Calvin, John   *28–30, 32, 112–13, 148–
   49, 157–59, 162, 169, 174, 233–34,
   344–53, 360, 363–64, 366*
Cameron, Euan   *162*
Caner, Emir   *234*
Carlyle, Thomas   *35–37*
Carson, D. A.   *53, 56–58, 63, 70, 72, 94,
   137, 210–11, 300*
Chamblin, J. Knox   *209–10*
Christman, Ted   *127*
Clowney, Edmund P.   *52, 56, 59, 78, 351*
Cocks, H. F. Lovell   *37*
Coker, Joe   *201, 213*
Conzelmann, Hans   *216*
Corbett, Steve   *328*
Crane, Catherine D.   *36*
Crawford, Michael R.   *147*
Cross, Anthony R.   *99*
Cyprian   *108–9, 169, 232, 334, 338,
   339–45, 348, 352–53, 359*

Dagg, John L.   *ix, xx, 5, 88, 152–53, 199*
Dana, H. E.   *222–23*
Danker, F. W.   *269*
Davies, Gwyn   *41, 42*
Davies, W. D.   *209*
Davis, Andrew M.   *187, 214, 224*
Davis, George B.   *221*
Davis, J. C.   *37*
Davis, Thomas J.   *149*
Dayton, A. C.   *221–22*
Denis, Philippe   *28*
Dever, Mark   *x, 47, 49, 63, 65, 77, 84,
   121, 127, 150, 170, 176, 182, 186,
   188, 190, 194, 201, 205–6, 212,*

215, 217, 224, 229, 235–37, 333–34, 363, 377
Deweese, Charles W.   *41–43, 171, 179, 192*
DeYoung, Kevin   *328*
Dobbins, Gaines S.   *223*
Drake, George A.   *37*
Duesing, Jason   *190, 224*
Dumbrell, William J.   *52–53*
Dunn, James D. G.   *105*

Elliott, John H.   *103*
Elwell, Walter A.   *209*
Engle, Paul E.   *177*
Erickson, Millard   *176, 239*
Evans, Robert F.   *336–37, 339–42*

Fee, Gordon D.   *104, 214, 314*
Ferguson, Everett   *107*
Ferguson, Sinclair   *57, 108, 112, 177, 333*
Fikkert, Brian   *328*
Finney, Charles   *204–5*
Finn, Nathan   *177*
Fitzgerald, Paul J.   *344*
Fletcher, Jesse C.   *222*
France, R. T.   *201*
Fraser, Antonia   *35*
Freeman, Curtis   *177*
Freeman, J. D.   *175*
Fuller, Andrew   *213*

Garland, David E.   *141, 216*
Garrett, Duane A.   *112*
Garrett, James Leo, Jr.   *186, 189*
Gentry, Peter J.   *50, 52, 154*
George, Timothy   *114, 148, 151, 162*
Gerhard, Friedrich   *208*
Gerrish, Brian A.   *162*
Gilbert, Greg   *84, 328*
Gingrich, F. W.   *269*
Godfrey, W. Robert   *148*
Golding, Peter   *50*
González, Justo L.   *336*
Gordon, J. M.   *151*
Graves, J. R.   *87, 204, 221–22*
Greear, J. D.   *179*
Grenz, Stanley   *179*
Griffith, Benjamin   *217, 236*
Grudem, Wayne   *57, 154, 239–40, 255, 277, 285, 287, 313, 319–20*
Gunton, Colin E.   *21*

Guthrie, Donald   *279*

Haight, Roger   *336–45, 348*
Hall, David W.   *6, 11*
Hambrick-Stowe, Charles E.   *39*
Hamilton, James M., Jr.   *55, 139, 141–42, 162*
Hammett, John S.   *x, 49, 63–64, 69, 88, 121, 123, 125, 129–30, 132, 154, 162, 165, 167, 171, 173, 175, 179, 181, 185, 187–94, 202–3, 224–25, 240–41, 281, 351*
Hardin, John   *xvi*
Harmer, J. R.   *249*
Harris, Josh   *168*
Hartman, Lars   *102–3*
Harvey, A. E.   *243–44*
Hawthorne, Gerald F.   *314*
Haykin, Michael A. G.   *28, 37, 145, 151, 378*
Heclo, Hugh   *13–14, 17–19*
Heinze, Rudolph W.   *162*
Hellerman, Joseph   *169, 172, 178, 183*
Hermas   *249*
Hirsch, Alan   *179*
Hiscox, Edward T.   *204, 207, 221*
Hoehner, Harold H.   *103*
Hoekema, Anthony A.   *54*
Hofius, Otfried   *141*
Hogg, David S.   *146*
Holmes, Michael W.   *249*
Höpfl, Harro   *346*
Horton, Michael   *50, 149, 351*
Hoskins, Paul M.   *59*
House, Paul R.   *53, 56*
Howell, R. B. C.   *221–22*
Howell, Roger, Jr.   *37*
Hunt, J. P. T.   *100*

Ignatius   *231–32, 248–49*

Jamieson, Bobby   *4, 154, 176, 334, 353, 359, 362–63, 379*
Jay, Eric G.   *249*
Jenson, Matt   *173, 350–51*
Jeschke, Marlin   *213, 223*
Jewett, Paul K.   *117*
Johnson, Andy   *377*
Johnson, William B.   *212, 236, 239*
Jones, Samuel   *236*

Keach, Benjamin   *39–40, 42, 215, 235*

Keller, Timothy   *328*
Kelly, Douglas   *32*
Kelly, J. N. D.   *279*
Kimball, Dan   *167*
Kimble, Jeremy   *209, 211–13*
Kingdon, Robert   *28–31*
King, Marty   *168, 175*
Kistemaker, Simon J.   *214, 216*
Kittel, Gerhard   *208*
Knight, George W.   *251–52, 267–68, 279*
Kolb, Robert   *111, 177*
Köstenberger, Andreas   *52, 92–93, 133*

Ladd, George Eldon   *83*
Lane, William L.   *277*
Laney, J. Carl   *202–3, 212, 214–15, 219, 223, 225*
Leeman, Jonathan   *5, 16, 20, 69, 165, 168, 171–72, 182, 184, 190, 192, 199, 200, 202, 205–7, 214–15, 217, 219–20, 224–25, 367*
Letham, Robert   *147–48*
Lightfoot, J. B.   *244, 249, 284*
Lindsay, Thomas M.   *244*
Louw, J. P.   *107, 109–10*
Lumpkin, William L.   *vii–viii, 38–40, 175, 191*
Luther, Martin   *30, 110–11, 134, 147, 159, 162, 174, 201, 230, 233, 303*

MacDonald, James   *48-49, 69*
Mack, Wayne   *170, 182, 190*
Mappes, David   *248, 252*
Marcel, Pierre   *115*
Marshall, I. Howard   *285*
Martyr, Justin   *108*
Maruyama, Tadataka   *29*
Maunder, Chris   *232*
McGoldrick, James Edward   *87*
McKee, Elsie A.   *234*
McKelvey, R. J.   *59*
McKinion, Steven A.   *108–10*
McKnight, Scot   *92*
Merkle, Benjamin L.   *x, 124, 170, 182, 190, 194, 224, 243, 253, 256, 281, 311*
Meuser, Fred   *303*
Milbank, Dana   *23*
Mohler, R. Albert, Jr.   *199, 201, 221*
Moody, Dale   *241*
Morden, Peter J.   *151–52*

Mounce, William D.   *251–52, 265, 267–68, 279, 315–16, 320*
Muller, Richard A.   *88*

Naylor, Peter   *152–53*
Nettles, Thomas J.   *121, 123*
Newton, Phil   *280, 287, 320*
Nolland, John   *201*
Norman, R. Stanton   *ix, 64–65, 211, 224–25*

Oberman, Hieko A.   *147, 162*
O'Brien, P. T.   *56–58, 60*
Oddy, Jeremy   *169*
O'Donnell, M. B.   *104*
O'Donovan, Oliver   *361–62*
Oliver, Robert W.   *152*
Owen, John   *37, 234, 239*

Packer, J. I.   *115, 120, 242, 333*
Packull, Werner O.   *234*
Parker, T. H. L.   *32*
Paul, Robert S.   *37*
Pelikan, Jaroslav   *145–46*
Pendleton, J. M.   *207, 210, 213, 215, 221–22*
Pennington, Jonathan T.   *133–34*
Piper, John   *177, 239, 261, 333–34, 352, 363*
Polycarp   *249*
Powell, Hunter   *356*
Pratt, Richard L., Jr.   *66, 112*
Putnam, Robert   *167*

Ramsay, William M., Sr.   *284*
Renihan, James   *235–36*
Reymond, Robert L.   *49, 88, 116, 148*
Reynolds, J. L.   *84–85, 186, 237, 239*
Robertson, A. T.   *314*
Robertson, O. Palmer   *50*
Robinson, C. Jeffery, Sr.   *28*
Robinson, Robert   *304*
Rott, Jean   *28*
Ryken, Philip G.   *351*
Samra, James   *183–85*
Sande, Ken   *306*
Sanders, Elizabeth   *15*
Sasse, Hermann   *147*
Saucy, Robert   *129*
Schaff, David S.   *221, 347*
Schaff, Philip   *221, 249, 347*
Schnackenburg, Rudolf   *98–99, 101–2*

Schreiner, Thomas R.   *54, 56, 72, 83, 102, 211, 215–19, 277, 281*
Schwöbel, Christoph   *351*
Sell, Alan P. F.   *33*
Simons, Menno   *213*
Skeat, T. C.   *252*
Spurgeon, Charles H.   *128, 151–53, 237, 303*
Stander, H. F.   *107, 109–10*
Stark, Rodney   *174*
Stayer, James   *234*
Stein, Robert H.   *92, 95, 99, 102, 176*
Stott, John R. W.   *60, 242*
Strauch, Alexander   *201, 270, 282, 284–85, 287–88*
Strawbridge, Gregg   *112*
Strong, A. H.   *238*
Swavely, Dave   *170, 182, 190*

Taylor, L. Roy   *250–51*
Thiselton, Anthony C.   *98, 141*
Thomas, Geoffrey   *33, 153*
Thompson, Philip E.   *40*
Thornbury, John   *87*
Tolmie, Murray   *38*
Treasure, Geoffrey   *28, 31*
Turner, David L.   *209*
Turner, Max   *54*

Van Neste, Ray   *154, 161–62*
Vickers, Brian J.   *155–58*
von Campenhausen, Hans   *233*

Waldron, Samuel E.   *251, 281, 289*
Walker, G. S. M.   *346*
Walker, Michael J.   *151–52*

Walton, Robert C.   *32*
Walzer, Michael   *5*
Wardin, Albert W.   *222*
Ware, Bruce   *119, 123, 147–48, 177*
Warfield, Benjamin B.   *115*
Watts, Michael R.   *33–34, 44*
Weatherford, Kenneth V.   *222*
Webb, Robert L.   *92*
Webster, John   *3, 5–6, 363*
Wells, David F.   *54*
Wellum, Kirk   *341*
Wellum, Stephen J.   *50–52, 83, 116–19, 341*
Wendel, François   *148*
White, B. R.   *33–34, 38, 40–41*
White, James R.   *55–56, 64–66, 278*
White, John   *209*
White, Thomas   *xxi, 190, 222, 224*
Wilhite, David   *173, 350–51*
Williams, Roger   *37*
Williams, William   *237*
Willis, G. G.   *174*
Wills, Gregory A.   *154, 175, 205, 209–10, 220–21, 223–24, 235*
Wilson, Douglas   *105*
Witherow, Thomas   *351*
Worden, Blair   *37*
Wright, D. F.   *101, 110*
Wright, Shawn D.   *88, 113, 115, 119, 148, 162*

Yarnell, Malcolm, III   *190, 224*

Zwingli   *111, 134, 147–48, 162, 174*

Subject Index

A

Anabaptists   *111–12, 174–75, 234, 351–52*
apostolic delegates   *279–80*
assembly
   as a requirement for church membership   *184–85*
   church as eschatological   *56–58*
Augustine
   conflict with Donatists   *342*
   teaching on local church   *340–42*
authority
   and tradition   *13–14*
   as God's gift   *xvi–xix*
   congregational   *66–69, 76, 185–86, 280–81, 353, 356–59*
   cooperation between leaders and congregation   *72–77, 186–87, 276–281, 298–299*
   cultural opposition to   *xv–xvi, 2, 11–13, 187*
   in everyday life   *xviii, 227*
   in the local church   *xviii–xix, 22, 353, 353–63*
   of leaders   *76–77*
   of persuasion   *71–72*
   of Scripture   *350–52*

B

baptism
   and the Great Commission   *93*
   and union with Christ   *99–101, 123–24*
   as cleansing from sin   *103–4*
   baptismal regeneration   *99–100, 102–3*
   biblical presentation   *91*
   defining baptism   *120–21*
   household baptisms   *97–98*
   immediacy   *94–95, 129–30*
   in Acts   *94–98*
   infant baptism   *39–40, 86, 93–94, 100–101, 105–6*
   in Jesus' name   *97*
   in the Epistles   *98–106*
   in the Gospels   *92–94*
   in the local church   *121–30*
   John the Baptist and Jesus   *92–93*
   mode   *123–24*
   of children   *126–29, 193*
   proper subject of   *123*
   relationship to church membership   *124–30, 176–77, 192–93, 369*
   relationship to circumcision   *100–101, 114–15*
   relationship to conversion   *95–97*
   relationship to the gospel   *122–23*
   relationship to regeneration   *102–3*
   relationship to unity among believers   *104–5*
Baptist
   history   *vii–x, 86–87*
   Particular Baptists   *38–41*

C

Calvin, John
   teaching on baptism   *111–12*
   teaching on elders   *233–34*
   teaching on local church   *344–49*
   teaching on the Lord's Supper   *149*
catechesis   *174*
church
   in relationship to Israel   *50–62, 346*

in relationship to the new
    covenant 49
church community
    as a unity and discipline 43–45
church covenants
    function 42, 178–79, 192
    in history 41, 43–45
church directory 304–5
church discipline
    and holiness 203–4
    and love 201–3
    biblical defense 200–204
    corrective 206–18
    excommunication 212–14
    for non-attendance 307
    formative 205–6
    Graves-Howell controversy 221–22
    historical decline in Baptist
        life 220–23
    how to treat excluded
        members 213–15
    in establishing meaningful member-
        ship 195–96, 199–200
    in the case of church leaders 217–18
    in the case of general offense 214–17
    in the case of personal
        offense 209–14
    in the Gospels 200–204
    in the New Testament 7–8
    Matthew 18 process 210–
        212, 306–307
    prudential questions 218–20, 224–26,
        305–7, 371–72, 379
    restoration as goal 208–9,
        215, 219–20
    restoring its practice today 223–26
    role of congregation in 67–69
    roots in the Old Testament 8, 216
church membership
    and accountability 183–84
    and corporate witness 189
    and love 189
    as a church office 11
    as an office 15–16, 372
    as citizens of a kingdom 171–72
    as covenant 177–79
    as members of a body 170–71
    as members of a family 172–73
    corporate responsibility and
        benefits 183–86
    individual responsibilities and
        benefits 181–83

in the New Testament 169
making membership
    meaningful 188–89
membership interview 193
members' meetings 194–95
recovering meaningful
    membership 190–91
regenerate 29, 55–56, 66, 83, 115–
    16, 173–74, 346–49
when to leave a church 196–97
church planting and revitalization
    as goal of plural eldership 291–94
    constitution and by-laws 292, 294
community 11
complementarianism 256–57
congregation
    authority in church discipline 212,
        216–17, 349
    involvement in accepting
        members 194
    involvement in choosing its
        elders 298–99, 344, 371
    submission to leaders xvii, 187,
        277, 279, 299
congregationalism 22–23
    and the new covenant 23, 49
    authority in church discipline 29–30
    biblical defense of 73–77
    biblical doctrine of 64–65
    condemned as heresy in 1560s
        France 27–31
    definition of 49
    for Particular Baptists 40
    in colonial America 34
    in Cromwell's England 35–38
    punished with execution in 1590s
        England 33–34
    Puritan historical roots 31–34
    theological foundation
        of 63–64, 66–69
consubstantiation 134, 147
consumerism 168
cooperation 18, 40–41, 376
corporate worship 184–85
covenant theology
    deficiencies 117–21
    explanation 116–20
Cyprian
    teaching on local church 338–40

D

deacons
  archdeacons   *230*
  benevolence   *327–29*
  biblical basis   *311–14*
  deaconess   *313, 317–19*
  diaconal duties   *230*
  in church history   *229–31*
  in Congregational churches   *231*
  in Eastern Orthodoxy   *230*
  in Lutheran churches   *230*
  in Presbyterian churches   *231*
  in Roman Catholic Church   *230*
  installation of   *326*
  origin of   *312–13*
  qualifications   *314–19*
  relationship to elders   *321–26*
  role of   *319–23*
denominations   *xvi, 241–42*
discipleship   *11–20, 276,*
  292–93, 295–96

E

early church   *107–10*
  baptism in the   *107–10*
  congregationalism in   *73–74*
elders
  and accountability   *274*
  and ministry of prayer   *300*
  as equippers   *275–76*
  as leaders   *271–72*
  as shepherds   *273–74, 303–5*
  as teachers   *274–75*
  authority in the church   *70–72,*
    272, 276–81
  compensation   *282–83*
  distinctions between elders   *249–52,*
    281–83, 298
  elder-ruled   *48*
  equipping the church for minis-
    try   *297, 372–73*
  function   *248, 271–76*
  in Baptist history   *235–38*
  in church history   *231–33*
  in early church   *231–32, 243*
  in Reformation   *233–35*
  in the New Testa-
    ment   *245–52, 283–86*
  lay elders   *286, 294*
  lead by example   *71*
  Old Testament roots   *243–44*

  pastor, elder, overseer as one
    office   *246–49*
  plurality of   *48, 239–40, 283–89*
  qualifications   *70, 247,*
    253–70, 292–93
  recent revival of the office   *238–42*
  relationships among elders   *302–3*
  relationship to deacons   *321–26*
  role in church discipleship   *305–7*
  senior pastor   *249–50*
  teaching elder vs. ruling
    elder   *250–52*
evangelism
  as the work of the
    church   *295–96, 372*
  in relationship to polity   *21–23*
expositional preaching   *293, 297–98*

F

faith and order   *5–6*
false professions   *126*
freedom of conscience   *35*

H

holiness in the church   *363–65*
Holy Spirit
  relationship to baptism   *96*
  work under the new covenant   *54–58*

I

individualism   *12, 19–20, 167*
infant baptism
  covenantal argument   *112–20*
  historical development   *107–20, 174*
institutions
  church as institution   *359–60*
  thinking institutionally   *13–20*

J

Jesus Christ
  as head of the church   *62,*
    63–64, 81, 289
  as king   *16*
  role in the ordinances   *83–84, 154–58*
  servant leadership   *272*

K

keys of the kingdom   *6–9, 337–38,*
    349, 353–54

L

leadership   *16–17*
    authority received from God   *33*
    developing leaders in the
       church   *308–9*
local church   *4–6*
    as autonomous   *64–65, 368–73*
    as an embassy   *171–72, 360, 368–69*
    as eschatological body   *57–58*
    as God's new humanity   *60–62*
    as God's temple   *59–60*
    as institution   *13–20*
    definitions throughout history   *335–49*
    not mixed   *58–59, 60, 114–16, 174,*
       341–42, 346–49
    role in discipleship   *12–19, 369–70*
Lord's Supper
    "breaking bread"   *137–39*
    close vs. open   *152–54*
    connection to Passover   *133–34, 157*
    corporate nature of   *136, 140*
    defining   *131–32*
    eschatological nature of   *135–36, 142*
    historic Baptist views   *150–53*
    history of   *145–54*
    how often?   *161–62*
    in early church   *145–46*
    in the Gospels   *132–39*
    in the local church   *158–63*
    in the Middle Ages   *146*
    in the Pauline epistles   *139–43*
    in the Reformation   *146–49*
    meaning of   *154–58*
    memorial view   *147*
    nature of   *155*
    Reformed/Calvinistic view   *148*
    relationship to the gospel   *155–56*
    relationship to the new cove-
       nant   *134–35, 155*
    role in the Christian life   *156–158*
    spiritual presence view   *149, 151–52*
    symbolic nature of   *134–35*
    unworthy recipients   *142*
    Where should it be given?   *160–61*
    Who should administerate?   *158–60*
Luther, Martin
    teaching on baptism   *110–11*
    teaching on elders   *233*
    view on Lord's Supper   *146–47*

M

mercy ministry   *379–80*
missions   *379*
moral evaluation   *15*

N

neo-evangelicals   *xv–xvi*
New Covenant   *52–62*

O

ordinances
    as opposed to sacraments   *88–89*
    relationship to polity   *4–5, 7,*
       360–63, 369
    relationship to the gospel   *84*
    role of church history   *85–88*

P

polity   *xv*
    as it defines local church   *1, 3–6*
    as it protects the gospel   *6–11, 353–59*
    in church life   *2–3*
    in everyday life   *1*
    in relationship to the gospel   *xxi, 5–6*
    in Scripture   *xix–xx, 3*
    in the Christian life   *xx–xxi, 9–10*
    not normative for today   *xix*
    relationship to authority   *xvi*
pragmatism   *18–19*
priesthood of all believers   *53–56, 66*
Puritans
    as Separatists   *32–34*
    Oliver Cromwell   *34–38*

Q

qualifications for elders
    apt to teach   *254–55*
    believing children   *267–70*
    controversial qualifications   *264–70*
    desire   *254, 286*
    family qualifications   *256–58*
    husband of one wife   *256–57, 264–67*
    manage household well   *257–58*
    moral qualifications   *258–63*
    not a new convert   *255–56*

situational qualifications   *253–56*

R

regulative principle   *32–34*
religious freedom   *36*

S

sacramentalism   *158–59*
Scripture
  as ground for church unity   *350–52*
  its centrality for discipleship   *20*
  SBC inerrancy controversy   *240–42*
  sufficiency of   *xx*
spiritual gifts
  among elders   *300–302*
  in context of the church member-
    ship   *182, 296*
Spurgeon, Charles
  teaching on the Lord's
    Supper   *151–52*
statements of faith
  Abstract of Principles
    (1858)   *82, 120, 221*
  Belgic Confession (1561)   *221–22*
  First London Confession
    (1644)   *39–42*
  in history   *vii–viii, 82, 370*
  Second London Confession
    (1689)   *82, 120, 150–51, 159, 190*
  Somerset Confession (1656)   *175*

submission
  as members to leaders   *170, 373*
  in relationship to faith   *20*

T

temple
  Christ as fulfillment   *59–60*
  in the Old Testament   *59*
Tertullian
  teaching on local church   *336–37*
transubstantiation   *134, 136, 146*

U

unity
  among local churches   *334–35, 352–*
    53, 365–66, 373–80
  between New Testament
    churches   *374–75*
  in the local church   *334–35,*
    352–53, 365–66
universal church   *3–4*

Z

Zwingli, Ulrich
  teaching on baptism   *111–12*
  teaching on the Lord's
    Supper   *147–48*

Scripture Index

Genesis

1:28 *15*
2:7 *257*
2:22 *257*
3 *xv*
3:6 *257*
3:13 *257*
3:15 *118*
15:6 *51, 55*

Exodus

1:8 *52*
10:2 *133*
12–14 *133*
12:15 *216*
12:26–27 *133*
13:3 *133*
13:6–7 *216*
13:8 *133*
13:14–15 *133*
18 *236*
19:6 *51, 364*
20 *71*
24:5–8 *135*
25:40 *59*
33:15–16 *59*
34:6–7 *263*

Leviticus

12:3 *101*

Numbers

11:27–29 *54*
14 *69*

Deuteronomy

1 *236*
4:10 *51*
7:18–19 *133*
10:16 *55, 101*
19:15 *211*
30:6 *55, 101*
32:15 *51*
32:17 *52*
33:12 *51*

Joshua

24:1 *51*
24:25 *51*

1 Samuel

6:7 *52*

2 Samuel

23:3–4 *xviii*

1 Chronicles

10:13–14 *300*
14:10 *300*
14:14 *300*

Job

1:1 *260*
31:32 *259*

Psalms

2:8 *300*
4:4 *263*
8 *15*

42:2 *59*
63:2 *59*
65:1–2 *59*
78:3–4 *133*
95:7 *303*
103:8 *263*

Proverbs

3:12 *202*
13:24 *203*
16:18 *255*
17:9 *210*
20:1 *261*
22:6 *270*
22:15 *203*
23:13–14 *203*
23:29–35 *261*
27:17 *287*
29:15 *203*
29:22 *263*

Ecclesiastes

1:10 *52*
4:9–12 *288*

Isaiah

2:2–4 *51*
9:6–7 *52*
11:1–3 *54*
11:1–10 *52*
11:11–15 *133*
25:6–8 *136*
32:15 *93*
40:3–5 *92*
40:3–11 *133*
40:11 *274*
42:1 *93*

42:6   *52*
42:16   *133*
43:2   *133*
43:5–7   *133*
43:16–19   *133*
43:20–21   *51*
43:25   *92*
44:2   *51*
44:3   *93*
44:22   *92*
49:1–2   *54*
49:6   *52*
52:13–53:12   *92*
55:3–5   *52*
56:4–8   *52*
59:2   *92*
59:12   *92*
61:1   *54*
65:17   *52*
66:18–24   *52*
66:22   *52*

Jeremiah

4:4   *55, 101*
9:25   *55*
13:11   *23*
23:5–6   *52*
31   *53, 55–56*
31:29–30   *53*
31:29–34   *52, 119*
31:31–34   *51–52, 101,
    119, 135, 364*
31:34   *23, 135, 357*
31:36–40   *52*
33:6–16   *52*
33:9   *52*
33:14–26   *52*

Lamentations

3:22–23   *52*

Ezekiel

11:19–20   *54, 119*
11:22–23   *59*
16:8–14   *103*
28:11–19   *255*
34:2–4   *273*
34:23–24   *52*
36:22   *8*
36:22–23   *360*

36:24–27   *364*
36:24–38   *52*
36:25–27   *54,
    61, 101, 119*
36:36   *52*
37:11–28   *52*
37:24–28   *52*
37:28   *52*

Hosea

1:6   *51*
1:9–11   *51*
2:1   *51*
2:7   *214*
2:23   *51*

Joel

2:28–32   *54, 119*

Malachi

3:1   *92*

Matthew

1:23   *59*
2:6   *246*
3:11   *54*
3:13–14   *93*
3:13–17   *93*
3:16   *123*
3:16–17   *97*
3:17   *93*
5:23–24   *207*
7:21–23   *83*
8:10   *20*
8–18   *209*
9:36   *303*
11:12–14   *92*
13   *174*
13:24–30   *341, 346*
13:38   *174*
16   *233, 335, 353, 358*
16:13–20   *xviii, 6*
16:17–18   *355*
16:18   *51, 59,
    63, 87, 200*
16:18–
    19   *200, 338, 349*
16:19   *16, 67,
    76, 172, 184*

17:10–13   *92*
18   *201, 209, 215, 219,
    306, 355, 358–60*
18:3–4   *93*
18:5   *93*
18:15   *183, 208*
18:15–20   *xviii, 64,
    67, 83, 203, 209,
    305, 358, 379*
18:16   *211, 306*
18:17   *3, 40, 184, 200,
    211–12, 307*
18:17–18   *16, 349*
18:18   *7, 76, 172, 184*
18:18–20   *16, 67, 200*
18:20   *7, 22, 184*
18:21–35   *209*
18:35   *209*
19:9   *213*
19:14   *93*
20:25–27   *313*
20:25–28   *329*
20:28   *227*
23:23   *352*
24:45   *269*
25:21   *269*
25:23   *269*
25:31–46   *328*
26:17–19   *133*
26:17–30   *56*
26:26   *134, 136, 155*
26:26–29   *84, 132*
26:27   *132,
    134, 136, 154*
26:28   *134–35*
26:29   *135*
26:31   *246*
27:51   *59*
28   *123, 358, 360*
28:1   *139*
28:18–19   *379*
28:18–20   *89,
    124, 295, 358*
28:19   *xx, 91–94, 97,
    121, 355, 360, 369*
28:19   *97*
28:20   *20, 205*

Mark

1:2–4   *92*
1:3   *92*

1:4–5 92
1:5 92, 123
1:6 92
1:7–8 92
1:9–11 93
4:17–19 126
7:21–23 219
10:13–15 93
10:25 262
10:42 240
10:42–44 272
10:45 227
14:12–16 133
14:22 134, 136
14:22–25 132
14:23 132, 136, 154
14:23–24 134
14:24 134–35
14:25 135
16:2 139

Luke

1:2 211
1:17 92
3:21–22 93
6:12–13 293
10:34 274
10:35 274
12:32 246
12:37 227
15:11–32 220
15:17 307
15:24 214
15:32 214
17:3–4 204, 208, 210
18:15 93
22:13 133
22:14–20 132, 140
22:15 133
22:17 136, 154
22:18 135
22:19 132–34,
  136–38, 154
22:20 119, 134–35
22:26–27 227
23 69
24:1 139
24:17–24 138
24:25–27 138
24:30 137–38
24:35 137–38

John

1 250, 322
1:12 174, 270
1:14 59
1:14–18 59
2:19 58, 60, 83
2:19–22 59, 137
2:20 73
2:23 51
3:1–15 61
3:3–6 137
3:7 260
3:15–18 328
3:23 123
4:1 375
4:1–3 355, 378
4:14–15 137
5–6 374
5:11–12 120
5:19 71
5:21 71
5:23 51
6 132, 136–37, 148
6:35 136–37
6:48 136
6:51 136
6:52 136
6:53–56 136
6:63 20
7–8 375
7:37–39 54
7:39 54
8:28 300
10:11 273
10:16 246
10:26 70
10:26–27 75
10:27 62, 303
12:31 216
13 75, 88, 227
13:1–18 313
13:1–20 272
13:34–35 12, 370
13:35 182
14 75
15:13 273
16:7 54
17 302
17:21 365, 370
20:1 139
20:19 139

20:23 349
21:16 246

Acts

1 30
1:4–5 54
1:22 355
1:23–26 xx
2 54, 56, 67, 114
2:21 7
2:33 54
2:38 7, 94–97, 121
2:39 114
2:41 xx, 89, 94,
  95, 125, 176,
  354–55, 361
2:42 64, 89, 137–
  39, 154, 275
2:42–47 178
2:46 137–39
2:47 xx
3:19 95
4:12 7, 51, 97
4:19 187
4:32 178
5 217
5:1–11 355
5:11 217
5:29 64
5:31 95
5:41 7
6 30, 312–14, 319–20,
  322–23, 328
6:1–2 312
6:1–6 73, 283,
  312, 321, 326
6:1–7 22
6:2–3 280
6:3–6 76, 185
6:4 300, 313
6:5 96
6:5–6 xx
6:8 282, 320
6:8–10 320
8 369
8:1 96
8:12 7
8:12–13 94–95
8:12–17 96
8:16 94, 97, 121
8:18–24 355

8:20–23   *359*
8:21   *89, 355*
8:22   *95*
8:36   *94*
8:36–38   *123*
8:38   *94, 176*
9:1   *266*
9:9   *94*
9:18   *94*
9:26   *266*
10:43   *95*
10:44   *97*
10:44–45   *96*
10:44–47   *97*
10:44–48   *105*
10:46   *97*
10:47–48   *94*
10:48   *7, 97, 121, 355*
11:14   *97*
11:15–17   *97*
11:16   *96, 105*
11:18   *95, 97*
11:19–24   *76*
11:22   *3*
11:30   *278,*
   283, 285, 322
13   *292*
13:1–3   *73, 76*
13:2   *296*
13:3   *280*
13:13   *282*
14:12   *282*
14:23   *4, 70, 76,*
   240, 279, 283,
   285, 292, 322
14:24–28   *76*
14:27   *3*
15   *283, 354–55*
15:1–35   *73*
15:2   *322*
15:2–3   *41*
15:4   *322*
15:6   *322*
15:7–11   *96, 105*
15:22   *76, 280*
15:22–23   *322*
15:37–40   *63*
16:4   *322*
16:15   *94–95, 97, 125*
16:30–33   *95*
16:31   *95, 97*
16:31–33   *125*

16:31–34   *95, 97*
16:33   *95*
16:34   *97*
17:10–12   *74*
17:11   *299*
17:30   *95*
18:7–8   *130*
18:8   *89, 95,*
   97–98, 125, 355
18:22   *3*
18:24–26   *74*
18:26   *206*
18:27   *xx*
19:1–7   *95–96*
19:5   *97, 125*
20   *285*
20:6–11   *139*
20:7   *xx, 89,*
   137, 139, 154
20:11   *89, 137, 139*
20:17   *xx, 70, 246,*
   278, 284–85, 322
20:21   *95*
20:28   *xx, 70, 76, 240,*
   246–48, 278, 284–
   87, 299, 321–22
20:28–29   *246, 273*
20:28–31   *187*
20:33–35   *283*
21:8   *320*
21:18   *322*
22:16   *95, 120, 122*
26:20   *95*
27:35   *137*
29:5   *121*

Romans

1:1–2   *51*
1:7   *364*
1:11   *51*
3:21–26   *55, 122*
4:9–12   *51*
4:25   *123*
5:1   *122*
6   *84, 100*
6:1–2   *369*
6:1–4   *71, 122*
6:2–5   *99*
6:3–4   *89, 122–23*
6:3–7   *89, 120*
7:1–3   *266*

8:1   *67*
8:9   *54, 76, 96, 105*
8:13   *300*
8:28–39   *60*
8:30   *270*
8:36   *374*
8:38–39   *300*
9:6   *55, 341*
9:24–26   *51*
10:9–10   *20*
10:13–14   *95*
10:17   *351*
12   *182*
12:1   *71, 122*
12:1–2   *184*
12:1–8   *301*
12:4–5   *171*
12:4–8   *182*
12:8   *187,*
   236, 248, 272
12:9–16   *178*
12:13   *259*
12:19   *208*
13:14   *71*
15:8   *227*
15:14–16   *71*
15:25–26   *374*
15:26   *xx*
16:1   *311, 313, 321*
16:1–2   *318*
16:1–16   *75*
16:5   *3, 375*
16:16   *374*
16:17–18   *203*
16:21–24   *75*

1 Corinthians

1:2   *3, 116,*
   364, 376, 379
1:10   *71*
1:13–16   *100*
1:17   *99*
3:1–23   *72*
3:9   *75*
3:11   *63*
3:16–17   *60*
4:2   *269*
4:7   *378*
4:15   *71*
4:16   *41*
4:17   *269*

5 *xx, 10, 22, 68,*
   210, 215–16, 306,
   357, 359–60
5:1–12 *64*
5:1–13 *67,*
   203, 214, 305
5:2 *184, 280*
5:3 *355*
5:4 *40, 184*
5:4 *22*
5:4–5 *7*
5:5 *76, 214, 216*
5:7 *133, 216*
5:9–13 *185*
5:11 *212, 214, 219*
5:11–12 *170*
5:12 *304*
5:12–13 *183–84*
5:13 *216*
6:2–5 *68*
6:4 *76*
6:9–10 *219*
6:11 *103, 120*
6:15–17 *171*
6:19 *60*
6:19–20 *75*
6:20 *71*
7 *105*
7:8–9 *266*
7:9 *266*
7:14 *105, 114*
7:32–35 *264*
7:39 *44, 266*
9:7 *246*
9:14 *186*
9:15 *370*
9:19–22 *210*
9:19–23 *61*
10:1–12 *140*
10:14–22 *139*
10:16 *132, 154*
10:16–17 *139, 361*
10:16–17 *132*
10:17 *140, 155*
10:21 *132, 140, 154*
10:31 *272, 295*
11 *156*
11:17 *140, 161–62*
11:17–34 *89,*
   132, 140, 355
11:18 *3, 51, 140*
11:18–19 *369*

11:19 *141–42*
11:20 *132,*
   140–41, 154
11:20–26 *76*
11:21–22 *141*
11:23 *89, 141*
11:23–26 *xx,*
   84, 133, 140
11:24 *132,*
   134, 141, 154
11:24–25 *133*
11:25 *134,*
   135, 141, 155
11:26 *64, 141–*
   42, 154, 361
11:27 *142*
11:28 *142*
11:29 *142*
11:29–32 *142*
11:30 *216*
11:33 *140–41*
12 *99*
12:1–31 *62*
12:4–7 *54*
12:7 *169, 182*
12:7–31 *75*
12:11 *300, 323*
12:12–25 *323*
12:13 *104, 120, 169*
12–14 *76*
12:16–21 *60*
12:20 *171*
12:25–26 *178*
12:26 *380*
12:26 *171, 212*
12:28 *236*
12:31 *182*
13:11 *19*
13:13 *182*
14:24–25 *185*
14:33 *378*
14:40 *78*
15:1–4 *123*
15:29 *98*
15:34 *307*
15:49 *15*
15:58 *71*
16:1–2 *xx*
16:1–3 *375*
16:1–4 *76*
16:2 *139*
16:3 *76*

16:15–16 *277, 285*
16:19 *374*
16:19–20 *75*

2 Corinthians

1:1 *364, 376*
2 *215–16*
2:5–8 *185, 220*
2:5–11 *67, 215, 307*
2:5–11 *215*
2:6 *280*
2:6–7 *359*
2:17 *262*
3:1 *xx*
3:18 *15, 78*
4:4 *216*
4:6 *20*
5:17 *76, 122*
6:14 *44*
6:14–18 *8*
6:16 *60*
7:10–13 *69*
8:1 *41*
8:1–2 *374*
8:4 *41*
8–9 *76*
8:18 *374*
8:24 *375*
9:9 *300*
9:12 *374*
10–13 *67*
13:5 *58, 207*
13:11 *71, 306*
13:12–13 *75*
13:13 *374*
13:14 *97*

Galatians

1 *299, 356–57, 371*
1:2 *3, 378*
1:6–9 *10, 22, 64, 204*
1:7–8 *76*
1:8 *65, 67, 279*
1:9 *378*
2:11–14 *204,*
   218, 287, 355
2:15 *355*
2:20 *154*
3:1–5 *96, 105*
3:6–9 *51*
3:26 *101*

3:26–29 *51*
3:27 *101, 122, 125*
5:7–12 *204*
6:1 *76, 211, 220*
6:1–2 *183, 208*
6:1–4 *203*
6:6 *186–7,*
    245, 275, 370
6:10 *172, 178, 328*
6:16 *52*
6:18 *71*

Ephesians

1 *123*
1:1 *364*
1:3–4 *75*
1:3–14 *60, 116*
1:5–7 *75*
1:13–14 *54, 75, 120*
1:15 *374*
1:17–19 *300*
1:22 *83*
1:22–23 *62, 75*
2 *123*
2:5–6 *57*
2:11–22 *59–60*
2:12 *51*
2:18 *60, 67*
2:19 *15, 51,*
    171–72, 376
2:20 *63, 350, 355*
2:21 *60*
2:21–22 *206*
3:4–6 *51*
3:17–19 *300*
4 *365*
4:1 *122, 365*
4:3 *43, 306*
4:3–6 *176*
4:5 *99, 104*
4:7 *296, 300*
4:7–16 *296, 301*
4:11 *70, 246–48,*
    273–74, 278,
    286, 313, 321
4:11–12 *372*
4:11–13 *206*
4:11–16 *21, 62*
4:12 *169, 297*
4:13 *300*
4:16 *183, 372*

4:16 *16*
4:20–24 *72*
4:25 *178*
4:26 *263*
4:29 *16*
4:32 *178*
5 *103*
5:21 *20*
5:22–24 *257*
5:23 *83*
5:25–26 *103*
5:25–27 *63,*
    75, 120, 189
5:27 *197*
5:30 *171*
5:32 *75*
6 *202*
6:4 *257, 270*
6:12 *303*
6:18 *375*
6:19 *187*
6:21 *269*

Philippians

1 *285*
1:1 *xx, 245,*
    284–85, 311, 314,
    321–22, 364
1:6 *72*
1:12 *295*
2:1–4 *306*
2:10–11 *156*
2:22 *71*
3:3 *51*
3:7 *51*
3:9 *51*
3:17 *308*
3:20 *15, 171*
4:5 *259*
4:8 *315*
4:21–22 *75*

Colossians

1:2 *364*
1:4 *374*
1:7 *269*
1:18 *83, 289*
1:21–23 *60*
2 *102*
2:11 *100*

2:11–12 *89,*
    120, 122–23
2:12 *100*
2:12–13 *57*
2:13 *100*
2:19–20 *171*
3:1 *122*
3:1–4 *72*
3:3 *57*
3:4 *187*
3:12 *364*
3:13 *306*
3:13–16 *178*
3:14 *182*
3:18 *257*
4:7 *269*
4:7–18 *75*
4:9 *269*
4:16 *41*

1 Thessalonians

1:4 *51*
1:7 *374, 378*
2:6–8 *71*
2:10 *364*
2:14 *375*
5:5 *124*
5:11–15 *178*
5:12 *187, 248, 272,*
    275, 277, 285
5:12–13 *170, 185–*
    86, 245, 299
5:14–15 *205*

2 Thessalonians

1:4 *378*
3:1 *187, 300*
3:6 *204*
3:14–15 *210, 214*
3:15 *183*

1 Timothy

1:19 *316*
1:20 *216*
2:8–9 *319*
2:9–11 *256*
2:12 *256, 319*
2:13 *256*
2:13–14 *257*
2:14 *257*

3   245, 257–58, 282,
    293, 299, 308,
    314–16, 320–21
3:1   254, 286, 293, 308
3:1–2   70
3:1–7   70,
    247, 292, 322
3:1–13   74
3:2   11, 70, 248,
    251–54, 256,
    258–59, 264–65,
    274, 301, 313–15,
    317–19, 321–22
3:3   259–63, 315
3:4   257, 267, 269
3:4–5   187, 248,
    254, 257, 272,
    277, 301, 315
3:5   257, 268, 322
3:6   255, 269, 317, 322
3:7   259–60
3:8   311, 315–16, 321
3:8–13   314, 318, 326
3:9   316
3:10   75, 317–18
3:11   269, 317
3:12   187, 264,
    311, 319, 321
3:13   329
3:14–15   74
3:15   172
3:16   316
4:2   316
4:11–16   71
4:13   275
4:13–15   298
4:14   48, 247
4:16   287, 373
5:3–16   328
5:9   265–67, 319
5:10   318
5:13   318
5:14   266
5:17   48, 70, 76, 187,
    236, 248, 251–52,
    272, 274, 277,
    282, 284–85, 301,
    314, 321–22
5:17–25   247
5:19   186,
    250, 299, 322
5:19–20   185, 187, 217

5:22   279
5:22–25   247
5:23   261
6:9   262
6:10   262

2 Timothy

1:6   247, 298
1:9   364
1:13   308
2:2   269, 276, 292
2:12   15
2:21   364
2:24   307
2:24–25   262
3:1–5   204, 219
3:3   318
3:16–17   64, 206, 297
4:1–2   275
4:2   293
4:3   76, 299
4:9–10   279
4:11   63
4:19–21   75

Titus

1   257, 268, 293, 299
1:5   4, 48, 246–47,
    279, 284–
    85, 322, 359
1:5–7   70, 247
1:5–9   70, 74,
    246, 292, 315
1:6   253, 256–58, 264–
    65, 268–70, 317–19
1:7   76, 246,
    261–63, 322
1:7–9   247
1:8   259–60
1:9   248, 252, 254,
    274, 313, 321
1:11   262
2:2   315–16
2:3   318
2:4–5   257
3   102
3:2   262
3:4–5   95
3:5   102, 120
3:9–11   217
3:12   279

Philemon

8–9   71, 355
10   71

Hebrews

2:5–18   67
3:1–6   59
3:5   269
3:6   60
3:14   60
4:14–16   60
5:12–14   206
6:2   104
7:1–10:18   104, 135
8   119
8:3–5   59
8:6–13   51
8:7–12   76
8:8–13   155
8–10   56
9:1–10:18   59
9–10   55
9–13   277
9:13   123
10   119, 219
10:15–18   101
10:19–22   60
10:19–25   67
10:22   104
10:24   287
10:24–25   178
10:25   xx, 51, 169, 307
11:8–19   51
12:6   202
12:6–11   202
12:11   20
12:15   184
12:18–29   56
13:2   259
13:5   263
13:7   xviii, 76, 185–86,
    245, 272, 275, 285
13:14   57
13:15   184
13:17   xviii, 76, 170,
    183, 185, 187,
    196, 245, 272,
    274, 277–78, 285,
    299, 304, 372
13:18   187
13:24   75, 285

James

1:1   *285*
1:5–8   *300*
1:18   *20*
1:19   *302*
1:20   *263*
1:21   *20*
2:15–16   *328*
3:2   *142, 206*
5:14   *48, 273, 284, 322*
5:19   *204*
5:19–20   *208, 210*

1 Peter

1:1   *285*
1:18   *72*
1:20   *157*
1:23   *20*
2:5   *60, 169, 184, 364*
2:9   *54, 364*
2:9–10   *51, 75*
2:11   *171*
2:25   *273, 303*
3:1   *210, 257*
3:1–2   *214*
3:4–6   *257*
3:18   *103*
3:21   *102, 122–23*
4:8   *306*
4:9   *259*
5:1   *250, 284, 322*
5:1–2   *246–47, 321*

5:1–5   *xviii*
5:2   *246, 262, 273, 278, 286*
5:2–3   *76, 240, 246, 285*
5:2–4   *70*
5:3   *186–87, 272*
5:4   *63, 70, 250, 273, 303, 309*
5:5   *48, 277, 322*
5:12   *269*
5:12–14   *75*
5:14   *71*

2 Peter

1:10   *58, 71*
1:16   *211*
3:18   *305*

1 John

2:19   *58, 60, 83*
2:20   *73*
2:23   *51*
3:15–18   *328*
4:1   *375*
4:1–3   *355, 378*
4:2–3   *51*
5:11–12   *120*
5:19   *71*
5:21   *71*

2 John

1   *250, 322*
7–8   *375*
13   *75*

3 John

1   *250, 322*
5–6   *374*
14   *75*

Jude

1:12   *246*
3   *87*

Revelation

1:10   *139*
2   *65*
2:20–24   *223*
2:27   *246*
3:19   *202*
5:9–10   *59*
5:10   *15*
7:17   *246*
12:5   *246*
19:15   *246*
21:2   *364*
21:10   *364*
22:5   *15*
22:19   *364*

Buiding Healthy Churches

Is Your Church Healthy?

*9Marks exists to equip church leaders with a biblical
vision and practical resources for displaying God's glory
to the nations through healthy churches.*

To that end, we want to help churches grow in nine marks of health that are
often overlooked:

1. Expositional Preaching
2. Biblical Theology
3. A Biblical Understanding of the Gospel
4. A Biblical Understanding of Conversion
5. A Biblical Understanding of Evangelism
6. Biblical Church Membership
7. Biblical Church Discipline
8. Biblical Discipleship
9. Biblical Church Leadership

At 9Marks, we write articles, books, book reviews, and an online journal. We
host conferences, record interviews, and produce other resources to equip
churches for the display of God's glory.

Visit our website to find resources in additional languages, such as Spanish,
Chinese, and Portuguese. You can also sign up to receive our free online
journal.

www.9Marks.org